Middle East
Monarchies

MIDDLE EAST MONARCHIES

The Challenge of Modernity

EDITED BY

Joseph Kostiner

LYNNE
RIENNER
PUBLISHERS

BOULDER
LONDON

Published in the United States of America in 2000 by
Lynne Rienner Publishers, Inc.
1800 30th Street, Boulder, Colorado 80301
www.rienner.com

and in the United Kingdom by
Lynne Rienner Publishers, Inc.
3 Henrietta Street, Covent Garden, London WC2E 8LU

Library of Congress Cataloging-in-Publication Data
Middle East monarchies : the challenge of modernity / edited by Joseph Kostiner.
    p.   cm.
  Includes bibliographical references and index.
  ISBN 1-55587-862-8 (hc : alk. paper)
  1. Monarchy—Middle East.   2. Middle East—Politics and government.   I. Kostiner,
Joseph.

JQ1758.A58 M53 2000
321'.6'0956—dc21

                                                                          99-051384

British Cataloging in Publication Data
A Cataloguing in Publication record for this book
is available from the British Library.

Printed and bound in the United States of America

⬁   The paper used in this publication meets the requirements
      of the American National Standard for Permanence of
      Paper for Printed Library Materials Z39.48-1984.

  5   4   3   2   1

Contents

PART THREE   CHALLENGES

Acknowledgments

The encouragement and assistance afforded by Asher Susser and Martin Kramer, the previous and current directors of the Moshe Dayan Center for Middle Eastern and African Studies, Tel Aviv University, were a continuous source of support and inspiration for the creation of this volume. The Adenauer Foundation, Israel branch, generously held the international conference that was the basis for the book.

The good advice and intellectual support of Gad Gilbar, at Haifa University, is much valued. Paul Rivlin's contribution was very helpful. The Dayan Center's administrative staff—Amira Margalith, Lydia Gareh, and Roslyn Loon—helped to bring this work to conclusion. Gill Dibner, David Mednikoff, Benzion Philiba, and Avi Muallem provided essential editorial assistance.

Last, but not least, the cooperation of all the contributors to this volume is duly acknowledged.

—*Joseph Kostiner*

Introduction

Joseph Kostiner

Eight active, quasi-absolutist monarchical regimes prevail in the Middle East. Several others that existed by the mid-twentieth century have since collapsed. Understanding of Middle East monarchies—the failure of some and prevalence of others—merits a special study, which is the focus of this volume.

*   *   *

The monarchical legacy of earlier Middle East empires (in this book, meaning the Arab and Ottoman Empires) inherited by their twentieth-century successors can be summarized by two main characteristics. First, monarchical principles were applied without official Islamic legitimacy. As is evident from Bernard Lewis's contribution to this volume (see Chapter 2), the title *malik* (king) was regarded as non-Islamic and therefore unlawful and corrupt. Until the twentieth century, Islamic rulers did not assume this title. A ruler's emphasis was rather on fulfilling the task of a *khalifa* (the prophet's substitute ruling over a community of believers, or *umma*), claiming his right to rule according to the *shari'a* (holy law). However, throughout all of Islamic history, Muslim rulers practiced at least two fundamentals of monarchic rule: individual-absolutist and dynastic-hereditary. These fundamentals were often expressed in two respective ruling principles: administrative and military apparati were established to serve the individual ruler, and a social system based on kin, ethnic, religious, and other solidarities was arrayed in hierarchical divisions. They also adopted additional monarchical facets, such as royal entourages and households. These basic principles marked the ruler's paramount power and position, the ruler wielding these prerogatives in hereditary fashion within a family or a dynasty. Second, without an official religious sanction, adoption and exercise of these qualities did not develop into a desired norm or into an official doctrine of monarchical rule. Monarchical principles in the Arab and Ottoman Empires evolved more haphazardly, typical of a regime created by a forceful seizure of government, following Persian, Greek, and Byzantine examples as well as local practices and arbitrary rulers' interests.

Islamic monarchies had to cope with the continuous challenges inherited in these characteristics: the need to legitimize and justify a rule, which, to borrow Jürgen Habermas's expression, was in a "legitimacy deficit,"[1] and the need to balance absolutist rule, based on administrative and military arms, with deference to ascriptive, religious, ethnic, and class divisions, to sustain dynasty and factional dynamism.

In tackling these challenges, two practices evolved: there was the monarchical practice of the central Ottoman government, as it evolved over several centuries and dominated the central provinces, notably the urban and village areas. There was also the practice that emerged in the peripheral areas, deserts, and nomadic regions, which were dominated by chiefdoms, namely, confederacies of nomadic and sedenterized tribal groups.

The monarchical legacy of the central government included varying aspects. Monarchical rule originated mainly from seizure or appropriation of rule by force (*mulk*), but it could then be legitimized by a vote of loyalty from the *bay'a* (people) and by a ruler's policies and actions, tempered in the interests of Islam and the Islamic community. Likewise, the ruler's edicts were aimed at achieving state interests, but he could shape them through application of the *shari'a* and cooperation with *ulama* (religious sages). Thus, seizure of power, directed to suit what was perceived as the common good for society in general and put in Islamic terms, became a principle in the legacy of classical monarchy.[2]

The ruler's actual source of power hinged on his family, clan, or tribe, namely, the extended kin-tie unit. As Ibn Khaldun (d. 1392) taught us, blood-ties can produce an effective *asabiyya* (group solidarity), which may lead to conquest, seizure of power, and the formation of an empire. *Asabiyya* can, nevertheless, fade away or degenerate and, in a few generations, lead to an empire's downfall. However, as Cornell Fleischer showed, Ottoman rulers' advisers and members of the intellectual elite (in the sixteenth and seventeenth centuries) were familiar with Ibn Khaldun's writings and their meaning. Unlike Ibn Khaldun's modeling, Islamic empires found ways to extend their existence and overcome the degeneration of their *asabiyya*'s weaknesses. They did so by adopting what Ernest Gellner termed (very generally) "the *mamluk* solution," or the devising of military and administrative bodies reliant on slave-soldiers and soldier-bureaucrats. Trained as useful tools for the ruler, they could be trusted both for their professionalism and, as bearers of slave status, for their personal subordination. First introduced during the late phases of the *abbasid* period, this institution reached its highest effectiveness during the classical age of the Ottoman Empire, as part of the *devshirme* system (the cultivation of a slave-based elite). Subsequently, modern armies and bureaucracies evolved to sustain the Ottoman Empire in its last 200 years.[3] The monarch's ability to transform his leaning post from kin-based *asabiyya* to more "routinized" state-based military-bureaucratic institutions, was a fundamental component in the above-mentioned legacy.

The extensions of group solidarities and pluralism in the empires were also a component in the monarchical legacy. Arab, and then Ottoman, states allowed the different tribal, ethnic, and religious mélange of peoples in their empires to remain intact and reproduce themselves. Although supreme decisionmaking, as well as paramount leadership titles, were the rulers' prerogatives, his control of society and relations with it were very mixed. Halil Inalcik's analysis shows that Ottoman political and economic elite groups, be they of the military, administrative, or religious sectors, depended on patriarchal domination (or patrimonialism), by which the sultan personally obtained and controlled loyalty from elite functionaries in return for affording them military and administrative ranks and economic benefits. The ruler also exercised the principles of divide and rule among elite groups, between the different kinds of soldiers and religious sages, between elites and the *riaya* (ordinary people) and among the various *millets* (religious denominations) and professional guilds. In addition, the ruler sanctioned the way they made their living and their sociopolitical status, but he did not attempt to penetrate their ranks or remold their structures. In return for their loyalty and service, such groups had, in fact, internal solidarity and autonomy.[4] Karen Barkey stresses that the Ottoman ruling institution, including the royal family and the top administration, often (both in the classical age and in the seventeenth and eighteenth centuries) maintained social control through bargaining, negotiations, and deal-striking with various powerful groups, even with bandits.[5]

Hence, the central government's monarchical legacy varied but was nevertheless characterized by a common logic. It provided a model of how to justify and legitimize what was basically capturing rule by force, with an Islamic agenda as a raison d'être for the state. It also demonstrated how kin-based organizations can coexist with bureaucratic institutions and how state control and centralization can be achieved on the basis of coalescing a mélange of groups, through patrimonial methods, as well as through rough bargaining. What characterized this legacy was political conduct flexible enough to adapt itself to changing circumstances.

The legacy of the peripheral, more nascent states, or chiefdoms, was similar but less institutionalized. The authority of a *shaikh* or *emir* of a tribal coalition hinged on *mulk* and was not fostered through *bay'a* and bureaucracy but rather via personal agreements with his own family branches and the heads of partner tribal groups. A ruler's stability and hereditary rights were likewise set. A ruler was, in principle, primus inter pares, his role fostered only by his own charisma and achievements.[6] The ruler's administration was based on patrimonial appointments, mainly of leading family members, but was minimal and nonelaborate. In most cases, administrative positions were not bureaucratized.

A ruler's success hinged on performing basic duties, such as defense and the caravan trade. The extension of his authority depended on achieving both internal stability and the territorial outreach of his chiefdom. Sometimes (e.g., in the Saudi case) a chiefdom committed itself to a religious mission that would enable the ruler to assume the authority of a religious imam and consolidate the solidarity among his chiefdom's tribal segments.[7]

The monarchical legacy of both chiefdoms and central government thus articulated a common aura of bargaining and negotiations, of personalized ad hoc arrangements, and of social pluralism. This was a legacy that could, if applied in a balanced manner, lend itself to changing state-building situations. Thus, the need to develop administrative arms and governmental capacity needed to be paralleled by encouraging separate group solidarities and pluralism, through segmentary policies. In twentieth-century terms, it could be argued that the need for development and modernity in technological, administrative-military, and economic spheres had to be mingled with a social order, based on ascriptive, ethnic, and other factional divisions, conducted through patrimonial policies. The problem in maintaining such balance accounts for many monarchical convolutions in the twentieth century.

A short discussion drawing on the scholarly background of this approach is called for. The monarch and his institution should not be regarded merely as the top of an ancien régime that may either remain intact or crumble by association with the upper, noble class. The monarch should be examined in two contexts. He is head of state, responsible for administrative-military order. He is also head of that state's society. In following the studies of Norbert Elias, the key factor is the monarch's ability to establish a code of behavior, or a set of practices, which can develop into a whole "monarchical code" or "civilization." Accordingly, the monarch should place himself above the sociopolitical system and interfere to regulate and award, through an assorted code of interactions, the social groups and their leaders, which compose this system. The monarch appears as the leader of all segments of society under an image of an overall patron—the "father" of his entire "flock." Thus, a monarch should avoid forging an upper class, which could place the monarch in an unwanted, partisan position vis-à-vis other groups. The need to both lead the administration yet preside over a pluralist social system, via personalized or patrimonial methods, is essential.[8]

The broader social cohesion in a monarchical society should therefore not be explained by criteria of national cohesion. Monarchs sometime refer to the societies that they control as "nation," but, to quote Alan Richards and John Waterbury, "what the monarchs want is a plethora of interests, tribal, ethnic, professional, class-based and partisan, whose competition for public patronage they can arbitrate. . . . The monarch's rule is to divide, chastise and regulate, but not to humiliate or alienate important factions."[9] The cohesion of such a mélange is mechanic, based on coalescing, on the monarchy itself as the linchpin of society, rather than on a nationalistic code, which would focus on the people rather than on the king. Society's diversity, rather than its uniformity, is a virtue.

Monarchical legitimacy can therefore not be coined in absolutist terms. As earlier mentioned, a monarch's right to rule is not sanctioned by Muslim ordinances; neither can they claim a real "people's" legitimacy, evident in a Western-type constitutional monarch, as discussed by Reinhard Bendix. Following Bryan Turner's analysis of Max Weber's theories, monarchies cannot claim legitimacy inherited in "substantive justice" or eternal, human, rights but rather in the monarchies' performance: laws, regulations, developmental ideologies, and the code that holds the hierarchy of segments together.[10] It is a practical, flexible legitimacy.

THE "KING'S DILEMMA"

Despite lacking religious sanction, monarchical regimes were the natural choice for the new, post–World War I regimes: after all, monarchical regimes were both a desired example taken from several European states and a follow-up of the dynastic rule that had prevailed in various quarters of the Ottoman realm. The accession of *mulk* in the new Middle Eastern states, based on the above-mentioned legacies, depended on the passage to becoming a new state. It applied to the transformation from empire and chiefdom structures to states' structures, each with its own political center, territorial demarcation, and socioeconomic composition.[11] Thus, several of the new monarchies had to struggle for integration against elements that resisted the new ruling elites. This led to the suppression of the Shi'ite revolt in Iraq in 1920, the subjugation of the Ikhwan (religiously zealot tribal groups) in the Saudi state (1929–1930), and the struggles of the Jordanian Emir Abdallah and the Yemeni Imam Yahya against tribal groups who opposed their supremacy. Egypt and Iraq had to establish their authority through complicated struggles against Britain for their independence. The new regimes mostly hinged on the ability of a leading family—a dynasty—to form (as Halliday demonstrated) a coalition among various social segments, drawing on earlier monarchical legacies, by using bargaining methods. In fact, the monarchical regimes had to cope with different class structures and socioeconomic formations. The more egalitarian and less stratified a society was, the easier it became for a monarchy to establish common causes leading to alignments with different segments. In more stratified societies, particularly with new, modernizing elites, the establishment of socioeconomic stability was much more problematic.[12]

A key question for the post–World War I period, and until the 1970s, concerns the fall of several monarchies. These regimes drew only partly on their legacies and presumed to adopt European political practices and institutions. In Chapter 3, Ami Ayalon stresses that the attempts by the kings of the Hijaz Egypt and Iraq to adopt a monarchical-majestic style by emulating European manners, as a means of trying to gain their foreign counterparts' respect, can be viewed as decorative but failing to establish an alternative, substantial political mode. These states' constitutions and political parties were acceded as a manifestation of modernization and enlightenment but failed to root themselves in their societies.

In reading the work of Bruce Maddy-Weitzman (Chapter 4) and Gabriel Ben-Dor (Chapter 6), several factors account for the monarchical failures and coups in Egypt (23 July 1952), Iraq (14 July 1958), Yemen (23 September 1962), and Libya (1 September 1969). First, it seems that some of the monarchical institutions "aristocratized" themselves. The former Ottoman ruling limits removed, the monarchical dynasties in Egypt and Iraq lashed out to enrich themselves by obtaining land. They thereby formed alliances with landowners, top administrators, and merchants who provided one another with wealth, legal titles to land, and security. Ruling dynasties became part of the wealthy landowning class.[13] In the interwar period there was a process of growing proletarization among agricultural workers, who became dwellers of shanty towns in the urban areas, which led to increasing tensions.

It also becomes evident that these monarchies had difficulties in accommodating the rise of an educated "new middle class," consisting mainly of government officials as well as professionals. The failure was twofold: first, while the monarchical regimes treated societal segments by applying mostly ascriptive, descent-based, or other segmentary criteria typical of monarchical legacies, these new groups exceeded the traditional social frameworks and confines reforming themselves in the manner of a modern class less affected than the ascriptive groups by corporate bargaining and kin-based structures. They were, therefore, quite beyond the government's manipulative reach. Second, these groups exposed new antigovernment perceptions, mainly concerning the neglect (e.g., Yemen and Egypt) of lower-class groups and inability to obtain full independence from colonial powers. Societies, such as the Egyptian, that were evolving into complex, stratified classes, with evident social gaps among them, became an insurmountable problem for some monarchical regimes. Third, middle-class elements occupied in the 1950s and 1960s the positions of middle-ranking army officers, ready to use the military power in their hands to topple their regimes. This problem was evident in Egypt and Iraq, as well as in the less developed societies of Yemen and Libya.

This process marked these monarchies' counterproductive attempts to establish their legitimacy. Egypt and Iraq failed to establish their legitimacy among their "people": as Ayalon shows, they did form parliaments and parties, and a formal constitutional regime, but avoided and failed to actually fulfill this pretension and did not transform authority, to use Reinhard Bendix's terms, from "kings to people."[14] Moreover, by transforming themselves into landowning aristocracies, these monarchies failed not only to establish popular legitimacy but also uprooted themselves from the monarchical codes that had earlier rendered them legitimacy. In addition, these states, as well as Yemen and Libya, failed to find legitimacy with surging modernizing elements such as army officers. The difficulties that monarchies faced with new social compositions, notably new-middle-class elements, led to what Samuel Huntington called the "king's dilemma,"[15] namely, the need to modernize while risking the activation of resultant hostile elements, which several times precipitated a monarchical downfall.

In reading F. Gregory Gause III's work (Chapter 11), it also becomes evident that these monarchies failed to align themselves to a foreign major power or superpower, which could possibly have intervened to save their existence. Without this kind of assistance their destiny could have been doomed.

"MONARCHIES' RESILIENCE"

This term, coined by Lisa Anderson,[16] relates to the monarchies' agility in recent decades. Unlike the coups that had overpowered several monarchies and threatened others, mostly in the 1950s and 1960s, that deemed monarchies obsolete by many observers in the region and in the West, the last three decades of the twentieth century witnessed a resilience in the activities and success of the institution.

This development can be attributed to some important regional and global processes. The enthusiasm of Middle Eastern societies for nationalist-socialist revolutions subsided following their limited success in achieving socioeconomic development. The messianic image of revolutionary regimes was marred, following Syria and Egypt's (two of the leading revolutionary states) defeat by Israel in 1967. The leadership of the revolutionary states in the 1970s and onward, typified by leaders such as Anwar al-Sadat in Egypt and Hafiz al-Asad in Syria, was less appealing than the revolutionary-charismatic personality of Jammal Abd al-Nasir in the two earlier decades. There were other factors that contributed to the upsurge of monarchs. Among these were the accumulation of oil wealth in the hands of Persian Gulf monarchs and their ability to use that wealth to evoke both internal development and international influence. Also important was the influential role that leaders such as the Saudi King Faysal had attained in the Middle East in the light of his part in helping to devise the oil boycott on some Western states and the Egyptian-Syrian cooperation in the 1973 war. The decline of the Soviet Union in the 1980s further weakened the challenge to the monarchies from revolutionary groups. Moreover, some monarchies succeeded in obtaining a superpower's defense for their survival.

Monarchs themselves definitely made use of the opportunities opened to them to reinforce their rule. Scholars have pointed out several explanations for such resilience. Michael Hudson stressed the initiatives to modernize, namely, the promotion of technological development, the raising of living standards, better education, and the activation of the economy. In so doing, monarchs followed the same course as revolutionary leaders and even surpassed them. They could assume the legitimacy of state developers and economic reformers by demonstrating organizational skills and initiating infrastructural projects, thereby beating the revolutionary leaders at their own claim to fame. Anderson (in her chapter in this volume as well as in an earlier article) emphasized the king's ability in coping with hurdles of state-building, by establishing valid institutions, social integration, basic game rules for a state, and/or myths (or a historical narrative) on which it can draw.

A most significant process in monarchies' resilience was the reinforcement of the monarchical institution, notably of the monarchs themselves as ex machina leaders, standing above the political system and reinstating the monarchical code in their relations vis-à-vis their societies. As we learn from the chapters written by Asher Susser, Remy Leveau, Joseph Kostiner and Joshua Teitelbaum, Uzi Rabi, and Joseph A. Kechichian (respectively, Chapters 7, 8, 9, 10, and 12), various practices and skills account for this development: first, the experience that Middle Eastern monarchs gained in dealing with their states' affairs and with opposition groups, which turned them into experts at survival and in devising legitimizing tactics. The Jordanian and Moroccan monarchs succeeded in surmounting most endangering mutinies. Second, linking themselves to state myths and/or leading religious ideologies: the Moroccan as leader of the independence movement and *amir al-muminin*, the Jordanian as the Hashemite offspring, and the Saudi as successor of the kingdom's founder and as *khadim al-haramayn* (custodian of the two holy places). Third, the monarchs learned to rule while rising above ethnic or other intergroup rivalries, acting as their mediators, and as self-styled patrons of all groups and defenders of minorities. The Moroccan king's action as a modern *marabut* (religious saint) and defender of the Berbers, the Jordanian king as the adjudicator or defender of the Palestinian–East Jordanian tension and champion of tribes, and the Saudi and Persian Gulf monarchs as balancing agents among Shi'ite and Sunni groups and tribal and regional segments, present several examples. Fourth, the monarchs were able to perform versatile personalized patterns of behavior, befitting the various individuals and social segments they sought to win over or co-opt. A monarch moved from a ritual in which he acted as a patron of a certain group, to preside over a tribal meeting to commemorate a local myth, to a meeting with businessmen, and then on to a governmental session. He would change roles and outfits accord-

ingly, each one with the special characteristics of the required code and eti-
quette, legitimizing himself with different groups. This enabled a monarch to
treat his people through intimate and traditional practices typical of their cultural grouping.[17] Monarchs were thus able to exercise the two fundamentals
of monarchical rule: generating state development and exercising patrimonial
segmentary social control.

According to Anderson's thesis, the monarchical code suited and espoused a society modeled around segments, each with a separate identity and
organizational framework, held together as a coalition in which the monarch
and his institution are the linchpin. Monarchies did not encourage the evolution of a uniform, assimilated, and organic "nation" in their states: such a development would have just emulated the endeavors of the rival revolutionary
states and would have eliminated the structural basis of the various segments
of society. This actual "primordial" practice allowed societies to retain their
traditional composition without having to transform. Minorities, various eco-
logical groups, and even majority populations favoring a traditional lifestyle
could find their stability and peace under a monarchical regime. This system
permitted the monarchs to appear as promoters of traditional values, of tribal
myths, and as defenders of minorities and ethnic groups. The ascriptive and
ethnic groups were personally linked to the king and fell under his protection.
He was thereby also able to become the medium through which such groups
were integrated into their state: the center that kept ties and open contacts
with all the groups in society. According to this argument the point made by
Hisham Sharabi and others lamenting the resilience of "neopatriarchy" can be
reversed: the patriarchal ascriptive loyalties and the monarchs' cultivation of
segmentary divisions mark a strong stabilizing factor of monarchies.[18]

In addition, unlike during the 1930s and 1940s, in recent decades kings
established strong ruling institutions in terms of bureaucracy and control able
to utilize finances to promote the societies they had envisaged. No practice of
constitutional government was allowed to interfere with this development.
Hazem Beblawi, Nazih Ayubi, and Kiren Chaudhry focused on the monarchies' ability to use the oil finances to develop a distributional welfare state,
or a "rentier state," notably the Gulf monarchies, to boost the inhabitants' living standards, either by engagement in trade, financial business, and immo-
bile property, or simply to employ them by the government and assure their
income. Furthermore, Gulf governments aimed at ensuring for their citizens
free, or almost free, benefits such as education, health insurance, and sometimes even housing (notably in Kuwait and Saudi Arabia). Ayubi, following
Khaldun al-Naqib, stresses that the welfare programs were supposed to cover
or compensate for the lack of political rights, and in the vein of "no taxation
without representation," as no major taxation was imposed (particularly in the
Gulf monarchies), there was also no adequate political representation.
Monarchies thus did not provide incentives for democratization but rather

preferable substitutes for it. Following Jill Crystal's point, it can be argued that new-middle-class groups, which endangered some Middle East monarchies in the middle of the century, integrated themselves into the rentier-state societies and patriarchal systems.[19]

Finally, monarchies' strength was evident in several innovative courses and their balancing means. The monarchs were in favor of technological development but balanced the subsequent social change both by allowing traditional, tribal, and Islamic practices to govern society and by allowing the welfare system to support any unfortunate failures of the changes. There was change, but it was with an eye to the individual and his traditional world. Societies thus still ran on traditional family-based codes with a welfare safety net to sustain them. Middle Eastern monarchism in the late twentieth century evolved into a system that was politically balanced, economically developmental, yet traditional and socioculturally integrative. Gregory Gause's argument—that monarchies' stability depends on superpowers' commitment to monarchies' stability—provides an additional, rather than a contradictory, factor to internal state-building explanations.

The resilience of monarchies is in fact evident when compared to the fate of revolutionary regimes in the region. After several decades these regimes have not only failed to produce "new societies" in the Arab world and array societies in "modern," stratified, class-based, and/or sectoral frameworks; they were also unable to develop an economy that would provide for the welfare of their populations and had to resort to material assistance from superpowers, European states, and even monarchical regimes. In recent years, revolutionary regimes therefore tended to withdraw from their revolutionary agendas and revert to hinging on coalitions consisting of family ties, personal business contacts, middlemen, and patrimonial appointments, which cut through the "modern" classes and resembled the more segmentary traditional societies. Monarchical resilience connotes the socialist Arab nationalist failure.[20]

As David Menashri illustrates in Chapter 13, the most evident monarchical failure in recent years—namely, the fall of the Iranian shah—was not so much a manifestation of deep-seated antimonarchical sentiment but rather a response to a failure of the shah's policies or, as Theda Skocpol noted, his inability to properly apply modernizing processes and balance them through welfare policies and tradition.[21]

Iran's experience, however, shows that a new set of challenges for monarchies may be at work and in ascent. The declining oil income hindered the monarchical governments' ability to perform welfare roles and infrastructural construction simultaneously. The rentier state has weakened. As Onn Winckler shows in Chapter 14, problems arise as the income sources of the economy have to be reinvigorated or sought out. Similarly, societies have to be cut off from government welfare and employment, but the monarchies prefer to prolong the welfare policies as they cannot restructure and fear the loss of their inhabitants' support and legitimacy. Moreover, with rising claims of unemployment, the salience of absent political rights becomes more evident. Under these circumstances, the personalized patriarchal touch of Middle Eastern monarchies may lose some of its attraction.

In Chapter 15, Gudrun Krämer shows the threat that Islamic fundamentalism can pose. This challenge is not only evident in military-terrorist activities, which can be suppressed, but—by inducing criticism of the tribal-personalized monarchical approach—in the name of *shari'a*-based equality set against monarchical supremacy in the name of a religious-based value system and leadership. In Chapter 16, Fred Halliday discusses whether fundamentalism, spurred by a declining rentier state, would be able to delegitimize monarchies, or whether they will be again able to diffuse this threat by traditional means; it remains a major question for the twenty-first century. But as time passes, Middle Eastern monarchs can perhaps smile when thinking that the regimes of Saddam Hussein and Hafiz al-Asad resemble today a monarchical dynasty rather than a triumphant revolutionary avant garde.

NOTES

1. Jurgen Habermas, *Legitimation Crisis* (London: Heinemann, 1976).
2. See Albert Hourani, *Arabic Thought in the Liberal Age, 1798–1939* (Cambridge: Cambridge University Press, rep. 1997), chapters 1–2.
3. Ernest Gellner, "Tribalism and State in the Middle East," in P. S. Khoury and J. Kostiner, *Tribes and State Formation in the Middle East* (Berkeley: University of California Press, 1990), pp. 109–126; Tarif Khalidi, *Classical Arab Islam* (Princeton: Darwin, 1985), pp. 117–127; Cornell Fleischer, "Royal Authority, Dynastic Cyclism, and 'Ibn Khaldunism' in Sixteenth Century Ottoman Letters," *Journal of Asian and African Studies*, 18 (1983), pp. 169–220.
4. Halil Inalcik, "Comment on 'Sultanism': Max Weber's Typification of the Ottoman Polity," *Princeton Papers in Near Eastern Studies*, 1 (1992), pp. 49–72.
5. Karen Barkey, *Bandits and Bureaucrats: The Ottoman Route to State Centralization* (Ithaca: Cornell University Press, 1994), chapters 1–2.
6. Peter Lienhardt, "The Authority of Shaykhs in the Gulf: An Essay in Nineteenth Century History," *Arabian Studies*, 2 (1975), pp. 61–76.
7. Philip S. Khoury and Joseph Kostiner, *Tribes and State Formation,* "Introduction," pp. 1–23.
8. Barrington Moore, *Social Origins of Dictatorship and Democracy* (Harmondsworth: Penguin, 1969); Theda Skocpol, *States and Social Revolutions* (Cambridge: Cambridge University Press, 1979); Norbert Elias, *The Civilizing Process* (Oxford: Basil Blackwell, 1982); Norbert Elias, *The Court Society*, trans. by E. Jephcott (Oxford: Basil Blackwell, 1983).
9. Alan Richards and John Waterbury, *A Political Economy of the Middle East* (Boulder: Westview Press, 1996), pp. 297–298.
10. Bryan S. Turner, *Max Weber from History to Modernity* (London: Routledge, 1993), pp. 185–208.

11. Compare with Perry Anderson's use of this concept, in his *Lineages of the Absolutist State* (London: Verso, 1974).

12. Compare with Theda Skocpol, *Social Revolution* (Cambridge: Cambridge University Press, 1979); see Nazih Ayubi, *Overstating the Arab State: Politics and Society in the Middle East* (London: Tauris, 1995), chapter 7; Khoury and Kostiner, *Tribes and State Formation*; see also Khaldun al-Naqib's discussion on this issue in I. Hijazi, et al., *Nahwa Ilm Ijtima^c Arabi* (Beirut: Center for Arab Unity Studies, 1986).

13. See Elie Kedourie, *Politics in the Middle East* (Oxford: Oxford University Press, 1991); Hanna Batatu, *The Old Social Classes and the Revolutionary Movements in Iraq* (Princeton: Princeton University Press, 1978); A. Ahmad, "Class, Nation, and State: Intermediate Classes in Peripheral Societies," in D. L. Johnson (ed.), *Middle Classes in Dependent Countries* (London: Sage, 1985).

14. Reinhard Bendix, *King or People: Power and the Mandate Rule* (Berkeley: University of California Press, 1978).

15. Samuel P. Huntington, *Political Order in Changing Societies* (New Haven: Yale University Press, 1968), pp. 177–180.

16. Lisa Anderson, "Absolutism and the Resilience of Monarchy in the Middle East," *Political Science Quarterly*, 106 (1991), pp. 1–25.

17. Ayubi, *Overstating the Arab State,* pp. 224–255; Ernest Gellner and John Waterbury (eds.), *Patrons and Clients in Mediterranean Societies* (London: Duckworth, 1977); J. Waterbury, *The Commander of the Faithful: The Moroccan Elite—A Study in Segmented Politics* (London: Weidenfeld and Nicolson, 1970).

18. Hisham Sharabi, *Neopatriarchy: A Theory of Distorted Change in Arab Society* (Oxford: Oxford University Press, 1988).

19. Michael Hudson, *Arab Politics: The Search for Legitimacy* (New Haven: Yale University Press, 1968); Anderson, "Absolutism and Resilience"; Kiren A. Chaudhry, *The Price of Wealth: Economies and Institutions in the Middle East* (Ithaca: Cornell University Press, 1997); Hazem Beblawi, "The Rentier State in the Arab World," in Giacomo Luciani (ed.), *The Arab State* (London: Routledge, 1990), pp. 85–98; Ayubi, *Overstating the Arab State,* pp. 224–255; F. Gregory Gause III, "Sovereignty, Statecraft, and Stability in the Middle East," *Journal of International Affairs*, 4 (1992); Jill Crystal, "Authoritarianism and Its Adversaries in the Arab World," *World Politics*, 46 (1994), pp. 262–289.

20. Elizabeth Picard, "Arab Military in Politics: From Revolutionary Plot to Authoritarian State," in Adeed Dawisha and William Zartman (eds.), *Beyond Coercion: The Durability of the Arab State* (London: Croom Helm, 1988); Jill Crystal, "Authoritarianism"; J. Migdal, *Strong Societies and Weak States* (Princeton: Princeton University Press, 1988).

21. Theda Skocpol, "Rentier State and Shia Islam in the Iranian Revolution," *Theory and Society*, 2 (1982), pp. 265–304.

PART ONE

Context

2

Monarchy in the Middle East

Bernard Lewis

The word *monarchy* has been, and at times still is, used in two different senses. One of them is indicated by its etymology, from two Greek words, the first meaning "single" or "alone," the second meaning "rule." In this sense monarchy means one-man personal rule—the rule of an individual—as contrasted in ancient and medieval times with aristocracy and oligarchy, or in modern times with democracy. Often the term also carries a connotation of arbitrary rule. The Arabic term used to render monarchy in this sense, *istibdad*, usually has this connotation and is contrasted with *shura* or *mashwara* (consultation). *Istibdad* conveys the idea of a ruler who governs in accordance with his personal desires and caprice without consulting those whom it would be appropriate to consult.[1] Traditional Islamic literature lays great emphasis on the importance of consultation, with both statesmen and men of religion.

The other connotation of the term "monarchy" relates not to the exercise but to the acquisition of supreme sovereign authority. In this sense monarchy means "hereditary," that is, dynastic rule, in which the headship of the state is transmitted from one member to another of the same family. It is membership of this family that confers legitimacy, that is, the primary basis of entitlement of whoever accedes to the supreme sovereign office after the death or removal of his predecessor. In this sense, the converse of a monarchy is a republic.

The two connotations of monarchy are not the same, though they may overlap. At some times and in some places, especially in recent years, they may even appear to be contradictory. In Europe, for example, the surviving monarchies are without exception constitutional democracies. Most of them have been so for a long time and show every sign of continuing along the same path. Most of the democratic republics, in contrast, have a brief and checkered history. The surviving tyrannies in the modern world are with few exceptions republics, not monarchies.

The Arabic term *malik* has been used to convey both meanings of "monarch." If you consult an English-Arabic or Arabic-English dictionary, you will be told with the laconic and sometimes specious certitude of lexicographers that *malik* equals "king" and "king" equals *malik*. This is, of course, misleading. There are times and places when that equation may be correct. But mostly, the connotations of these terms, and for that matter of other equivalent terms in various languages, differ considerably.

In talking about the use of royal titles among the Arabs, we are not obliged to rely only on literary evidence, itself often based on fallible human memory. We have hard evidence in the literal sense—coins and inscriptions, many of them dated—where we can follow the development and ramification of royal titulature.

The earliest uses of the title are on the whole positive. There were the kings of Kinda and of Hira, known from the literary tradition. The oldest surviving inscription in the Arabic language, an epitaph of 328 C.E. found at Namara, commemorates a "king (*malik*) of all the Arabs, who wore the diadem. . . . No king until this time had attained what he had attained."[2] The last Byzantine emperor to rule over Egypt and the Syrian lands before the advent of Islam, Heraklius, adopted the king-title *basileus*, in addition to the usual Byzantine title *autokrator*, to celebrate the Christian victory over the infidel Persians, in particular the recovery of the Holy Land and the Holy City of Jerusalem. The term *basileus* brought with it an echo of the ancient kings of Israel celebrated in the Bible and of Christ the king.

But among the ancient Arabs kingship often had a negative connotation. The Bedouin, like other nomads, dislike any kind of central authority. An Arabic word, *leqah*, is explained as meaning "those who had never submitted to a king," and there is a poem attributed to the pre-Islamic Arabic poet Abid ibn al-Abras in which he says in praise of his own tribe: "They refused to be servants of kings, and were never ruled by any. But when they were called on for help in war, they responded gladly."[3]

The earliest specifically Islamic references to kings and kingship are mostly negative and very much resemble the picture that emerges from the Hebrew Bible, particularly from the Book of Samuel, of the events that led to the troubled emergence of the Israelite monarchy. In both Quran and *hadith* the word *malik* is sometimes used as a divine epithet, in which case of course it has a positive meaning. As applied to mortals, it often carries a connotation of presumption and even of paganism.[4] Both David and Solomon appear in the Quran and both are positively portrayed. But both are prophets and, though depicted in royal splendor, are not designated by the word *malik*. The only one of the ancient Israelite kings expressly designated as such in the Quran is Saul, in the Quranic version called Talut, and he has the same rather equivocal image in the Quran as in the Book of Samuel.[5]

In the early Islamic centuries the words *king* and *kingship* often retain this rather negative connotation, especially when contrasted with *caliph* and *caliphate*. An early narrative preserved by Tabari records a conversation between the caliph Umar and the Persian convert Salman: "Salman said that Umar said to him: 'Am I a king or a caliph?' And Salman answered: 'If you have taxed the lands of the Muslim one dirham, or more, or less, and applied to unlawful purposes, then you are a king not a caliph.' And Umar wept."[6] The contrast between *kingship* and *caliphate* is clearly indicated in this anecdote. The essential difference is not between elective and dynastic succession, since the latter very rapidly became the norm in the caliphate, too, but between arbitrary rule and government in accordance with the divine law.

The term *malik* was thus used in the early Islamic centuries to denote rulers whose authority was primarily military and political—or, as we might say, "secular"—rather than religious and whose manner of ruling was arbitrary and personal rather than lawful and religious. But the dynastic principle was not seriously challenged and was argued in an extreme form by the Shia for whom the only legitimate dynasty is that of the descendants of the Prophet. The title *king* (*malik*) was not replaced but rather overtopped by more exalted titles with an imperial rather than a royal connotation. These may be Arab, like *sultan*, or Persian, like *shah* and *padishah*, or Turkish and Mongol, like *khaqan* and *khan*.

As the use of these titles became more general among Muslim dynasties, the title *king* acquired another and different negative connotation—that of subordination with the rise of independent principalities within the caliphate; the title was used by many of the new princes. Their titulature makes it clear that it was no longer a title of sovereignty. The king, the *malik*, was less than the caliph and the sultan, and while asserting his own authority he nevertheless recognized the higher authority of a suzerain. Another distinctive feature is that the king in this period does not claim kingship of any place or people. His title is simply *al-malik*, usually followed by some adjective, such as "the Excellent," "the Perfect," and the like.

The title *king*, followed by an enumeration of the peoples and lands over which kingship is claimed or exercised, was at first used principally of foreign and infidel rulers. These include the Byzantine emperor, the king of Nubia, and various Christian European kings collectively known as *muluk al-kuffar* (the kings of the unbelievers) or even as *muluk al-kufr* (the kings of unbelief). Tabari tells a revealing story about an exchange of diplomatic messages between the Byzantine emperor Nikephorus and the caliph Harun al-Rashid. Nikephorus addressed the caliph as "Harun, king of the Arabs." From the point of view of the emperor this was no doubt a correct title, since he himself used the title *king* (*basileus*) and was king of the Romans. He was doing Harun the honor of giving him the same kind of title as he used himself.

But for the caliph—"the commander of the faithful"—to be called "king of the Arabs" was a double insult. It implied that he was only a king—and only of the Arabs! He expressed his anger in his reply to the emperor, headed "From Harun, Commander of the Faithful, to Nikephorus, Dog of the Romans" (*Mim Harun, amir al-muminin ila Niqfur, kalb al-Rum*).[7]

In later medieval centuries, both territorial and ethnic titles begin to appear in Muslim royal titulature. Some of these are rather vague: for example, *Malik asl-Barrayn wal-Bahrayn* (King of the Two Lands and the Two Seas), used by the Mamluks and later adopted by the Ottomans. For the Mamluks the two seas were the Mediterranean and the Red Sea; for the Ottomans, the Mediterranean and the Black Sea. An even earlier title used by the Seljuks was *Malik al-Mashriq wal-Maghrib* (King of the East and the West), which looks rather like a claim to universal sovereignty. Another interesting title is *Malik al-Muluk* (King of Kings), clearly a translation of the Persian *shahanshah*. The Buyid dynasty also used such titles as *Malik al-Umam* (King of the Nations) and even *Malik al-Dawla* (King of the State). Some titles appear to be ethnic. Thus, Mamluk sultans called themselves, as part of a string of titles, *Malik al-Arab wal-Ajam* (King of the Arabs and Persians); perhaps a fair translation would be "King of the Arabs and everyone else."[8] In Ottoman times this becomes *Malik al-Arab wal-Ajam Awal-Rum* (King of the Arabs and non-Arabs and the Rum), *Rum* at that time meaning the Ottomans and the Ottoman lands. These are not claims to ethnic leadership but rather denote the assertion of universal supreme sovereignty.

Titles defining a territorial or national kingdom, commonplace in Europe, were until the twentieth century almost unknown in the Islamic world. A few Turkish rulers in pre-Ottoman Anatolia, no doubt influenced by the usage of the peoples whom they had just conquered, sometimes struck coins or wrote inscriptions with territorial titles. But these are rare and atypical and were of brief duration. In the later medieval and subsequent centuries the petty sovereignties and autonomous principalities typical of the Islamic Middle Ages had for the most part disappeared. Most of the Islamic Middle East was divided among a small number of major states, the rulers of which used imperial rather than royal titles. The term *malik* survived principally in two contexts: as a component, of no special significance, in the string of titles and honorifics used by the Ottoman and other emperors; and as a designation for European and other infidel rulers. It was in the latter but not in the former context that the term denoted sovereignty and related to a particular place and people. In Turkish these monarchs were usually given the title *kiral*, a loanword from Slavic or Hungarian. In Arabic they were called "*malik*," sometimes replaced by the explicitly condemnatory term "*taghiya*" or "*taghut*," with a connotation of insolence and usurpation.

In the twentieth century the *malik* title enjoyed both a revival of popularity and an improvement in status. This change is a reflection of Western, more particularly British, usage and derived its popularity and prestige from the sovereign institution of what was then the greatest empire in the world. The first modern Muslim ruler to use the title appears to have been Sharif Hussein, who declared himself king of the Hijaz in 1916. He was followed by his son Faysal, who proclaimed an Arab kingdom in Syria in 1920 and, after the failure of that adventure, became king of Iraq in 1921. In 1922 he was followed by the ruler of Egypt, where the ruling dynasty had changed its titles several times. The line of Muhammad Ali came to power in Egypt as Ottoman pashas. They changed their titles successively to *khedive*, to declare their autonomy under the Ottoman sultan, and then to *sultan*—using the Ottoman suzerain's own title—to declare their independence. In the same way the title *king*—that used by the ruler of Britain himself—served to proclaim independence from Britain.

Others followed. The most important was Ibn Saud, who in 1926 proclaimed himself king of the Hijaz and sultan of Najd. In 1932 the two were merged in a kingdom with a new name—Saudi Arabia. Later in Morocco, Jordan, and Libya adoption of the royal title served the same purpose as it had in Egypt at an earlier date, namely, that of declaring independence against a European suzerain power.

Through all these changes, the dynastic principle and the practice of hereditary succession remained powerful, deep-rooted, and virtually universal in the Islamic Middle East. Even in the nomadic tribes, the *shaikh* is normally chosen from among the members of one family, who have a recognized hereditary claim to the headship of the tribe and very often to the custody of some sacred place or object—the palladium or ark of the covenant, so to speak. Similar practices may be observed also among Iranian and Turkic nomads. The principle of primogeniture—of succession from father to eldest son in the direct—is a European idea. It was not accepted among the ancient Arabs, and it never took root in the great Muslim dynastic empires. Descent in the male line from the founding and the ruling families was the sole requirement. The most usual practice was for the ruler to designate his successor, choosing whichever of his uncles, brothers, nephews, or sons might be the most suitable. Sometimes the ruler might designate more than one in line, though this was neither usual nor required.

The advent of Islam changed this only briefly. The death of the Prophet posed an immediate question of succession. As Prophet, he could have no successor. But the Prophet had not only created a religious community; he had also founded a state, which was rapidly becoming an empire, and that state urgently needed a sovereign. At a very early date the famous split occurred between the Sunni and the Shi'ite views, the Shia doctrine being frankly dynastic. According to them, only the lineal descendants of the Prophet are entitled to rule as his successors. Since the Prophet had no descendants in the male line, a unique exception is made in favor of the descendants of his daughter, Fatima. The Sunni view, in contrast, as formerly set forth, was that the caliphate should be elective. This should not be understood in modern terms of universal suffrage. The juristic concept of election means that on the death of the caliph the most suitable successor is chosen by a small college of qualified electors.

The first four caliphs after the death of the Prophet were indeed elected in the sense that none of them had a hereditary claim to the succession. If one asks the pragmatic question—did the elective system work?—the answer must surely be that it did not. Of the four elective caliphs three were murdered—the last two by fellow Muslims—and the whole system collapsed in a bloody civil war. The emergence of the dynastic caliphates and sultanates was the result.

Republican, that is, nonhereditary, sovereignties were not unknown in the Islamic world. We have descriptions from Arabic and Turkish writers of the Italian republics in the Middle Ages and of the Dutch and English republics in the seventeenth century. But they showed no great interest in this form of government. The first European republic to obtrude itself forcibly on Muslim attention was the French republic. Early reactions to it were almost uniformly negative. The Ottoman historian Asim at the beginning of the nineteenth century likens the politics of the French republic to "the rumblings and crepitations of a queasy stomach."[9] But republicanism, often confused with democracy, began to exercise an increasing fascination, and during the twentieth century republicanism—and with it republican forms of government—developed rapidly. The earliest republics were those established in the Muslim territories of the fallen Russian Empire, when the temporary relaxation of pressure from the capital after the revolutions of 1917 allowed a brief interval of local independence and experimentation. In May 1918, after the dissolution of the short-lived Trans-Caucasian Federation, the Azerbaijani members of the Trans-Caucasian Parliament declared Azerbaijan an independent republic—the first Muslim republic in modern times. It was of brief duration and in April 1920 was conquered by the Red Army and reconstituted as a Soviet republic. The same pattern was followed by other Turkic and Muslim peoples of the Russian Empire, whose short-lived national republics were all in due course taken over and reconstituted as Soviet republics or regions within the USSR. The first Muslim republic to be established outside the Russian Empire seems to have been the Tripolitanian Republic, proclaimed in November 1918. It was later incorporated in the Italian colony of Libya. The first independent republic that remained both independent and a republic was that of Turkey, established on 29 October 1923. Republican institutions were created by the French in the mandated territories of Syria and Lebanon.

In the aftermath of World War II, the decline of the once dominant British Empire and the rise to power and prominence of the United States and the Soviet Union contributed to the devaluation of royalty and the new popularity of republics. In one country after another monarchs were overthrown, by coup or revolution, and replaced by presidents and leaders presiding over republics of various complexions: Egypt in 1953, Sudan in 1956, Iraq in 1958, Tunisia in 1959, Yemen in 1962, Afghanistan in 1973, Iran in 1979. In many of these states the term *republic* denotes neither the Islamic converse of arbitrary rule nor the Western converse of dynasticism.

The institution of kingship or, more specifically, the use of royal titles, was under attack from various sides: by liberals and leftists who saw a republican form of government as more in accord with their ideologies and aspirations; by Muslim fundamentalists who had revived the tradition of Islamic condemnation of royal pomp and titulature; and more generally by those who felt that monarchy was old-fashioned and republics were modern and progressive.

Monarchies are now clearly a minority in the Middle East, yet the dynastic principle has remained extremely powerful even to the present day. The last and most enduring of the great Islamic empires, that of the Ottomans, took its name and identity from the founding and ruling dynasty—the House of Osmon (Uthman). In the same way, Saudi Arabia, probably the most Arab and most Islamic of the states in the region, takes its name and identity from the founding and ruling dynasty. More remarkably, even in the modern, avowedly secular regimes of Syria and Iraq, it is striking that both Saddam Hussein and Hafiz al-Asad seem determined to found dynasties or at least to ensure the succession of their sons. Both royalty and democracy are under siege in the Middle East, but dynasticism, it would seem, is alive and well.

BIBLIOGRAPHICAL NOTE

The numismatic and epigraphic evidence in the use of *malik* in medieval Islamic states was reviewed and analyzed by Hasan al-Basha, *Al-Alqab al-Islamiyya fil-tarikh wal-wathaiq wal-athar* (Cairo: Maktabat al-Nahda al-Misriyya, 1957), pp. 496–506, and al-Basha, *Al-Funun al-Islamiyya wasl-wazaif ala al-Arabiyya*, 3 (Cairo: Maktabat al-Nahda al-Misriyya, 1966), pp. 1139–1142. The literary evidence relating to pre-Islamic Arabia was examined by Emile Tyan, *Institutions du droit public musulman*, 1, *Le Califat* (Paris, 1954), pp. 75–84, and Francesco Gabrieli, *Tribu e Stato nellantica poesia araba*, in his *L'Islam nella storia* (Bari, 1966), pp. 9–26. The reappearance of monarchical titles and their use by Muslim rulers have been studied by Wilferd Madelung, "The Assumption of the Title Shahanshah by the Buyids" and the "Reign of the Daylam Dawlat al-Daylam," *Journal of Near Eastern Studies*, 28 (1969), pp. 84–108 and 168–183, and by C. E. Bosworth, "The Titulature of the Early Ghaznavids," *Oriens*, 15 (1962), pp. 210–233. The revival and use of the term in the nineteenth and twentieth centuries was studied by Ami Ayalon, "Malik in Modern Middle Eastern Titulature," in *Die Welt des Islam,* 23–24 (1984), pp. 306–319. On royal titles in general, see Bernard Lewis, *The Political Language of Islam* (Chicago: University of Chicago Press, 1988), pp. 96ff.

NOTES

An earlier version of some parts of this chapter was published in my article, "Malik," in *Cahiers de Tunisie*, Tunis, 35, no. 139–140 (1987), pp. 101–109.

1. B. Lewis, "Usurpers and Tyrants: Notes on Some Islamic Political Terms," in Roger M. Savory and Dionisius A. Agius (eds.), *Logos Islamikos: Studia Islamica in honorem Georgiii Michaelis Wickens*, Papers in Mediaeval Studies 6 (Toronto: Pontifical Institute of Mediaeval Studies, 1984), pp. 259–267.

2. *RCEA (Repertoire Chronologique d' Epigraphie arabe)*, 1 (Cairo 1931), n. 1.

3. The *diwan*s of Abid b. al-Abras and Amir b. al-Tufayl, ed. and tr. Sir Charles Lyall (Leiden, 1913), p. 64; text, p. 81 (London, printed for the trustees of the "E.J.W. GIBB Memorial" by Luzac).

4. See, for example, Quran 12, where *malik* is commonly used for pharaoh; cf. 27, 34, where the queen of Sheba remarks to Solomon: "When kings enter a city, they pillage it and make its nobles destitute. Thus do kings."

5. Quran 2, 247 ff.

6. Tabari, *Tarikh al-Rusul wal-Muluk*, 1, p. 2754.

7. Ibid , 3, pp. 695–696.

8. Al-Basha, *Al-Alqab al-Islamiyya fil-tarıkh wal-waıhu'iy wal-athar* (Cairo, 1957), pp. 497, 502–505; *RCEA*, 6, p. 2177, 7, pp. 2377, 2378, 2707, 2734, 2760; 9, p. 3509; 10, p. 3739; 11, pp. 3273, 4308; 12, p. 4554.

9. Ahmad Asim, *Tarikh* (Istanbul, n.d.), 1, p. 78.

3

Post-Ottoman Arab Monarchies: Old Bottles, New Labels?

Ami Ayalon

The fall of the Ottoman Empire at the end of World War I confronted its former Arab provinces with the need to redefine their political communities. Gone was Ottoman suzerainty with its age-old, clear, and simple order. As provinces were about to turn into states, with international boundaries, capitals, and local governments, their future political identity and system of rule were anything but obvious.

As for setting up political regimes, the new states had several options to consider. One distinct choice was the long-familiar order of unchallenged autocracy, subject to no controls, of the kind that had marked Ottoman rule during the empire's heyday and, more recently, under Abd al-Hamid II. Another option—less well-known but now conspicuously present in the neighborhood—was the novel model of a republican regime, with popular sovereignty and elective government, which the Turkish heir to the Ottoman state was about to adopt—an imported idea that would take a leader of Ataturk's caliber to introduce. There were other possibilities: nonabsolute monarchy, limited by constitution and parliament, as practiced in certain Western states, above all in Britain; and some other variations of kingship, familiar in certain local polities mostly in the Arabian Peninsula—tribal chieftaincies headed by widely accepted leaders with or without regal titles. As it happened, the great majority of Arab states opted for a monarchical order of one brand or another. Only in a few places this did not occur: either where no state was set up (as was the case in mandatory Palestine and the provinces of Tripolitania and Cyrenaica),[1] or where the French, who came to rule parts of the region, imposed a nonmonarchical regime. Elsewhere, kingship and monarchy became the fashion, and it remained so until after midcentury.

It is hardly surprising that monarchy was widely preferred in the Arab states. For one thing, it represented the most familiar kind of regime, an "intelligible government" in Walter Bagehot's words, a straightforward idea: "The mass of mankind understand it, and they hardly anywhere in the world understand any other."[2] For another, monarchy—in the literal sense of a "single-person rule"—was compatible with Arab and Islamic thought as sanctioned by generations of Muslim jurists. It was just as compatible with the region's experience of government both before and during centuries of Ottoman rule. But perhaps more significant was a more recent cause for the lure of kingship: the contemporary Western example, in which royal power seemed to be associated with a dignified international status. Kings and queens in Europe—above all, again, those of Britain, the mightiest power of the day—were widely acknowledged symbols of proud dominion. Majestically sovereign and subordinate to no other human sway, these Western monarchs featured an attractive model. With the decline and later disappearance of the caliphate, joining the international circle of respectable royalties seemed to many leaders in the region the obvious course to follow. Establishing monarchies thus corresponded not only to the tradition of the region but also to what seemed norms of modern international prestige.

The Western example of royal government had an additional facet that the new Arab polities now had to consider. In some of Europe's most powerful states, kingship was constitutional and parliamentary, with representative institutions and responsible governments. Impressed with the global prominence of these monarchies, the new states could import the additional components of the foreign model, assuming that they were marks of modernity and maybe a recipe for might. This, of course, was optional, and rulers in the region did not necessarily have to buy the whole package: they could choose to borrow only the kingly title and certain regal trappings in order to acquire the standing that they seemed to entail while rejecting the other ingredients of the foreign formula.

The monarchies that emerged in the Middle East following World War I may be discussed under two headings, distinct from each other by their approach to this last choice. One category would comprise monarchies in tribal societies, whose rulers sometimes borrowed the Western royal titulature but little else. These were set up or continued to exist where foreign influence was relatively limited—mostly, though not exclusively, in the Arabian Peninsula. The other would include kingdoms of a more modern type, whose leaders tried to assimilate not just the royal title but also some of the other institutions of the European example, thereby accepting certain constitutional restrictions on the king's sway, at least in theory. Such states were set up in those parts of the region that had been gradually exposed to Western influences during the previous century, namely, Egypt and the countries of the Fertile Crescent. States of the latter kind represent a far more instructive case, and the greater part of the discussion below will be devoted to them.

The first Arab ruler in the twentieth century to proclaim himself king, however, did not belong to the last category of modern-style monarchs in the Middle East. This was the Hashemite Sharif Hussein bin Ali, ruler of the Hijaz, who did so during the war while rebelling against his Ottoman masters. Hussein squarely belongs in the group of old-type, traditional kings. Still, it will be useful to examine his case first, since in more ways than one he blazed the trail for subsequent Arab monarchs.

The sharif's coronation took place in the Grand Mosque of Mecca, on the morning of 2 Muharram 1335/29 October 1916. Local *ulama* and notables came to offer Hussein a solemn vote of confidence, as *malik al-bilad al-arabiyya* (King of the Arab Lands).[3] There seemed to be little novelty in this event: not only did it follow the conventional procedure for recognizing a new ruler; it also recalled a tradition, with roots as deep as the early Abbasid period, of Muslim potentates defying imperial or caliphal authority by declaring their own autonomous or independent state. Even when Hussein introduced a new flag, and later a new coin bearing his name, he was merely treading a familiar path.

Still, there was a new aspect to the sharif's gesture. Hussein was the first Arab ruler in many centuries to assume the title *malik*, the closest Arabic equivalent to "king." This choice of title was not without significance. The word *malik* (plural: *muluk*) had had a vicissitudinal history, in which commendatory and derogatory connotations had alternated over the centuries with the changing circumstances of power and status. For hundreds of years prior to the nineteenth century *malik* had been an uncomplimentary title: Muslim rulers had not taken it for themselves, and it had served mostly to designate foreign monarchs, implying an inferior kind of power. The title had often been accompanied by an indication of territory, so as to emphasize the limits of the foreign king's or queen's domain (whereas Muslim rulers had usually professed sovereignty "of Islam" or "of the believers"). This attitude, however, had begun to change in the later part of the nineteenth century. European kings, no longer the "petty rulers" they had once been, had come to be viewed in the Middle East as eminent symbols of potency and high standing. Disregard and disdain had gradually given way to a more complimentary view, and *malik* had concomitantly lost its pejorative connotations, becoming a respectable title instead.[4]

By the time Sharif Hussein had to consider his options, declaring himself as *malik* and even adding the qualifying reference "of the Arab Lands" had ceased to be problematic for a Muslim ruler. Nor did the *ulama* of Mecca seem to have had much difficulty in sanctioning a new and more commendable semblance of kingship. Abdallah, Hussein's son, relates in his memoirs how the mufti (the leading professional jurist) of Mecca, the *qadi al-qudat* (leading judge) of the Hijaz, and other religious functionaries came to persuade the sharif to accept the kingly title.[5] Hussein also received the blessing of another known *alim*, Rashid Rida, who sent him a letter to congratulate him and reproduced the report on the coronation ceremony, first published in the sharif's organ *al-Qibla*, in his own journal *al-Manar*.[6] Becoming a "king," then, was now not only acceptable but also desirable. Like his predecessors in the Abbasid era—the Samanids, Buwayhids, Ghaznavids, and others—the sharif would thereby be declaring his autonomous standing, indeed his sovereignty, versus his former lord. He would thus acquire a powerful claim for supremacy over his dangerous neighbors in the Peninsula, the Saudis,[7] and strengthen his position among his own tribal constituencies. Like his esteemed contemporary monarchs in Europe, he further would be presenting a claim to the international standing over which he had been bargaining with Great Britain and which, he felt, he rightly deserved. If the ruler of Montenegro was entitled to a recognized kingly status, he insisted in his negotiations with the British, was not the sharif of Mecca similarly qualified?[8]

A month before his coronation Hussein issued postage stamps for his state in order to proclaim his rebellion against the sultan "self paying and incontrovertible, to the four corners of the earth."[9] Now he rushed to proclaim to the world that he had made himself king, both by promptly notifying the Allies and neutral powers of this by telegraph and by providing a detailed account of his coronation in *al-Qibla*, a state bulletin designed mostly for foreign consumption.[10] Thus, already before the Ottoman Empire's final demise and while the fate of the caliphate was still in the murky future, proclaiming kingship was revived as marking a claim to sovereignty by an Arab leader seeking to play the modern international game. The world's superpowers were puzzled and quite discontent about the sharif's demand and forced him to negotiate it with them. Ultimately they compromised over the scope of Hussein's "kingdom," and he was recognized as king "of the Hijaz" rather than "of the Arab Lands." His claim to a royal status, however, was acknowledged and accepted by them.

Hussein bin Ali's kingdom survived for less than a decade. He himself would eventually go down in history as a ruler of the old type who ran his tribal realm along the same traditional lines as those reflected in the ceremony of his coronation.[11] But his gesture of proclaiming a monarchy portended a policy line of a novel brand that would become the vogue in Arab countries after the war. Leaders of the new states set up on the Ottoman ruins hurried to duplicate the sharif's move, for the same objectives: to obtain regional and international dignity and domestic prestige. The old, condemnable image of royalty was abandoned and forgotten; after all, it was the *khadim al-haramayn* (custodian of the two Holy Places) of Islam, backed by the guardians of religious values, who showed other rulers the titular way to a respectable status. Kingship, including the very important principle of heredity, had become an attractive option.

First to follow in Sharif Hussein's footsteps were his own sons. In July 1919, a General Syrian Congress of notables and national activists convened in Damascus to examine the country's political future under Emir Faysal, the sharif's third son. Responding to questions of the King-Crane Inquiry Commission, the Congress stated that the most appropriate way to exercise self-determination was by establishing a sovereign monarchy with Faysal as king. Several months later, when news of France's uncompromising demands appeared to put this intended sovereignty in jeopardy, the Congress moved to preempt the danger. In March 1920, it proclaimed the kingdom of Syria and appointed Faysal as king with the honorific "his majesty" (*sahib al-jalala*). Faysal duly deserved both the post and the title, the statement of the Congress read, because of "his untiring efforts for the country's liberation"; kingship and independence, then, were two sides of the same coin. In a more curious, and somewhat less known, episode, a group of twenty-nine Iraqi notables gathered in Damascus on the very same day and declared the foundation of a sovereign monarchy of Iraq, with Faysal's brother Abdallah as king and his other brother Zayid as deputy. The two declarations, all but identical in structure and phrase, closely associated the notion of monarchy with the claim to "full and absolute political independence." This royal status, the Syrian and Iraqi dignitaries insisted, should help in elevating the country to the "highest degree of progress, so it can become an active member of the civilized world."[12]

In the event, the Syrians were not permitted to retain their monarchy. The demand for sovereignty linked to Faysal's kingship was a far cry from France's own plans for the country. The French imposed republican governments in their mandatory territories in Syria and Lebanon—"republican" in the sense that it had no hereditary ruler—to the profound dismay of Syrian leaders and politicians. Some of the latter continued to busy themselves searching for a king to be installed in Damascus, insisting that this was the form of government most befitting Syria's political tradition and expectations. Sometime in the late 1920s they even secured a *fatwa* from local *ulama* to the effect that monarchy was more compatible with Islamic principles than was a republic,[13] but to no avail. By contrast, the other group that had published its statement in Damascus in March 1920, proclaiming an Iraqi kingdom, did see its demands realized, albeit in a somewhat different format. The Iraqi monarchy was set up in August 1921 by British design, with Faysal at its head, an outsider whom the country was required to accept. Once installed, however, the outsider king became an expression of national sovereignty. The first Iraqi constitution, formulated some three years later, stated in a single article that "Iraq is a sovereign state, independent and free . . . the government is [a] hereditary monarchy." Years of Iraqi struggle against British tutelage would later demonstrate that independence and freedom rather represented a wish more than a reality. But there was no mistaking the belief of the Iraqi leadership that the quest for sovereignty and freedom was pronouncedly reflected in the majesty of a throne.

In Egypt, Sultan Fu'ad declared himself king in March 1922, following the British unilateral granting of formal independence to his country. Officially an Ottoman province until World War I, Egypt had been in practice an autonomous monarchy since the early decades of the previous century. Its ruler, entitled *khedive* until the outbreak of the war, became "sultan" thereafter as a mark of insubordination to his former Ottoman lord, the sultan. As the war ended, the new masters to be defied were the British, and this the Egyptian monarch did once again by assuming the title of his royal counterpart and oppressor (as Bernard Lewis put it, "to assert his independence against the Ottoman sultan, the Khedive of Egypt became a sultan; to assert his independence against the king of England, the sultan of Egypt became king"[14]). Fu'ad announced "to the whole world," in one breath, that "Egypt is a sovereign and independent state as of today, and we assume the title 'His Majesty the King of Egypt.'" Sovereignty and kingship were closely intertwined, Fu'ad suggested, and the state had to have all "the trappings of an international personality and the circumstances of national dignity befitting its independence" (*li-yakun li-biladina ma yattafiqu ma'a istiqlaliha min mazahir al-shakhsiyya al-dawliyya wa-asbab al-'izza al-qawmiyya*).[15]

In Egypt, as in Iraq, more years of struggle were needed to realize fully the wish for complete sovereignty and independence. Meanwhile in Cairo, as in Baghdad, the throne continued to epitomize the proud claim to that coveted status. Other Arab rulers also sought to benefit similarly from the prestige associated with kingship during the interwar period: Abd al-Aziz (Ibn Sa'ud) who proclaimed himself "king of the Hijaz" in 1926, "king of Najd" in 1927, and "king of Saudi Arabia" in 1932; and Imam Yahya of Yemen, who in 1926 began to use the royal title in his diplomatic contacts.

We now come to the other important characteristic that marked some of the post-Ottoman Arab monarchies, along with the claim to a prestigious international status. The example of modern Western European monarchies, we have noted, also featured constitutions, elected parliaments and responsible cabinets, political parties, and a free press. Such ideas were not entirely new in the Middle East: in several places there had been some limited beginnings of constitutionalism already prior to the Ottoman fall. Then as now, monarchs accepted the idea without enthusiasm: rulers in the region, as elsewhere, did not wish to see their power limited and would have been happier without constitutions and the constraints that they entailed. Then as now, however, they had to submit to pressures: from without—by foreign powers inducing them to modernize their government—or from within—by often powerful local interests that sought to have a say in government and by the educated elites who demanded the emulation of the foreign model. Then as now, again, monarchs in the region were made to acknowledge that constitutions and elected assemblies were part and parcel of contemporary international fashion, a sign of modernity and progress. This had been a major consideration for the enactment of the Tunisian constitution of 1861 and the formation of the Grand Assembly there, for the foundation of *majlis shura al-nuwwab* (Consultative Council of Delegates) in Egypt in 1866, and for the promulgation of the Ottoman constitution a decade later. In the twentieth century this reason seemed to carry even more weight: Was it not the constitutional states that emerged victorious in the great war while nonconstitutional regimes were defeated and crumbled? Samanid-, Buwayhid-, or Ghaznavid-type autocracies, these kings were told, were no longer fit for modern states. The argument sounded sensible, and along with foreign and domestic pressures it led some of the Arab kings to accept the alien instruments, even though this meant sharing their authority with others. They hoped, however, to keep the constitutional limitations on their own power at a bearable minimum—not entirely an unrealistic aspiration, as the example of the Young Turks' constitutional tyranny had recently demonstrated.

When the Syrian Congress moved to set up a monarchy with Faysal as king, its members, local leaders and strongmen, did not intend to give up their own political leverage. The regime they will establish, they announced in June 1919, will be a "civil representative monarchy" (*malakiyya madaniyya niyabiyya*) based on "broad decentralization" (*al-lamarkaziyya al-wasi'a*). Royal authority, then, will stem from, and be dependent upon, the political constituency and its wishes. Several months later, when the Congress again convened to proclaim the monarchy, its statement was yet more specific and precise: Faysal was declared a "constitutional monarch" (*malik dusturi*), whose rule would be "based on civilian representative foundations" with a "representative monarchical government answerable to this assembly." The Congress promptly proceeded to prepare a draft constitution for Syria, featuring these principles, which was ready in early July 1920, just a few days before the kingdom collapsed. A very similar formula appeared in the declaration by Iraqi notables in Damascus, who sought to install Abdallah in Baghdad as a "constitutional monarch" with a "national government responsible to the people" (*hukuma wataniyya mas'ula amam al-sha'b*).[16] In both cases, prominent local notables chose the constitutional model, hoping to retain their influence in the new state. In the former case, the incumbent monarch unenthusiastically accepted the restrictive formula. In the latter, his brother was never given a chance to consider the option until a much later time, in another place, and under quite different circumstances.

When Faysal moved to Iraq after the defeat of his troops in Maysalun later that month, he was again faced with pressures to introduce a constitution by his own lieutenants, local leaders, and the British. A provisional Council of State, consisting of Iraqi notables and appointed by the British, administered the affairs of the country. The council, which approved Faysal as king of Iraq in July 1921, also demanded that the state should have a "constitutional, representative, and democratic government, limited by law" (to wit: confined by local interests). The Anglo-Iraqi Treaty of the following year likewise contained a stipulation for a constitutional system of government.[17] Such was also the case with Fu'ad in Egypt, who faced similar firm demands for a constitution, by domestic forces (mostly the group later to be known as the "liberal constitutionalists") and still more by the British.[18] Both kings succumbed to the pressure after some bargaining over the division of authority.

But however reluctant Faysal and Fu'ad may have been to accept the burden of a constitution, they were certainly aware of the clear benefit it involved, namely, an appearance of modernity. When still in Damascus, addressing the Syrian Congress that proclaimed him king, Faysal articulated this awareness. "Europe is closely observing us," he reminded the assembly, "and will pass a favorable or unfavorable judgment on us according to the political course we choose to follow and our future acts." This foreign appraisal was of essential importance for Syria's future, he argued, hence it was incumbent upon Syria "to establish a constitution that would prescribe for each of us, ruler and ruled, their rights and duties."[19] Egypt's King Fu'ad publicly subscribed to the same concept. In 1923, granting a constitution by royal decree, he noted his desire to assure the country of "happiness, progress, and all that which is enjoyed by free and civilized nations." Such goals, he suggested (in a phraseology conspicuously reminiscent of the preamble to the Ottoman *hatt-i Sherif* of Gülhane nearly a century earlier), could only be "properly attained if the country had a constitutional regime akin to the most modern and advanced constitutional regimes of the world." Embracing this kind of a system would therefore allow Egypt to "take its deserved place among the nations and peoples of the modern world."[20]

The progressive image associated with constitutions and parliaments could be expected to have another important advantage for the new monarchies in the domestic front: it could lend them more legitimacy, not instead of but alongside the traditional legitimacy that was based on popular respect for hereditary rule and the religious injunction to obedience. Essentially secular in nature, this new kind of legitimacy would gain support mostly from members of the important educated elites who called for the adoption of constitutional institutions. In the post-Ottoman, and especially postcaliphate, eras governmental legitimacy in the new states was a delicate issue; principles beyond question in the past became questionable and open to political contest. Under the confusing circumstances, the importation of tools associated with powerful and stable governments elsewhere could be expected to help in consolidating the popular stature of the royal house, defusing potential sources of threats to its hold on power. Again, it was imperative that the price of conceding authority remained minimal and always controllable. While accepting constitutions, however reluctantly, kings could thereby claim the legitimacy of a balanced, attentive, representative government according to modern standards.

Constitutional monarchies in the post–World War I Middle East were new creations. Bearing an old title refurbished to inspire respect of a new kind, their heads purported to fulfill the quest of their subjects for sovereignty. Where a struggle for independence was under way, they symbolized leadership of that struggle. By accepting constitutional regimes they also claimed to possess an entry ticket to the modern world, one that should enhance their acceptance at home. It seemed to be an attractive formula, enough to induce other rulers in the region to join the club of constitutional kings later on. Three of them would embrace the concept and the claim to legitimacy that came with it: Emir Abdallah, who became king in 1946 and enacted a constitution right away; Muhammad Idris al-Sanusi of Cyrenaica, who followed suit by becoming Libya's constitutional monarch in 1951; and Sultan Muhammad V of Morocco, who assumed the title *malik* in 1957 and promulgated a constitution in 1963. In these three states, as in Syria, Egypt, and Iraq in the 1920s, royal title and constitution were closely associated with independence and modernity.

To what extent, we may ask, did the novel labels confirm the content of the bottles? In other words, did these modern-type monarchies actually enjoy a dignified standing at home and abroad? And were their regimes truly constitutional? On both scores, it seems, there was dissonance between claim and reality. The political circumstances under which these kings were installed perforce rendered their claim to proud sovereignty rather wishful. The first of them—Faysal in Syria—may have been the linchpin of a bold quest for honorable independence for a moment, but he was scarcely given a chance to exercise that status. The kings in Egypt and Iraq were crowned under the custody of a power that imposed visible limitations on their freedom, and they remained shackled by such foreign controls. One need merely recall the passionate struggle that preceded both the Anglo-Iraqi Treaty of 1930 and the Anglo-Egyptian one six years later to appreciate the impact of the restrictive foreign presence, which persisted after the conclusion of these treaties as well. It inevitably tarnished the image of local monarchs as symbols of independent authority. Nor were the British, with their often high-handed policy toward Cairo and Baghdad, helpful in enhancing the international status of these kingdoms. Quarrels with domestic rivals, who made extensive use of the new freedom to criticize, further undermined the standing of monarchs as consensual national leaders. At times their public position was eroded to the point of nondignity: in 1932, according to an account by the U.S. chargé d'affaires in Baghdad, when King Faysal appeared on the streets of the Iraqi capital, the only ones to take any notice of him were foreigners who paused and lifted their hats.[21]

Likewise, in the domain of constitutional and parliamentary life the new monarchies represented a claim rather than a reality. It may have been an earnest claim, backed by a sincere readiness to modernize the state through introducing certain ingredients of the recipe for success. Yet by adopting constitutions and parliaments, these monarchies did not necessarily become constitutional and parliamentary. There was a gap between the foreign model and its local implementation, for which there were many reasons—social, cultural, and political—whose examination cannot be undertaken here (such a gap, it will be noted, similarly occurred in the nonmonarchical Arab states that ventured to experiment with constitutionalism; mandatory Syria is the obvious example). It is important to bear in mind, however, that the kings themselves contributed their share—a truly major share at that—to the constitutional failure. They did so both in the way in which they charted the ground rules, retaining maximum autocratic powers for themselves and thus rendering the constitutional game itself largely futile, and in the manner in which they continued to exercise these prerogatives, playing by the rules of their self-authored book. In these states, Elie Kedourie assessed, parliaments and elections were "a make-believe and a deception." This is a harsh judgment, but it is hard to disagree with Kedourie that the constitutional record of the interwar Arab monarchies was "disappointing, not to say dismal."[22] The performance of these monarchs did not help in underscoring the advantages of the modern principles over the old and in making them popular. Instead, it bitterly alienated the small but important groups of those who had initially favored the change. Consequently, the novel style of government these kings claimed to have adopted failed to generate a new kind of domestic legitimacy for their rule.

Elsewhere in the region there were kingdoms of an older type, devoid of the pretense to modernity that was associated with imported political institutions. They emerged, or continued to exist, in the region's periphery—in the Arabian Peninsula, its center and southwestern and eastern flanks, some of them still tribal polities to become full-fledged monarchical states only at a later time. The mostly desert emirate of Transjordan also properly belonged in this category during the first half of the century, and so did in many ways Morocco. The monarchies of this group did not open themselves up to the outside world, did not strongly aspire to equalize their international prestige with that of world powers, and had no desire to join the League of Nations. Nor were their rulers under the same pressures, domestic or foreign, to share their authority with other partners as were their modernizing counterparts. Moreover, they did not seek—to use, again, Kedourie's biting phrasing—to "complicate matters for themselves by promoting education."[23] These old-type monarchs looked inward rather than outward. They were content to remain sultans, emirs, and imams, not reproductions of the kings of Europe. Nor did they seek a new kind of legitimacy. Instead, they retained the traditional basis of their domestic status, even when adopting the title *malik* for expediency, relying as ever on autocratic authority, prestigious pedigree, and the readiness of their subjects to obey them, as marked by the time-honored *baya*. Such an inclination of the ruled, enhanced by the traditional Islamic call for obedience, was particularly strong when the ruler was of a recognized sharifian origin, as in the Hijaz, Transjordan, and Morocco, or an imam, as in Yemen, or even an advocate of Wahhabi-Hanbali ideas, as in Saudi Arabia. To exercise control, the rulers of these states resorted to the equally traditional manipulation of domestic forces, usually leaning on a closely loyal circle of family members and confidants, whom they entrusted with political and administrative tasks, and dominating over other groups with a mix of manipulation, occasional subventions, and coercion. They co-opted potential allies by offering them access to resources and at times involving them in decision-making and played less forthcoming groups against each other.[24] Such policies remained as serviceable and satisfying as ever. Constitutions, parliaments, elections—all were little known, irrelevant, or outright objectionable ideas.

In light of the above observations, one may wonder whether the dissimilarities between the monarchies that professed modern principles and those that did not were all that great. Put another way, were the bottles bearing different labels truly different in their contents as well? Considering the gulf we have noted between claim and reality in the former group of states, the answer to this dilemma appears to be negative. In the international arena, the major foreign actors demonstrated in their behavior that they cared little about such differences. Having encouraged the foundation of liberal-type parliamentary states in the Arab countries, the European powers showed them no more respect as sovereign entities than they offered to their more traditional colleagues, in whose countries they had equally important interests. The situation in the arena of intraregional relations was similar: most Arab leaders accorded little importance to claims of modern principles. Status and prestige in the newly evolving inter-Arab system—a novel name for a less-novel game—continued to derive from more traditional considerations, with the domestic regime of each actor having little or no bearing on his place in it (this would change somewhat in the second half of the century). Finally, at home, the modern style of royalty had a rather limited import. By associating themselves with claims to honorable sovereignty that were slow to materialize, and by advocating constitutional principles they themselves often disregarded or vitiated, the more modern monarchs lost as much legitimacy as they had hoped to inspire. Such an erosion of legitimacy scarcely occurred in the more traditional monarchies, in Najd and Saudi Arabia, Yemen, Abdallah's Transjordan, and elsewhere, where rulers never sought more than the compliance of their subjects in accordance with the region's time-honored values and Islamic rules. Monarchies of both types alike, so it seems, survived, although they did mainly because of this last kind of traditional legitimacy.

Kingship, the fashionable form of government in the Middle East during the post–World War I years, began to lose its attraction by midcentury. Prod-

ucts of the colonial era and often allies of foreign occupiers, royal houses in
the region came to be identified in the minds of many with the nation's enemies. The wave of leftist-inspired, antimonarchical revolts that swept the area
after World War II eliminated some of the reigning kings and came to dominate several other states as well. First to be toppled by their own subjects
were the constitutional monarchs in Cairo and Baghdad, attesting perhaps to
the frailty of the modern ideas they had professed. They were followed by the
monarchs in Yemen—whose downfall was inspired by and engineered in revolutionary Egypt—and, some time later, in Libya. "The throne is not necessarily the seat of a just king," the Free Officers declared in Egypt, "and when
a just king does ascend to the throne, there is no guarantee that he would so
remain." Kingship, they asserted, is based on "corrupt foundations and false
logic; a regime of this kind is doomed to vanishing."[25] In Egypt, the "whole
nation" was "unanimous in wishing to see the monarchical regime disappear
forever."[26] The officers who several years later put an end to the monarchy in
Iraq and assumed control of that country similarly claimed to have "liberated
the country from the domination of a corrupt group which was installed by
imperialism to lull the people."[27] And the head of the Yemeni Revolutionary
Council, which deposed the imam, defined the primary goal of the revolution
as putting "an end to those things that have blocked all progress in Yemen—
tyranny, reaction, corrupt government, and the evil system of monarchy."[28]

Those monarchs who were not eliminated—all of them from the more
traditional group in the Arabian Peninsula, Jordan, and Morocco—were stig-
matized by the exponents of revolutionary ideologies as symbols of imperialism, reaction, and mischief. But they withstood the revolutionary wave,
which peaked in the 1950s and 1960s, and survived, marking the vigor of traditional patterns of rule in significant parts of the region. More curious, in
most of the places where kings were removed, their rule was not replaced by
truly participatory republics. Rather it was substituted with a form of government strikingly akin to monarchies in all but name: in the central role of autocratic authority, the exclusive power of a small ruling elite, the highly limited
weight of other governmental institutions, and, in some places, even in the serious consideration of the option of heredity.

NOTES

1. In an episodic instance, the "Republic of Tripolitania" was established in November 1918, the first "republic" in the Arab Middle East. It turned out to be short-
lived. See al-Tahir Ahmad al-Zawi, *Jihad al-abtal fi tarablus al-gharb* (Cairo: Mat-
bua't al-najah, 1950), pp. 222ff.

2. Walter Bagehot, *The English Constitution and Other Political Essays* (New
York: Appleton, 1924), p. 101.

3. The ceremony is described in *al-Qibla* (Mecca), 22, 3 Muharram 1335/30 October 1916.

4. See Ami Ayalon, "'*Malik*' in Modern Middle Eastern Titulature," *Die Welt des Islams*, 23–24 (1984), pp. 306–319.

5. Abdallah bin Husayn, *Mudhakkirat* (Jerusalem: Matbuat Bayt al-Maqdas, 1945), pp. 129–130. See also Elie Kedourie, *In the Anglo-Arab Labyrinth* (Cambridge: Cambridge University Press, 1976), pp. 144ff.

6. Eliezer Tauber, "Rashid Rida's Political Attitudes During World War I," *The Muslim World*, 65 (1995), p. 116; *al-Manar*, XIX, 15 December 1916, pp. 435ff. Rida would later reproduce the full texts of the Syrian Congress proclamations of July 1919 and March 1920 concerning the coronation of Faysal as king of Syria (see below).

7. Ernest Dawn, *From Ottomanism to Arabism* (Urbana: University of Illinois Press, 1973), pp. 48–49.

8. Ronald Storrs, *Orientations* (London: Nicholson and Watson, 1937), p. 207, reporting a conversation with Abdallah. Storrs recalled that, "oddly enough," he had "this same argument from Sultan Hussein during the forty-nine days' discussion that preceded his accession to the throne of Egypt."

9. Ibid., p. 220.

10. Abdallah, p. 131. On *al-Qibla*'s mostly external use, see *al-Qibla*, 11 December 1919, p. 2. Cf. Joshua Teitelbaum, *The Rise and Fall of the Hashemite Kingdom of Hijaz, 1916–1925: A Failure of State Formation in the Arabian Peninsula*, Unpublished Ph.D. dissertation, Tel Aviv University, 1996, pp. 139–152.

11. See Teitelbaum, especially chapters 4–6.

12. Text of the General Syrian Congress statement of July 1919 in *al-Manar*, XXI, 28 June 1919 [*sic*], pp. 221–223. Text of the 8 March 1920 declarations on Syria and Iraq in ibid., XXI, 17 June 1920, pp. 434–447. See also Aaron S. Klieman, *Foundations of British Policy in the Arab World* (Baltimore: Johns Hopkins University Press, 1970), pp. 46–47 and passim; Philip S. Khoury, *Urban Notables and Arab Nationalism* (Cambridge: Cambridge University Press, 1983), pp. 89–91.

13. Yehoshua Porath, *In Search of Arab Unity, 1930–1945* (London: Frank Cass, 1986), p. 9; Philip Khoury, *Syria and the French Mandate* (Princeton: Princeton University Press, 1987), pp. 337–340, 351–359.

14. Bernard Lewis, *The Political Language of Islam* (Chicago: Chicago University Press, 1989), p. 53.

15. Text of Fu'ad's declaration of 15 March 1922 in *al-Hilal* (Cairo), 1 April 1922, pp. 607–608.

16. *Al-Manar*, XXI, 28 June 1919 [*sic*], p. 221; XXI, 17 June 1920, pp. 440, 444, 447.

17. Majid Khadduri, *Independent Iraq, 1932–1958* (Oxford: Oxford University Press, 1960), pp. 13ff.

18. Elie Kedourie, "The Genesis of the Egyptian Constitution of 1923," in his *The Chatham House Version and Other Middle Eastern Studies* (Hanover and London: Brandeis University Press, 1984), pp. 160–176.

19. *Al-Manar*, XXI, 17 June 1920, p. 437.

20. *Al-Muqtataf* (Cairo), May 1923, p. 498.

21. Quoted in Elie Kedourie, *The Chatham House Version and Other Middle Eastern Studies*, pp. 245–246.

22. Elie Kedourie, *Democracy and Arab Political Culture* (Washington, D.C.: The Washington Institute for Near East Policy, 1992), pp. 86, 87.

23. Ibid., p. 83.

24. For some typical examples, see Teitelbaum, esp. chapter 6; Joseph Kostiner, *The Making of Saudi Arabia, 1916–1936: From Chieftaincy to Monarchical State* (New York: Oxford University Press, 1993), esp. chapter 2; Sarah Yizraeli, *The Remaking of Saudi Arabia*, Occasional Papers Series, Moshe Dayan Center for Middle Eastern and African Studies, Tel Aviv University (Tel Aviv, 1997).

25. Abd al-Rahman al-Rafiʻi, *Thawrat 23 Yulyu 1952* (Cairo: Dar al-Maʻarif, 1959), pp. 68–70.

26. Declaration of the republic on 18 June 1953, quoted in ibid., p. 81.

27. Quoted in Hisham Sharabi, *Nationalism and Revolution in the Arab World* (Princeton: Van Nostrand, 1966), p. 166.

28. Quoted in ibid., pp. 171–172.

4

Why Did Arab Monarchies Fall?
An Analysis of Old and
New Explanations

Bruce Maddy-Weitzman

Views regarding Middle Eastern monarchies have changed considerably during recent decades. During the heyday of radical Arab nationalism, which corresponded roughly with the first generation of modernization theories in the social sciences, monarchies were often depicted as representing narrow social bases; unrepresentative of increasingly literate and politicized populations; unfit for governing developing, increasingly complex societies (as opposed to modernizing officer classes); and destined for the dustbin of history.[1] More recently, the shortcomings of a generation of revolutionary regimes in the Arab world compelled a reexamination of previous thinking. The "monarchical way" has sometimes come to be seen as a preferred system providing much-needed balance, stability, and authority for societies experiencing the upheavals of social, economic, and cultural change. Morocco and Jordan, neither of which are wealthy distributive states, especially come to mind in this regard.[2]

Given that monarchies are currently viewed more kindly, it may be a bit difficult to return to the zeitgeist of an earlier era, during which monarchies were on the defensive everywhere. Moreover, the resources available to state structures and ruling institutions in the 1990s were much more far-reaching than those that existed back in the 1950s. Nevertheless, it is my view that there is much to be learned from such a comparative examination.

A necessary building block for comparative analysis is to examine the explanations for the fall of Arab monarchies during the 1950s and 1960s. Inevitably, such an examination must focus on two of the Arab world's "majors": Egypt, where the 150-year-old monarchy was overthrown in a bloodless coup in 1952, and Iraq, where the thirty-eight-year-old Hashemite dynasty was bloodily toppled six years later. Not coincidentally, perhaps, both were monarchies with "modern" labels—those that tried to combine European models of constitutional monarchy with more traditional values and norms of rule (see Ami Ayalon, Chapter 3, in this volume). The other two cases of fallen royal rule, Yemen (1962) and Libya (1969), will be referred to only secondarily— Yemen, because its geographical remoteness, tribal complexities, and particular form of monarchy, the Zaydi imamate, render it problematic for comparative purposes; and Libya, because the tenuous nature of both the Libyan state and the Sanussi monarchy, epitomized by the ease in which Qaddafi overthrew the old order, limits its analytical usefulness as well.

Such a venture must touch on political science–types of questions: the question of legitimacy, or the lack thereof, as an explanatory variable; issues connected to modernization processes and theories; and the more recent concern with the "state," not only as an expression of a dominant social class but also as an institution that stands apart, or at least is semiautonomous, from society. It also, however, must deal with more traditional historical questions, such as whether or not the monarchies' downfall was inevitable, what were the concrete issues and grievances creating problems for the old regimes in domestic and foreign relations spheres, and the nature of that particularly elusive notion—the quality of leadership—that is a crucial determinant of any political outcome. It must also take into account the spirit of the times: the example of the Egyptian Free Officers and the spread of Nasirist influences throughout the region had a direct bearing on the other three countries under scrutiny.

HISTORICAL ROOTEDNESS
AND THE LEGITIMACY QUESTION

An examination of the essential features of the monarchical regimes in question touches on the extent to which they were rooted in the society, in terms of both political culture and institutional reach. This, in turn, may be related to the depth of their legitimacy.

Ilya Harik, in an important article in the four-volume *Arab State* project, noted that most modern Arab states—monarchies and republics alike—possess considerable sources of their own legitimacy that predate nineteenth-century colonialism.[3] However, legitimacy derives from many aspects having varying weights. Consequently, the possession of historical sources of legitimacy was not sufficient, in and of itself, to insulate regimes from transformatory upheaval: three of our four cases of fallen Arab monarchies (excluding Iraq) come under Harik's rubric of states possessing indigenous sources of legitimacy. Neighboring non-Arab Iran is a hybrid case in this regard: monarchical rule is central to Iran's political tradition; at the same time, the Pahlavi dynasty was decidedly new, and even more "artificial" or "invented," than the Hashemites next door in Iraq.

In any event, Harik's typology belies the notion of Arab states being purely artificial creations and that such artificiality is the source of all of the subsequent troubles that they experienced. Moreover, one may note that the most historically "artificial" of Arab entities—Jordan—is ruled by a monarchy that has displayed surprising durability and attained considerable legitimacy. Thus, either a state's artificiality or historical rootedness alone are not sufficient explanations for the fall of monarchies. One must probe deeper into the sources and limitations of their power and examine the depth of their social, economic, and political control.

The Islamic component of regime legitimacy seems an appropriate place to begin such an inquiry. For the Sanussis in Libya and the imamate in Yemen, Islam was central to their ascent and maintenance of power, although neither possessed religious legitimacy outside of their immediate communal-territorial base. Hashemite legitimacy in Iraq, by contrast, seems to have drawn relatively little strength from the fact that the new (post-1920) foreign ruling family was *ashraf*. After all, there were other *ashraf* in Iraq as well. Moreover, Faysal and his successors did little in the way of turning it into a central resource of their rule.

One observer of the monarch's fall in 1958 noted the repugnance of many Iraqis with the horrible murder and mutilation of members of the Prophet's house.[4] But this shouldn't obscure the consensus among scholars that the Iraqi royal house was viewed with disdain, or worse, by much of the politically conscious portions of the society. Hana Battatu pointed to two events that sealed the fate of the monarch's image: the death of King Ghazi in 1939, widely believed by Iraqis to be the work of British hands and possibly with the complicity of Nuri al-Sa'id—the crown prince—and the queen; followed by the return of the monarchy in 1941 on the backs of British troops.[5] By contrast, Phebe Marr focused on the extremely unpopular Crown Prince Abd al-Illah between the mid-1940s and 1958 as the decisive factor in the widespread rejection of the monarchy.[6] Ironically, the Iraqi monarchy has been consciously rehabilitated in recent years by Saddam Hussein in order to promote an organic, historical link between his regime and earlier manifestations of Iraqi nationhood. This effort focuses on the personage of King Faysal I and his son Ghazi, but not on those who reigned and ruled during the monarchy's final two decades— Abd al-Illah, young King Faysal II, who came of age in 1953, and of course the strong man of the regime, Nuri al-Sa'id.[7]

Unlike in Iraq, the Egyptian monarchy made a number of efforts to employ Islam as a resource for legitimation. The convening of a Caliphate Congress in Cairo by King Fu'ad in 1925, and Farouk's later hankering after the caliphate during the late 1930s, were illuminated by Elie Kedourie.[8] Michael Winter has pointed out that the monarchs assiduously sought the support of al-Azhar for their ambitions and that the *ulama* were the palace's staunchest allies against its *wafdist* and other political rivals. Al-Azhar itself became an arena for palace-government rivalry.[9] In addition to their overt political aspects, palace actions belonged to ongoing efforts by the monarchy and aligned conservative and state-oriented Islamic groups to develop a cultural "language of monarchy."[10] On the whole, however, Farouk's own hedonistic personality, al-Azhar's vulnerability to charges of being merely an appendage to the existing order, and the successes of the opposition Muslim Brotherhood made it difficult for the monarchy to cultivate Islam as a legitimizing resource.

Other reasons for the lack of legitimacy among the two "modern" royal regimes were more central. One feature common to both was the failed attempt to legitimate the monarchy through parliamentary institutions. Nadav Safran highlighted the contradictions inherent in the 1922 constitution between royal prerogatives and a liberal-democratic regime.[11] Indeed, the resulting parliamentary regime was largely a shell game: for the upper classes, parliament was a tool for maintaining their power and privilege; for the lower classes, its discussions were, at best, remote from their real concerns. The Egyptian Wafd's transformation over time from the repository of national sentiment to one of the pillars of the corrupt, dominant order (regardless of its repeated clashes with the palace) symbolized the bankruptcy of the existing system. By the 1940s, the Wafd was neither capable nor willing to address the severe social and economic strains plaguing Egypt. The fact that Farouk was forced to save his throne in 1942 by bowing to Britain's diktat, backed by tanks surrounding his palace, to appoint a more pliable *wafdist* prime minister, did not help its image either.[12]

As for Iraq, its parliamentary framework was even farther away than Egypt's from serving as a legitimizing institution. Not only were Iraqi cabinets chosen largely from the same small pool of politicians; during the last four years of the regime's survival, political parties were completely banned from activity, and more than 80 percent of the parliamentary seats during the 1954 elections were uncontested.[13]

FOREIGN POLICY ISSUES VERSUS DOMESTIC ISSUES

The collective Arab failure in the 1948 war with Israel contributed heavily to the delegitimation of Arab regimes at home. Indeed, as Abd al-Nasir testifies, his own experience at the front strengthened his determination to address the root causes of the army's defeat.[14]

Nonetheless, determining the relative weight of domestic versus foreign policy issues in the undermining of the Egyptian and Iraqi ancien regimes is an enormously complicated if not impossible task. The poor performance of Egypt's army against Israel was one source of difficulty. Even more central was Egypt's problematic relations with Britain, an ongoing source of domestic political tension beginning in the mid-1930s. By 1951, the guerrilla warfare against the British Canal Zone base, spearheaded by extraparliamentary groups such as the Muslim Brotherhood, was helping to bring Egypt to a state of near chaos, epitomized by Black Sunday, the burning of parts of downtown Cairo in January 1952. At bottom, according to Raymond William Baker, the meaning of the Egyptian revolution to its supporters was that it epitomized both the negation of Egypt's colonial past and the promise of a new political community.[15]

Interestingly, the foreign policy grievances among Egyptians did not have a particularly "Arab" cast: Egypt may have been primus inter pares among Arab states since guiding the founding of the Arab League in 1944–1945 and may have spearheaded the Arab war coalition in 1948 against Israel,[16] but there were no particular "Arab" issues on Egypt's agenda during the early 1950s. In this respect, the contrast with Iraq's prerevolutionary context is striking.

It is generally recognized that the Iraqi regime's utter identification with Great Britain, beginning with Britain's restoration of the Iraqi monarchy in 1941, followed by the abortive Portsmouth Treaty of 1948, and culminating in the Baghdad Pact in 1955, was a central reason for its decline in legitimacy and the alienation of its political classes. Concurrently, Iraq's intelligentsia and urban lower and middle classes were profoundly influenced by Iraqi communist activity during the 1940s and 1950s[17] while being identified almost entirely with radical pan-Arabism and anti-Westernism. Nuri al-Sa'id's failure to react adequately to the British-French-Israeli attack on Egypt in 1956 was seen by his enemies as a natural continuation of existing pro-British, anti-Arab nationalist policies. Some observers believe that his inaction sealed the regime's fate.[18] A recent study of British-Iraqi relations takes a somewhat different approach, holding that initially the benefits of the Baghdad Pact for the regime outweighed the costs but that after Suez it became more of a liability.[19]

The Yemen case is also interesting regarding the mix of foreign policy and domestic political variables. Manfred Wenner ascribed crucial importance to Imam Ahmad's obsession (following in his father Yahya's footsteps) with ridding the British from southern Yemen. This led Ahmad and his son, Crown Prince Muhammad al-Badr, to seek powerful outside patrons, even at the price of opening up the insulated kingdom. The result was that Soviet and Egyptian protégés quickly sought to undermine the existing order. Had the imamate remained secluded, Werner contents, the revolution might have been considerably postponed.[20] To be sure, as Dana Adams Schmidt has pointed out, the imam was equivocal regarding the penetration of modern influences that he himself had authorized, well aware that a strengthened military could boomerang against him.[21]

In any case, one must also recognize the crucial importance of Abd al-Nasir's decision to send troops to support the new republican regime. Without it, the "royal" forces may have well succeeded in restoring at least a semblance of the ancien regime. Leigh Douglas, for his part, has placed initial blame for the monarchy's decline on Imam Yahya. His efforts to extend his rule to non-Zaydi areas antagonized the Shafi'i community in the southern areas of the country. Moreover, by the mid-1930s, his policy of rigid isolation created discontent among a young generation of urban intellectuals, and the imam's expression of hereditary dynastic aspirations aroused opposition among many of the *sayyid* families that had traditionally provided Zaydi imams.[22]

As for Libya, Qaddafi's view of Abd al-Nasir as a model and father figure was central to his political identity and program,[23] and stood in sharp contrast to the ruling order's worldview. In retrospect, Qaddafi's seizure of power was the last concrete success of radical pan-Arabism, which, ironically, had by then begun its inexorable decline as a workable political idea.

STATE, CLASS, AND LEADERSHIP VARIABLES

Although initial discussions of political upheaval in the Arab world during the 1950s focused on the themes of national self-determination and liberation from foreign rule,[24] scholarly analyses during the 1960s and 1970s focused more on social forces. Manfred Halpern helped pioneer the idea of the rise of the so-called new middle class, spearheaded by the military, which was eager to modernize society and the body politic under the ideological rubrics of nationalism and social reform. Kings, he declared, would no longer be able to survive by virtue of being royal. Whether or not this had previously been the case can be questioned; nonetheless, their tasks had multiplied immeasurably as a result of complex modernization processes. They would succeed or fail, Halpern wrote, according to their ability to resolve conflicting domestic pressures and move their societies forward. The old regime in Iraq had failed to do so: Nuri, he stated, should have parceled out 6 million empty acres to the masses and thereby taken the lead in instituting what he called a "peaceful and constructive revolution."[25] Again, one might dispute the likely results of such a measure; nonetheless, Nuri's strategy was clearly one of resisting political and social reform, leading, in Halpern's eyes, to the regime's inevitable fall.

Samuel Huntington broke additional ground in emphasizing the connection between political institutions and social forces. Political systems that have the capacity to expand their power and simultaneously broaden participation within the system are, he wrote, unlikely to undergo revolutions.[26] As Ervand Abrahamian showed in his work on the Iranian revolution, the evolution of political institutions did not keep pace with social and economic change.[27] Most traditional systems, wrote Huntington, face the "king's dilemma," in which survival may be threatened by the very forces that the regime seeks to include. If, in contrast, the old regimes seek merely to maintain the social and political status quo, their fates would be similar to those of Farouk and the Iraqi Hashemites. Like Halpern, he emphasized that the middle class was making its debut in the epaulettes of the colonel and stipulated that military officers play a highly modernizing and progressive role, at least during the early stages of political modernization. In the Iraqi case, he wrote, the overthrow of Nuri did not break the prevailing pattern of praetorian politics but did mark a qualitative change in that it opened the way for the bureaucratic and professional classes to enter politics.[28]

One of the main shortcomings with the new-middle-class idea was that neither it nor the army was actually one class—socially, politically, or ideologically. P. J. Vatikiotis emphasized that the conspiring Free Officers in Egypt had different political views and lacked ideological cohesiveness; it was their generational links, he stipulated, comprising their social and economic backgrounds, formative and adolescent experiences, and subsequent frustrations that generated their common desire for change and catalyzed their drive for power.[29] Eliezer Be'eri's important work on army officers pointed to their self-image as "pioneers of national liberation and social reform for the entire nation."[30] In Morroe Berger's view, the Egyptian military sought, upon assuming power, to create a new middle class to represent, rather than being a branch of an already existing social grouping.[31]

The publication at the end of the 1970s of Batatu's mammoth work on the underlying social and class factors of Iraqi's repeated political upheavals established a benchmark against which all other "society-based" analyses will be measured. The alliance between former sharifian officers, the Hashemite house, and the big landowners and tribal shaikhs, backed by Great Britain, was sufficient to establish the Iraqi kingdom. By the late 1940s, however, British Foreign Office officials, including Foreign Secretary Ernest Bevin, were warning that Nuri's exclusive reliance on the "old gang" to run the country would not be sufficient to manage the social and political strains appearing among the new urban *effendi* class and the military.[32] Indeed, most observers during the 1950s viewed matters as a race against time. Would the large-scale development projects undertaken in the 1950s following the influx of oil revenues sufficiently trickle down to the populace before opposition boiled over and the regime lost control? Nonetheless, despite the widespread discontent, Britain's last ambassador in Baghdad, Sir Michael Wright, did not deem Iraqi society in 1958 as having reached the acute revolutionary situation that characterized Egypt six years earlier.[33]

Some refinements of Batatu's underlying premises were in recent years undertaken by Marion and Peter Sluglett, who emphasize the gap between the ruling landed and commercial elites, and the 44 percent of holders of corporate commercial and industrial capital, that is, the developing middle sector of property owners, merchants, traders, workshop owners, and small manufacturers who had no access to the state;[34] and by Sami Zubaida, for whom communal perspectives conditioned the various aspirations for the Iraqi national entity.[35]

Historical and social science research in more recent years has been heavily influenced by the work on the state and social change, spearheaded by Theda Skocpol, who questions the value of legitimacy as an overriding explanatory variable. What is more important, she writes, is to understand that states are actual organizations that control territories and people; a state may remain stable even after it loses its legitimacy, as long as it retains a coercive and effective organization. The ebbing of a regime's legitimacy in the eyes of its own cadres and other politically powerful groups may figure as a mediating variable in an analysis of regime breakdown. But the basic causes will be found in the structures and capacities of state organizations, as those are conditioned by developments in the economy and class structure and also by developments in the international situation.[36]

This approach is useful in looking at the collapse of the Iranian monarchy in the late 1970s. As Said Arjomand showed, the influx of oil revenues conferred an unprecedented degree of autonomy on the state but resulted in the state apparatus's disregarding of all social and political forces, including those who should have been its natural allies, the new middle and professional classes.[37]

Roger Owen has sought to augment Batatu's work by "bringing the state back in" in his analysis of pre-1958 Iraq. Instead of asking "whose state was it" (for Batatu, it was the alliance between the landowning politicians, other property owners, and the shaikhs), he suggests first asking what type of state the various social forces were struggling to control. His central point is that the ruling elite was "unable to create a sense that they were at the center of a single, unique coherent entity with an unchangeable claim to universal allegiance." The "colonial" state created by Britain and run by this elite thus made way for those who sought to construct a new type of Iraqi state whose capacity to impose itself on society would be much greater.[38]

At bottom, all scholars agree that both Iraqi and Egyptian societies were in the midst of profound social and economic upheaval, brought on by demographic pressures (population growth and increasing urbanization); the expansion of the educational system, which created larger politically conscious publics; stagnant or distorted economies; frustrations among the younger generation of military officers; and dysfunctional and discredited political systems. Many of these factors were present in Yemen and Libya as well.

INEVITABILITY AND THE QUESTION OF LEADERSHIP

Emphasis on the structural weaknesses of fallen monarchies tends to give their fall a deterministic quality. Nonetheless, one should distinguish, as Batatu has reminded us, between different levels of causation.[39] Said Arjomand's analysis of the shah's fall took this into account: while emphasizing the structural aspects of his overthrow, he also points to another, more "traditional," factor in the regime's downfall—the shah's physical and mental weakness that made him almost congenitally averse to asserting his authority against the opposition at crucial junctures.[40] This leads us to question whether the Arab monarchies under scrutiny were doomed or not, at least at that moment in time.

In the case of Iraq, Kedourie makes the strongest argument possible in favor of inevitability. The rabid anti-British feelings of large sections of the ruling classes, he writes, stemmed from a "nagging feeling that it was a make-believe kingdom, built on false pretenses and kept going by a British design for a British purpose."[41] Thus, its end was implicit in its beginning. At the same time, Kedourie did not shrink from analyzing some of the specifics of the regime's shortcomings. On the organizational level, the state machine expanded and became top-heavy over the years, without showing any responsibility (a carryover from Ottoman attitudes, in his view). Ideologically, the adoption by the political elites of pan-Arabism—as opposed to Iraqi nationalism—was deemed a fatal flaw, since others were better suited to carry the pan-Arab banner than they. Meanwhile, the crown prince's efforts to punish those in the army who had revolted against him created widespread hatred against him.[42] The bulk of the officer corps was drawn from poor and middle classes, unlike other state institutions such as the parliament and cabinet. Consequently, states Batatu, "it mirrored societal views. The royalists thus possessed little more than the appearance of power and had for some time lost its authentic premises."[43] Not surprisingly, then, Qasim and his fellow conspirators had no intention of keeping it on in any form, although the physical liquidation of the royal family may not have been preplanned.

As for the organizational-structural aspects of the situation, Batatu points to the increasing autonomy of the state from society as a consequence of the huge influx of oil revenues, as well as to the failure of Nuri and Abd al-Illah to turn the state's autonomy to its advantage and come to grips with existing structural imbalances. As a result, the 1958 "revolution" (he, unlike some others, believes that it should be called such) was "unavoidable."[44]

In this he takes strong issue with the U.S. ambassador to Iraq at the time, Waldemar Gallman, who has insisted that the monarchy's overthrow was merely a seizure of power by a small, determined group of conspirators and that the mobs that filled the Iraqi streets were merely hoodlums recruited by agitators.[45] Clearly, Gallman underplayed the deeper social forces at work. Nonetheless, the actual success of the conspirators should not be taken as a foregone conclusion. Even Batatu takes care to highlight the uncertainties. No more than 3,000 troops were involved in the overthrow, two-thirds of which had no ammunition and the remainder only a few rounds. It is his view that the 100,000 persons who took to the streets during the first few days (spontaneously or otherwise) had a greater importance in determining the outcome than had been supposed. Physically, they clogged the streets, rendering potential countermoves by forces loyal to the old regime difficult; even more important, they paralyzed the will of the monarchy's supporters and gave the coup an irresistible character in people's mind.[46]

Bad judgment and an overall failure of leadership seem to be common threads running through all accounts of the fall of the Iraqi regime. To be sure, Nuri was keenly aware of the army's importance as a pillar of the regime and thus pampered the officer corps. It was this policy that apparently led to Nuri's overconfidence in 1958 regarding his ability to handle any unrest. Majid Khadduri pointed to Nuri's inability to communicate his ideas to the public, and his appeal to reason rather than emotion (as compared to Abd al-Nasir). Similarly, Lord Birdwood lamented Nuri's failure to communicate more frequently and directly to the people. Nuri's advanced age was also a factor, according to Khadduri, leading him to grow careless and overconfident and to underestimate his opponents. Birdwood also has posited that Nuri was preoccupied with giving concrete institutional expression to the recently formed Arab Union, which he formally headed, leaving the running of Iraq to lesser lights and further lowering his alertness to possible threats.[47]

As for the royals, no one has a good word to say about Ab al-Illah, who is widely depicted as shallow, manipulative, obsessed with the Syrian throne, and with extremely ambitious prerogatives. Popular animus was directed, often viciously, against him: he was, to his detractors, an "Anglo-Arab" incarnate, whose taste ran to foxhounds, swans, British tailors, and the company of Englishmen.[48] His and Nuri's mutual distaste for and rivalry with one another were well known and became debilitating. His heavy hand over Faysal II, even after he came of age, prevented the youngster from assuming any kind of substantive role, although he may not have had the aptitude for it in any case (unlike his cousin Hussein in Jordan). The crown prince's behavior, according to Marr, brought the whole monarchical system into disrespect. His actions dovetailed with Nuri's repression of institutions and parties between 1954 and 1958. Thus, she declares, the main reasons underlying the regime's weakness were, at bottom, the failure of political leadership and the direction of its foreign policy.[49]

Despite such underlying and ultimately fatal flaws, Marr is not a determinist. On the question of inevitability and leadership, Marr speculates that had the crack royal brigade resisted at the al-Rihab Palace, the revolt might have been put down then and there. Its commander, she notes, wanted to fight, but the crown prince refused to allow it. His was a failure of will, she writes, possibly in the mistaken notion that he would thus be able to save his life and that of the young king.[50]

The coup in Egypt clearly had even more an air of inevitability about it than in Iraq, no small irony in that the monarchy in Egypt cannot be said to have been a foreign implant, as in Iraq, and that it still possessed considerable power to manipulate the political scene to its advantage. The problem in Egypt was that the palace, and the groups aligned with it among the large landowners, big bourgeoisie, senior military echelons, and smaller political parties, though recognizing the rampant deterioration of the situation, developed no coherent strategy for arresting it.

Although the inevitability of the coup in Egypt seems obvious in retrospect, one must still look at the various factors that made this so. Joel Gordon's recent study assigns the responsibility for the failure to check the army on both the palace and the political establishment.[51] The increasing signs of dissent in the army, highlighted by the Free Officers' victory in the Officers' club elections at the end of 1951, challenged the palace's hegemony over the army. The election should have triggered alarm bells in Farouk's court. Indeed, panic may have even set in shortly afterward: according to Sadat's memoirs, one of Farouk's confidants told him that following the Cairo burnings of January 1952 the king had begun smuggling gold out of the country and preparing a list of those who would accompany him into exile.[52] On the whole, however, Farouk, like Nuri six years later, suffered from overconfidence in his ability to contain and control the army. Egypt's civilian political elite, for its part, was on the whole unwilling to sacrifice partisan and personal interests for the sake of political reform. The return of the Wafd to power in 1950 seemed to hold out some last chance for improvement, but such hopes were quickly dashed. The palace, wafdist, and non-wafdist politicians all continued to maneuver for narrow advantages until the end. The fact that senior military officers were not really of the ruling class, as Vatikiotis has pointed out, would contribute to the military's passivity at the moment of truth.[53] The same may have been true in Iraq.

Most revolutions bring together various political and social groups who often have disparate interests. Such was certainly the case in Iran in 1979. Such was certainly the case in Egypt's Urabi revolt of 1882 and the 1919 "revolution." Such was the case in Yemen in 1962, where there was no ideological uniformity among the conspirators, apart from a general desire for reform and the abolition of the imamate—a sine qua non absent from earlier attempted revolts there.[54]

Regarding Egypt circa 1952, Baker is of the view that the Free Officers were rebelling as much against their military superiors, out of revulsion of fat, corrupt, and lazy senior officers, as against the monarchical regime.[55] This would seem to complement Gordon's point about their initial willingness to maintain an emasculated monarchy. Nonetheless, as Vatikiotis points out, the antiregime tracts distributed by the Free Officers while in opposition did attack the king and the monarchy as an institution as well. Vatikiotis makes two additional useful points regarding the system of authority and control: the absence of a British military mission from 1948 onward served to weaken the inhibitions against sedition among the military; and the Wafd's brief period of liberalization in 1950–1952 made it easier for the Free Officers to operate.[56] As for the coup itself and the alleged U.S. role, the Central Intelligence Agency had been in touch with the Free Officers for some time, although it did know their exact plans,[57] and U.S. officials held considerable hopes that Egypt's reforming officers would provide the necessary tonic to the rampant instability plaguing the country. Nonetheless, the initiative for the coup clearly came from within.

In examining the aftermath of the coup, Gordon contests what he calls Vatikiotis's "Machiavellian" view that the Free Officers were guided by a coherent strategy of asserting absolute power and control, manifested by the swift abolishment of the monarchy, the purging of Egypt of political parties, and the adoption of agrarian reform. It is Gordon's position that the Free Officers did not initially plan to demolish the liberal system, abolish the monarchy, or impose a military dictatorship. He points to their initial proclamation of having acted in the name of the constitution to preserve order and restore "sound" parliamentary life. Thus, not only was Farouk exiled, and not killed, as in Iraq, the throne was formally transferred to his six-month-old son, Ahmad. It was only one year later that Egypt was proclaimed a republic and the monarchy abolished. Nonetheless, one must note that there seems to have been little debate among the Free Officers, either before or after 23 July 1952, regarding the maintenance of the monarchy, indicating perhaps that they viewed the whole issue as secondary.

The intention of the Free Officers, Gordon writes, was to destroy the political power of the pasha class, root out corruption in the bureaucracy, and purge "traitors" from the military high command.[58] Their self-view as "guardian of the nation" was very common to politically engaged military elites. Unlike numerous cases of military intervention in Turkey, however, the military plotters in all four cases under examination were seeking to profoundly alter the old order, not simply to stabilize it and improve its functioning.

CONCLUSION

Hindsight is always 20–20. Nonetheless, it is difficult to see how the overthrow of the old regimes in Egypt and Iraq, and probably Libya and even Yemen as well, could have been avoided, given the existing combination of internal and external factors. Structural changes and dislocations had given rise to oppositional-revolutionary politics in all four countries; regional and international environments grievously exacerbated the domestic political order throughout the Arab world; rulers were woefully lacking in leadership skills; and the dominant social groups underpinning monarchical rule had hardly a clue about how to reform the existing system in order to forestall upheaval. None of the countries in question had yet become sufficiently "modernized" states (as opposed to "modern"), that is, they had developed neither the sufficient capacity to address the growing grievances of their increasingly politicized populations nor the means of efficient repression familiar to Arab politics during more recent decades. In the face of strong radical-nationalist currents, monarchies had not sufficiently fashioned themselves as the repositories of the national will and the nation's hopes (compare Morocco again, and perhaps Jordan as well). Consequently, their ability to creatively manipulate diverse political forces was fatally diminished. By the time of the actual coups, the monarchical regimes had squandered most, if not all, of their symbolic capital. They were thus utterly bereft of support when "Nasir and his generation" executed their coup d'état in July 1952, when Colonels Arif and Qasim carried out their coup de grâce against the Iraqi Hashemites in July 1958, and when the young Colonel Qaddafi emulated his idol, Abd al-Nasir, in September 1969. The Yemeni imam in 1962 was an exception because he escaped to fight another day and he had a patron in Saudi Arabia. Even so, he only postponed the day of reckoning.

A final caveat: the structural and personal limitations on the ancien regimes that led to their failures are all too apparent, as are the enormous expansion of state capacities after their overthrow. One must nevertheless also note that while bureaucracies mushroomed they continued to function in familiar modes. Berger's study of Egyptian bureaucrats in 1957 finds them to be the direct lineal descendants of the previous bureaucratic corps.[59] Egypt's relatively high level of "stateness" vis-à-vis other Arab states characterized both the pre- and post-1952 regimes. For Iraq, by contrast, the elusive formula for nation-building and state-building, whose absence was first noted plaintively by Faysal back in 1930,[60] remained beyond the reach of the post-Hashemite radical praetorian regimes.

Neither Libya nor Yemen, for their parts, had any prerevolutionary bureaucracies to speak of and entered into the process of modernization thanks to oil (Libya directly, Yemen indirectly via remittances and aid). But Yemen's search for a workable formula for national unity has been a painful one and remains ongoing. A post-Qaddafi Libya may experience similar difficulties, although there the struggle may be to "capture the state," as opposed to the Yemeni realities of multiple power centers and a relatively weak central government.

NOTES

1. Daniel Lerner, *The Passing of a Traditional Society* (New York: Free Press, 1958); Manfred Halpern, *The Politics of Social Change in the Middle East and North Africa* (Princeton: Princeton University Press, 1963).

2. John Entelis, *Culture and Counter-Culture in Morocco* (Boulder: Westview Press, 1989); I. William Zartman, "King Hassan's New Morocco," in I. William Zartman (ed.), *The Political Economy of Morocco* (New York: Praeger, 1987), pp. 1–33; John Damis, "Sources of Political Stability in Modernizing Monarchical Regimes: Jordan and Morocco," in Constantine P. Danopoulos (ed.), *Civilian Rule in the Developing World: Democracy on the March?* (Boulder: Westview Press, 1992), pp. 23–51.

3. Ilya Harik, "The Origins of the Arab State System," in Ghassan Salame (ed.), *The Foundations of the Arab State* (London: Croom Helm, 1987), pp. 19–46.

4. Lord Birdwood, *Nuri al-Said: A Study in Arab Leadership* (London: Cassell, 1959), p. 267.

5. Hana Batatu, *The Old Social Classes and Revolutionary Movements in Iraq* (Princeton: Princeton University Press, 1978), pp. 343, 764–766.

6. Phebe Marr, *The Modern History of Iraq* (Boulder: Westview Press, 1985), pp. 123–125.

7. Ofra Bengio, "Iraq," in Ami Ayalon (ed.), *Middle East Contemporary Survey*, Vol. 13, *1989* (Boulder: Westview Press, 1991), pp. 372, 374–375.

8. Elie Kedourie, "Egypt and the Caliphate Question, 1915–1952," in Elie Kedourie (ed.), *The Chatham House Version and Other Middle Eastern Studies* (Hanover, N.H.: University Press of New England, 1984), pp. 177–207.

9. Michael Winter, "Islam in the State: Pragmatism and Growing Commitment," in Shimon Shamir (ed.), *Egypt: From Monarchy to Republic* (Boulder: Westview Press, 1995), pp. 44–48.

10. Avriel Butovsky, "Language of the Egyptian Monarchy," *Harvard Middle Eastern and Islamic Review*, 1 (1994), pp. 52–66.

11. Nadav Safran, *Egypt in Search of Political Community* (Cambridge: Harvard University Press, 1961), pp. 108–121.

12. P. J. Vatikiotis, *A History of Egypt*, 2nd ed. (London: Weidenfeld and Nicholson, 1981), pp. 347–349.

13. Marr, *Modern History of Iraq*, p. 115.

14. Gamal Abdul Nasser [Abd al-Nasir], *Egypt's Liberation: The Philosophy of the Revolution* (Washington, D.C.: Public Affairs Press, 1955), pp. 21–23.

15. Raymond William Baker, *Egypt's Uncertain Revolution Under Nasser and Sadat* (Cambridge: Harvard University Press, 1978), p. 1.

16. Bruce Maddy-Weitzman, *The Crystallization of the Arab State System, 1945–1954* (Syracuse: Syracuse University Press, 1993) , pp. 13–21, 55–90.

17. Hanna Batatu, "The Old Social Classes Revisited," in Robert A. Fernea and Wm. Roger Louis (eds.), *The Iraqi Revolution of 1958* (London: I. B. Taurus, 1991), p. 213.

18. Edith and E. F. Pentose, *Iraq: International Relations and National Development* (London: Ernest Benn, 1978), pp. 199–201.

19. Matthew Eliot, *"Independent Iraq": The Monarchy and British Influence, 1941–1958* (London: I. B. Tauris, 1996), p. 160.

20. Manfred W. Werner, *Modern Yemen, 1918–1966* (Baltimore: Johns Hopkins University Press, 1967), pp. 176–189.

21. Dana Adams Schmidt, *Yemen: The Unknown War* (New York: Holt, Rinehart and Winston, 1968), pp. 41–42.

22. Leigh Douglas, *The Free Yemeni Movement, 1935–1962* (Beirut: American University of Beirut Press, 1987), pp. 9–15, 30–33.

23. Francois Burgat, "Qadhdhafi's Ideological Framework," in Dirk Vandervalle (ed.), *Libya, 1969–1994* (New York: St. Martin's Press, 1995), pp. 49–50.

24. John Marlowe, *Arab Nationalism and British Imperialism* (London: Cresset Press, 1961); Fayez Sayegh, *Arab Unity: Hope or Fulfillment?* (New York: Devin-Adair, 1958).

25. Halpern, *Politics,* p. 359.

26. Samuel Huntington, *Political Order in Changing Societies* (New Haven: Yale University Press, 1968), p. 275.

27. Ervand Abrahamian, *Iran Between Two Revolutions* (Princeton: Princeton University Press, 1982).

28. Huntington, *Political Order,* p. 202.

29. Vatikiotis, *Nasser and His Generation* (London: Croom Helm, 1978), p. 109.

30. Eliezer Be'eri, *Army Officers in Arab Politics and Society* (Jerusalem: Israel Universities Press, 1969), p. 366.

31. Morroe Berger, *Bureaucracy and Society in Modern Egypt* (Princeton: Princeton University Press, 1957), p. 185.

32. Wm. Roger Louis, *The British Empire and the Middle East* (Oxford: Clarendon Press, 1984), pp. 309–310, 148–150.

33. Louis, "The British and the Origins of the Revolution," in Fernea and Louis (eds.), pp. 45–46, 56.

34. Marion Farouk-Sluglett and Peter Sluglett, "The Social Classes and the Origins of the Revolution," in Fernea and Louis (eds.), *The Iraqi Revolution,* pp. 131–134.

35. Sami Zubaida, "Community, Class and Minorities in Iraqi Politics," in Fernea and Louis (eds.), pp. 197–210.

36. Theda Skocpol, *States and Social Revolutions* (Cambridge: Cambridge University Press, 1979), pp. 30–32.

37. Said Amir Arjomand, *The Turban for the Crown: The Islamic Revolution in Iran* (New York: Oxford University Press, 1988).

38. Roger Owen, "Class and Class Politics in Iraq Before 1958: The 'Colonial and Post-Colonial State,'" in Fernea and Louis (eds.), pp. 154–171.

39. Batatu, "The Old Social Classes Revisited," p. 214.

40. Arjomand, *The Turban for the Crown,* pp. 117–119.

41. Kedourie, "The Kingdom of Iraq, a Retrospect," in Kedourie (ed.), *The Chatham House Version,* p. 278.

42. Ibid., pp. 270–278; Marr, *Modern History of Iraq,* pp. 123–125.

43. Batatu, *The Old Social Classes,* pp. 805–806.

44. Ibid., pp. 115–116.

45. Waldemar Gallman, *Iraq Under General Nuri, 1954–1958* (Baltimore: Johns Hopkins University Press, 1964), p. 205.

46. Batatu, *The Old Social Classes,* pp. 805–806.

47. Majid Khadduri, *Arab Contemporaries* (Baltimore: Johns Hopkins University Press, 1973), pp. 40, 42; Birdwood, *Nuri al-Sa'id,* p. 257.

48. Jan Morris, *The Hashemite Kings* (London: Faber and Faber, 1959), p. 197.

49. Marr, *Modern History of Iraq,* pp. 113–125.

50. Ibid., pp. 156–157.

51. Joel Gordon, *Nasser's Blessed Movement* (New York: Oxford University Press, 1992), p. 56.

52. Anwar al-Sadat, *In Search of Identity* (New York: Harper and Row, 1977), p. 102.

53. Vatikiotis, *Nasser and His Generation,* pp. 109–110.

54. Robert Stookey, *Yemen: The Politics of the Yemen Arab Republic* (Boulder: Westview Press, 1978), p. 225.

55. Baker, *Egypt's Uncertain Revolution,* p. 29.

56. Vatikiotis, *Nasser and His Generation,* p. 106.

57. Miles Copeland, *The Game of Nations* (London: Weidenfeld and Nicholson, 1969), pp. 48–59; Barry Rubin, *The Arab States and the Palestine Question* (Syracuse: Syracuse University Press, 1981), pp. 218–219.

58. Gordon, *Nasser's Blessed Movement,* pp. 5, 59.

59. Berger, *Bureaucracy,* p. 37.

60. Bengio, "Faysal's Vision of Iraq: A Retrospect," in Asher Susser and Aryeh Shmuelevitz (eds.), *The Hashemites in the Modern Arab World* (London: Frank Cass, 1995), pp. 139–151.

5

Dynasts and Nationalists: Why Monarchies Survive

Lisa Anderson

The Middle East and North Africa host the only major ruling monarchs in the world. At a time when most of the world's historical thrones were overthrown long ago and nearly all the surviving kings, queens, and emperors have been satisfied to become symbols of their states—continuing to reign in exchange for surrendering the right to rule—Middle Eastern kings are conspicuous by both their number and their power.

This remarkable feature of Middle Eastern politics provokes several questions. Why are there so many ruling monarchs in the Middle East? How have those that survived done so? What difference does the institution make for the nature of politics or policy? The conventional answers to these questions are often inconsistent or unverifiable. Tradition and culture are routinely called upon to explain the prevalence of monarchy in the Middle East and North Africa but, as I have argued elsewhere,[1] none of the existing monarchies, with the possible exception of Morocco, predate the late nineteenth century (although, obviously, the ruling families trace ancestral lineages quite far—in several cases to the Prophet Muhammad himself). Moreover, Islam's provisions for the administration of the community of the faithful—notably the requirements for *shura* (consultation) and for explicit expressions of acquiescence and *bay'a* (allegiance)—do not constitute clear endorsements of monarchy as we conventionally understand it. In fact, the monarchies of the Middle East and North Africa are as often associated with British imperial influence as with any local cultural and traditional prescriptions.

Neither local traditions nor British influence account for the broad despotic power enjoyed by the monarchs of the Middle East. Neither British parliamentary practice under the crown nor the Islamic provisions for coronation provide precedent or justification for the virtually unfettered absolutism that has characterized much government in the postwar Middle East. The regimes of European imperialism did little to foster local accountability, of course, but the contemporary absolutism is unprecedented in the region, thanks in large measure to advances in military and communications technologies monopolized by the state. Moreover, on this score, the monarchies are virtually indistinguishable from the ostensibly republican governments. Certainly President Saddam Hussein of Iraq is no more—and probably less— accountable to popular sentiment than was King Hussein of Jordan; Libya's Colonel Qaddafi is hardly more responsive to his citizens than Saudi King Fahd is to his subjects.

The astonishment with which we view the stability of the Middle Eastern monarchies since 1975 is as much a measure of our prejudices—monarchy usually strikes Western observers, especially Americans, as a quaint anachronism perpetually on the verge of demise—as of the unique adaptability of the monarchs themselves. In fact, one significant monarch did fall during that period—Iran's shah—but that constituted the only significant regime change in the entire region between 1970 and the end of the Cold War. It appears that after several decades of considerable political turmoil in the Middle East, the music stopped: the occupants of the rulers' chairs—thrones or otherwise—in 1970 proved able to hold on to them for more than twenty years. Most observers attribute this stability to both wealth afforded the region by oil revenues after 1973 and the influence of détente in the Cold War rivalry between the United States and the Soviet Union during the 1970s. None of these factors was unique to the monarchies of the region.

If, in many important respects, the monarchies are little different from their neighbors—novel governmental forms in relatively new states, largely unaccountable to their subjects or citizens but able to hang on to power for longer than most observers have predicted—is there no political significance to the pomp and circumstance that attaches uniquely to monarchy?[2] Is it entirely contingent and essentially inconsequential that Presidents Ben Ali of Tunisia and Asad of Syria indulge in elections in which they win 98 percent of the vote, while the late Kings Hasan of Morocco and Hussein of Jordan did not run for their office at all?

Few self-respecting political scientists would be comfortable with that conclusion. Institutions, such as crowns or presidencies or parliaments, should matter, both as predictable effects of identifiable causes and as discernible causes of specific effects. Equally important, there is empirical evidence—not conclusive but certainly suggestive—that monarchy does have measurable consequences for policymaking procedures and outcomes in the Middle East. Even the most casual observer of the funeral of Israeli Prime Minister Yitzhak Rabin in Jerusalem in November 1995 had to notice that far more than half the representatives of Arab governments were led or sent by monarchs, including those of Jordan, Morocco, Oman, and Qatar. Indeed, Jordan and Morocco had been among the oldest and closest of Israel's interlocutors in the Middle East.

If institutions and policy are politically significant, we should be able to draw inferences about the nature and prospects of today's monarchies from their characteristic institutional features and policy postures. This chapter is an exploration of both the utility of monarchy in the process of state-formation and its unusual suppleness in the face of the project of nation-building. As such, the study of this relatively uncommon regime type reveals the important intervening role that regime type in general may play in mediating between the often simultaneous and rarely unrelated processes of state-formation and nation-building.

STATE-FORMATION AND THE MONARCHS

In my earlier work on Middle Eastern monarchies, I proposed that all of the states of the Middle East confront the imperatives of state-formation and that monarchy provides a regime particularly compatible with that project.[3] Like the regimes of seventeenth-century European absolutists, most of the regimes of the Middle East are centralized, personalistic, and actually or potentially coercive. These features are typical of (perhaps even required by) the project of state-formation. Old privileges and institutions are under challenge and new rights and procedures are ambiguous. The magnitude of the transformation produces exceptional uncertainty and amplifies the importance of statecraft, personal skills and relationships, and brute force in government.

In all of these respects, monarchy may have an advantage over its republican counterpart in that the monarchs, very much like their European precursors, are expected to rely on personal attributes and virtues. They are neither sustained nor burdened by the impersonal rules and procedures of routinized bureaucracies and consolidated legislatures, as ostensibly republican rulers are expected to be. Of their personal virtues, military valor is particularly highly prized—witness some of the Middle Eastern monarchs with experience piloting fighter planes, including the late King Hussein of Jordan and the former shah of Iran—and it is utilized to convey both the personal courage of the incumbent and the importance and legitimacy of government-sponsored coercion. State-formation makes the same demands of republican governments for coercion—of new taxpayers, conscripts, smugglers, and citizens—which is why they are so often led by military regimes. But monarchy has the advantage of the easier association of military virtues with other desirable qualities—compassion, piety, learning—in the person and the office of the king.

Clearly the institutional flexibility and inclusiveness of monarchy is an important element of its remarkable resilience in the Middle East; as I have suggested, there is an "elective affinity" between this regime type and the demands of state-formation. What I would like to explore here are the complex links between monarchy and another, probably *the* other, significant project in the Middle East: nation-building.

NATION-BUILDING AND THE MONARCHS

As we know, issues of nationalism and nation-building have been major pre-occupations in the Arab world for more than a century. From the early polemics in the waning days of the Ottoman Empire, to the anti-imperialist campaigns of the interwar period, to the embrace of unity, freedom, and social justice by Jammal Abd-al Nasir and the Ba'th Party in the 1950s and 1960s, Arab nationalism in particular has played a crucial role in shaping politics in the Middle East and North Africa. In playing such a large role, the nationalists captured and diverted our attention, provoking long and learned debates about the future of the ideology and its adherents, to the neglect and often outright dismissal of other political, social, and cultural identities. Yet the persistence of the monarchies—never full participants or eager supporters of Arab nationalism—testifies to the importance of other, alternative efforts at defining and redefining political and cultural identities in the Middle East and North Africa.

There is a vast and provocative theoretical literature on the nature of nationalism in general and of its various manifestations in the Middle East.[4] I will not rehearse that literature here, but I would like to make several general points about nationalism itself and how we have addressed it. It is by now conventional to observe that what analysts once took to be obvious—that national and ethnic identities are "primordial" features of human existence, found in nature and subsequently mobilized for political claims—borrowed too much from the lexicon of the nationalist ideologues themselves. Most students of ethnic—or, more broadly, identity—politics now agree that identities are "social-constructed." Social meaning and political significance are attached to biological or historical facts to create the accepted understanding of religious, racial, sexual, or ethnic characteristics.

In the Middle East today—as for the entire twentieth century—questions of political identity are elastic, open, and often highly contentious. The very arbitrariness of the historical installation of most of the states in the region, including the monarchies, created the need to devise formulas for legitimation, to write "national" histories and traditions, and to develop civic myths with the state institutions. Nationalists usually address these complex issues by simplifying them: nationalism is inherently egalitarian and exclusivist. Accountable equally and only to other members of their nation, its advocates define that nation's membership, sharpen its limits, and cement its contours.

Monarchs, by contrast, thrive on multiplicity and avail themselves of considerable ambiguity and nuance in defining the members of their realm. In fact, although we ordinarily think of monarchy as brittle,[5] there is ample evidence that these regimes are both accommodating and effective in appealing to a wide variety of political, social, economic, and even foreign constituencies. Our problem is not so much identifying the "natural" constituency of monarchy in the middle East—there seem to be a plethora of actual and potential constituents—but in determining the circumstances in which monarchs choose to appeal to one over another.

In part the complexity of comparing nationalist and monarchical regimes reflects the fact that the fundamental constitutive principles of monarchy and nationalism are very different, indeed, virtually contradictory. As Benedict Anderson puts it in his study of nationalism, "in fundamental ways, serious monarchy lies transverse to all modern conceptions of political life."[6] Monarchy celebrates and reinforces identification with both the narrowest of loyalties—the family—and the broadest of universalist attachments—to a transcendent God. What it avoids—indeed rejects—is an exclusive or singular ethnic, linguistic, or cultural identity.

Monarchy emphasizes the primacy of kinship in the arrangements for succession, and it symbolizes the link with the transcendent in the various formulas that accord monarchs divine rights to rule. Ethnic markers, notably language but also regional origin or even ideological commitment, are far less significant than God and family, and the institutions associated with such loyalties—vernacular newspapers, cultural associations, political parties—are discouraged if not prohibited. As F. Gregory Gause III points out, the Gulf monarchies, "portray themselves to their own people and to the world as the embodiment of Arabian tribal values and (more in some cases than others) of Muslim piety. The governments supply money to support tribal and religious institutions and allow them space to operate publicly. Such public space is largely denied to other types of social and political organization, like political parties or, with some limited exceptions, a free press."[7]

Lest we assume that the privileging of God and family over nation is a feature peculiar to the Middle East, we need only to recall that just as the Saudis insist upon their role as "custodians of the holy mosques" in Mecca and Medina and the king of Morocco is formally described as "commander of the faithful," the British monarch reigns as the head of the Church of England. Even more striking is the royal preference in both Europe and the Middle East for social and political ties based on kinship rather than rationality. Well into the twentieth century the royal families of Europe scoured the aristocracy of the continent looking for suitable matches for their offspring—and often married their children to spouses who hardly spoke the same languages. So, too, the Arab monarchs do not hold Arab ethnicity per se as an important criterion for their spouses: two of the four wives of King Hussein of Jordan have been non-Arab women; his widow is an American by birth. As in Europe, the best royal marriages are to cousins rather than to spouses defined

as nationals. King Hussein's first wife was, as he put it, "a member of the
Hashemite dynasty who lived in Cairo . . . a distant cousin," and when the
marriage was dissolved, she returned to her native Egypt.[8]

The crucial distinction is not one between the Middle East and the West
but between profoundly different principles of political identity and loyalty.
As Ernest Gellner has reminded us, "modern man is not loyal to a monarch or
a land or a faith, whatever he may say, but to a culture."[9] This chapter exam-
ines the conceptions of identity and loyalty that "lie transverse" to modern
nationalism as they are revealed in the theory and practice of the modern
Middle Eastern monarchs, through exploration of the elaboration of explicit
and implicit theories of sovereignty, the constitution of societal identity
groups, and the construction of legitimating myths.

THE MANDATE TO RULE:
THE DIVINE RIGHT OF THE FAMILY

The right of kings to rule is predicated upon the acceptance of hereditary distinctions and religious grace. It requires the existence of certain kinds of "social capital," including personal and filial loyalty and religious faith. Monarchs must therefore work to reinforce these values, both in justifying their
own right to rule and in maintaining a societal environment in which such beliefs thrive.

Reinhard Bendix distinguishes two types of monarchical authority, reit-
erating a distinction made by Machiavelli in *The Prince:* "Kingdoms known
to history," writes Machiavelli, "have been governed in two ways: either by a
prince and his servants, who, as ministers by his grace and permission, assist
in governing the realm; or by a prince and by barons, who hold their positions
not by favor of the rulers but by antiquity of blood."[10] Monarchs may be
obeyed by their "servants" because the realm is construed as the king's property. Alternately, the king may mediate among and balance the private domains of the "barons" who acknowledge his authority as primus inter pares
(first among equals). In both cases, kinship and hierarchy are crucial, and in
neither case are ordinary people part of the administration except as recipients, nor are they represented in government counsels; instead, said Bendix,
"a king governed his country like a giant household."[11] This conception of the
king's domain as a household or family reinforces both notions of kinship
and hierarchy; it is, of course, quite familiar in the Middle East.

Indeed, the Middle East is home to the only country in the world named
after its ruling family. The primacy of that family is encoded in law: in March
1992, the government of Saudi Arabia issued a document—the Basic System
of Government—as close to a constitution as the country has; Article 5 unam-

biguously declares that responsibility for the country resides in the sons and grandsons of Abd al-Aziz al-Saud. Sovereignty rests with the al-Saud family; the "people" with whom nationalists are ordinarily concerned are conspicuous by their absence.[12]

Yet even though they are not sovereign in monarchies, the "people" are an important component of the system, for what is a king without subjects? Not only is the royal family itself endowed with a specific right to rule; royal authority is demonstrated and confirmed in the king's discharge of his paternal responsibilities to his metaphorical children—his subjects. The familial metaphor is deliberate and repeated: King Hasan of Morocco has described his country as a family, routinely referring to his people—particularly his military forces—as his children.[13] King Hussein of Jordan carefully cultivated identification with Jordan as kindred ties: "Invariably I have been at pains to build up a family feeling in Jordan so that I may be, if you like, the father of a large family just as much as the king of a small country."[14]

Like the fathers they aspire to be, kings have many roles and multiple responsibilities. The Moroccan constitution of 1972, for example, outlined the position of the monarch, declaring

> the king, Commander of the Faithful, supreme representative of the nation, symbol of its unity, guarantor of the perpetuity and continuity of the state, shall insure that Islam and the Constitution are respected. He shall protect the rights and freedoms of citizens, social groups, and communities. He shall guarantee the independence of the nation and the territorial integrity of the kingdom within its authentic boundaries.[15]

There is no mention of popular sovereignty; it is the king who is ultimately responsible as representative, guarantor, protector of the nation, the state, Islam, citizens, social groups, communities, and the kingdom itself.

Not only are the king's responsibilities multiple, so too are his realms: the domain traced by Morocco's "authentic" boundaries, for example, is open to interpretation. This is not simply a reflection of Morocco's claims to the Western Sahara nor merely kings' special interest in Moroccan communities elsewhere in the world, however important those may be. As Anderson points out,

> In the modern conception, state sovereignty is fully, flatly, and evenly operative over each square centimeter of a legally demarcated territory. Not in the older imagining, where states were defined by centers, borders were porous and indistinct, and sovereignties faded imperceptibly into one another. Hence, paradoxically enough, the ease with which premodern empires and kingdoms were able to sustain their rule over immensely heterogeneous, and often not even contiguous, populations for long periods of time.[16]

It is perhaps not surprising, therefore, that many of the Middle Eastern monarchies have substantial outstanding questions about their borders, including most famously Morocco's claim to the Western Sahara, Jordan's ties with the West Bank, and Kuwait's dispute with Iraq.

Unlike nationalist regimes, monarchies acknowledge, sustain, even encourage heterogeneity among their subjects. Monarchs are better able to serve as the central focus in balancing, manipulating, and controlling societies characterized by such vertical cleavages, particularly when those are reinforced by "antiquity of blood." The continued emphasis on tribal and familial divisions in the Arabian Peninsula not only reinforces the legitimacy of the constitutive principle of kindship but also permits the monarchs to exercise their skills as patrons and mediators.

The contrasting language policies of Morocco and Algeria illustrate the superior capacity of monarchies to subtain the ambiguities of multiple identities among their subjects. Language is a particularly important component of developing nationalism—indeed, to many theorists, including Gellner, it is the most important:

> In a traditional social order the languages of the hunt, of harvesting, of various rituals, of the council room, of the kitchen or harem, all form autonomous systems: to conjoin statements drawn from these various fields, to probe for inconsistencies between them, to try to unify them all, this would be a social solecism or worse, probably blasphemy or impiety, and the very endeavor would be unintelligible. By contrast, in our society it is assumed that all referential uses of language ultimately refer to one coherent world, and can be reduced to a unitary idiom.[17]

As the uses of language coalesce around a single conception of the world, the choice of idiom becomes crucial.

Both Morocco and Algeria style themselves Arab countries, but they include large Francophone elites and substantial Berber-speaking populations. Shortly after independence, there were widespread calls to discontinue the use of French—the language of colonialism—in education, government, and daily commerce. The Algerian government, which had nationalized all the remaining French-owned property at the end of the war of independence, began a dramatic Arabization campaign, outlawing the use of French in public forums, painting out French-language street signs, and importing primary school teachers from Egypt and elsewhere to fill Arabic-language positions Algerians themselves could not staff. Suddenly many highly educated Algerians conversant only in Berber and French found they could not read street signs, practice law, and otherwise participate as full members of the Algerian nation for whose independence they had fought so hard. The Berber cultural movement, which many observers view as the precursor of a full-fledged nationalist movement, appeared within half a decade.

By contrast, the Moroccan government, having achieved independence without a major war, permitted French nationals to remain after independence, owning property and staffing important parts of the government bureaucracy. As a result, over the succeeding several decades, while paying lip service to Arabization, the Moroccans deliberately dragged their feet. Ultimately, they pursued a strategy of Moroccanization instead, whereby Moroccan nationals were to be favored in the economy and public administration. This had the advantage of appealing to the anti-imperialist sentiment still alive in North Africa without provoking a self-consciously Berberiat backlash. By the mid-1990s, and partly in response to the contagion of the upheavals in Algeria, the Moroccan government that had previously discouraged efforts to promote Berber language and culture permitted the teaching of Berber in the schools and authorized daily broadcasts of Berber-language news on the state-owned television station. As Mark Tessler observes, "the monarchy remains a crucial element in the political formula that unites Arabs and Berbers."[18]

The popular sovereignty implicit in nationalist ideologies implies not only equality among citizens but also identity—even interchangeability—among the people. In their formal public roles as conscripts, taxpayers, and voters, citizens all resemble each other, and citizenship requires skills, such as literacy, that can be taught and measured in quantity. The theories of legitimation that accompany and support monarchy, by contrast, discourage formal interchangeability among subjects. Monarchies promote and defend definitions of the roles of kings and their subjects that emphasize inequality, diversity, and personal fealty. As a result, kings not only endorse societal diversity, inequality, and multiplicity as constitutive principles of politics; they deliberately create and maintain complex social structures in practice.

DEFINING CLIENTS: SOCIAL BASES OF RULE

Monarchical rule requires a household to supervise, clients to satisfy, and constituencies to balance. Rulers must establish the criteria for membership in those households and constituencies and patronize the resulting groups. One of the mechanisms to reinforce the primacy of kinship over nationalism is to nourish and strengthen existing kinship patterns and loyalties. Royal marriages not only serve to cement particular families to the monarchy, obliging them to lend support to the king, but also to reinforce the importance of kinship as a constitutive principle of society. This not only emphasizes the social and political distinction between the privileged families tied to the royals and the common people but also denies the very notion of equality that undergirds the nationalist conception of citizenship. The creation of kinship relations and the resulting political alliances is an important function of royal marriages. Abd al-Aziz Ibn Saud, founder of the state named after its ruling family, consolidated his realm in Saudi Arabia through dozens of marriages, many with wives drawn from the leading tribal families, fathering nearly a hundred children.[19]

Nonkin constituencies may also serve to symbolize the primacy of personal loyalties and ascriptive identities, simultaneously creating dependent "protégés" of the king and reinforcing the importance of such criteria in social and political organization. King Hasan of Morocco long argued that among his obligations as commander of the faithful is protection of the people of the Book, for example, and he has taken a long-standing interest in Morocco's Jewish community. The 18,000-member Jewish community of Morocco, though considerably reduced from its 250,000 at independence, is the largest and most prosperous Jewish community in the Arab world. Jews are represented in parliament and in the Casablanca City Council, and the Jewish community retains control of its own courts and schools. Solicitude toward the Jewish community, as Mark Tessler points out, is an important element in the monarchy's self-image: "Hasan takes personal pride in this situation, regarding himself as the protector of Moroccan Jewry. Most Moroccan Jews believe the king is sincerely concerned about his welfare. Moreover, Hasan is carrying forward an historical tradition of the Moroccan monarchy's conviction that it is responsible for the well-being of all citizens of the country."[20] Out of this concern has grown the king's interest in Arab-Israeli rapprochement; Moroccan-Israeli contacts may date back to the mid-1960s. The public record shows that by the mid-1970s Yitzhak Rabin had made a secret trip to Morocco as part of the king's efforts to facilitate the contacts between Israel and Egypt that eventually produced the Camp David Accords.

The Moroccan monarch has made no secret of his particular concern for Israelis of Moroccan origin, whom he continues to consider a part of his domain. In 1986, he received the leaders of the World Association of Moroccan Jewry—including a number of Israelis—saying, "Let this association serve as a bridge between the Jewish world and the Arab world, for it is our community that links the two," and he decreed that Israeli Jews of Moroccan origin have not forfeited their Moroccan citizenship and are free to return at will.[21]

Religious minorities are formally recognized in some republican regimes in the Middle East: Lebanese of all confessions, for example, have reserved seats allocated to them in their states' parliaments. As the early and important role of Christians in the development of Arab nationalism suggests, however, nationalism is designed to permit minorities equal—not privileged or even singular—status in politics and society. From that perspective, it must be counted a failure of the nationalist project that some states continue to distinguish among themselves on the basis of religion.

By contrast, monarchies can favor religious minorities without betraying their principles; on the contrary, such favoritism reinforces the arbitrary power of the king to create and legitimate social distinctions and to sustain the resulting groups as his clienteles and constituencies. The late shah of Iran gloated about the Iranian National Assembly: "I am proud that as a symbol of tolerance, these minority groups [Jews, Zoroastrians, Assyrians, and Armenians] actually enjoy proportionately more representation than does our population at large."[22] This boast would hardly make sense to an advocate of popular sovereignty, but it is virtually universal among the monarchies. In Jordan, where Islam is the religion of the state and by law both the head of state—the king—and the prime minister must be Muslims, Christians have always enjoyed representation disproportionate to their numbers. And this has not gone unnoticed. As Philip Robins reports about the late Jordanian king, "There is a general perception within the Christian community that King Hussein is well disposed toward them and he has assumed the role of protector."[23]

However predisposed to personal, informal, familial, or patronage relations they may be, many of the monarchies of the Middle East and North Africa have had to confront the appearance of social groups organized around common ideological commitment or economic interests. Morocco has numerous political parties and labor unions; Jordan's political parties and newspapers include representatives of a variety of nationalist positions. The kings of Morocco and Jordan accommodated these developments in royal fashion, using their patronage to encapsulate and incorporate potential challenges based on ideology and interest. As Tessler remarks of Morocco:

> Despite structural pluralism, the palace remains dominant. Most members of Morocco's political class, including the leaders of most political parties, owe their position to its support. Hasan presides over a national political machine that operates on the basis of clientelism; and, sitting atop this network of patron-client hierarchies, the king rewards his supporters, punishes his enemies, and generally keeps others dependent on his favors. [Thereby] he assures that elections and multiparty politics do not evolve into political competition he is unable to control.[24]

Whether the monarchies can sustain their capacity to assign privileges, dispense largesse, and provide protection on the basis of personal loyalty is open to question. For decades, analysts have predicted that the rise of a new middle class—educated nonroyals with a collective interest in more egalitarian political theory and practice—would spell the downfall of the monarchies of the Middle East and North Africa.[25] Yet the monarchies have proven able to effectively convey the very real costs entailed in abandoning the monarchical regime for what may be, at least in the short run, far less stable, open-minded, even—ironically—less liberal alternatives. The resulting dilemma is apparent even to the most reluctant of monarchy's beneficiaries. As Robins observes, in Jordan "the wariness and reluctance of the Christian community to relinquish its formal position of privilege is beyond dispute. Even one of the articulate, younger supporters of the notion of democracy was only willing to contemplate an end to this special status if there was a trade-off with the legalization of political parties."[26]

MYTH-MAKING: THE INVENTION OF TRADITION

Combining deference and loyalty in metaphors of family, and celebrating the diversity and incomparability of the kings' varied protégés, the monarchs of the Middle East and North Africa provide an alternative conception of society and government to the egalitarian populism of the nationalists of the region. Yet like the nationalists they confront the dilemma of novelty: the need to create a history consistent with the present.

All of the countries of the Middle East and North Africa greeted the second half of the twentieth century with the task of establishing the criteria for, and desirability of, membership in the polity. For the republican regimes, nation-building demanded the specification and celebration of the collective merits of the distinctive "people" whose sovereignty they reflected. Schools, printing presses, and broadcast stations disseminated the civic myths and official histories of the Turks, Persians, Arabs, and Jews as ancient and virtuous nations destined to light the way for all others.

Throughout the heyday of nationalism in the Middle East—roughly the quarter century after the end of World War II—the region's monarchies were on the defensive. Several fell to nationalist regimes, including those of Egypt, Iraq, and Libya, and the remaining monarchs were preoccupied with fending off challenges from foreign and domestic foes. By the time the dust settled—or perhaps more accurately, when oil reserves proved to have favored the region's monarchies—the kings were ready to redress their neglect of official civic myths.

As for the nationalists, the development of suitable histories for the monarchies required hard work and inventiveness. The requirements of the project were somewhat different, however, for the nationalists' emphasis on the equality and equivalence of citizens was replaced by the multiplicity and often incommensurability of the groups tied through their links with the royal family. The oil-producing monarchies of the Persian Gulf devoted substantial resources to the discovery and creation of appropriate symbols. As Jill Crystal tells us, in 1972, when Shaikh Khalifa acceded to the throne of Qatar, the country "was sadly lacking in a civic myth," but in the next few years the emir gave high priority to developing symbols that would clarify and legitimize his claim to rule. Among the principal results was a museum built around the old shaikh's palace: "The selection of the palace as a centerpiece linked the ruling family to all the other pasts displayed within: the stone age, the nomadic days, the Islamic era, the pearling days, the oil boom, the state projects."[27] The museum conveys graphically the notion that through history, as today, the royal family embraced and united varied, seemingly unrelated, times, places, and people.

Similar projects in other Persian Gulf countries proliferated, producing museums devoted to the *turath*, or "heritage," of the various realms, and glossy books packaging their history were quickly produced. Unlike the nationalists, who celebrated the exploits of "national" heroes like Sallah al-Din, Sulayman the Magnificent, Xerxes, and King David, most of the monarchs could not construct a story in which their predecessors played a large role on the world stage. Interestingly, however, the need for a local heritage coincided with changing styles in historiography, and many of the scholars employed to work on the archaeology, ethnography, and history of the monarchies of the Middle East— schooled in modern social history—considered the political history adopted by the nationalist historiographers passé. They melded the most advanced technologies and styles of historiography with the purposes and needs of the monarchs, emphasizing local tradition, kinship—with the reconstruction of elaborate tribal genealogies—and Islam and its local observance.[28]

Outside the Gulf, the monarchs face somewhat more complex challenges. In Jordan, even by the early 1950s, courtesy of King Abdallah's decision to annex the West Bank and grant citizenship to the Palestinians who took refuge in his realm, a substantial proportion of the population had no tribal identity and was already committed to an elaborate nationalist program. As a result, the nationalist theme is routinely played by the monarchy; like those of his subjects who are devoted to their tribal heritage, the nationalists too will fit under the inclusive wing of the benevolent king. As Yezid Sayigh points out, in their "continuing attempt to inculcate a sense of their own history into the Jordanian popular mind . . . members of the royal family have often stressed their tribal, Islamic and Arab nationalist credentials to their constituencies."[29]

Indeed, according to the late King Hussein himself, after they were galvanized by the subjugation of the Arabs in the waning days of the Ottoman Empire, "the Arabs turned for leadership to Mecca and the Hashemite dynasty." Sharif Hussein, leader of the dynasty, determined "to liberate the Arab world."[30] In their own view, then, the disappointments that followed what Jordanian historians know as the "Great Arab Revolt" do not tarnish their Hashemite credentials as Arab nationalists, permitting them to co-opt and even to claim precedence among the nationalists.[31]

Moreover, as Yezid Sayigh observes, the presence of the Palestinians also presented an opportunity to King Hussein to demonstrate his skill at balancing the competing needs of his various constituents and to retain the ambiguous relationship between territorial boundaries and personal clienteles that is so characteristic of monarchy.

> In historic overview, the Hashemites' insistence on absorbing and welding both communities into one society has been responsible for the present degree of stability in Jordan. Ultimately, if the key to the Hashemite throne's early success in establishing its authority was its command of the state and the army, then its long-term success lay in the balance it contrived, determining the place of each socioeconomic group or ethnic community within the country's social, economic and political life.[32]

Chafe though they might, the Palestinians in Jordan, like the nationalist Istiqlal Party in Morocco, have been transformed into yet another of the various groups in society who are beneficiaries of royal patronage. In Morocco, King Hasan adroitly utilized claims to the Western Sahara to demonstrate his own nationalist credentials and to put the nationalist political parties—once his serious rival—on the political defensive, following his agenda rather than setting one of their own. Nationalist rhetoric has been appropriated by these monarchies as effectively as tribal genealogy and Islam to identify and isolate yet another of the king's myriad constituencies.

CONCLUSION

The persistence of the monarchies of the Middle East and North Africa reflects not only the adequacy of the regime for undertaking the project of state-formation but also—and equally important—the urgency and complexity of identity politics in the region. Perhaps better even than the recent revival of Islamist political movements as challenges to secular nationalist ideologies, the persistence of the monarchies illustrates the ambivalence and ambiguity of political identity in the region. At midcentury, ethnically based nationalist movements seemed to have triumphed; Turkey and Israel had appeared as products of nationalist movements, and Arab nationalism appeared poised to capture the loyalties and governments of Arabs everywhere. More than fifty years later, the Arab nationalist project is in disarray, and religion complicates ethnicity even in Turkey and Israel.

The monarchies of the region, long despised and ignored, particularly by Western social scientists, might well be viewed as instructive indicators of the limits and limitations of the secular nationalism that once seemed destined to overwhelm all other political identities. Monarchy is not only well-suited to early stages of state-formation; it may also be far better adapted than we have suspected to the complex cosmopolitan world in which diverse communities interact through international finance and trade, labor migration, and global communications. Certainly in the absence of an egalitarian, populist world culture, monarchs can avail themselves of useful experience in balancing varied international and domestic constituencies to draw resources from beyond their putative borders.

Certainly, as political scientists and historians we must recognize that most conventional discussions of the relationship between state and nation, or between state-formation and nation-building, neglect an important intervening variable: regime type. Most discussions of the development of nationalism focus on economic and technological determinants—the shift from agrarian to industrial society, the development of the printing press and other media for dissemination of vernacular-language materials. These may well be significant, particularly in the early stages of the world historical development of nationalism. In the Middle East, however, nationalism is not correlated with levels of industrialization or with literacy; the early associations have come uncoupled. This suggests the desirability of examining other influences on the contours and trajectory of identity politics, and regime type appears to be a provocative vantage point. Indeed, regime type appears to have been significant elsewhere. The French government, for example, did not undertake language rationalization seriously until the late nineteenth century,[33] well after the last of the monarchist restorations was defeated. Thus the relationship between political identity and government legitimacy is too close not to merit closer scrutiny, of which this chapter is merely a beginning.

NOTES

1. Parts of this argument are based on my earlier foray into the study of Middle Eastern monarchs. See Lisa Anderson. "Absolutism and the Resilience of Monarchy in the Middle East," *Political Science Quarterly*, 106 (1991), pp. 1–15.

2. For an elaborate case for the importance of symbolic politics in a monarchy, see M. E. Combs-Schilling, *Sacred Performances: Islam, Sexuality, and Performance* (New York: Columbia University Press, 1989).

3. Anderson, "Absolutism and the Resilience of Monarchy," supra.

4. Among the particularly provocative books on nationalism in general, see Ernest Gellner, *Nations and Nationalism* (Ithaca: Cornell University Press, 1983); Benedict Anderson, *Imagined Communities: Reflections on the Origins and Spread of Nationalism* (New York: Verso, 1991). For the debates on Arab nationalism specifically, see Rashid Khalidi et al. (eds.), *The Origins of Arab Nationalism* (New York: Columbia University Press, 1991); Fouad Ajami, *The Arab Predicament: Arab Political Thought and Practice Since 1967* (Cambridge: Cambridge University Press, 1992); Tawfic Farah (ed.), *Pan-Arabism and Arab Nationalism: The Continuing Debate* (Boulder: Westview Press, 1987).

5. See, for example, Samuel P. Huntington, *Political Order in Changing Societies* (New Haven: Yale University Press, 1968).

6. Anderson, *Imagined Communities*, p. 18.

7. F. Gregory Gause III, *Oil Monarchies: Domestic and Security Challenges in the Arab Gulf States* (New York: Council on Foreign Relations, 1994), pp. 10–11.

8. King Hussein, *Uneasy Lies the Head: The Autobiography of His Majesty King Hussein I of the Hashemite Kingdom of Jordan* (New York: Bernard Geis Associates, 1962), p. 69.

9. Gellner, *Nations and Nationalism*, p. 36.

10. Cited in Reinhard Bendix, *Kings or People: Power and the Mandate to Rule* (Berkeley: University of California Press, 1978), p. 225.

11. Ibid., p. 248.

12. Gause, *Oil Monarchies*, p. 106.

13. John Waterbury, *The Commander of the Faithful: The Moroccan Political Elite—A Study in Segmented Politics* (New York: Columbia University Preas, 1970), p. 150; Alain Claisse, "Makhzen Traditions and Administrative Channels," in William Zartman (ed.), *The Political Economy of Morocco* (New York: Praeger, 1987), p. 49; Richard Parker, *North Africa: Regional Tensions and Strategic Concerns* (New York: Praeger, 1984), p. 21.

14. Hussein, *Uneasy Lies the Head*, p. 247.

15. The Constitution of the Kingdom of Morocco (1972).

16. Anderson, *Imagined Communities*, p. 19.

17. Gellner, *Nations and Nationalism*, p. 21.

18. Mark Tessler, "Image and Reality in Moroccan Political Economy," in Zartman (ed.), *The Political Economy of Morocco*, p. 225; see also Lisa Anderson, "North Africa: Changes and Challenges," Special Issue on Embattled Minorities Around the Globe, *Dissent*, Summer 1996; "Human Rights in Morocco," *Human Rights Watch/Middle East*, 7, 6 October 1995, p. 33.

19. David Holden and Richard Johns, *The House of Saud* (London: Pan Books, 1981), p. 14.

20. Mark Tessler, "Explaining the 'Surprises' of King Hassan II: The Linkage Between Domestic and Foreign Policy in Morocco. Part III: The Hassan-Peres Summit and Other Contacts with Israel," *University Field Staff International Reports*, Africa/Middle East, no. 40, 1986, p. 9.

21. Cited in ibid., p. 5.

22. His Imperial Majesty Mohhamed Reza Shah Pahlavi, Shahanshah of Iran, *Mission for My Country* (London: Hutchinson, 1960), p. 169.

23. Philip J. Robins, "Politics and the 1986 Electoral Law in Jordan," in Rodney Wilson (ed.), *Politics and the Economy in Jordan* (London: Routledge, 1991), p. 203.

24. Mark Tessler, "Image and Reality in Moroccan Political Economy," p. 218.

25. The first statement of this thesis was by Manfred Halpern, *The Politics of Social Change in the Middle East and North Africa* (Princeton: Princeton University Press, 1963); more recently it appeared in Nadav Safran, *Saudi Arabia: The Ceaseless Quest for Security* (Cambridge: Harvard University Press, 1985).

26. Robins, "Politics and the 1986 Electoral Law," p. 204.

27. Jill Crystal, *Oil and Politics in the Gulf: Rulers and Merchants in Kuwait and Qatar* (New York: Cambridge University Press, 1990), pp. 163–164.

28. For an example of a useful and instructive volume utilizing the resources of one of the several historical research centers that sprung up in the Gulf in the late 1960s and early 1970s, see Frauke Heard-Bey, *From Trucial States to United Arab Emirates* (London: Longman, 1982). Although not formally an "official history," this book reflects the royal patronage of the Centre for Documentation and Research in Abu Dhabi, and it concentrates on the tribal structure of society, the Islamic basis of

society, traditional economies, and, belatedly, "external influences" in the making of the UAE.

29. Yezid Sayigh, "Jordan in the 1980s: Legitimacy, Entity, and Identity," in Wilson (ed.), *Politics and the Economy in Jordan*, p. 171.

30. Hussein, *Uneasy Lies the Head*, p. 87.

31. Among the more prolific of the Jordanian documenters of Hashemite devotion to Arab nationalist causes is Sulayman Musa. See his *al-haraka al-Arabiyya* (Beirut, 1970). Other perspectives are offered in Mary C. Wilson, *King Abdallah, Britain, and the Making of Jordan* (Cambridge: Cambridge University Press, 1987); Ernest Dawn, *From Ottomanism to Arabism* (Urbana: University of Illinois Press, 1973).

32. Sayigh, "Jordan in the 1980s."

33. David Laitin, *Language Repertoires and State Construction in Afrira* (Cambridge: Cambridge University Press, 1992).

6

Patterns of Monarchy in the Middle East

Gabriel Ben-Dor

The idea of a monarchy[1] is a simple one, indeed one of the most simple ideas in politics. It is based on the premise that one person has to be the head of the political community; in addition, that one person has to personify solidity, stability, and continuity. The structure of the monarchy seems to yield all that—and more: the majesty of the state and the drama and pageantry that are so useful in the ritual aspects of politics. And for most of the existence of the human race, it was indeed taken for granted that this form of government, if not necessarily the best, was the most natural form and that it would remain as the most widespread one for a long time, if not forever.

Yet the age of revolutions swept most monarchies away,[2] making them synonymous with irrelevance, ossification, and obsolescence.[3] One of the first targets of political revolutions and revolutionaries was the whole idea of monarchy. Monarchy became the symbol for tyranny (although in retrospect we may well argue wrongly so, for most great acts of repression have been committed not by monarchies, and certainly few if any monarchs have been associated with atrocities such as the ones committed by Hitler and Stalin). Monarchy also seems to contradict many key ideas of modern politics in general. Monarchy is hereditary, by its very definition, whereas modern politics is based on achievement and attainment. Monarchy is based on class and distinction of birth, whereas modern political ideology likes to emphasize equality, at least at birth. Monarchy is stability, modernity is change.

Of course, there are alternative models of the relationship between modernity and monarchy, other than putting an end to monarchy altogether. There has been an evolution, making monarchy more and more restricted, in the form of a written set of rules and laws, making other parts of the political community more and more powerful while leaving the monarch to the ceremonial and other functions of the head of state. This has been the case in Britain, Sweden, the Netherlands, Belgium, and Denmark, all well-known and accepted Western democracies, some of them among the most advanced postindustrial democracies in the world. This evolutionary model is very interesting because it retains many of the most attractive ritual aspects of monarchy while putting an end to some of the most objectionable ones to the modern mind.[4]

There is even a tendency to think today in terms of restoring monarchies. Such ideas exist in Russia, eight decades and more after the communist revolution that put an end to czarist rule there. One can argue that this tendency has to do with the general nostalgia in Russia for an old order that is no longer in existence, or with the general tide of nationalism and religious patriotism that longs for a kind of order that is not apparently attainable in the modern competitive democratic order. There are such ideas also in Romania, another former communist country that suffers from the lack of a strong ideological and symbolic center for the political community. Beyond that there are such ideas in Greece, a country that has had a stormy experience with republican democracy, involving the transfer of power to "republican" rulers only recently.

This means that the days of monarchies are not over yet.[5] They may survive in several important places for quite some time, and in other cases they may even make a comeback, although concrete examples of that are yet to be seen. But it is not necessary to accept generalizations to the effect that it is the verdict of history that monarchies are irrelevant while at the same time making republics the tide of the future. Of course, we may have to make many important distinctions between different kinds of monarchies and to ask why it is that monarchies have survived in certain instances and disappeared in so many others. For example, it would be tempting to ask why so many successful, enduring constitutional monarchies seem to be associated with Northern and/or Western Europe—the notable exception being the restoration of the monarchy in Spain—and whether this has to do with any kind of social stability, political culture, or standard of living. To the best of my knowledge, there are no established answers to these questions in general, so it is futile to try to look for applications for the Middle East. And, of course, the history of monarchy in the Middle East has been very different in any case.[6]

The main difference lies in the fact that monarchy in the European cases is now a constitutional monarchy and has been one for many decades, following a complex and rich pattern of evolution—also a fairly lengthy one. In the Middle East, monarchies[7] are, as a rule, like European monarchies of old, in which the monarch actually rules[8] in addition to symbolizing the legitimacy of the system. This alone makes all the difference in the world. The shah of Iran, prior to his overthrow, was the center of power and by far the most dominant force in Iranian politics for several decades.[9] The king of Jordan is the overwhelming political actor in his country, and King Hussein's work and career was most intimately associated with the political history of the state.[10]

The king of Morocco is actively and heavily involved in running the current affairs of state,[11] and such has been the pattern in that country from time immemorial.[12] The rulers in Saudi Arabia and the Persian Gulf have also been the direct rulers of the countries in question,[13] as had been the case with the kings who had been overthrown by revolutions as well—the kings of Iraq before 1958 and the imam of Yemen prior to 1962.[14]

It is obvious that a radical style of politics in countries that have grave problems with legitimacy is not conducive to maintaining a monarchy[15] when the monarchy is not constitutional but "active"—a good term that is an antonym to "constitutional" but does not mean "absolute"—for many different reasons. Of course, in radical politics, when there is so much at stake, constitutional issues in general tend to count for little, as constitutions need to depend on a long tradition of constitutional acceptance that has never existed in the Middle East. And a monarch who is so strongly associated with the ancien régime is likely to be the very first target of the revolutionary forces, as practical experience in the region has indeed shown persuasively (the one possible exception I can point to is Egypt before 1952).[16] Hence, we need to keep in mind that radical politics, being such a dominant fact of life in the recent history of the region, makes monarchy a doubtful institution in terms of surviving revolutionary onslaughts.

So perhaps the most important thing to bear in mind is that, unlike in Europe, the idea of constitutional monarchy has never grown deep roots in the Middle East.[17] Where monarchs exist, they rule and dominate, so that in a period of political change they become the first and most obvious targets. Even today, as we look around, we do not really see constitutional monarchies in the region.[18] Would the shah have survived if he had been a constitutional monarch? It is uncertain, and there is little point in speculation. But once everyone became accustomed to the idea that monarchs rule and do not act merely as constitutional figureheads, it is virtually impossible to turn the clock back, so that once revolutionary forces and trends come to the fore, it is not feasible to allow the monarchy to survive by curtailing its powers and transforming it into a constitutional one. This is one of the casualties, so to speak, of the patterns of the development of the monarchy in the region.

Why is this so? Strictly speaking, this is the focus of the other chapters in this volume, but some points need to be made here. Clearly, this is partly a matter of the historical legacy of the peoples of the Middle East, who were used to a single ruler or at least a single dynasty dominating the state,[19] enjoying legitimacy as the protector of the faith and as the "commander of the faithful," as the Islamic phrase has it (even today in Morocco, for example). One may speculate, again, at what point the peoples of the area exactly had the opportunity to break away from such a constraining concept of monarchy and make the transition to a more limited one (and, I hesitate to say, a more modern one). But clearly they did miss the opportunity, or perhaps they never really wanted it and rejected it more or less consciously. Now it may be too late. It is difficult to believe that in this day and age constitutional monarchy may be introduced at such a late stage of political development. The one case in which this may be more or less feasible, given some very big changes, is Iran, but that, too, is far-fetched speculation more so than a realistic option within the existing political agenda of the country.

Why, then, do some monarchies survive and do quite well? Their number is still significant. Morocco, Jordan, Saudi Arabia, the Persian Gulf shaikhdoms (which are, properly speaking, monarchies in the more or less generic sense of the term) are important examples in the political history of the Middle East. Of course, what they might have in common may teach us something about the politics of the Middle East. At first glance, it is difficult to generalize about such things. Obviously, what they do have in common is that they have more or less avoided—or, I should say, contained—the radical trends of politics and have managed to impose, continually, a more conservative one. But to some extent this only begs the question, because it is not clear whether conservatism has saved the monarchy or whether monarchy has saved conservatism.

It seems to me that a most relevant consideration is the fairly close approximation of tribalism and monarchy. In a tribal society, as in a monarchy, there is one single person who, as a rule, heads the political system, both symbolically as well as in terms of practical political activity on the everyday level. And in a tribal society, too, there is the strong idea of heredity and hereditary rights and privileges, continuity, and dynasties. Where such tribal structures exist, there is a good correspondence between monarchy on the central level and the social structure in the country at large. But where social revolution or development upsets the hereditary balance of tribal society, monarchy may quickly become irrelevant and be overthrown by the forces of change—some might say progress.

Let us dwell on this point for a minute. Obviously, in the cases of Saudi Arabia and the various entities in the Gulf, this theory fits reasonably well. We are dealing in these cases with basically tribal societies where the ancient, traditional balance has not yet been upset. There has been a good deal of urbanization, and there is the emergence of a middle class and various other social-structural manifestations of what used to be called "modernization."[20] But, in general, the argument seems to hold that these are tribal-rooted societies, and in such societies an institution such as the monarchy is very much in place. One may well ask whether this means that social change, which seems as inevitable as anything else on the horizon, will sweep monarchy away with time. Before answering this question, let us take another look at the other surviving monarchies in the Middle East.

In the case of Jordan, there is also the strong tribal element, at least in the Bedouin, or non-Palestinian, part of Jordanian society. That entity used to be based on a confederation of tribes, which was headed, appropriately enough, by a monarch. Of course, we know that by now the non-Bedouin element, which represented more than half of Jordanian society, is a very different social entity that has practically nothing in common with the tribal tradition of the Bedouins. The Palestinians in the country have nothing in common with the past of the monarchy; if anything, they have every reason to resent that historical association. In addition, there is the question of social change in the non-Palestinian parts of Jordanian society as well. There is a growing rate of urbanization, and the ancient tribal ways of life are changing quickly for hundreds of thousands of Jordanians.[21] The question is to what extent these changes will undermine the ideological or cultural attachments to the old idea and institution of the monarchy, once the old tribal realities no longer exist in the form known in the past.

Many of the same considerations apply also to Morocco. Of course, in that country there is no major split, such as in Jordan, between the two main components of the population. Yet there is a strong identification of the monarchy with the old tribal ways, which used to be so dominant in the political anthropology of the country, as exemplified, documented, and analyzed in John Waterbury's *Commander of the Faithful.* In the case of Morocco, we are witnessing, I think, perhaps the clearest identification of the monarchy with the ancien régime, which used to be the case in Europe before the revolutions. And for that very reason, radical forces and, in general, the forces of discontent, which are many, tend to regard the monarchy as the prime target for their activity. If and when the level of discontent rises to that of a possible revolution, it is not likely that the leaders or the masses will settle for a transition to a constitutional monarchy but will want to wipe it out altogether, as in Iran in 1978 and 1979. So we may argue that one reason for the difficulty of such monarchies to survive is that they still do too much, much more than is the case around the world in this day and age.[22]

At this point it is necessary to take another look at the relationship between tribal structures, on the one hand, and monarchy in the Middle East on the other. On the surface, there may be a contradiction between the argument advanced by Lisa Anderson as to the lack of authenticity and long-standing cultural roots of the monarchy, on the one hand,[23] and the strong relationship to tribal structures on the other. Yet the contradiction is more apparent than real. Monarchies were partly created by the events and manipulations engineered by European colonial strategies and policies in different political systems in the region and sustained by European support. The success of these attempts depended not necessarily on social structure as such but more on the degree of the European penetration and the ability of the foreign power to manipulate the local political forces.

However, with time, once the European presence receded and eventually disappeared, the survival of the monarchy became very dependent on the authentic local social configuration. The less tribal and more urban a society, the less the power of the monarchy relative to the radical forces of change in the cities. Hence, it was possible for the British to bring about monarchies in Egypt as well as Kuwait, Jordan, and Iraq, but the social, tribal structures in Kuwait and Jordan proved strong and gave the monarchy overwhelming support, whereas the more urban centers of politics in Egypt and Iraq led to the radical waves of revolution that then put an end to the ancien régime, including the monarchy itself. All in all, even though the early strategies of monarchical rule were sustained by European, mainly British, support and thanks to state institutions that the British helped initiate, their survival did and does depend on their ability to fit in with authentic social forces and structures. This is not surprising: there are many historical examples of externally imposed structures that then may or may not prosper and endure, depending on their relationship with the concrete circumstances and conditions in the given society.

As for the sociological composition of monarchical elites, there are, of course, differences and variations on this theme, again depending on the concrete local circumstances of each case. However, certain general attributes of such elites do seem to be justified by the historical record:

1. Monarchies in the Middle East tend to require and utilize religious legitimacy to a high degree. Monarchy and religion in general seem to have a strong universal relationship, but in the case of the Arab world, the necessity to find a relationship with religious legacies is evident in several states, perhaps as part of the quest for authenticity. This may take the form of claiming descent from the family of the Prophet, or of being the guardian of holy places, or of defending the faith, or of purifying it from the corruption of external as well as domestic impurities. In contrast, most intriguingly, modern Islamic fundamentalists are not enthusiastic about monarchy—probably because they are radicals—and the first Islamic state in the region, Iran, emphasized its self-identity as an "Islamic republic."

2. Monarchical establishments in the region tend to be relatively large. Ruling families proliferate, due to large families and the need to intermarry with the ruling families of powerful tribal and other notable families' groups as a basis for cooperation and loyalty. Hence, there are royal families, such as that in Jordan, with just several branches and others with multiple branches and princes, such as that in Saudi Arabia. The size of royal families in the area tends to be disproportionately large compared to other parts of the world.

3. There seems to be little direct relationship between royal elites on the one hand and class structure as such on the other. Monarchies are not necessarily the paragons of upper classes as such, nor are they the creatures of some authentic aristocracy. Their distance, therefore, from other strata of society is not socially great. This is more an example of segmentation than of rigid horizontal divisions. There is more fluidity within the royal elite, and

there is more contact between that elite and other elites in society than is normally the case for classic "active" monarchies.

4. Royal families do not tend to be ethnically different from the mainstream of society but instead tend to be representative of it. Family ties then differentiate it from others, and power is used, as Manfred Halpern has pointed out, to accumulate wealth, more than the other way around. In other words, monarchy in the Middle East, once established, is large in terms of size, strongly dependent on religious legitimacy, uses tribal and family ties to solidify political support as well as social stability, and uses political power for the accumulation of wealth rather than opening itself up to political influence by the independently wealthy.

These seem to be the main social themes of monarchy. There are, needless to say, considerable variations on these themes, because the specific and concrete historical and social circumstances differ so much from one case to another; some societies are larger than others, some are more divided than others ethnically, class divisions differ, and even the degrees of attachment to religious symbols and loyalties vary considerably. Such variations are to be expected in a region as large and diverse as the Middle East, and they do not detract from the value of the generalizations about the nature of monarchy as such. However, we need to be conscious of the considerable differences between the various monarchies, even in the face of the basic similarities in the circumstances of their creation and their fate in relationship to social structure.

In the light of all this, it is not easy to find a common denominator for the survival of monarchies in the region. We can only say that wherever tribal structures and modes of behavior have remained an important ingredient of the regime, monarchy, the corresponding form of central rule, has also tended to survive, whereas in an age of change and revolution, the collapse of the old tribal structures[24] has also eroded the monarchy to the point of disappearance. All this raises the question of the future of monarchy in the Middle East. And, of course, answers to such a question have to come from the general scene around the world and from the concrete social and political conditions of the region itself.[25]

Overall the outlook seems pessimistic, even if the further erosion of monarchy may take quite some time yet. No additional countries are likely to adopt a monarchical form of government, nor is there much of a prospect for the restoration of the monarchy where it has disappeared, with the possible exception of Iran (but more on that later). Yet at the same time many pundits believe that it is only a question of time before monarchy comes to an end in several political entities in the Gulf and, eventually, in Morocco, Saudi Arabia, and Jordan as well.[26] Of course, we need to be on guard against oversimplification. Such things do not happen overnight, and much depends also on the personalities concerned. Another ruler instead of the shah may have survived in the late 1970s in Iran. Another ruler instead of King Hussein may not have survived in Jordan since the 1950s. As for the new king in Jordan, Abdallah II, much depends on his personality, ability, and policies, as they evolve. And all this is true also with regard to Morocco, the Gulf, and Saudi Arabia.

Yet even when we take into account the personality factor[27] it is difficult to be optimistic about the survival of monarchies. They have been assaulted by great and potent forces,[28] and even though the tides of radicalism may abate—indeed may already have abated to a significant extent—the Islamic version will be around for a long time. Thus, a reversion to other versions of radicalism in the future is at least as likely as the establishment and institutionalization of a stable kind of conservatism in regional politics, which indeed would be closely associated with a monarchical form of government. And once the tide of radical politics does strike and brings about revolution, it is not likely that the postrevolutionary regime will restore the monarchy, even if it adopts a more and more conservative posture in the later stages of its existence. There have been no examples of restoring former monarchies in the Middle East thus far.

Under what conditions could monarchies fare better in the future in this part of the world? Speculating about this may be somewhat unrealistic and beyond the realm of practical political analysis, but let us attempt it all the same, mostly on the assumption that this is a good heuristic exercise; even if the results are basically negative, the analysis itself will shed some light on the political forces at work.

1. As I have argued before, monarchies in general would fare much better in a less radical and more conservative style of politics in any given country and, of course, across the region in its entirety, given that there is much penetrability of boundaries and intensive ties of communications between the various regional political systems.[29]

2. Discrediting one radical regime is not likely to create much nostalgic longing for monarchies. But is it possible to imagine a succession of failures by several radical regimes that might create some momentum for nostalgia for an earlier age that was not quite so bad?[30] This might be true in Egypt, Iraq, and Iran, perhaps not in countries that have not had experience with monarchy, as in the cases of Syria and Algeria.[31] But in the other cases, a change is not beyond imagination—though very unlikely indeed.

3. The Middle East is heavily influenced by the example of the outside world in general and of the Western world in particular. Elsewhere I have argued that this is a discernibly important motivating force for more democratization in the region and that this tendency is likely to grow in the foreseeable future, with important practical changes in regional politics.[32] The question of monarchy is a case in point as well. If we see other cases of transition to democracy coupled with the restoration of monarchies, this might prove to be

a potent force in the politics of Middle Eastern countries. For example, restoring the monarchy in Romania while making a successful transition to democracy might look attractive.[33] Even more important, bringing back the Romanov dynasty to Russia while democratizing that country might whet the appetite of prospective monarchists around the world—the Middle East included. This may not be very likely, but one cannot rule it out.

4. As mentioned above, in this day and age monarchies cannot be divorced from monarchs. One has to think about the possibility that some very attractive and even charismatic monarchs, or prospective monarchs, will appear on the scene, perhaps at the very time when republican leaders will be discredited due to inefficiency or corruption, or both. Still, it is also possible that there will be coalitions and alliances between republican leaders and prospective monarchs for various expedient reasons. Republican leaders may want to use royal figureheads to enhance legitimacy or national unity, as well during times of ethnic strife or other kinds of dissent and centrifugal tension. It is possible to imagine such a chain of events in a country like Iran, assuming, for example, a military coup or some other form of violent revolution or counterrevolution wins out against the current regime. In such a case, there may be a quest for legitimacy, which takes place to a large extent by the use and manipulation of political symbols, of which monarchy often is the prime example. Although the regime of the late shah may not be particularly popular today, as it never was during its existence,[34] it still may exercise a certain fascination when the current regime outlives its usefulness. However, that is not a particularly likely scenario either. Should the shah's family produce an outstanding political figure who might rally massive support around him, things might look up for the family, but that is not something that we can predict at this time.

5. Finally, it is necessary to ask whether the entire question of monarchy is really relevant, beyond the formalities concerned. In other words, does monarchy really make a meaningful difference to the countries concerned? To a large extent, the answer is that it does not. As the example of the constitutional monarchies in Western Europe amply demonstrates, the similarities between the European monarchies and European republics are very great, certainly greater than the differences dividing them. Yet the differences separating them are negligible compared to the differences between them and other political systems in other parts of the world, such as the Middle East.[35] Hence, it is possible to argue that whether a state is a monarchy or a republic is a minor issue in the political lives of the peoples involved, carrying little impact for significant issues, such as the performance of the rulers, the quality of life of the ruled, their rights, and the ability of the regimes to produce the political goods desired by the people.[36]

This point is worth stressing, because analysts of political history at times tend to attribute an exaggerated importance to structural factors, such as the formal-constitutional morphology of regimes, or their electoral systems, or the presidential-versus-parliamentary nature of democratic political systems in Western Europe and North America.[37] Although such questions are of obvious relevance to our understanding of political systems, they are not of decisive importance. What is of greater relevance is the behavioral, or cultural, aspect of politics, namely, how the ruler and the ruled perceive each other and what kind of habits and traditions form the background against which people understand and interpret the rules of the political game in the country.[38] It is only within this framework that monarchy becomes important, because it has an impact on these traditions and perceptions. In the case of the Middle East, monarchy in the past by and large failed to provide a useful check against the tyranny of those in power at any given day, as is the case in constitutional monarchies.[39]

In many instances, monarchies have indeed been able to act like republican regimes. In some cases, they have simply copied and adapted the repressive methods of using police, security forces, and the other structural and administrative wonders imported from the outside world, either directly from outside the region or else from the republican regimes themselves. This form of governmental technology is a most useful tool for securing and maintaining power, and its attractions are almost irresistible to republicans and monarchists alike, as both are determined to use a broad range of means to protect their power. This gives the monarchies a freedom to act and room to maneuver, simply on account of the confidence they secure.

In addition, monarchies have deliberated between putting together a political bloc of their own in the region, on the one hand, and taking part in more diverse regional alliances on the other. Whereas in the 1960s, during the so-called Arab Cold War,[40] monarchies tried to protect themselves as a bloc against the radical onslaught, this radical tide later receded on the inter-Arab scene, and monarchs started to pursue more diverse and complex regional political games, as we can see from the numerous twists and turns in the regional policies of the kings of Jordan.[41]

Finally, the general growing stability of regimes in the region[42] has allowed monarchies to pursue a richer variety of policies. Because republican regimes no longer opposed or subverted monarchies—because they were monarchies and more pragmatic solutions were pursued[43]—monarchies were allowed a lot of leeway in terms of access to alliances, as well as in terms of working out diverse domestic policies, without too much apprehension about the immediate dangers flowing from them. Yet all of this freedom to be like the republican regimes basically derived from the fact that the monarchies have been as repressive as the nonroyal regimes. So the difference between the two types of governmental morphology on the crucial issues of legitimacy and freedom has not been very decisive, to say the least.

Instead, monarchy was in the past—and still is today—part of the problem of legitimacy and arbitrary rule in the Middle East.[44] It is because of this that monarchy has not been popular there in earlier decades, and with the quest for a better future it has become irrelevant in most cases. And it is because of this that restoration is no more likely than the survival of those monarchical regimes still in existence today.[45]

NOTES

1. See Reinhard Bendix, *Kings and People* (Berkeley: University of California Press, 1987).

2. See Charles Tilly (ed.), *The Formation of National States in Western Europe* (Princeton: Princeton University Press, 1975); and Leonard Binder et al., *Crises and Sequence in Political Development* (Princeton: Princeton University Press, 1971).

3. The potentially relevant literature on monarchies is so voluminous that there is no point in even trying to list it here. I would like to acknowledge my indebtedness to the excellent discussion of the dilemmas of modern monarchy in historical perspective in a variety of societies in Samuel P. Huntington, *Political Order in Changing Societies* (New Haven: Yale University Press, 1968). The analysis in classic literature continues to be germane to the situation today in the so-called developing countries. On the problems specific to the Middle East, see Manfred Halpern, *The Politics of Social Change in the Middle East and North Africa* (Princeton: Princeton University Press, 1963). On the historical background in the Middle East, again there is a huge number of relevant works. One of the more intriguing ones is Elie Kedourie, *Politics in the Middle East* (London: Oxford University Press, 1992).

4. It is noteworthy that in the European context monarchies in the northern part of the continent exhibit remarkable stability, and they have also managed to come to terms with constitutional development in an evolutionary manner. The record of the South (Greece, Spain, and Italy) has been far more sketchy.

5. There are also interesting examples of monarchy in other parts of the world. There is the major case of Japan, the one country in Asia that normally impresses pundits with its adaptability and ability to come to terms with the challenges of modernity, but there are also other examples, such as that of Malaysia.

6. See the stimulating discussion in Lisa Anderson, "Absolutism and Resilience of Monarchy in the Middle East," *Political Science Quarterly,* 106 (1991), pp. 1–15.

7. On the etymological background to monarchy in the Middle East, see A. Ayalon, "Malik," *Encyclopedia of Islam*, Vol. 6 (Leiden: Brill, 1987), pp. 261–262. On the implications of this analysis, see Anderson, "Absolutism and Resilience of Monarchy in the Middle East," p. 7.

8. See Albert Hourani, *The Emergence of the Modern Middle East* (Berkeley: University of California Press, 1981).

9. See, for example, Marvin Zonis, *Majestic Failure: The Fall of the Shah* (Chicago: University of Chicago Press, 1991).

10. See Joseph Nevo and Ilan Pape (eds.), *Jordan in the Middle East, 1948–1988: The Making of a Pivotal State* (London: Cass, 1994).

11. I. William Zartman (ed.), *The Political Economy of Morocco* (New York: Praeger, 1987).

12. See John Waterbury, *The Commander of the Faithful: The Moroccan Political Elite—A Study in Segmented Politics* (New York: Columbia University Press, 1970).

13. James Piscatori (ed.), *Islamic Fundamentalism and the Gulf Crisis* (Chicago: University of Chicago Press, 1992).

14. Alan Richards and John Waterbury (eds), *A Political Economy of the Middle East: State, Class and Economic Development* (Boulder: Westview Press, 1990); James A. Bill and Robert Sprinborg, *Politics in the Middle East* (New York: Harper, 1994); Michael Hudson, *Arab Politics: The Search for Legitimacy* (New Haven: Yale University Press, 1977).

15. This argument appears in numerous sources, perhaps most eloquently in the writings of Huntington and Hudson.

16. See Gabriel Ben-Dor, "The Continuity of the Egyptian State and the Ambiguity of the Revolution," in Shimon Shamir (ed), *Egypt from Monarchy to Republic: A Reassessment of Revolution and Change* (Boulder: Westview Press, 1995).

17. Anderson, "Absolutism and Resilience of Monarchy in the Middle East." See also Gabriel Ben-Dor, *State and Conflict in the Middle East* (New York: Praeger, 1983).

18. See James A. Bill and Carl Leiden, *Politics in the Middle East* (Boston: Little, Brown, 1984).

19. See the intriguing thesis in Hisham Sharabi, *Neopatriarchy: A Theory of Distorted Change in Arab Society* (New York: Oxford University Press, 1988).

20. See Halpern, *The Politics of Social Change in the Middle East.*

21. See Nevo and Pappe (eds.), *Jordan in the Middle East.*

22. In a sense, the question is that of the state. The primary consideration in the societies in question seems to be, above all, that of building and maintaining a viable modern state. When that attempt seems to lead to failure, and the ruling monarchy is identified too closely with the state, the entire structure of the state may be under assault. A less close identification allows change in regimes and policies without shattering the structure of the state. See Gabriel Ben-Dor, "Stateness and Ideology in Contemporary Middle East Politics," *Jerusalem Journal of International Relations,* 9 (1987), pp. 10–37.

23. Anderson, "Absolutism and Resilience of Monarchy in the Middle East."

24. Fu'ad I. Khuri (ed.), *Leadership and Development in Arab Society* (Beirut: American University of Beirut, 1981).

25. Compare with the European experience, as articulated in Reinhard Bendix, *Kings or People* (Berkeley: University of California Press, 1978).

26. It is important to note also the problem of succession and the general difficulty in making transitions from one ruler to another, with particular reference to monarchies. This is analyzed in J. C. Hurewitz, *Middle East Politics: The Military Dimension* (New York: Octagon Press, 1974), who points to the "hovering" of Islamic politics in general between hereditary and "elective" monarchies. Quoted in Anderson, "Absolutism and Resilience of Monarchy in the Middle East," p. 8.

27. The issue of personality in politics is one that political science finds difficult to tackle (though historians have dealt with this literally for ages). Recently, attempts have been made to transplant psychological theories and insights into the study of politics, but myriad problems remain. For a classic exposition of this problematique, see Fred Greenstein, "Personality and Politics: Problems of Evidence, Inference, and Conceptualization," in Seymour Martin Lipset (ed.), *Politics and the Social Sciences* (New York: Oxford University Press, 1969), pp. 163–204.

28. See Gabriel Ben-Dor, "Prospects of Democratization in the Arab World: Global Diffusion, Regional Demonstration, and Domestic Imperatives," in Rex Bry-

nen, Bahgat Korany, and Paul Noble (eds.), *Political Liberalization and Democratization in the Arab World: Volume 1, Theoretical Perspectives* (Boulder: Lynne Rienner, 1995), pp. 307–332.

29. This argument is developed more fully in Ben-Dor, "Prospects of Democratization in the Arab World."

30. Of course, the failure of the current elite in general might be a harbinger of change, but normally it is more customary to assume that since the present regimes as a rule are pretty arbitrary and authoritarian their failures are likely to lead to more democary (of course, of the republican variety). See, for instance, Saad Edin Ibrahim, "Crises, Elites, and Democratization in the Arab World," *Middle East Journal*, 47 (1993).

31. See I. William Zartrman (ed.), *Political Elites in Arab North Africa* (New York: Longman, 1982).

32. Ben-Dor, "Prospects of Democratization in the Arab World."

33. A relevant example of the 1970s in a Southern European country has been that of Spain, where monarchy and democracy have coexisted happily since 1980, with a fairly active participation of the constitutional monarch in maintaining the legitimacy and the vitality of the democratic system of government in that country. Yet somehow this example has been all but ignored in the various arguments over the question of monarchy and democracy in the Middle East, perhaps because Spain has not been considered a major or important country by key local leaders and intellectuals.

34. Zonis, *Majestic Failure*.

35. In other words, comparison easily shows that the categories that belong together are not those of monarchies as such, because monarchies in the Middle East on the one hand and those in Western Europe on the other are worlds apart, which is also the case with republics. Yet it may be more relevant to ask to what extent monarchies within the Middle East contrast with nonmonarchies, and even that comparison is only partially useful. For instance, it has been suggested that monarchies in the Arab world have been more accomodating toward the peace process, which may be true, at least to the extent that no monarchies have been actively rejectionist. Still, the first major breakthrough on the Arab side of the peace process was by the president of Egypt and the second by the chairman of the PLO, whereas the current rejectionists are all republicans (Iran, Lybia, and to some extent, perhaps, Syria). So it is not certain that the right variable for the comparison is the one between monarchies and republics but perhaps more between conservatives and radicals, to use a simple alternative formulation.

36. Of course, some will argue that all this is in the eyes of the beholder. That is to say, pundits study what they think is important in terms of their own values and convictions, but that is not good enough. What we study or do not study in politics should derive from some consistent model of what politics is and what makes a difference in political life. In other words, we need a paradigm of politics in which certain things matter more and others matter less or not at all. See the classic by Thomas Kuhn, *The Structure of Scientific Revolutions* (Chicago: University of Chicago Press, 1968). Of course, it is very difficult to put together such a paradigm in the study of Middle East politics, and this has been the case literally for decades. See Manfred Halpern, "Toward Further Modernization of the Study of New Nations," *World Politics*, 17 (1964), pp. 157–181; and Halpern, "Middle Eastern Studies: A Review of the State of the Field with a Few Examples," *World Politics*, 15 (1962), pp. 108–122.

37. For a good look at that kind of tradition, see Joseph LaPalombara, *Politics Within Nations* (Englewood Cliffs, N.J.: Prentice Hall, 1974).

38. Of course, the argument over our ability to study scientifically the difficult cultural issues of politics has been raging for decades. See Gabriel Ben-Dor, "Political Culture Approach to Middle East Politics," *International Journal of Middle East Studies,* 18 (1976). The debate on this is as vigorous as ever. See, for example, Lisa Anderson, "Democracy in the Arab World: A Critique of the Political and Culture Approach," in Brynen, Korany, and Noble, *Political Liberalization and Democratization in the Arab World,* pp. 77–92; and Michael C. Hudson, "The Political Culture Approach to Arab Democratization: The Case for Bringing It Back In, Carefully," in ibid, pp. 61–76. See also Simon Bromley, *Rethinking Middle East Politics* (Austin: University of Texas Press, 1994). Although this debate demonstrates the enormous difficulties and pitfalls inherent in the utilization of culture for political analysis in the Middle East, I honesty do not see how one can claim to understand regional politics with any degree of profundity without dealing with cultural questions in some depth.

39. Kedourie, *Politics in the Middle East.*

40. Malcolm Kerr, *The Arab Cold War* (London: Oxford University Press, 1971).

41. See Gabriel Ben-Dor, "Jordan and Inter-Arab Relations," in Nevo and Pappe, *Jordan in the Middle East.*

42. Ben-Dor, *State and Conflict in the Middle East.*

43. See Fouad Ajami, *The Arab Predicament* (Cambridge: Cambridge University Press, 1981).

44. Hudson, *Arab Politics: The Search for Legitimacy.*

45. This is not to say that monarchies are "doomed." One should not be deterministic about such things: history provides ample checks against deterministic generalizations of this kind. But looking into the future involves probabilities, or chances, and the chances of monarchies in the long run just do not appear to be good. On the need to live with genuine uncertainties about the future of macrodevelopments in politics, see Reinhard Bendix, *Nation-Building and Citizenship* (New York: Wiley, 1964).

PART TWO

Case Studies

7

The Jordanian Monarchy: The Hashemite Success Story

Asher Susser

The Jordanian monarchy has proved to be one of the most resilient regimes in the modern Middle East. It has been blessed with two especially astute kings, Abdallah I, the founder of the kingdom, and Hussein, the creator of modern Jordan as we know it. Jordan's kings have been talented, courageous, and pragmatic practitioners of the craft of politics and the art of diplomacy. The roles of Abdallah and Hussein in providing leadership and in maintaining elite cohesion by serving as the "unifying essence" of the political order were of immeasurable importance at critical junctures. But Jordan has never been a one-man show, and above and beyond the roles and personalities of its monarchs, a variety of other factors have contributed to the originally unexpected longevity of the Hashemite Kingdom. These are mainly the following: (1) the evolution and crystallization of a cohesive civilian and military elite, the "king's men," motivated by self-interest in preserving their political patrimony; (2) the loyalty of the armed forces and the domestic security establishment, which is largely a function of the cohesion of the civilian and military elite; and (3) the consistent interest of external powers, in the region and beyond, in Jordan's continued stability as an essential component of the regional status quo. As Jordan is situated at the strategic core of the Fertile Crescent, between Israel and Iraq and Syria and Saudi Arabia, as well as at the heart of the Palestinian question, the destabilization of Jordan could have potentially horrendous consequences for the region as a whole.

The Hashemites, as descendants of the Prophet Muhammad (*Ahl al-Bayt*), who himself belonged to the Meccan house of Hashim of the Quraysh tribe, have traditionally enjoyed considerable religious and political reverence and prestige, bearing the noble title of sharif (pl. *ashraf*) to denote their honorable lineage. It was, therefore, not incongruent with their special status that it was they who, in the modern era of Middle Eastern history, raised the banner of Arab revolt against the Ottomans during World War I. In the eyes of the leader of the Arab revolt, Sharif Hussein bin Ali, the emir of Mecca, it was only natural that he and his sons, Faysal and Abdallah, assume the leadership of the nascent Arab nationalist movement. Arab nationalism under his aegis was to be the vehicle for establishing a Hashemite Arab kingdom that was to encompass almost all of the Arab *mashriq*, on the ruins of the Ottoman Empire. That kingdom, however, never came into being, and Hashemite ambition for pan-Arab leadership was to remain an unrealistic dream.

In 1921, in partial fulfillment of British wartime commitments to the Hashemites, in what was to become known as the "sharifian solution," Faysal was installed by the British as king of Iraq; Abdallah was allowed to establish himself as emir of the far more modest territory of Transjordan. These two artificial creations were carved out of portions of the Fertile Crescent to serve a coalescence of British imperial and Hashemite interests. They greatly expanded the Hashemite domain, which hitherto consisted solely of the kingdom in the Hijaz, proclaimed by Sharif Hussein during the Arab revolt.

The three Hashemite kingdoms had mixed fortunes. The Hashemite kingdom in the Hijaz proved to be no more than a fleeting episode of Middle Eastern history. Faysal was more fortunate. Imposed by the British on an incoherent conglomeration of Sunnis and Shi'ites, Arabs, Kurds, Christians, and Jews in Iraq, Faysal struck a fragile balance between his alliance with Britain and his association with the local Sunni Muslim Arab nationalist urban elite. He was consequently able both to deal with Britain and to maintain his stature as a nationalist. Iraq was the first of the mandated territories to achieve independence and, in 1932, became the first Arab state to join the League of Nations. Faysal, however, died shortly thereafter, in 1933. Hashemite Iraq lingered on for another twenty-five years, plagued by thinly veiled military dictatorships, coups and countercoups, and other intermittent outbursts of political violence. The end came in July 1958, when the Hashemite monarchy of Iraq was destroyed in a chilling exhibition of brutality and blind hatred.

Oddly enough, the most successful of the Hashemite monarchies appeared at the outset to be the most artificial and least likely to cross the threshold into the family of nations. Originally, Abdallah's Transjordan was a decisively tribal, desert emirate, with no resources, a tiny population, no natural political center, and not much of a sophisticated political class. Against what appeared to be all odds, an often hemmed-in and beleaguered Hashemite kingdom survived the trebling of its population with a disaffected Palestinian majority; the assassination of its founder, King Abdallah; the mental derangement of his successor, Talal; the challenge of Arab radicalism; prolonged confrontation with Palestinian nationalism; humiliating defeat in the conflict with Israel; and, most recently, the passing of King Hussein after forty-six years at the helm. Paradoxically, at least some of the explanations for Jordan's longevity are to be found in its initial artificiality. In their state-building enterprise, Abdallah and the British had to start from scratch. In contradistinction to Iraq, they were almost entirely undisturbed by domestic opposition, in what was a relatively small and underdeveloped political society. They established law and order and an effective political, economic, and administrative center, or "core area," where none had previously existed; encouraged the formation of a loyal Transjordanian elite with a vested interest in the status quo; and transformed the traditionally rebellious Bedouin into the military backbone of the state. This was all achieved in the space of a quarter of a century of practically uninterrupted domestic tranquility that preceded the 1948 war.

The 1948 war and its consequences, revolution in the Arab world, and the regional effects of the Cold War all combined to revolutionize Jordan's domestic, regional, and international situation. Nonetheless, the solid foundations of the "Jordanian entity" established by Abdallah and the British, coupled with the skillful stewardship and good fortune of King Hussein, helped Jordan to weather the various storms that would follow in fairly rapid succession.

Two of Jordan's permanent features—its strategic location and its homogeneous population—have contributed over the years to its relative stability. Jordan's geopolitical centrality has convinced many actors, regional and international, to support Jordanian stability in order to forestall regional havoc. Jordan's population, more than 90 percent being Sunni Muslim Arabs, is the most homogeneous in the Fertile Crescent. The political cleavage between Jordanians and Palestinians, though potentially explosive, lacks the historical depth of ethnic cleavages such as that between Kurds and Arabs or the religious chasms that have separated Sunnis and Shi'ites or Muslims and Christians for centuries. The Hashemite monarchy in Jordan, the modest remnant of a great ambition, remains today a model of stability and a monument to Hashemite tenacity and pragmatism.[1]

FROM ANARCHY TO MONARCHY

Abdallah Settles In

When Abdallah established himself in Transjordan in 1921, the country was no more than the peripheral backwater of Syria to the north and Palestine to the west. The entire population was only about 250,000, about half being nomadic or seminomadic Bedouin tribes. Salt was the largest town on the East Bank, with only some 20,000 inhabitants; Amman, at the time, was a little Circassian village of just over 2,000 people ensconced in the environs of the ancient ruins of Roman Philadelphia.

Abdallah was especially well received by the Circassian and Christian minorities, who, from the outset, regarded his arrival as the harbinger of a benevolent central authority that would protect them from the ravages of the prevailing anarchy. The Circassian farmers of Amman and its vicinity were weary of living under the constant threat of Bedouin raids. The Christians of Transjordan, like most other Christian Arabs in Syria, were favorably disposed toward the Hashemites. Abdallah appealed to them in a "special way as a *sharif* and a Muslim of undoubted credentials who was, at the same time, tolerant and fair-minded."[2]

This was not true of other segments of the population, settled and nomadic alike, who were initially unsympathetic to the pretentious outsider. Arab nationalists among the urban Muslim population were strongly opposed to Abdallah. They were led by Syrian *istiqlalis*, political fugitives of Faysal's ill-fated former Arab government in Damascus who had consequently become "cynical about the Hashemite leadership in general." They were beginning to develop distinctly republican sentiments "and no longer envisaged the Arab future exclusively in terms of dynastic monarchies."[3] Even so, some of these nationalists—Syrians and otherwise—were co-opted into Abdallah's fledgling administration. He had little choice. Qualified Transjordanians were hard to come by. To compensate for the paucity of competent Transjordanian administrators, Abdallah also recruited a considerable number of Palestinians, three of whom were to rise to prominence as prime ministers for much of his reign.[4]

In terms of scale, Transjordan was eminently manageable. Upon his arrival in the country Abdallah had a reliable military force at his disposal, which, though small, was sufficient to contend with any local opposition. With relatively minor effort and moderate resources, and with the occasional assistance of British airpower, he rapidly subdued tribal opposition. As for the villagers, the land policies initiated by the British mandatory authorities from the late 1920s went a long way toward securing their loyalty to the regime. As they were allowed to certify legal rights and title to their land, the value of their property was increased; coupled with fair and light taxation, the lot of the cultivators was markedly improved. Within just a few years, Transjordan was to become the "land of the Emir Abdallah" in a way that Iraq was never the land of King Faysal I or his successors.[5]

Abdallah deliberately chose Amman as his capital. He preferred to start there from scratch, amid the hospitable Circassians, rather than in the main town of Salt, the more obvious choice at the time, where the local population was more circumspect and thus less reliable. Moreover, in its initial phase, Abdallah's regime was heavily reliant on outsiders, newcomers to Transjordan. These were mainly the Syrian *istiqlalis* as well as Palestinians who had migrated to Irbid and Salt since the 1880s or to Amman since 1920.[6] This in turn gave rise to domestic opposition from the ranks of the younger generation of educated townsmen from Irbid, Salt, and Karak, the so-called petty bourgeoisie professionals, as well as from tribal leaders, who vented their displeasure with the rule of the *ghuraba* (foreigners).[7]

Abdallah, Hussein, and the Jordanization of the State

By the mid-1920s, Abdallah had settled in and could dispense with the services of the *istiqlalis*, who were becoming more of a liability than an asset. They were a problem for Abdallah's British mentors, who could accommodate neither their nationalist tendencies nor their anti-French proclivities. Abdallah was not entirely happy with them, either, and getting rid of them not only removed an unnecessary irritant in the emir's relationship with the British but also paved the way for the ever-increasing inclusion and co-optation of the fledgling local political class that desperately sought government office. By the late 1930s, though the upper echelons of the administration still remained in the hands of former Palestinians, two-thirds of the bureaucracy (excluding the British officials) were already staffed by original Transjordanians (60 percent Arabs and 7 percent Circassians); Arabs from other countries occupied the remainder.[8]

Under Hussein, who came to power in 1953, the Jordanization of the bureaucracy was completed, partly as a deliberate break with the past and partly in response to the Palestinian challenge. Very shortly after his accession to the throne, Hussein opted for a new generation of leaders to fill the senior offices of state. These were almost all original Jordanians, born during World War I and thereafter, who hailed from the urban centers of the East Bank. Since the mid-1950s, Palestinian prime ministers have become the rare exception rather than the rule.

Under Hussein, the military, the state bureaucracy, the developmental machinery, economic potential, and overall administrative capacity were all significantly expanded. The annexation of the West Bank after the 1948 war and the tripling of Jordan's population set the stage not only for domestic strain and increasing opposition to the regime from the ranks of its new disenchanted Palestinian majority but also for the rapid economic, bureaucratic, and institutional development of the state. The level of "stateness," significantly enhanced from the 1950s onward, transformed Jordan into a markedly different entity from what it had been during Abdallah's time.[9]

Paradoxically, the challenge of Arab radicalism of the Nasserist and Ba'thi strands actually served to further the monarchy's entrenchment. The pan-Arabist onslaught against the seemingly anachronistic, pro-Western monarchies captured the imagination of the Palestinians, who impatiently anticipated deliverance by the revolutionaries from their post-1948 predicament. The dangerous combination of Palestinian disaffection fanned by the external enemies of the status quo in Jordan reinforced the mutual interest of the East Bankers and the monarchy[10] in the struggle to preserve what had become their political patrimony. The fact that this challenge coincided with the rapid expansion of the institutions of state enabled the regime to reward and maintain the loyalty of its original Jordanian subjects with ever-increasing incorporation into the bureaucracy, the military, and the other arms of the internal security apparatus, thereby enhancing the mutual interest in the existing political order. Moreover, as of the early 1970s, in the aftermath of the civil war of 1970–1971, many Palestinians were removed from the bureaucracy to the extent that it has now become an almost exclusively Transjordanian domain. The East Bank political elite—urban and tribal alike—has by and large been co-opted by the regime.

The monarchy and the state in Jordan evolved simultaneously. The monarchy was the first effective seat of central and centralizing government Transjordan had known for centuries. The monarchy and the state thus developed hand-in-hand, to a degree that the two became indistinguishable in the eyes of friend and foe alike. This was never true of Hashemite Iraq, though it was similar to the evolution of other Middle Eastern monarchies that have lasted, like Saudi Arabia and Morocco.

As opposed to his brother Faysal in Iraq, Abdallah did not have to contend with a vibrant nationalist movement that might have hindered his common cause with the British to consolidate the monarchy. The urbanized elite was not only small but also divided between northerners (Irbid and Salt) and southerners (Karak and Ma‘an) who competed for royal favor. Coupled with the traditional cleavages between the nomads and the settled population, as well as tribal rivalries and the relatively low level of politicization (in terms of independent political organizations like parties, clubs, and unions or an active and critical press), these factors all combined to facilitate the emir's domination of the political "space." A kernel of opposition was ever-present among segments of the educated elite in Salt and Irbid, which had traditionally close ties with Palestine and Syria, respectively. They, however, remained ineffectual and incapable of overcoming the obstacles that retarded the development of a coherent nationalist movement that might have seriously challenged not only the British presence but also the regime it had ushered into existence.

The Integration of the Tribes

Perhaps the most significant of all Abdallah's achievements was the pacification, incorporation, and co-optation of the tribes into the machinery of the state. This was obtained by the skillful wielding of a combination of force and favor. Tribal rebellions against the emir's authority during the first few years of his rule were effectively suppressed by his own forces, assisted on occasion by the Royal Air Force. As John Bagot Glubb, the legendary former commander of the Arab Legion, subsequently explained, the greater mobility of modern armed forces and airpower put an end to Bedouin military advantage.[11]

Tribal loyalty was also bought with offers of land, government positions, and tax exemptions.[12] As the influence of his government spread throughout the country, Abdallah's rule "began to take on all the hallmarks of neopatrimonialism. He used the power he had to . . . [direct] the flow of government resources to increase the stature of those who supported him and to isolate and undermine those who did not."[13] Generally Abdallah tended to direct his patronage toward the more powerful tribes to facilitate the retention of their preeminence and thereby win their support.[14]

However, the most effective and comprehensive vehicle of tribal integration and co-optation was through recruitment to the Arab Legion. In a revolutionary turn of events, those whose traditional lifestyle had been antithetical and even hostile to any form of centralized governmental control, or to state-inspired law and order, were transformed into the backbone of the state.[15] To this day the Bedouin remain the core of the armed forces, predominantly represented in all the frontline formations, especially in the armored corps and the elite infantry units, officers and enlisted personnel alike.

This process began in the early 1930s, when Glubb established the Desert Patrol, manned entirely by Bedouin soldiers. Recruitment to the Legion became an especially attractive proposition for the tribesmen, who had been driven to the verge of pauperism since the emergence of the state. The consolidation of central government increased the burden of taxation and finally put an end to the flow of protection money the tribes had hitherto extracted from the settled population. Saudi raids and a cycle of locust infestation and drought decimated their flocks between 1929 and 1936, thus adding to their misery and increasing their willingness to accept military service on behalf of the state.[16] The Legion henceforth "provided a structure through which the state could reach large numbers of tribesmen. This, in turn, provided a channel through which the tribes could conceptualize the state as a positive institution, providing resources and training, instead of threatening their livelihoods."[17]

Service in the Arab Legion contributed decisively to the transformation of tribal allegiance into loyalty to the commanding officer and, ultimately, to the monarch. It was the king who now assumed the mantle of the "shaikh of shaikhs"—the supratribal leader.[18] Moreover, the Hashemite kings of Jordan—Abdallah and Hussein—tracing their lineage to the Prophet, could double as religious leaders or bearers of the religious heritage, thereby further enhancing their appeal to tribal soldiers.[19] Preferential enlistment of the Bedouin consolidated the legitimacy of the monarchy through a patron-client relationship, superbly characterized as the "quintessential monarchical/tribal-military axis."[20]

The monarchical-tribal symbiosis has come to full fruition in a relation-ship whereby the monarchy or the state (for the tribes and, indeed, for most East Bankers, these were to become synonymous) ensured the preferential status, prestige, and economic well-being of the tribes, who in return were to serve the regime with unswerving loyalty. Moreover, the state itself has con-sciously highlighted the extraordinary role of the Bedouin tribes in the devel-opment of the state and has deliberately promoted Jordan's tribal heritage as a "symbol of Jordan's distinctive national identity."[21] Yet at the same time it is the tribes who have, in their own self-perception and in the perception of oth-ers, become the standard-bearers of the Jordanian identity, or Jordanianism,[22] intimately interwoven with the monarchical institution.

The Trials of Transition from Abdallah to Hussein

The Arab Legion, in contradistinction to other armed forces in the Arab world, was slow in developing an indigenous officer corps. In Egypt, Syria, and Iraq it was these men of the sword who were to be the spearhead of revo-lution and the institution of military regimes. In Jordan, however, the role of the army, based for most of Jordan's history on selective recruitment and not conscription, has been very different. Instead of serving as the vehicle of rev-olution, the military has been the unflinching protector of the existing order. Until the mid-1950s, the Legion was led by British officers. In 1955, follow-ing the rapid expansion of the Legion after the 1948 war, British officers numbered 100 or more, and it was they who held the commands of most regi-ments and all higher formations, as well as all sensitive staff appointments.[23]

Following the dismissal of Britons by Hussein in 1956, a new generation of relatively young and junior urban officers, among whom Saltis were espe-cially prominent, rose rapidly to the vacated senior commanding echelon of the military.[24] Under the influence of the so-called Free Officers in Egypt, they too sought to overturn the status quo in Jordan by combining with the civilian opposition of the day, led by Prime Minister Sulayman al-Nabulsi, also from Salt. The officers and Nabulsi met with ignominious failure, outmaneuvered by the king in the notorious Zarqa Affair of April 1957, when Bedouin enlisted men turned against their own commanders, refusing to obey orders and as-saulting and locking up Free Officers the moment they realized that the objec-tive was to challenge, or, more likely, even to overthrow, the monarchy.[25] The officer class that developed thereafter, particularly in the combat formations, was disproportionately composed of the traditionally loyalist men of Bedouin and Circassian origins. Instances of insubordination and betrayal remained few and far between; most important, they were all nipped in the bud.

The Zarqa Affair and Hussein's countercoup reestablished royal primacy and the traditional balance of power. After an interlude of wavering indeci-sion that had threatened the regime with disintegration, the king, who was then not yet twenty-two, reasserted his political supremacy as the "corner-stone" or "linchpin" of the system, as the unquestioned head of the "king-government-army condominium."[26]

The transition from Abdallah to Hussein had been completed. The king-dom was now Hussein's in every sense that it had been Abdallah's before. This was all the more remarkable considering Hussein's youthful inexperi-ence and the considerably more difficult domestic and regional contexts in which the new king had to function. For the great majority of his reign, Ab-dallah did not have the Palestinians to deal with as a serious domestic chal-lenge, and Abd al-Nasir had yet to appear on the scene. Some observations on Hussein's character, his regime, and his opponents are therefore in order.

In the 1957 crisis, Hussein displayed those traits that have been ascribed to him ever since: political acumen, tactical sophistication, and personal courage and determination of the highest order. In this and in subsequent hours of trial, those traits emboldened and rallied loyalists and contributed much to the demoralization of adversaries.[27] The monarchy's opponents, do-mestic and external, rarely displayed the courage, sacrifice, or determination of the king or the cohesion and sense of purpose that motivated the king and his allies. After all, it was never quite as crucial for Abd al-Nasir and his Jor-danian allies to overthrow the regime as it was for Hussein to survive. Hus-sein had inherited from his predecessors the "faith in the role that devolved on him as the standard-bearer of the Hashemite house and his resulting determi-nation never to give up."[28] Moreover, his life in all probability depended on it. Abd al-Nasir "lacked the singleness of purpose in wishing [Hussein's] de-struction," and other enemies "who may have had that singleness of purpose lacked the resources."[29]

The Power Structure: The King and His Men

Hussein, in contrast, had substantial resources at his disposal. Those were the structures inherited from Abdallah, recast in an adjusted dye to suit the re-quirements and sensibilities of a new generation. Original Transjordanians were elevated to the highest offices in the land, and the army was "Arabized." Essentially, the power structure set up by Abdallah and the British was kept intact, though it was expanded to cope with the ever-increasing needs of a modernizing state forced to contend with a variety of domestic and external opponents.

The palace was the real and uncontested seat of power. It was a relatively small, efficient, and compact operation. The king reigned and ruled from the top of the decisionmaking pyramid, directly overseeing all foreign and do-mestic policies of any import. Former Premier Zayd al-Rifa'i characterized the system as "highly personalized," where decisions were made by the king with input from his advisers and, at times, from the prime minister and the cabinet. It was a fact of political life, according to Rifa'i, that there was no institutionalized decisionmaking process. The king was, in effect, the system's "unifying essence," and his influence permeated all spheres of the country's political life.[30]

Though the Hashemite Kingdom is a constitutional monarchy, the Jordanian system has been variously described as a form of "controlled constitutionalism" or as "monarchical absolutism."[31] The constitutional balance of power is heavily weighted in the monarchy's favor. The monarch is the head of all three branches—executive, legislative, and judicial—and as the supreme commander of the armed forces has complete control over the army. It is the king's prerogative to legislate by royal decree, to appoint and dismiss prime ministers, to convene, prorogue, and dissolve parliament, and to call for or postpone elections. Moreover, solely at his own discretion, the king can declare either a state of emergency or institute martial law, according the government sweeping powers to curtail political freedoms. Thus, in the aftermath of the Zarqa Affair, in April 1957, political parties were banned and martial law was imposed. Though martial law was rescinded at the end of 1958, the ban on parties remained in force continuously for thirty-five years, until 1992, when martial law, reimposed with the outbreak of war in June 1967, was also finally abolished.

The cabinet was more of an executive arm of the palace than a policymaking body, though central figures in the cabinet (usually the prime minister, the minister of interior, and the minister of information) were members of the king's informal inner council. Together with the crown prince, other key members of the royal family, the chief of the royal court, some alternating veteran politicians, and the commanding officers of the military and the domestic security organs—a circle of twenty or so—they became known most appropriately as the "king's friends" or the "king's men,"[32] as indeed they have been, through thick and thin.

The depiction of Jordan's struggle for survival as one of a lonely but "plucky little king" propped up by foreign aid is inaccurate. Without detracting from the quality of leadership, personal courage, political acumen, and fortitude of the Hashemite kings—Abdallah and Hussein—one cannot ignore the indispensable role of the East Bank political elite (of urban and tribal origin alike) and their cohesion and determination in the preservation of their political patrimony. After all, it is those same East Bank politicians, soldiers, and bureaucrats who, with the king, form the backbone of Hashemite Jordan. In weathering Jordan's trials—from the challenges of Nasserism, Palestinian nationalism, and Islamic fundamentalism to the transitions from Abdallah to Hussein and from Hussein to Abdallah II—more credit is due to this political corps of Majalis, Rifa'is, Talls, Badrans, Tarawnas, Khasawnas, and many more than is generally given.[33] It is they who not only share in the onus of government but also shield the king from popular criticism for policies that are essentially his own, thereby allowing him to remain above the unseemly fray of domestic politics.

Prime ministers are appointed by the king, and their cabinets are formed in close consultation with the monarch. However, it is the government that is exposed to parliament, the press, and the public on a routine basis, fulfilling the role of political lightning rod by frequently absorbing and deflecting criticism for policies whose true origins are in the palace. As such they have been invaluable assets that the king has never failed to appreciate.[34] The consistent cooperation of the East Bank elite is nurtured with great care. The king invests considerable effort and skill to cautiously maintain the equilibrium between the various local constituencies in the distribution of power and influence. In sensitive appointments, a calculated effort is made to allot positions more or less equitably between northerners and southerners and between the various Bedouin tribes, especially in the appointment of officers in the major military formations and the security organs, in which the king is always intimately involved. The Christian and Circassian minorities are similarly accorded their due, more or less.

This stabilizing and supportive role of the East Bank elite was demonstrated most impressively during the potentially precarious two-year period of transition, between Abdallah's assassination (July 1951) and Hussein's assumption of his constitutional powers (May 1953) and yet again after Hussein's death (February 1999). Abdallah's son and heir, Talal, had suffered extended periods of mental instability, and there were times when Abdallah and his closest confidants had seriously considered dropping him from the line of succession. In fact, when Abdallah died he had no clear successor. However, as Alec Kirkbride, Abdallah's almost lifelong companion as British Resident and, subsequently, ambassador, summed up the situation: "The small group of political leaders, which the late monarch had gathered round the throne, firmly held on to the reins of power, and while they were not friends amongst themselves, they had the wisdom to see that their failure to pull together could only bring harm to all concerned."[35]

After a brief interlude of palace intrigue, during which Abdallah's younger son, Na'if, tried to secure the throne for himself, it was Talal who, despite his obvious shortcomings, was preferred by most of the key players in the ruling elite, including the three elder statesmen (Ibrahim Hashim, Tawfiq Abu al-Huda, and Samir al-Rifa'i), as well as the ever-influential Kirkbride. Characterizations of Na'if were hardly complimentary, and he was by no means an obviously more worthy successor. Between the two, there was not much to choose from. There was, however, one overriding advantage in Talal's favor: he was the father of Hussein, who, though only sixteen at the time, was presciently regarded by the old guard as the most promising successor to Abdallah. Once Talal became king, Kirkbride noted, "there could be no further doubt about Hussein's right to follow his father as sovereign."[36]

Talal became king in September 1951. During all of his unhappy reign, which lasted less than a year, Prime Minister Tawfiq Abu al-Huda was the real power behind the throne and the true master of the Jordanian political scene.[37] In August 1952, Talal, not unexpectedly, was declared unfit to rule due to mental illness and was deposed. Hussein, at the time, was still a minor. He therefore acceded to the throne only nine months later, in May 1953. In the interim, the Hashemite Kingdom was essentially without a king, ruled instead by a Regency Council of three stalwarts of the regime (Ibrahim Hashim, of Nablus, Transjordanian since the 1920s; Sulayman Tuqan, of Nablus; and Abd al-Rahman al-Rashidat, of Irbid—that is, two East Bankers and a Palestinian from a family closely associated with the Hashemites since Abdallah's early days), along with Abu al-Huda, still firmly entrenched as prime minister. The prolonged absence of a monarch had no unsettling ramifications on the nature of the Jordanian state, as the king's men shifted into gear to secure the monarchy, which they fully realized was intimately linked to their own political survival. Indeed, the regency proved "that at a certain time . . . the establishment could keep on top in the rough-and-tumble of domestic challenges, without the Hashemite ruler as a continuous prime mover."[38] There is no reason to believe that the king's men of today are any less capable or determined to do the same if need be.

The key to the capacity of the king and the elite to maintain the domestic status quo rests with the military and the internal security organs and their loyalty to the monarchy. By extension this also means the loyalty and devotion of the Bedouin, whose role in the military has been so central. Hussein, needless to say, was always acutely aware of this reality, especially ever since the Zarqa Affair.[39]

Hussein's preoccupation with the army and the tribes, their well-being, and their loyalty was therefore a major part of his functioning routine. He maintained regular and close contact with the tribes and frequently expressed his identification with and commitment to the protection of Jordan's tribal heritage. The extent to which the Bedouin tribes are associated with the regime has created such a profound perception of mutual dependence that any critique of the tribes or tribalism could be construed as a veiled attack on the monarchy itself.[40] Hussein, in one such instance, first reminded his listeners of his own noble tribal ancestry, as a descendant of Hashim and Quraysh, "the noblest Arab tribe of Mecca that was honored by God and into which was born the Arab Prophet Mohammad." He then went on to declare unequivocally that "whatever harms our tribes in Jordan is considered harmful to us, as this has been the case all along, and it will continue to be so forever."[41]

As for the army, Hussein invested considerable energy, time, and resources to ensure the privileged status of the men of the armed forces. The army has its own extensive welfare services, education, housing and medical facilities, and generous patronage, salaries, and other benefits that include privileged access to the palace. Moreover, the king maintained constant contact with all echelons of the service, making routine visits to General Headquarters and to the men in the field, with whom he fostered a particularly intimate camaraderie.[42]

The Palestinians and the Monarchy

Although it is true that the regime and the entire power structure is heavily reliant on the East Bank elite, urban and tribal, it would be erroneous to portray the Palestinian component of the population as necessarily opposed to the monarchy and the status quo. In the 1950s and 1960s, in the heyday of Abd al-Nasir, many of Hussein's Palestinian subjects identified more with the president of the United Arab Republic than with their own sovereign. Much the same could be said of Palestinian identification with the *fida'iyyun* in Jordan in the late 1960s. A great deal has changed since then. The Nasserist panacea evaporated in the wake of humiliating defeat in June 1967, and the *fida'iyyun* were crushed and expelled from Jordan in the 1970–1971 civil war.

Many Palestinians have since willingly thrown in their lot with the Jordanian Kingdom. From the outset, it was state policy to absorb and integrate the Palestinians. However, since Palestinian loyalty was often suspect, they were rarely found in the upper echelons of the machinery of state, among the king's friends, or in the military, especially after the civil war. At the same time, their contributions to the modernization of the Jordanian state and its rapid economic development have been most impressive. Skilled Palestinian manpower (whether employed in Jordan itself or in the Gulf), their enterprise, and their relatively high levels of education, coupled with large amounts of foreign aid for Palestinian refugee rehabilitation, have all been assets of progress that, in retrospect, have outweighed the onerous impact of the Palestinians as a potentially destabilizing political liability.

Economically and socially, if not politically, the Palestinians have been well integrated into the state and the fabric of society. This is especially true of those who came to the country (as refugees and nonrefugees alike) in the early years after the 1948 war. Many of them have moved up into the middle, upper-middle, and upper classes of Jordanian society, so much so that it is they who predominate in the private sector of the Jordanian economy; they have by now acquired a vested interest in the continued stability of the political order.[43] Significant segments of this Palestinian community were alienated from the Palestine Liberation Organization (PLO) because of the civil war,[44] and in recent years a variety of regional developments has reinforced this trend of Palestinian acceptance of and loyalty to the monarchy and the Jordanian state.

A "sea-change of sorts has occurred."[45] First of all, the major irritant in Jordan's relations with its Palestinian citizens has been mitigated considerably. In the more distant past, Jordan's relative moderation toward Israel was perceived by many Palestinians to be inimical to their most immediate interests and aspirations. Now, however, in an era of Middle East peacemaking, in which the PLO is as full a partner as Jordan, this no longer holds as true. Moreover, in recent years a number of Hussein's major policy decisions further endeared him to his Palestinian subjects: the disengagement declaration from the West Bank in 1988, the political liberalization set in motion in 1989, and Jordan's stand by Iraq in the Gulf War.[46] Jordan's peace with Israel and the shift away from Iraq, though less popular, have not markedly altered the generally favorable appraisal of many Palestinians of their lives as Jordanians. Certainly in comparison to the lot of Palestinians elsewhere, their experience in Jordan has, for the most part, been secure, benevolent, prosperous, and difficult to improve upon elsewhere in the Arab world, including in an independent Palestine.[47]

The co-optation of the major segments of Jordanian society into the state has thus been achieved through the evolutionary political, social, and economic processes of modern-day state-building. Traditional devices of co-optation, such as the marriage of representatives of key sectors of society into the royal family, as has been the practice in Saudi Arabia, for example, have never been a realistic option for the tiny Hashemite family. They comprise but a few score, compared to the literally thousands of Saudi princes, readily available not only for such politically expedient marriages but also to occupy the highest offices of state. The king's men in the Saudi case are invariably members of the family. The comparative needs for and modes of co-optation have therefore been very different in these two neighboring Arab monarchies.

LEGITIMACY AND THE RESTRAINED USE OF FORCE

The Style of Governance

As a rule the Hashemite kings have been determined to exercise their extensive constitutional powers to the full while demonstrating an ingrained reluctance to use force against their own subjects, lest any such violence undermine their incessant quest for legitimacy among their own people and in the Arab world at large. Not that force was never employed, but it was usually a last resort—the exception to the rule. One such exception was the civil war of 1970–1971. The presence of the armed *fida'iyyun* in Jordan in the late 1960s and their creation of a kind of "state within a state" was an unprecedented threat to the very existence of the monarchy. Hussein, no doubt, was acutely aware of the danger from the outset, but hesitated for more than two years before taking the plunge into bloody confrontation. Even then the decision to finally crack down on the *fida'iyyun* was only reached after considerable pressure by the king's men.[48]

But it was also characteristic of Hussein to implement his decisions, once finally made, with relentless determination. The *fida'iyyun* were expelled from the country completely, their infrastructure destroyed; needless to say, they were never allowed back. Throughout the struggle, however, Hussein was at pains to convince his own public that the action against the *fida'iyyun* had been taken to restore law and order and was by no means to be construed as a campaign against Palestinians per se.[49] Judging by the evolution of Palestinian attitudes toward the regime after the civil war, it would appear that Hussein's explanations were accepted, by and large, by his Palestinian subjects.

In contradistinction to Kanan Makiya's characterization of Saddam's Iraq, Jordan is not a totalitarian "monarchy of fear."[50] Compared to most other Arab states, Jordan is a relatively liberal state. The regime is neither particularly intrusive nor oppressive, and the rather suffocating atmosphere in the capitals of some other Arab states is hardly the norm for Amman. Moreover, the Hashemites have developed a tradition of magnanimity toward former domestic enemies. Would-be assassins, plotters, rogues, and traitors have invariably not only been forgiven for their deviation but also rehabilitated and even appointed to high office, occasionally in the most sensitive positions in the domestic security apparatus. The recipients of this royal largesse, who owe not only their careers but also their lives to the monarch in person, have for the most part reciprocated with grateful and loyal service. The instances are far too many to enumerate, but suffice it to say that this practice included Abdallah al-Tall, sentenced to death in absentia for his implication in the assassination of King Abdallah, as well as Ali and Ma'an Abu Nuwwar and Nadhir Rashid (who, after his pardon, became chief of domestic security and later served as minister of interior). All were key conspirators in the Zarqa Affair who fled into exile and were later allowed back into the country and the king's good graces.

Survival and Performance

Hussein, like Abdallah before him, succeeded over the years in earning the respect of the great majority of his subjects and in imparting to them an enduring perception of Hashemite legitimacy in the Weberian sense of the term, that is, the acceptance of his authority with an infrequent need to resort to force and coercion. In part, this legitimacy rested on the prestigious ancestry of the Hashemites, the projection of their role as defenders of Islamic holy places, and as the instigators and leaders of the Great Arab Revolt against the Turks. However, these factors in and of themselves are not decisive. More important is the fact that the monarchy, for the most part, has consistently been able to provide its subjects with relative prosperity, economic and social development, and benevolent and not overintrusive government in an atmosphere of stability and individual security. This legitimacy of competence, performance, and ancestry was systematically buttressed by a deliberate promotion of Hussein's image as a courageous leader,[51] coupled with his personal and humane touch, whereby the king's accessibility to the citizenry and his receptivity to their private needs and requests highlighted his role as "the ultimate Jordanian gift-giver."[52]

In September 1992, Hussein returned to Amman from cancer surgery in the United States. Hundreds of thousands, and possibly over a million people, turned out to line the streets of the capital to welcome his safe return. Granted, the festivities were not entirely spontaneous. The day had been declared a national holiday by the government, and the people were made aware of what was expected of them. Even so, the celebrations, which went on for days throughout the kingdom, did seem to reflect the widespread and genuine popularity of the king and the loyalty to Hussein as "an enduring unifying symbol of stability."[53] Hussein ruled the country for more than half of its existence, becoming a "key symbol of the Jordanian nation." Indeed, in the way he had come to embody "cultural notions of history, tradition, and peoplehood shared by the people of Jordan he [was] also a metonym for the country."[54] The outpouring of sorrow and mourning by the masses of the Jordanian people upon the death of Hussein was a genuine expression of loss for a leader who had assumed the mantle of father figure for the nation in its entirety.

Monarchies, Republics, and Succession

The legitimacy of the regime has been enhanced, perhaps more than any single factor, by the fact that the experience of monarchy in Jordan can be summed up in relative terms as a success story. Hussein survived against the odds for more than forty years since it was said of him that "his days [were] numbered." And he finally succumbed to cancer, not to his political rivals.[55] Long gone are the heady days of Nasserism, when Arab politics were defined by the dichotomy separating the so-called progressive revolutionary regimes from their reactionary rivals. The former were the "positive neutralist" republican officer regimes, with Abd al-Nasir as the embodiment of the ideal type, promising power, deliverance from the West, the liberation of Palestine, and a socialist paradise; and the latter were composed of the monarchies who were seen by the predominant ideological trend as anachronistic pro-Western waifs and lackeys of imperialism, destined by the masses and the determinist forces of history to be relegated to political oblivion.

For almost two decades, the monarchies dug in to face the progressive onslaught, assuming a usually defensive and, at times, pathetically apologetic demeanor. For many of Hussein's subjects, especially among Palestinians, Abd al-Nasir's brand of Arab socialism was the unquestioned wave of the future and the guaranteed avenue to modernity, progress, and victory. Any comparison between the monarchy and the republics, in terms of their relative legitimacy and promise to fulfill the aspirations of the people, left the Hashemite Kingdom trailing way behind.

Jordan was the only Arab state that emerged from the 1948 war with much of its ambition in hand. The regime attained its major political and military objectives and at war's end sought nothing more than to preserve the status quo. For the Palestinians, however, the war had been an unmitigated disaster. Their prime ambition was to turn back the clock of history, which in their minds was predicated on the transformation of Jordan into their vehicle of liberation. The fundamental points of departure of the regime and many of its Palestinian citizens were therefore diametrically opposed. Unfortunately for Hussein, mounting Palestinian disaffection coincided with the popularization of the messianic, antimonarchist, anti-Western, pro-Soviet, and Arab-socialist Nasserism, which expounded the attractive republican antithesis to everything the Hashemite monarchy represented. After all, Hussein appeared to be no more than a youthful monarch, drawing his legitimacy from a conservative vision of Arabism, as enshrined in the old-fashioned Arab Revolt, dependent for his survival on the very same Western powers that—in the eyes of Palestinians—were responsible for their calamity.

In June 1967, the regional context in which the monarchies functioned changed dramatically. The messianic promise of Nasserism was shattered in humiliating defeat. The dichotomy of the 1950s and 1960s, distinguishing the progressives from the reactionaries, became an irrelevant anachronism in the real world of Arab politics once it transpired that the progressive formula for power and modernity was nothing but an illusion. In an Arab world that now became more realistic and pragmatic, ideology gradually disappeared as a determinant of inter-Arab relations. The "end of pan-Arabism"[56] legitimized the twentieth century–type territorial state in the Arab world—Jordan included—and the Hashemite Kingdom was finally accepted as an equal member of the Arab family of nations. This would have seemed unthinkable only a short while before. The fact that the Jordanians had also acquitted themselves honorably on the battlefield, in contrast to some of their progressive neighbors, only added to their newly earned respectability.

The officer regimes had taken pride in their "revolutionary" detachment from the past. Relying neither on historical precedent nor prestigious ancestry, religious credentials, and democratic election, their legitimacy depended almost entirely on competence and performance. Invariably they failed to meet the unrealistic expectations that they themselves aroused in their peoples. The monarchies, and certainly the Hashemites, were less presumptuous and less ideological. They promised less and delivered more than the false republican messiahs. The "unity, freedom, and socialism" of Abd al-Nasir and the Ba'ths came to naught on all three counts. The more pragmatic Hashemite parallel of the time differed only slightly in formulation—"unity, freedom, and a better life"—but it proved to be a lot more realistic. With all its problems, the unity between the East Bank and West Bank was the most enduring Arab union and may be revived in one form or another in the future. Jordanians also enjoy a greater measure of political freedom than do most other Arabs, and they know it. In fact, they probably know that they lead a better life than most other Arab peoples, certainly better than those living with the paltry remains of the socialist paradises of the Free Officers.

Nowadays, in stark contrast to the earlier period of Hussein's reign, Hashemite legitimacy is actually enhanced by the comparison to revolutionary republics. It was Hussein who, more often than not, could claim relative success in comparison with the Arab revolutionary republics and project an image of self-assurance and confidence about the future.

It is not that the institution of monarchy is inherently more legitimate than republican regimes. It is, to a large degree, legitimacy by default, reinforced by the failure of the competition to deliver. Consequently, there is far less reason in the Middle East of today to question the institution of monarchy per se, especially since its adaptability and resilience have defied the predictions of both revolutionaries and political theorists. Moreover, monarchy is very much in keeping with centuries of Islamic political tradition, Sunni and Shi'i alike. The Muslim world has been accustomed to dynastic rule since the Umayyads of the seventh century, and orderly and bloodless succession—hardly the rule in the republics—has had a reassuring effect on the public and maintained their confidence in the political system. The ultimate irony of this republican-monarchical rivalry is to observe the ultrarepublican-socialist-revolutionary rulers of Ba'thi Syria and Iraq earnestly engaged in the creation of "republican dynasties" of their own, desperately grooming their sons for succession in vintage monarchical style.

Hussein, having experienced serious illness, became acutely aware of his own mortality, and in the early 1990s he began to contemplate the Jordan he would leave to his heirs. Instilling faith in the monarchy, Hussein sought to reassure his people that their state, as opposed to the neighboring republics, was "not one tied to an individual, a party, a faction or a class" but was a state founded on the legitimacy of the Hashemite family, with its noble descent from the Prophet Muhammad and the legacy of the Arab Revolt. Jordan under the Hashemites, according to Hussein, was a state with a mission: to serve as a model of "freedom, democracy, pluralism, and respect for human rights" for the Arab world, spurning tyranny, dictatorship, and totalitarian regimes.[57]

On a more practical level, Hussein in October 1994 announced the formation of a Hashemite family council that would include all the descendants of his great-grandfather, Hussein bin Ali. It would be they who would choose from among themselves the most qualified heir to Hussein and Crown Prince Hasan, his brother and designated successor. This, he noted, would be a "democratic monarchy," reviving the Islamic pledge of *baya* (allegiance), as closely as possible to the practices of the early days of Islam.[58] Such painless intrafamilial accord, however, was not to be.

The Jordanian people were stunned by Hussein's decision in late January 1999, just days before his death, to depose former Crown Prince Hasan. (Hasan had been elevated to the position of crown prince in 1965, when he reached the age of eighteen. Hussein opted then to pass over his own infant son, Abdallah, the first son from his marriage to Princess Muna who had been crown prince since his birth in 1962, in favor of an adult successor.) Precisely because the order of succession had been so clear for nearly thirty-four years, the Jordanian people, as opposed to their fellow Arabs in countries like Syria and Iraq, lived with the comforting and stabilizing assurance that they knew who was next in line. It is true that there were those, within Jordan and without, who had their doubts about Hasan's capacity to fill Hussein's shoes, but he was widely respected for his intellect, experience, and international stature. He was said to be less popular than Hussein, less instinctively charismatic, and not as well accepted in the Jordanian army and domestic security establishment, the backbone of the regime. But Hasan was a known quantity, and the Jordanian people had generally become accustomed to the idea that he would follow in his brother's footsteps. His sudden and rather brutal removal therefore had an immediately unsettling effect.

Apart from doubts, justifiable or not, that Hussein may have had about Hasan's competence, the seemingly most plausible reason for his decision was Hussein's ultimate desire to ensure succession to his own descendants, rather than to those of his brother. Until Hussein's last days, he and Hasan were unable to agree on who would follow Hasan in the line of succession—Hussein's fourth son, Hamza (from his marriage to Queen Nur), or Hasan's only son, Rashid. Hussein was determined to ensure the eventual accession to the throne of Hamza, his favored (and reputedly most talented) son. The only way to do so, once he realized that he had very little time to live, was to remove Hasan and appoint Abdallah to succeed him as king and to have Abdallah appoint his younger brother Hamza as crown prince. The constitution provided for only two possible successors: the king's eldest son or one of the king's brothers. Hamza was neither, and since Hussein did not have the time to go through the process of altering the constitution, his choice fell on Abdallah, literally at the last moment, and apparently to Abdallah's own surprise.

Despite the dramatic last-minute change of successor, the transition from Hussein to Abdallah II was smooth, stable, and reassuring. Abdallah, the thirty-seven-year-old British- and U.S.-educated new king, was until his appointment as crown prince a career officer in the Jordanian army, his last post being that of commander of the Special Forces with the rank of major general. He had little political experience, but his greatest assets were the continued consensual acceptance of the monarchy as the "unifying essence" of the state and the support he enjoyed in the armed forces and the other arms of the security establishment. Moreover, Jordanians, for the most part, had faith in Hussein's political judgment and rapidly accustomed themselves to the new choice. Hasan's own remarkably gracious and majestic acceptance of his brother's decision—at least as far as the public appearance was concerned—was in itself an important factor that facilitated this adjustment.

The regional and global context of Abdallah's ascension to the throne is far more congenial than was the case for Hussein in his early years. The so-called Arab Cold War[59] between Abd al-Nasir and his rivals is over, the Arab-Israeli conflict has transformed into a peace process, and the Cold War between the superpowers is a past memory. The level of "stateness" bequeathed by Hussein to his successor is far more impressive compared to that which he inherited, in terms of the size, competence, and sophistication of the bureaucracy, the military, and the security establishment. The reservoir of experienced politicians, officers, and bureaucrats to serve in the historical role of the king's men has, therefore, been greatly enhanced and is no less loyal, capable, and cohesive than were its predecessors. In the current circumstances there is no shortage of able and experienced senior politicians and officers to coach Abdallah through the transition, as other king's men had done for his father during an earlier era. According to Jordanian sources, Abdallah was initially guided by an archetypal team of such king's men. In Amman they were referred to as *al-Abdayn, wal-Zaydayn, wal-Fariqayn*, that is, the two Abds (chief of the Royal Court and former prime minister, the southerner Abd al-Karim al-Kabariti; and the incumbent prime minister, the northerner Abd al-Rauf al-Rawabda); the two Zayds (Speaker of the Senate and former prime minister Zayd al-Rifa'i, the Amman-born boyhood friend and lifelong confidant of King Hussein; and former chief-of-staff and prime minister Emir Zayd bin Shakir, a Hashemite and cousin to Hussein and, like Rifa'i, a longstanding confidant of the late king); and the two lieutenant generals (Chief of Domestic Security Samih al-Batihi; and the commander of the armed forces, Abd al-Hafiz Mar'i al-Ka'abina). Batihi and Kabariti were the two key figures at the new king's side.

There are no noticeable chinks in the armor of the military and its loyalty to the existing order, and Abdallah's career in the armed forces stands him in good stead with this mainstay of the regime. And lastly, Jordan's external supporters are no less prepared than previously to grant support, both political and economic, if need be.

A worst-case scenario would be the unlikely implosion of the regime. This might happen if Abdallah, contrary to expectations and initial performance, proves to be inept, and the royal family and the political and military elite, instead of compensating for the king's shortcomings, degenerate into power struggles that filter down into the army. Then the monarchy may not survive the ordeal. Were such a scenario to become a reality, it would be virtually impossible for Jordan's external supporters to do much about it. Their support in the past was of crucial importance to a determined and cohesive regime that had consistently kept its own house in order. That would remain an essential precondition for effective external assistance of whatever nature.

Jordan does face potentially destabilizing challenges that are, however, unrelated to the succession. The most urgent, at present, is the kingdom's faltering economy, the issue highest on the agenda of King Abdallah II.

CONTENDING WITH THE ISLAMISTS AND SOCIOECONOMIC CRISIS

The Islamist Phenomenon in Jordan

Having withstood the trials and tribulations of succession and transition, the challenges of Arab radicalism and Palestinian militancy, and the ravages of war and domestic strife, the monarchy is currently confronted with problems of a different nature—those resulting from the potentially disruptive combination of Islamic fundamentalism and protracted socioeconomic crisis. The ideological vacuum left by the demise of pan-Arabism has been filled in Jordan, as in other parts of the Arab world, by two concurrent but conflicting processes: the entrenchment of the territorial state, on the one hand, and the rise of Islamic fundamentalism on the other.

The main opposition in Jordan has thus been transformed, since the late 1970s and early 1980s, from an essentially secular Arab or Palestinian nationalist opposition into an Islamist challenge, influenced by the overarching regional trend, the Iranian revolution, and Jordan's economic woes. As of the late 1980s, Jordan had been struggling with high unemployment and other socioeconomic fallout from the structural imbalance between a rapidly growing population and dwindling resources. Foreign aid (from Arabs and others) is less readily available, and the slogan of the Islamists that "Islam is the solution" had an authentic appeal to the swelling ranks of the disenchanted.

The regime and the Islamists, however, have established an informal modus vivendi, an uneasy standoff between protagonists who are not mortal enemies. Now that the challenge to the status quo emanates from the religious right rather than the secular left, the regime and the Islamists find themselves on opposing sides of the ideological barricades. This was not always so. In fact, the Muslim Brethren in Jordan and the regime were long-standing political allies in the confrontation with the Nasserist and Ba'thi secular Arab socialists of the 1950s and 1960s, who were perceived to be dangerously threatening to both. The monarchy tended to defend itself in Islamic terms against the Nasserist onslaught and—as opposed to the republics—never resorted to anti-Islamist socialist and pseudosocialist rhetoric and policy. When all political parties were banned in 1957, the ruling did not apply to the Muslim Brethren, who formally functioned as a charitable association, and thus remained the only legal political group in the country, until parties were legalized once again in 1992. There is, therefore, no residue of bad blood between the regime and the Islamists, as there was and is, for example, in Egypt, Syria, and Algeria.

Moreover, the Hashemites are not a religiously illegitimate minority regime like the Alawis in Syria. On the contrary, the regime now tends even more than before to highlight its noble Islamic ancestry as descendants of the family of the Prophet and to emphasize and publicize its religious rectitude. The regime can boast Islamic credentials that most of the Islamists respect, even though they are at loggerheads with what is an essentially secular and Westernizing monarchy.

The decisive factor in this modus vivendi, however, is the balance of power, which is politically and constitutionally very much in the regime's favor. The monarchy, confident in its power and reluctant as always to resort to repression, has chosen to contend with the new political and socioeconomic challenges by initiating a process of democratization. The process, set in motion by the parliamentary elections of 1989—the first since 1967—is firmly controlled by the regime. It is confined by the constitution, a new national charter approved in 1991, and laws governing political parties and the press, which were all designed to ensure the unrivaled superiority of the monarchy, domestic security, and state interest, as defined by the regime. Political pluralism and guarded liberalization were intended primarily to deny the Islamists a monopoly on political society. The objective was to allow for the formation of political parties from all sectors of the establishment as well as the opposition to compete with the Islamists while co-opting the Islamists into a system that upheld the status quo.

None of this was concealed. King Hussein and former Crown Prince Hasan were quite explicit in demarcating the boundaries of the democratic experiment. They explained that democratization was a means to "guarantee the stability of the Hashemite Kingdom" at a time of prolonged domestic crisis. Political pluralism and openness were the "safety valve in Jordan," and democracy was "one of the most important pillars of national security." Nobody would be permitted "to exploit democracy to liquidate it." Pluralism and tolerance were the antithesis to Muslim extremism, whereas Jordan rejected "intellectual terrorism and [had] never condoned violence, fanaticism, malice, and anarchy," having opted for "tolerance with firmness that [could] best ensure security."[60] In the worldviews of both the regime and the Islamists, then, democratization was neither a value nor a virtue but an instrument. For the regime it was a sophisticated means of control. For the Islamists it was an opening to enhance their public posture and influence without engaging the regime in a head-on confrontation that they were bound to lose.

The Islamists, for the most part, have accepted the rules of the game. The lessons of 1957 and 1970, when the regime took extreme and even brutal action against its opponents, have left an indelible imprint on the minds of Jordan's political public and have an obvious deterrent effect. It is clear to all and sundry that the regime is capable, albeit reluctantly, of putting an end to the democratization process, even of crushing the opposition, if and when it feels unduly threatened. Again, Hussein left little to the imagination when he "remember[ed] the 1950s" and expressed concern lest there be a repetition of the practices that had led then to the "faltering of [Jordan's democratic] march."[61]

The Muslim Brethren and their political party, the Islamic Action Front (IAF), emphasize their belief in the evolutionary, and not revolutionary, Islamization of society. They studiously highlight their support for domestic stability, uphold the constitution and the national charter, recognize the religious legitimacy of the Hashemites, and do not challenge the monarchy in principle. Even when the regime takes action against them directly they usually shy away from confrontation, the doves invariably outnumbering the hawks in the leadership of the movement. Leaders of the Muslim Brethren were said to be "aware of the state of distrust" toward them and of the need, therefore, to remain "in harmony with the regime" rather than pose a challenge that "could seriously undermine [their] own political future."[62]

Generally abiding by the rules set by the regime also has its advantages. The Muslim Brethren factions in Jordan enjoy relatively far more political freedom than do their counterparts in other Arab countries, such as Egypt, Syria, Algeria, and Tunisia.[63] The more radical Islamists in Jordan, who have refused to accept these rules, have been penalized accordingly. The Islamic Liberation Party, avowedly antimonarchist, seeking the reestablishment of the caliphate, is a marginal and illegal movement, its members spending much of their time behind bars. A more extraordinary but instructive case is that of the maverick former parliamentarian and president of the engineers association, Layth Shubaylat. An outspoken independent Islamist who does not belong to the Muslim Brethren, Shubaylat is probably the only prominent politician who has publicly called for the amendment of the constitution in order to reduce the power of the monarchy and to establish a truly democratic system in Jordan. In the summer of 1992, Shubaylat, along with some lesser figures, was brought to trial on charges of treason, accused of conspiring to overthrow the regime by revolution. Shubaylat was sentenced to twenty years in prison but was granted amnesty by the king. It was widely believed in Jordan that the charges were politically motivated, intended to silence Shubaylat and to send a warning to the Islamists in general not to overstep the bounds of the political process set by the regime. The case did not silence Shubaylat for long (and he subsequently ended up in jail on other charges and was pardoned again), but the warning no doubt helped to keep the mainstream Islamists in check.

Jordanians, Palestinians, and Economic Recession

In the 1990s, partly as a consequence of the economic hardship and partly as a result of the peace process, latent Jordanian-Palestinian tensions resurfaced, albeit in a different mode, shaped more by socioeconomic factors rather than the ideological cleavages of old.

"Black September" and the 1970–1971 civil war was a traumatizing formative experience that accelerated the coalescence and consolidation of the divergent group identities of Jordanians and Palestinians alike. The conflict widened the distinctive divide between the communities and endowed both Jordanians and Palestinians with a more profound and coherent sense of national consciousness, fueled by mutual distrust and acrimony. However, during the decade of prosperity, from the mid-1970s to the mid-1980s, these tensions, for the most part, receded.

King Hussein developed an ambivalent approach to these phenomena. On the one hand, he made a deliberate effort to promote and reinforce the particularist Jordanian loyalty, identity, and statehood. His former slogan — "Jordan is Palestine and Palestine is Jordan"—which was intended to preserve and nurture the union between Jordanians and Palestinians on both banks of the river, was gradually superseded by a new formula: "Jordan is Jordan and Palestine is Palestine." Hussein thus promoted the East Bank as the separate inviolate political patrimony of the Jordanians and recognized the Palestinians' right to self-determination and statehood on the *other side* of the river. On the other hand, as Hussein was fully conscious of the disruptive potential inherent in the fractious rise of intercommunal tension, his version of Jordanianism never excluded Jordan's citizens of Palestinian origin on the East Bank. On the contrary, Hussein consistently upheld the essential national unity of all Jordanians, from whatever origin (*min shatta al-manabit wal-usul*), and repeatedly warned, in the strongest of terms, against any attempt to sow dissension between the members of the "one family" of Jordanians.

Some conflicting aspects of Jordanian domestic policy since the civil war have emanated directly from this duality in the king's thinking. As already mentioned, as part of the effort to secure the Jordanian entity, many Palestinians were removed in the early 1970s from the bureaucracy and the military, thereby further reducing their representation in the machinery of state. At the same time, however, in accordance with the genuine desire to integrate the Palestinians and to benefit from their skills, they were encouraged—or at least not restricted—in pursuing careers in most other walks of life. This has resulted in the development of an almost "built-in" functional cleavage, whereby the Jordanians control the institutions of state and the Palestinians predominate in the private sector, the financial markets, and the economy in general.

However, with the faltering economy of recent years the government has been induced to cut back its own spending. The regime is now less capable of generously rewarding soldiers and bureaucrats on its payroll, resulting in disaffection among original Jordanians who are beginning to feel disadvantaged in comparison to many of their Palestinian compatriots. In April 1989 and again in August 1996 riots broke out in protest against price hikes of basic commodities. In both instances the core of the troubles was in the more tribal south, always the bedrock of support for the regime. Contrary to past experience, the traditionally less reliable Palestinians played no part in the disturbances. It would be wrong to infer that historical roles are being reversed, or that there has been a serious erosion in the historical association and fundamental loyalty of the more tribal south to king and country. But the ramifications of the functional cleavage in an era of economic uncertainty are taking a toll that requires the regime's urgent attention.

This is all the more so following the Oslo Accords and Palestinian advances toward statehood in the West Bank and Gaza. Many Jordanians have become increasingly suspicious of what is seen as potential Palestinian dual loyalty. Latent tensions between Jordanians and Palestinians have since resurfaced with a "saliency unheard of since the dark days of Black September."[64] Jordan's more liberal political system of recent years has made room for ultranationalist Jordanian rumblings that have freely entered the public discourse. Spokesmen for this trend have been quite uninhibited in their contention that "Jordan for the Jordanians" had to be protected from possible Palestinization, reflecting their fears of Palestinian irredentism, demographic weight, and economic power.

Ironically, at a time when the Palestinians in Jordan are more willing than ever to integrate into the Jordanian state, they are being spurned by a significant segment of their East Bank compatriots. Though not a majority trend, or entirely coherent or monolithic, this ultra-Jordanianism is significant in that its key spokespersons are not marginal figures from the political periphery but have actually emerged from the core of the East Bank elite. Some of them are ultraroyalists, whereas others emphasize the priority they place on their loyalty to the Jordanian state and its interests above and beyond their loyalty to the monarchy.[65] The latter people are critical of Jordan's policies, particularly on the peace process, which they regard as having drawn Jordan far too intimately into the Israeli-Palestinian orbit and away from its natural Arab hinterland to the east. They are by no means antimonarchist in principle, but they have serious reservations about any intimate association with the Palestinian state of the future; they do not believe that the peace treaty with

Israel was Jordan's timely strategic choice, or that it will be the promised panacea for the country's economic problems. It is, therefore, not uncommon for representatives of this latter school to join forces with other opponents of the peace treaty from the Islamist right and the secular left.

Protracted economic difficulty and widespread disappointment with the "peace dividend" resulted in increasing criticism of the regime. Hussein responded by curtailing the democratization process, including the introduction of restrictive measures, on the press for example, by royal decree. Though hardly a novelty in terms of his political style, the king's undisguised and direct intervention in the domestic political fray was damaging to his personal stature, as criticism was more commonly leveled against him personally.

Shortly after his accession to the throne, Abdallah II indicated his readiness to reconsider some of his father's restrictive impositions. What exactly will be done in this regard remains to be seen.

CONCLUSION

The monarchy today has to contend with a variety of domestic challenges, most of which are extensions of socioeconomic strain. These are problems of a new order that are not readily solvable by the monarch's own decision or by the extreme measures of old—force and repression—as these were effectively employed against the political threats of Arab radicalism and Palestinian militancy. The regime can still suppress the opposition, but that, needless to say, would have no bearing on the growth rates of either the population or the economy. Moreover, certain measures that are indeed essential to addressing the economic challenges, such as a major reduction of dependents on the government payroll, are politically dangerous. Downgrading the public sector, manpower reductions in the bureaucracy and military, and accelerated development of the private sector might fuel the feelings of East Bankers that they are becoming "economic, political, and social losers"[66] and thereby erode the power structure of the regime itself, so laboriously cultivated since the early days of the emirate.

The monarchy appears to be having difficulty in adjusting to the new challenges. Yet it would be an exaggeration to suggest that the regime cannot cope with them. As long as the Hashemite kings remain more or less as astute as they have been; are supported by a relatively cohesive elite and loyal security establishment; and are buttressed by a range of external powers who have a vested interest in Jordan's political and economic stability, the Hashemite monarchy, with a little help from its friends, is more likely than not to identify the core problems and eventually come up with the appropriate solutions.

However, an estimable change in any one of the above stabilizing factors could mean a different story altogether.

NOTES

1. This section has been adapted from Asher Susser, "Introduction," in Asher Susser and Aryeh Shmuelevitz (eds.), *The Hashemites in the Modern Arab World: Essays in Honour of the Late Professor Uriel Dann* (London: Frank Cass, 1995), pp. 1–5.

2. Kamal Salibi, *The Modern History of Jordan* (London: I. B. Tauris, 1993), p. 85.

3. Ibid., pp. 85–86.

4. Alec Kirkbride, *From the Wings: Amman Memoirs, 1947–1951* (London: Frank Cass, 1976), pp. 152–153.

5. Michael Fischbach, "British Land Policy in Transjordan," in Eugene Rogan and Tariq Tell (eds.), *Village, Steppe, and State: The Social Origins of Modern Jordan* (London: British Academic Press, 1994), pp. 80–81; Salibi, *The Modern History of Jordan,* p. 49.

6. Salibi, *The Modern History of Jordan,* pp. 98–99.

7. Ibid., p. 106; Mary Wilson, *King Abdallah, Britain, and the Making of Jordan* (Cambridge: Cambridge University Press, 1987), pp. 64–65; Schirin Fathi, *Jordan: An Invented Nation?* (Hamburg: Deutsches Orient-Institut, 1994), pp. 92–94.

8. Naseer Aruri, *Jordan: A Study in Political Development, 1921–1965* (Ann Arbor: University of Michigan Microfilms, 1967), p. 82.

9. Paul Kingston, "Breaking the Patterns of Mandate: Economic Nationalism and State Formation in Jordan, 1951–1957," in Rogan and Tell, *Village, Steppe, and State,* pp. 187–216.

10. Uriel Dann, *King Hussein and the Challenge of Arab Radicalism: Jordan, 1955–1967* (New York: Oxford University Press, 1989), p. 8.

11. John Bagot Glubb, *The Story of the Arab Legion* (London: Hodder and Stoughton, 1948), p. 8.

12. Toby Dodge, *An Arabian Prince, English Gentlemen, and the Tribes East of the River Jordan: Abdallah and the Creation and Consolidation of the Trans-Jordanian State,* Occasional Paper 13, Centre of Near and Middle Eastern Studies, School of Oriental and African Studies, University of London, 1994, p. 4.

13. Ibid., p. 6.

14. Ibid., p. 25.

15. Riccardo Bocco and Tariq Tell, "*Pax Britannica* in the Steppe: British Policy and the Transjordan Bedouin," in Rogan and Tell, *Village, Steppe, and State,* p. 108.

16. Ibid., pp. 108–109.

17. Dodge, *An Arabian Prince,* p. 28.

18. Fathi, *Jordan,* pp. 96–97, 127; Linda Layne, "Tribesmen as Citizens: 'Primordial Ties' and Democracy in Rural Jordan," in Linda Layne (ed.), *Elections in the Middle East: Implications of Recent Trends* (Boulder: Westview Press, 1987), p. 128.

19. Laurence Axelrod, "Tribesmen in Uniform: The Demise of the Fida'iyyun in Jordan, 1970–1971," *Muslim World,* 68, no. 1 (1978), p. 44.

20. Ibid., p. 26; Laurie Brand, "'In the Beginning Was the State. . .': The Quest for Civil Society in Jordan," in Augustus R. Norton (ed.), *Civil Society in the Middle East* (Leiden: E. J. Brill, 1995), pp. 153–154.

21. Linda Layne, *Home and Homeland: The Dialogics of Tribal and National Identities in Jordan* (Princeton: Princeton University Press, 1994), p. 103.

22. Fathi, *Jordan,* pp. 259, 264.

23. James Lunt, *Hussein of Jordan: A Political Biography* (London: Macmillan, 1989), p. 13; Dann, *King Hussein,* p. 32.

24. Dann, *King Hussein,* p. 35.

25. Ibid., pp. 58–59; Robert Satloff, *From Abdallah to Hussein: Jordan in Transition* (New York: Oxford University Press, 1994), pp. 166–168.

26. Dann, *King Hussein,* p. 3; Uriel Dann, "Regime and Opposition in Jordan Since 1949," in Menahem Milson (ed.), *Society and Political Structure in the Arab World* (New York: Humanities Press, 1973), p. 146; Satloff, *From Abdallah to Hussein,* p. 170.

27. Dann, *King Hussein,* p. 67.

28. Ibid., p. 165.

29. Ibid., p. 169.

30. Fathi, *Jordan,* p. 125.

31. Ibid., p. 124.

32. See Dann, *King Hussein,* p. 4; Satloff, *From Abdallah to Hussein,* p. 7.

33. Asher Susser, *On Both Banks of the Jordan: A Political Biography of Wasfi al-Tall* (London: Frank Cass, 1994), pp. 176–177.

34. Ibid., p. 175.

35. Kirkbride, *From the Wings,* p. 140.

36. Satloff, *From Abdallah to Hussein,* pp. 15–16; Kirkbride, *From the Wings,* pp. 141–142.

37. Satloff, *From Abdallah to Hussein,* pp. 13–72.

38. Dann, "Regime and Opposition," p. 157.

39. Satloff, *From Abdallah to Hussein,* p. 168.

40. Layne, *Home and Homeland,* p. 104.

41. Ibid., p. 105.

42. Samir Mutawi, *Jordan in the 1967 War* (Cambridge: Cambridge University Press, 1987), p. 16.

43. Fathi, *Jordan,* p. 221.

44. Yezid Sayigh, "Jordan in the 1980s: Legitimacy, Entity, and Identity," in Rodney Wilson (ed.), *Politics and the Economy in Jordan* (London: Routledge, 1991), p. 173.

45. Brand, "'In the Beginning,'" p. 159.

46. Ibid.

47. Ibid.

48. Susser, *On Both Banks,* pp. 136–138.

49. Ibid., p. 141.

50. Samir al-Khalil (pseud.), *Republic of Fear: The Inside Story of Saddam's Iraq* (New York: Pantheon Books, 1989).

51. Mutawi, *Jordan in the 1967 War,* p. 3.

52. Layne, *Home and Homeland,* pp. 146–153.

53. Asher Susser, "Jordan," in Ami Ayalon (ed.), *Middle East Contemporary Survey (MECS),* Vol. 16, 1992 (Boulder: Westview Press, 1995), pp. 535–537.

54. Layne, *Home and Homeland,* pp. 143–144.

55. Anthony Nutting, former British minister of state for foreign affairs, quoted in Dann, *King Hussein,* frontispiece.

56. Fouad Ajami, "The End of Pan-Arabism," *Foreign Affairs,* 57 (1978/79), pp. 355–373.

57. Susser, "Jordan," *MECS*, Vol. 16, 1992, p. 537.

58. Susser, "Jordan," *MECS*, Vol. 18, 1994, p. 432.

59. Malcolm Kerr, *The Arab Cold War: Gamal 'Abd al-Nasir and His Rivals, 1958–1970* (Oxford University Press, 1971).

60. Susser, "Jordan," *MECS*, Vol. 15, 1991, pp. 500–501; Vol. 17, 1993, pp. 451–452.

61. Susser, "Jordan," *MECS*, Vol. 17, 1993, p. 464.

62. Susser, "Jordan," *MECS*, Vol. 16, 1992, p. 544.

63. Susser, "Jordan," *MECS*, Vol. 17, 1993, p. 458.

64. Susser, "Jordan," *MECS*, Vol. 18, 1994, p. 438.

65. Tariq al-Tall, "Al-ustura wasu' al-fahm fi al-alaqat al-Urdunniyya-al-Filas-tiniyya," *Al-Siyasa al-Filastiniyya* 3 (1996), pp. 152–165.

66. Brand, "'In the Beginning,'" p. 160.

8

The Moroccan Monarchy: A Political System in Quest of a New Equilibrium

Remy Leveau

Since Hasan II came to power in Morocco in 1961 and until his death in 1999, the country fared comparatively well relative to its neighbors. Relations between the monarchy, the government, and the subjects of Morocco are still quite stable. But this stability is in large part due to the remarkable personal skills of Hasan II, and it would not be prudent to conclude from Morocco's current equilibrium that the Moroccan system of government can survive in the long term unless it undergoes significant reform.

Authoritarian pluralism as managed by the monarchy may have suited Morocco when the country was largely rural, as far as its economy and society were concerned, at the beginning of the 1960s.[1] Due to demographic evolution, urbanization, and integration with the outside world and the relative progress of mass education, it had become, toward the end of the 1990s, a universe of middle-class groups and large cities that have not turned into unmanageable metropolises. Integrated into regions with strong local identities, Morocco's medium-sized cities are still linked with the surrounding rural areas. The coastal axis from Kenitra to Al-Jadida has dominated the Moroccan economy, with more than 60 percent of the investments and other advantages, since the days of the protectorate, but it does not play an overburdening role for the whole of Moroccan society.

For a long time opposition to Algeria, which began almost the day after Morocco's independence and manifested itself in the dispute over the Western Sahara,[2] has constituted the major political focus that helped unify the monarchy and the people, through their common struggle against domination by a neighbor country, made wealthy by oil revenue and endowed with a political model that was presented as exemplary. Notwithstanding isolated incidents of political unrest (the most violent being the military coups of 1971 and 1972),

Morocco has experienced an original political system, which, in fact, is quite modern in its functioning. Monarchy has offered Morocco a set of political practices—adjusted in turn by Mohammad V and Hasan II—that meet the needs of a modern state and allow for the effective concentration and application of power.[3]

In a similar way, the Moroccan economy is the result of an arrangement controlled by the political forces that dominate Moroccan society while allowing more autonomy than in neighboring countries. Because of the absence of oil revenues, the government has not been allowed to establish itself as the distributor of national resources, taking charge of the basic needs of the population in exchange for submission. Indeed, the method of subsidizing indispensable products (such as flour, sugar, tea, oil, and butane) was used in the 1970s but to a lesser extent than in Egypt and Algeria. These subsidies constituted 3 billion dirhams of the 1996–1997 budget. More accessible to the outside world, the Moroccan monarchy has been capable of finding various resources, including foreign aid and revaluation of debts.[4] But it was obliged, far earlier than its neighbors were, to submit itself to the strictness of a structural adjustment program as early as the mid-1980s. The country could not continue the war over the Western Sahara without reducing costs elsewhere. Budget reductions indeed resulted in various violent incidents that shook the country in 1981, 1984, and 1990. On each occasion, the state was able to preserve its monopoly on the legitimate use of violence without resorting to extreme repression.

Nevertheless, a strong feeling of *hiba* (fear) has come to characterize the relationship between the people of Morocco and their king. For a long time, the people were unprotected against arbitrary heavy-handed measures, and any opposition to the state was viewed as treason. Gradually, the government has come to accept that allegiance to the state can entail moderate expressions of opposition to official policy. In addition, the increasing interaction between Morocco and the outside world and the appearance of political moderates, who oppose the regime but do not threaten it by calling for radical change, will help encourage respect for human rights and democracy in Morocco.[5]

THE FUNCTIONING OF MONARCHY

Within the functioning of Moroccan body politics, qualitative change is considerable even under the appearance of stagnation. In many respects, a comparison with Spain under Franco might be useful, though with some nuances. Indeed, the Moroccan monarchy is not the by-product of a civil war, yet for a long time it brutally disregarded the political parties representing the urban middle class. Right after independence, reliance upon a rural middle class, which seemed frightened by the disorder that urban intellectuals had

promised, was the regime's strategy. The monarchy has implemented a conservative modernization while recuperating the programs and the individual
competencies of its opponents. By opening itself to the outside world, it has
found resources that have made economic growth easier, at a lower cost, but
that have gradually limited the possibility of imposing absolute authoritarianism. At the end of the 1970s, the opening-up was aimed primarily at balancing Algerian pressures in the context of the rivalry over the Western Sahara,
but it also aimed at finding a compromise with the business world in order to
readjust the balance of payments. Morocco's increased accessibility to international markets and social trends is now irreversible and has had a profound
effect on large segments of society. Significant emigration of Moroccans to
Europe has further tied the country to the outside world. Tensions within the
society persist today and, often, are probably due to the Islamist currents that
exist in Morocco (as they do in most Arab-Muslim countries). Monarchy in
itself does not represent immunity to these tendencies, yet one may think that
a monarchy would be more capable of countering their influence than would
other governmental forms.[6]

Before reexamining in detail the functioning of the Moroccan monarchy,
it is necessary to underline the presence of the king in other areas, as an entrepreneur and as the producer of models and symbols. At this point, it will be
difficult for the new king to modify substantially his way of functioning and
behaving. At the most, he will be able to establish a political alternation, the
principles of which have been set since the end of the 1980s.

Moroccan monarchy, in its current form, is a historical-political construction, intended to persuade people to believe in the perenniality of its
structures. Through their faith in the institution of monarchy, the people grant
the monarch legitimacy in the eyes of both his partners and his opponents.
The symbolic power of the monarch as the commander of the faithful can be
very effectively converted into real power.[7] By following this path, the
monarchy has influenced the state's modernization and ensured the preservation of a strong national identity and the keeping of a unitarian framework.
Today, it has to accomplish another transformation, by drawing again on a
strong symbolic role, to entrust real power in autonomous, democratically
elected institutions in charge of the arbitration of conflicts and of the distribution of resources within society. Because of the very natures of the power
structure and of Hasan II's personality, such transformation of succession effectively evolved upon his death.

In that respect, the comparison with Spain under Franco remains valid.
One cannot expect the sovereign to be at the same time both Franco and Juan
Carlos. But, like the Caudillo, he will have presided over Moroccan society's
deep change, helping the birth of a new middle class not dependent exclusively upon the state and, through the development of a stratum of entrepreneurs, more developed than that of most Arab countries,[8] especially those

marked by single-party structures. The logical outcome of such an evolution would be a transformation of the political system to guarantee these new social groups control over the decisions that concern their personal security or the establishment of the rules and laws under which they will conduct their own affairs.

The efforts to fight corruption—taking place in Morocco since the last three months of 1995—have the advantage of illustrating the system's contradictions and showing the monarchy in search of populist support, mobilizing for its own benefit the theme of the fight against the "big ones" and against drug dealers and smugglers. This effort uses the resources that the monarchy controls directly, allowing the sovereign to adjust initiatives on the political level by finding an issue for negotiation with representatives of various parties. In themselves, these attempts have not always resulted in agreements satisfactory to the king. In fact, it requires an alternative process, which would have relieved the monarchy of part of its responsibilities in the management of the unpopular structural adjustment but would have thereby led it to lose its capacity to control society. Demonstrating that arbitrary power enabled the king to fight efficiently against the "big ones." By showing that nobody was protected against inquiries into one's own illegal though long-tolerated wealth, he could recover the initiative without having to accept his partners' conditions. Thus, he could put a group with emancipation ambitions back in its place. He set a limit to the perverse effects of corrupt practices upon normal economic functioning, which endangered, because of these practices' importance and duration, the structural adjustment process or Morocco's entry into a customs union with Europe. Criticism from abroad also motivated, in part, the cleaning-up campaign, and so did the will to allay the opposition, which had launched a campaign parading the slogan of the moralization of public life. From that angle, it was useful to undertake the cleaning-up initiative before experimenting with an alternation of the political system.

The king's speech on 3 March 1996 supports this conclusion. By announcing his satisfaction with the "clean hands" operation—the Moroccan way—he gave remarkable support to its main proponent, Driss Basri. Nevertheless, the question regarding the Ministry of the Interior's place in relation to the functioning of Moroccan institutions constitutes Morocco's main political problem today; it is far more important than any constitutional reform. That problem has existed since independence inasmuch as Mohammad V had always wanted, already at the time when the Istiqlal and the Union Socialistes des Forces Populaires (USFP) parties held the prime minister's office (under Balfrej's and Abdallah Ibrahim's governments), to control both the ministry and the institution of national security through two personalities faithful to the king (Driss M'hammadi and Mohammad Laghzaoui). The king had also kept direct control over the appointment of the authority of agents whose records were supervised by the royal cabinet. When the monarchy recovered direct control over public affairs, starting in May 1960, again it was a faithful person, Si Bekkai, who was placed in charge of the Ministry of the Interior. After Mohammad V's death, the head of the royal cabinet, Ahmad Rida Guedira, took over that office and was given the responsibility to organize a constitutional referendum (held in December 1962) as well as parliamentary and local elections.[9]

These arrangements provided the new sovereign with a direct source of popular legitimacy, relying especially on the votes of rural Moroccans, unlike the modern nationalist parties that found their support within the urban middle class, and vis-à-vis the newly independent Algeria that presented itself as a model for the whole of Maghrib. Since then the political parties have been suspicious of the monarchy, an institution they believe is curtailing their role while maintaining a charade of limited democracy. Paradoxically, it was during that period when the monarchic control was growing tougher—leading to the dismissal of parliament in 1965—and when the Ministry of the Interior was in the hands of General Muhammad Oufkir, a minister who accentuated its autonomy and eventually plotted a conspiracy against the king. Hasan II did not again make the error of concentrating in the same hands police powers as well as control over the military. Driss Basri's rise rested upon the role that he played, starting in 1980, in the repression of urban riots and in the preventive elimination of General Ahmad Dlimi, who had been involved in a conspiracy against the king. After this episode, King Hasan closely supervised his officers by means of the gendarmerie forces and through military surveillance of both the police and the Ministry of the Interior. During the 1980s he also extended his influence to foreign affairs by leading the fight against the Polisario and its international support networks set up by Algeria. Similarly, control over the Moroccan communities in Europe lies with the Moroccan consular network, in which agents dispatched by the Ministry of the Interior set the mode.

The interior minister oversees all police activity—which in Morocco ranges from legal practices to less palatable tactics such as disappearances and torture—but his authority extends policing. He has proven an efficient manager and an apt administrator, causing opposition parties to be reluctant to share power with him for fear they might be cheated or undermined from inside. Until now, this network has been functioning exclusively for the sovereign's benefit. However, one cannot deny the reluctance the interior minister must feel when the king is searching for other relays. In January 1995, King Hasan chose to keep Basri in his office rather than establish an alternative that would have been founded upon his removal from power. Furthermore, the royal cabinet's official statement, announcing the establishment of a technocratic government under the leadership of Minister of Foreign Affairs Abd al-latif Filali, established the link between extending the interior minister in his post and the defense of the "sacred institutions" of the country—the monarchy.

Considering this, could one assume that the interior minister is in the position of being the protector of the monarchy in the event of an unexpected succession crisis? Indeed, prospects for the king's succession are rather ambiguous. Morocco's original constitution, enacted in 1962, was designed to ensure that succession would always be by the sovereign's eldest male descendant. Shortly after the military conspiracies against the king came to light, the constitution was altered to allow the *ulama* to select a successor from among the "princes of the blood," allowing them to exclude the previous king's eldest son under certain circumstances. If Muhammad VI decides accordingly, the best means he has to guarantee that his wish will be executed is to somehow institutionalize the interior minister as the custodian of his will. It is highly probable that other powerful actors in the political system, especially the military, might attempt to "enlighten" the *ulama*'s choice, if only to escape the control of a minister whom they find particularly heavy-handed. But a solution that would base succession upon putting aside the king's eldest son with Basri's support network would also risk leading the country into a civil war of uncertain duration.

In contrast, in a period of political transition, the king accepts the neutralization of one of his key ministers, if the control of public affairs were given to a prime minister from the opposition. The king's 1996 speech focused on invoking constitutional changes, such as a referendum and elections. The legislative assembly would consist only of members elected by way of universal suffrage and would have its role completed by a senatelike second assembly, representing the regions and the most important socioeconomic groups. This reconfiguring of the legislative bodies to which King Hasan has referred during the 1990s, through his evocation of the German Laender's model, requires the help of an expert in German politics. The evolution of the political system, which would profoundly alter the functioning of the Moroccan state, could be justified by the need to offer a new framework of integration to the Western Sahara if a reconciliation is going to take place quickly. Similarly, Morocco could approach the Western Saharan issue by applying a model of varying levels of regional autonomy, such as in Spain and Italy. This could be especially useful in the integration of the Rif, if Morocco bows to pressure from the European Union to intensify antidrug enforcement efforts.

Power-Sharing

The debate over constitutional change must not obscure the fact that Morocco's most important institutional problems are not really constitutional; rather, they concern the interactions and power-sharing between the monarchy and Morocco's political parties. The latter have the power to do little more than refuse to serve as a rubber stamp for the king's policies. Even opposition leaders are obligated to kiss the hand of the king upon being presented to him, an expression of allegiance that has handicapped Moroccan politics. As a result, no party openly questions the monarch's central symbolic role or even his special privileges in foreign relations and defense. Indeed, Hasan II's wisdom, experience, and skill in managing Moroccan foreign relations made him an appropriate leader. His cautiousness and, since the plots against him in the early 1970s, his suspicion of his generals served to reassure those who, like the king, feared the entry of the military into the political arena. King Muhammad VI has a major example to follow. The military remains a potential actor outside of the political system. It is expected, in the normal course of events, to ensure the country's defense from Algeria. But when the Western Saharan conflict is settled,[10] its role ought to diminish. The army could then start changing, as far as the number of troops and missions are concerned, but such change would be painful to the old generations. Moreover, the military is still the last resort in the case of urban riots and regional separatism. Thus, it is rather unlikely that the structural adjustment measures will concern the army any more than the various "clean hands" operations: the fight against corruption and drugs would probably not exceed the occasional dismissal of an embarrassing military man.

If the military still constitutes a group that might potentially place itself outside the system, the Islamist movements might become allies; indeed their apparent absence in the Moroccan scene is intriguing. It is advisable to distrust a purely mechanist or essentialist reasoning for that very reason. It would be unwise to conclude that because the king is referred to as "commander of the faithful" that the country is somehow immunized from the Islamist contagion. Doing so neglects the fact that the Moroccan monarchy is an evolving political construction, drawing more efforts made by the nationalist movement in fighting the French rule over the protectorate than to the institutions of a modern state inherited from that period. The construction of the monarch's image as the religious symbol of national unity is largely due to the Istiqlal Party of the 1930s, when the Rif's rebellion in 1925 presented itself, under Abd al-karim's leadership, as a republic hostile to Spanish and French colonizers as well as to the Alawite dynasty.[11] The nationalist movement that started in 1934, however, chose the contrary, that is, to free the monarch from the colonizer's grasp by emphasizing the religious dimension of the monarchic institution. Morocco's leaders, especially the Western-educated intellectuals, assumed that the monarchy's role, once independence was obtained, could be restricted to a symbolic dimension. The advocates of this approach, however, underestimated the popular effect of restoring the sovereign's image. Mohammad V's first aim after independence was to master internal and international difficulties by assuming real power, ensuring the formal dismissal of the French general-resident and establishing cooperation with the Istiqlal.[12] Thus, the ruler was granted powers that he only partly delegated to the government, keeping for himself effective control over the army and the security services, as well as decisive influence over the functioning of the Ministries of the Interior and Justice. He could therefore easily recover direct control over governmental authority in May 1960, after the national movements efforts in this direction had worn out.

Subsequently, Hasan II legitimized his seizure of power by holding a popular referendum to ratify the constitution of December 1962. Hasan's rule was further legitimized in response to the emergence of the Algerian threat. In the wake of the direct conflict between the two countries, the king restored the national pact focusing on defense, independence, and Moroccan unity. He also reinvigorated the social and economic modernizations promoted by the Moroccan elite. Without abundant oil rent, Morocco did not dream to develop heavy industry but exercised a policy of import substitution (goods such as sugar, tires, cars, textiles, and petroleum products) as well as agricultural modernization (improved irrigation practices and the use of fertilizers). The monarchy derived a certain level of legitimacy from these programs, yet they did not adequately meet the needs of the Moroccan society at large. These changes helped to develop a new urban middle class, which was less willing to accept the monarchy's absolute authority, a development that has been accompanied by corruption and clientelism. One can interpret the futile military coups of 1971 and 1972 as attempts to seize power by members of the new middle class with rural origins, much like the Free Officers in Egypt. Those abortive efforts to topple the monarchy prompted the king to reinforce the religious underpinnings of his rule, to crack down on opposition groups, and to resume negotiations with the nationalist parties in an attempt to reach a minimal consensus.

This approach led to a new political pact with the opposition, the abolition of the state of emergency, the release of political prisoners, and the organization of national and local elections, which took place during 1976–1977. Political parties in favor of the monarchy won, but a substantial portion of the national and local representation fell into the hands of the opposition. This pact also aimed to cope with the latent threat of the military and the perceived rise of the Islamist movements that challenged both the monarchy and the parties. Pluralism then appeared as a means to fight those two threats by allowing a growing functional role for the Istiqlal, the USFP, and the trade-union movement, associated with the downtrodden. Istiqlal's religious inheritance is still present today, a reference point and legitimation of the effort to establish a Salafi model combining Islam with modernity. For that matter, Allal al-Fassi is a far more significant author than is Malik Bennabi, who is used as a reference by the Algerian Islamists.

However, if the monarchy has not been able to prevent the emergence of a rival Islamism, it has not allowed it to organize as a religious party, following the Algerian Front Islamique (FIS) model. Through the Ministry of Religious Affairs, the Habous administration has retained supervision of Morocco's religious foundations, and through the Ministry of the Interior the government has been able to control and infiltrate Islamist groups. The government encourages *ulama* associations representing official Islam so as to leave Islamists be—as long as they don't practice or advocate violence. The merger that took place, with the government's approval, between Reform and Renewal (Reforme et Renouveau; under Abdallah Benkirane's leadership) and the Popular Constitutional Democratic Movement (Mouvement Populair Constitutionnel Democratique; under the leadership of Abd al-karim Khatib, a former minister and leader of the Moroccan Liberation Army), as well as the election of nine moderate Islamists to the parliament in November 1997, reflect this trend. Similarly, the relationship between the government and the Moroccan Islamic movement's oldest leader, Shaikh Abdallah Yasin, may have evolved into one of mutual acceptance that can, to a certain extent, resemble the relationships between the monarchy and the parties. But the threat today emanates, perhaps, from some groups of new intellectuals, originally close to official Islam.

On the occasions of the Gulf War and the Madrid conference, the new intellectuals have been able to condemn the Moroccan government's choices for not being consistent with Islam. Their approach is comparable to that of al-Azhar's *ulamas,* who, in recent affairs, have condemned Faraj Fawda or divorced from Abu Zayd because of their supposed lack of respect for Islam. In light of those initiatives the Moroccan leadership became inclined to react sharply to such challenges. It will probably try, at the same time, to find a means to avoid radicalization of the opposition in order to prevent it from going underground and use, with some leaders who support these trends, recovery tactics similar to those that have worked with the opposition parties and the trade unions. It seems particularly important to make them cooperate with the Makhzin, preempting a possible political-doctrinal fight about the legitimacy of the succession. At the beginning of the twenty-first century, the uncertainties surrounding Mula'i Hasan I's succession have lasted some five-plus years. That period has witnessed the prince's struggle to gain the support of any religious and foreign powers.

During the 1972 constitutional revision, the abolition of the reference to the right of primogeniture, which had been inscribed in the 1962 constitution, seems to have been a concession made to the *ulama* who found the provision contrary to Islamic rules as well as Moroccan tradition. It seems that the change took place just after the 1971–1972 military coups, when the government urgently attempted to gain legitimacy by both reinvigorating official Islam and resuming the dialogue with opposition parties. It was also agreed that the late king's choice for succession would have to be confirmed by the religious leaders who have, according to tradition, the power to depose the ruler. Those uncertainties suited Hasan II yet will marginalize the modern and rational side of the Moroccan political system and reinforce the roles of religious actors. It is probable that the *ulama* will not be the only ones to express their choice. Islamist nonestablished currents and religious groups will be able to function in competition with great mosques' Islam of the establishment. The participation of civil society, parties, trade unions, and associations will then be marginalized. In contrast, actors outside the system possessing the means to exert pressure and influence—such as the army, the Interior, the entrepreneurs from Suss and Fez who dominate the coastal border's economic activities, and the drug dealers and smugglers who escaped the cleaning-up—may be tempted to intervene. King Muhammad VI will have to cope with such challenges.

Unsuccessful pretenders to the throne may form a network of opposition that will have to be appeased or destroyed for the new monarch to survive. A new monarch will seek to legitimize his power via referendum or elections, but the succession procedure may be destructive if it gives rise to a conflict over the justification—religious or otherwise—for the monarchy. Ironically, the very methods used to justify monarchy—referenda and elections—may introduce doubt into the minds of Moroccans concerning the institution that those methods are designed to bolster. Despite the imperfect nature of Morocco's democracy, Moroccans, having been exposed to democracy and monarchy simultaneously, are beginning to question whether they are subjects or citizens. The growing Moroccan urban middle class, despite internal divisions, and the educated youth have reached a consensus that Morocco should move toward pluralism, democratic debate, and respect for human rights. This has been the price of the monarchy's effort to legitimize itself.

Any questioning of this pact might again lead part of the opposition to seek abolition of the monarchy. It is more likely, however, that in time of crisis it will accelerate the move toward a parliamentary monarchy. The components of the problem have existed since 1962, and they resurfaced again in 1992, when Hasan II announced his plan for a constitutional revision, a plan rejected by the opposition. The first Moroccan constitution had been based on the 1958 French constitution. Maurice Duverger used to characterize the original as an "Orleanist" type of text, the prime minister being responsible both to the head of state, who appoints him (and may dismiss him), and to the assembly that approves him by a vote of confidence. That model suited the Moroccan monarchy perfectly, for it found in it such devices (besides the ordinary means of control over government) as the state of emergency (which it used in 1965 to dismiss parliament) and the royal decree. The most important aspect of the parliament's power in the Moroccan system was its responsibility to enact a budget and the right of deputies to question ministers.

Furthermore, the parliament offered legitimate social standing, revenue, and visibility to opposition leaders. The king did not neglect to consult them, give them rewarding missions, offer them presents, or grant them favors that indicated that they belonged to his circle, to the Makhzin, and to court society. By yielding to one of the last requests made by the opposition, which called for the election of all the members of the assembly by way of universal suffrage, the king overcame a formal obstacle to the monarchy's acceptance in society. Nevertheless, he still retained the means to balance the power of the first assembly through a second chamber representing the regions and professions.

The elections of November 1997 allowed the king to appoint Prime Minister Abderdiamane Yousoufi, leader of the Moroccan Socialist Party, which obtained the best electoral results but without an absolute majority. He had to form a coalition with the Istiqlal Party and to keep Driss Basri as interior minister; some other departments (Foreign Affairs, Justice) were given to ministers directly subordinated to the palace. The implementation of this policy may establish a political pattern resembling the cohabitation, under the Fifth Republic in France, between a president and a prime minister, and would coalesce from opposite ends of the political spectrum. Even though that situation ought to have happened with the last elections, it does not mean that Morocco is witnessing a decrease in the conservative majority and a rise in monarchist opposition.

Hasan II stated several times his desire to see the socialist opposition share responsibility for economic and social measures that must be taken in order to boost a policy of structural adjustment and full economic integration with the European Union. Despite the consensus that exists within the opposition concerning such policies, one must not forget that it goes with a high abstention rate (37 percent), together with blank ballots and invalid votes (15 percent). Assuming that the government will function according to the French cohabitation model, the king will lack neither the means nor the resources to make foreign and defense policies. The government will be ready to use its credit in the country's economic and financial relations with Europe, the United States, and international financial bodies. The new constitution also maintains, for the monarch's benefit, provisions allowing intervention by the king that could always be justified by external threats and Islamist pressures.

These changes carry a political price. They imply that the monarchy will relinquish at least a part of the control over Morocco's political system held by the Ministry of the Interior. For a long period, Moroccan politics was dominated by a fear of the security services. Although the Moroccan government became significantly less repressive during the 1990s, it has maintained the threat of repression to help guarantee the stability of the regime. Further complicating the liberalization of Moroccan society is the potential for "backlash violence," whereby the long-repressed would express anger toward their former repressor. Perhaps Morocco will follow the example set in Latin America, where backlash meant enactment of sweeping amnesty legislation.

One of the predictable effects of change will concern the clear separation and clarification of the economic and financial relations between the monarchy and the state. The shadowy areas are very important, and the resources and privileges of the palace greatly exceed those of ordinary constitutional monarchies. It is not so much the place of the royal family "holding," or the fact that the monarch is the country's largest landowner, that will create a problem; rather it is his intervention in major state contracts and his control over public corporations that ought to be clarified. The surrender of a certain margin of political and financial power and the clarification of succession procedures are part of a reconciliation of the monarchy with a codified political field that the monarchy has successfully avoided since 1960 by cultivating religious legitimization for its power. If Muhammad VI merely goes on governing as Hasan II skillfully did, changes in the system may gradually evolve. In the meantime, the political show goes on. The new king knows how to keep the initiative—and how to flatter his audience—by letting his faithful executants play the role of honest arbiters.

By accepting a framework drawn up by the monarchy, the opposition shows its submission to royal power and to transferring certain prerogatives from the parliament and giving government some of the king's privileges. In compromising with the leaders of the Kutla Party to form a government, Hasan II had to accept some constraints. However, one notices that in the dialogue between the king and the Kutla Party unconditional allegiance allowed for a major change in behavior. This is expressed by a greater firmness concerning fundamental choices, with eagerness to see the king consider changes, but without a power struggle.

CONCLUSION

In sum, Moroccan society appears to be under tight constraints due to an extremely quick change. This engenders both irreversible modernization pressures as well as obstacles. The latter are felt especially in the institutions. They center around the passage from a monarch's omnipresent real power, both feared and desired, to a symbolic role, as the management of public affairs would be transferred to a prime minister responsible to the parliament. Urbanization and gradual industrialization have already engendered changes in Moroccan society far deeper than those brought by colonization in the first half of the twentieth century. Customs have been upset, and young people seem freed from the previous cultural framework (without, however, breaking totally from the previous generation and from the image of the sovereign-father).[13] But the explosion of individual freedom is such that any arrangement, even among the Islamists, ought to be considered temporary if new forms of collective expression are not recognized.

The same goes for women's emancipation, the most important aspects of which are education and participation in the workforce. Collective social action merely reflects the new reality that also influences marriage, family life, number of children, and other social choices.

A deep feeling of vitality exists within Moroccan society. The press, opinion polls, and intellectual debates give more evidence to that vitality than do opposition parties and trade unions, which are too strained, even internally, by a long, conflictual coexistence with the monarchy.

The tradition of monarchy is heavy for the new generation to assume, but it also grants the country a strong identity during a time of transition within an unstable region. One may assume that the Moroccan monarchy, poorly qualified to take upon itself negotiated gradual change, is preparing the conditions for a gradual mutation now affected by the accession to power of King Muhammad VI. However, uncertainties still remain, and Hasan II did not quite clarify the situation. But, like Franco, he established a whole set of mainly external constraints that will bring Morocco closer to Europe. By using economic devices, he influenced society and, ultimately, created the conditions for a controlled change that may happen without him and will contradict the method of government that characterized his reign.

NOTES

1. Remy Leveau, *Le fellah marocain defenseur du trone* (Paris: Presses de la FNSP, 1985).

2. Khadija Mohsen-Finan, *Sahara occidental. Les enjeux d'un conflit regional* (Paris: CNRS, 1997).

3. John Waterbury, *The Commander of the Faithful: The Moroccan Political Elite* (London: Weidenfeld and Nicholson, 1970); William I. Zartman, *Destiny of a Dynasty: The Search for Institutions in Morocco's Developing Society* (Columbia: University of Developing Society, University of South Carolina Press, 1964).

4. Remy Leveau, "Stabilite du pouvoir monarchique et financement de la dette," *Maghreb-Machrek* (1987).

5. Remy Leveau, "Le pouvoir marocain entre la repression et le dialogue," *Le Monde Diplomatique*, October 1993.

6. Remy Leveau, "Reussir la transition democratique au Maroc," *Le Monde Diplomatique*, October 1993.

7. Waterbury, *Commander of the Faithful.*

8. Said Tangeaoui, *Les entrepreneurs marocains. Pouvoirs, societe et modernite* (Paris: Karthala, 1994).

9. Leveau, "Le Fellah marocain defenseur du trone."

10. In December 1997 an agreement signed in Houston under the auspices of James Baker, former U.S. secretary of state, acting in the framework of a UN mission,

decided a referendum on the future of the territory to be held in December 1998. It was postponed until December 1999 for giving more delay in the establishment of the electoral lists.

11. Abdallah Hammoudi, *Master and Disciple: The Cultural Foundations of Moroccan Authoritarianism* (Chicago: Chicago University Press, 1997).

12. Zartman, *Destiny of a Dynasty*.

13. Monnia Bennani-Chraibi, *Soumis et rebelles. Les jeunes au Maroc* (Paris: CNRS, 1994).

9

State-Formation and the Saudi Monarchy

Joseph Kostiner & Joshua Teitelbaum

The institution of the monarchy in the kingdom of Saudi Arabia has tradition-ally been regarded as fundamentally congruent with the kingdom's basic so-ciocultural characteristics, a factor that has accounted for the institution's durability and popular support. The Saudi royal family, which heads the monarchy, is integrally linked with it and structured to befit the tribal forma-tions that underpin Saudi society.

The royal family was formed through political marriages of the al-Saud clan with the leading families of the major tribal groups, urban centers, busi-ness community, and religious sages, forming, in fact, a biological, intermar-ried elite of many of the leading Saudi Arabian families. Loyal but less prominent families and tribal groups are accommodated through financial transfers and by serving as officers in the Saudi internal militia, the Saudi Arabian National Guard (SANG).

The royal family itself thus became subdivided into kinship groups echo-ing some of the tribal formations of society. In so doing, the Saudi leaders ac-commodated themselves to the prevailing principles of tribal loyalty and identity, a stratagem that allowed them to prevail.

The Saudi monarchy also evolved in congruence with the Wahhabi reli-gious tenets of most of society. The Saudi king has also been the leader, the imam of the Saudi-Wahhabi community of believers and subordinate only to the Holy Law, the *shari'a*. Moreover, the Saudi royal family was careful to honor and cultivate the *ulama* (senior sages) and maintain their position as in-terpreters of the *shari'a*, sometimes turning them into policy advisers and partners in marriage.[1] The public norms of proper Wahhabi conduct were ac-cepted as the formal code of behavior of Saudi Arabian society, and the royal family saw to the enforcement of this code by a special "morals police," known as the Committee for the Encouraging of Virtue and the Prevention of Vice (*hay'at al-amr bil-ma'ruf wal-nahi an al-munkar*).

The Saudi monarchy has also evolved in congruence with the modernization process. The royal family initiated the oil industry and the utilization of oil income to advance the country technologically and develop infrastructure, health, and education services, as well as business and welfare. Members of the royal family were among the first Saudi Arabian students at Western universities, obtaining skills that enabled them to staff top bureaucratic and business positions. They have become closely associated with turning Saudi Arabian society into a wealthy and technologically advanced community.[2]

This congruence with the sociocultural underpinnings of Saudi Arabian society does not inform us, in itself, as to the dynamics through which the royal leaders adapt themselves to these political and sociocultural changes. In order to explain them, it is necessary to focus on the dynamics of state-building in Saudi Arabia.

STATE-BUILDING

The evolution of the Saudi monarchical institution is inextricably linked with the kingdom's state-building process. It was formed and shaped according to the formation of the Saudi state. The state-building approach emerges from the assumption that a state is a flexible social institution that changes over time. It may acquire, develop, or lose state attributes, or "stateness." A state's main underpinnings—borders, central government, and sociopolitical cohesion—may change, strengthen, or attenuate.[3] The process of state-building unfolds in stages: every several decades a new type of state order, or social contract, emerges, focusing on new conceptions of those underpinnings aimed at tackling the challenges of a certain period. New challenges spur a new state-building order. The Saudi state has a particularly convoluted history of state-building, as it turned from a nascent, tribal chieftaincy, to a more organized, monarchical state, and finally into a wealthy, bureaucratized state. The history of Saudi Arabia, is, in fact, a sequence of state-building—or -rebuilding—stages.

Viewed through the prism of state-building, the Saudi monarchy can be divided into three main functions, each harboring a specific complex of problems. First, the monarchy functions as a ruling institution. The leading members of the royal family assumed the positions of main government ministers, top administrators, and regional governors. As such it developed as a patriarchal elite—the *umara* (sing. *emir*, or "senior princes")—linked with the lower ranks of society through bureaucratic and personal contacts as benefactors and arbiters. This took place via the *majlis* (open meetings), whereby an emir meets with his "constituency." *Umara* have become the apex of patron-client networks, providing jobs and other benefits to constituencies. However, the Saudi rulers also developed their ruling position as a separate elite group that, despite its members' connection with commoners, kept a corporate structure, distinct interests, and a superior economic position in Saudi Arabian society. Hence, the monarchy was characterized by a basic dilemma. The need to maintain a balance between Saudi rulers as a leading, self-perpetuating elite group and as patriarchal shaikhs providing for their constituencies was evident, but could it be maintained? How could the leading princes sustain supreme, elitist positions while keeping their grip on society via bureaucratic and clientelist contacts? Under what circumstances was Saudi society ready to accept such arrangements, and how did those arrangements evolve?

The Saudi monarchy's second function was as the royal family. Taking their cue from tribal practices, the al-Sauds intermarried with other notable families, thereby swelling their ranks; the family now numbers in the thousands. As the family drew on its members as a reservoir for filling government positions, problems often developed when members were called upon to act as a unified body in support of the government and their royal prerogatives, yet they found themselves divided according to groups and factions, and by generation. During the last several decades, at least several such factions, emerging from intermarriages, were active: the Al al-Shaikh, named after the founder of the Wahhabi *da'wa*, or "doctrine," Muhammad bin Abd al-Wahhab; the Jilawi; the Thanayan; and the Sudayri. More recently, sons of founder and patriarch Abd al-Aziz al-Saud have given their names to form new sub-branches, such as the al-Faysal and the al-Fahd. The last two decades have witnessed the supremacy of the Sudayri clan, led by King Fahd and his six full brothers, as seen in their assumption of the leading positions in the kingdom. A member of one faction obtaining a powerful position was often the reason for a fierce rivalry to prevent the concentration of too much power by one group. There were also personal rivalries among candidates for the throne.[4] A second monarchical dilemma is therefore twofold: to maintain unity through a balance among the many royal branches with respect to power and position, particularly regarding the line of succession to the throne, which has traditionally run through the sons of Ibn Saud; and to provide candidates that would not only be from the right family branch but also suitable for the job.

A third function of monarchical rule has been its integration with the Wahhabi religious establishment and adoption of the Wahhabi principles. As imam the king is regarded as the leader of the Wahhabi community, which refers to the majority of the core of the Saudi Arabian population in Najd. The senior religious sages, notably the Al al-Shaikh and other renowned families, often intermarried with the al-Sauds. The Saudi royal leaders were able to establish mechanisms that gave them control over religion by integrating religious services and high-level personnel with the state institutions. The *shari'a* was recognized as the law of the state, and Wahhabi courts became state courts. The problems of this arrangement inhere in its exclusiveness. It was an arrangement contrived by leading elites of princes and senior *ulama* based on the principles of a formal, Wahhabi "high culture." As such, it excluded nonelites who interpreted Wahhabi principles differently: those nonelites, particularly younger, lower-ranking clerics and tribesmen, have occasionally disagreed with the way in which the Wahhabi *dawa* was being applied and have turned it into a vehicle of opposition against Saudi state Wahhabism, as represented by the state and personified by the royal family, in what has amounted to a struggle to control the discourse and tenets of Wahhabism.[5] A third monarchical dilemma thus concerns the ability of the monarchy to either maintain continuous control over the Wahhabi religious establishment and its version of state religion and overcome opposition movements that manifest an antistate—or at least anti–al-Saud—version of Wahhabism.

An examination of the institution of the Saudi monarchy, its different functions, and how it has been coping with the complexes of problems that have arisen is best facilitated through a discussion of the main phases of the kingdom's state-building. The first phase evolved during and after World War I. The Saudi state was then nascent, a chieftaincy based on ad hoc arrangements among settled and nomadic populations; it was lacking an elaborate central government (composed only of some members of the al-Sauds, leading tribal figures, and clergy), clearly defined borders, and basic socionational cohesion. The need to cope with new economic and strategic conditions that evolved during the war—mainly due to the collapse of the Ottoman Empire, the emergence of British dominance, and the creation of the Arab state system—forced the Saudi chiefdom to develop more elaborate state attributes to give the state increased durability.

The ruling groups adapted to these changes by becoming a monarchy. The ruler, Ibn Saud, assumed new qualities: he emerged as a leader in the expansion and the occupation of territory, an expert in foreign relations who secured British support for the state, and then as a unifier of the main Saudi provinces—Najd and the Hijaz—by representing and balancing their interests one against the other. In 1926, a state government was established in the Hijaz, and in 1932 a state budget was announced. A regional administration was also established. Yet all these innovative arrangements also attested to the maintenance of chieftaincy-based tribal practices: the tribal practice of balancing different populations was articulated in a new state structure—a monarchy. Lower-ranking population groups were bound in personal and family loyalties to particular princes, as the royal family emerged as a biological elite tying itself to the most important families in the kingdom.

Making the Wahhabi interpretation of Hanbali *fiqh* (religious codes) the state law was accomplished by the imposition of senior *ulama* as the arbiters of the *shari'a*, a move executed in a special *fatwa* after the subjugation of the

Ikhwan in 1930. These senior *ulama* were personally appointed by the king and some were intermarried with the royal family.[6]

Hence, the royal family functioned as a unifying elite in a postexpansionist era, an embryo government in a state with growing capacity, the imposer of Wahhabi law. All these functions were established on the basis of familiar tribal practices. The monarchy's institutions symbolized the making of the new Saudi state yet were responsible for maintaining acceptable and therefore familiar, time-honored Arabian traditions.

FAYSAL'S ORDER

Ibn Saud built an encapsulated monarchy that included a combination of modern institutions and tribal practices. Yet the state had difficulties in meeting the challenges of the post–World War II era, namely, radical Arab nationalism, utilization of oil revenues, and the need to satisfy a growing population with educational opportunities, health, and welfare. A new type of state was called for. In the 1950s and early 1960s three versions of state order vied for dominance: King Saud (r. 1953–1964) wanted to maintain the existing order, which had been evolving since the 1930s; his half-brother Prince Tallal led an attempt to establish a constitutional monarchy; and his half-brother Faysal (prime minister, 1958–1960, 1962, and 1964; king, 1964–1975) sought to introduce a reformed, technologically developed but conservative order. Faysal prevailed, and a new state order was established. This we call "Faysal's order."

Faysal's order was based on a balancing act among the competing forces in Saudi Arabian society. The most important principle of the order was maintaining the authority of the Saudi monarchy. Faysal objected strongly to the initiatives of the so-called Free Officers of the late 1950s and early 1960s, who called for limiting the absolute authority of the monarch via a Western-style constitution. Claiming adherence to the holy law and the Quran, he underlined the authority of the Saudi king as the imam of the Wahhabi Muslim community. The king was above any other political or proposed constitutional restraints and could be limited only by the *shari'a* as interpreted by the senior *ulama*.

Faysal further buttressed the monarchy with an unprecedentedly elaborate administrative and bureaucratic order, entrenching and founding twenty government ministries. The roles of professional ministries—in areas such as petroleum, public works, education, planning, justice, and commerce and industry—were key in extending the influence of the royal family and the monarchy into all spheres of public life throughout the realm. The establishment of the Ministry of Justice in 1970 locked the senior *ulama* in an official role. He accepted their right to staff it, and they in turn were integrated into the state bureaucracy. A burgeoning civil service, which grew from 62,000 to

336,000 between 1960 and 1980, turned the monarchy's government, operating by decree, into the unquestioned ruler and organizer of the kingdom. Reorganization and expansion of the armed forces were also a priority. The monarchy, held by the al-Sauds, thus became the political center, main economic entrepreneur, welfare provider, and planner of Saudi Arabia's future.

Although not giving up the primacy of the al-Sauds, it was Faysal's order that enabled the absolute power of the monarch to be checked by other means. Faysal, as the head of the family, succeeded in obtaining the princes' consent to establishing a balance between the two main branches of the royal family: that of Fahd and his six full brothers (the Sudayris) and the other leading princes, including then Crown Prince Khalid and Fahd's would-be crown prince, Abdallah (sometimes referred to as the Jilawi faction, which derived its strength from the Eastern Province). The candidates of these two factions alternated in important positions, thereby preventing an absolute concentration of power in one particular branch, as King Saud (r. 1953–1964) had tried to do, a move that provoked a rebellion among the princes. Faysal divided the control over Saudi Arabia's main military force: the regular army was put under the control of Sultan, Fahd's full brother and minister of defense and aviation, whereas SANG, responsible for internal security, was under half-brother Abdallah.

Faysal also set, and personally met, the standards required of a Saudi king: he combined religious devotion with understanding of the uses of technology, planning, and education in society. The monarch had to be at once a firm-handed patriarch and a believer in modern, professional consultation and growth. He devised an effective security strategy in coping with the great powers and the Egyptian military intervention in Yemen while preserving the traditional Saudi regime. He demonstrated an aptitude for coping with changing conditions and steering the kingdom successfully. Faysal thus strengthened the absolute rule of the Saudi monarch while setting high standards in his abilities to govern.

The second principle of Faysal's order concerned a new balance between social change and tradition. Faysal, judging by his speeches and early activities, had an instrumental view of modernization. He was interested in his people attaining skills and improving their health, so as to develop the national infrastructure. First priority was given to substantially improving education, health services, and communications.

Although its far-reaching consequences might not have been completely to his liking, Faysal accepted the fact that social change was inevitable. It came in the form of educated professionals with new value systems, nomad sedentarization and urbanization, a growing population, more evident social stratification, a new, consumer-geared lifestyle, and many other manifestations. A principle goal of the first Five-Year Plan was to balance these changes. It called for "maintaining economic and social stability within the existing religious and social framework." Faysal wanted a dynamic, healthy, and modernized society that lived well, but he also wanted it to remain religiously conservative and socioculturally traditional. He maintained a strong Islamic establishment, backed by government authority, which promoted Wahhabi values through mosque preaching and the "morals police." Social change was also balanced by maintaining a second, important set of values—those connected to tribalism. Thus, the social supremacy of the royal family, in alliance with some tens of merchant families, formed a dominant elite of political and economic figures who operated their own patron-client networks. Accordingly, those high-ranking people gave employment and status to their lower-class clients, thereby gaining their political support. The elite was thus able to control society both politically and economically. The resulting networks—sometimes based on authentic lineage lines or at least resembling them—maintained tribal values, hierarchy, and order in society. The kingdom was pervaded by personal-patrimonial appointments in the administration, and familial and personal contacts were used as bases for political factions and business associations. They created an atmosphere of favoritism in the state bureaucracy, which was, however, a modus operandi based on family and personal contacts familiar to society and congruent with its lines of cohesion.

As a third principle, Faysal was careful to base Saudi ruling methods on a new social postulate. In a kind of social contract, a new economy from oil wealth was introduced, aimed at meeting all of his subjects' needs. It was the instrument that provided for all the government's activities, but it also permitted raising the living standards of the entire population, giving Saudi Arabians the security of advanced health care and a new educational system. In order to attenuate the effects of an inevitable stratification, Faysal devised an elaborate welfare system to compensate society's lower echelons. There was no income tax, health services and education were free, and food, electricity, and water were heavily subsidized. Social-security laws were enacted, and welfare and community centers were opened in the provinces. This economy was intended to function as a bottomless pot of gold, maintaining a rentier state far into an even more promising future. This, then, was the balance inherent in Faysal's economy. It constituted a drastic, unfamiliar innovation but was meant to satisfy all: to stimulate those who benefited from it and compensate those who were offended by the change.[7]

Thus, Faysal's monarchical order provided a regime that defined royal functions, social welfare, and social cohesion.

THE CHALLENGES TO FAYSAL'S ORDER

Faysal's balancing act between tradition and modernity—within the royal family (between the Sudayris and the other branches) and among various components of society—seemed to many in the West to be a recipe for relative stability upon which the Saudi monarchy could build as it strode into the late 1970s and 1980s. But during the 1990s problems arose that constituted a challenge to Faysal's order.

At the turn of the twenty-first century there are three main challenges to Faysal's order with respect to the monarchy: problems of a weakening leadership and the succession; threats to the sociopolitical arrangement; and an Islamic, sometimes "Islamist," opposition threat to the Saudi monarchy's monopoly on Islam. Observers of Saudi Arabia were vividly reminded of these challenges in 1995 and 1996. In mid-November 1995, a bomb exploded at a joint U.S.-Saudi military installation in Riyadh; it was followed by another in June 1996, this time at a complex housing U.S. Air Force personnel in al-Khubar.

With respect to the succession, our attention is first drawn to the age factor.[8] King Fahd (b. 1921) has been hospitalized several times during the past few years. In late November 1995, he was hospitalized with a stroke. Fahd can no longer put in long working hours and is reported to be mentally frail. Other members of the second generation of princes, such as the crown prince and commander of SANG, Abdallah bin Abd al-Aziz, and Sultan bin Abd al-Aziz, the defense and aviation minister (who is next in line for the throne), are also in their seventies. Abdallah has assumed the running of day-to-day affairs. Saudi Arabia will soon see a changing of the guard, as a new generation takes over the reins of power. The kingdom is therefore at a crossroad, and the succession—how it will be accomplished and what effects it will have—is a crucial issue of immediate concern.

Sensing the problem presented by its septuagenarian leadership, the royal family in 1992 moved to codify the succession process for the first time. In a new statute (*al-nizam al-asasi lil-hukm*, or the Basic System of Governance), it was determined that the grandsons of founding patriarch Abd al-Aziz would now also be eligible for kingship. Previously, this had been limited to the sons of Abd al-Aziz.

Although it is widely believed that Defense Minister Sultan will become crown prince when Abdallah becomes king, the possibility now exists that given Sultan's age and the new edict, Abdallah may choose another heir from among the grandsons of Abd al-Aziz. Sultan has been reported to be concerned that he will now be forced to lobby to become heir apparent.[9]

If, however, the al-Sauds do not move to the grandsons' generation soon, a distinct possibility exists of a Soviet-era Brezhnev-Andropov-Chernenko syndrome, whereby aging rulers pass away or become incompetent in quick succession, leading to extended instability and a sense of no one being at the helm.[10] A way to avoid this would be for Fahd—if he is able—to either bypass Abdallah and even Sultan and indeed choose an heir from the third generation. But going to the third generation also threatens an internal battle over maintaining the balance among the family factions, as each of Ibn Saud's sons has a favorite son whom he wishes to see in power.

In sum, the succession, though not yet at crisis point, threatens Faysal's order with respect to the monarchy. The fact that the royal family has an aging leadership may bring about a confrontation that would challenge the balance Faysal established between the factions of the al-Sauds. A new consensus would have to be reached to head off a crisis, but that would require new arrangements beyond Faysal's order.[11]

The royal family's ability to cope with this issue was sorely tested by Fahd's November 1995 stroke. On 1 January 1996 the royal court announced an order from Fahd to Crown Prince Abdallah commanding him to "undertake the affairs of state while we enjoy rest and recuperation." Abdallah replied in the affirmative, stressing his love for his brother and his sincere hope that Fahd would soon return to take up his duties.[12]

This formula stressed the problematique of the change in rule: according to the royal family, Fahd would return, but it remained unclear whether the step was taken amid rancor or disagreement. According to one report, Fahd's hand had been forced.[13] But even if there had been problems, they were most likely over timing alone, for there had never been any real question among family members that Abdallah would eventually replace Fahd. On 22 February 1996 it was announced that King Fahd had resumed his duties and in a letter to Abdallah stated that he had rested and was fully recovered.[14]

So ended the interregnum. What emerged clearly from the episode was that although Fahd was certainly ill, he and his full brothers were presumably extremely reluctant to pass the baton permanently, as long as there was a chance that he would recover. Abdallah, the half-brother, thus ruled solely on a temporary basis under Fahd's titular supremacy. Although all knew and agreed that Abdallah would eventually replace Fahd, taking that step earlier than absolutely necessary would have brought about the struggle for the position of crown prince that everyone wanted to avoid. The crisis had been resolved successfully, at least until further crucial decisions were needed.

As monarch, Faysal had projected an image of Islamic propriety. He had fought alongside Ibn Saud and had been the viceroy of the Hijaz, presiding over what has been described as the "Wahhabification" of the *haramayn*, the importation of Najdi religious values and traditions into the more cosmopolitan and—in the Wahhabi view—heterodox Hijaz.[15] "Faysal [had] underlined the King's absolute authority as Imam of the true Wahhabi Muslim community," combining "religious devotion with understanding of the uses of technology, planning and education in society."[16]

In contrast to Faysal's order, the royal leadership of the 1990s has shown itself lacking: it failed to prepare adequately for a threatened invasion by Iraq and thus had to rely on foreign forces, and it failed to effectively limit the results of an economic recession. Serious questions have arisen in Saudi Arabia over the suitability of the al-Sauds to lead the country into the next century.

Much of the criticism of the Saudi monarchy comes from the so-called new middle class,[17] the group comprising academics, members of the professions, educated technocrats, and middle-ranking businessmen that emerged as a result of economic abundance and Faysal's defensive yet modernizing reforms.[18] They challenge the personal favoritism and cronyism that characterizes the Saudi monarchy. The new middle class has been sorely affected by lower oil income, which had led to the economic downturn of the 1990s. As a result, the bureaucracy and private sector were unable to siphon off a swelling pool of university graduates, which was fed on the other end by one of the world's highest rates of population growth. The economy and population growth thus also threatens the second component of Faysal's order, namely, the social contract that has allowed the al-Sauds to rule nearly unchallenged, in exchange for easy access to basic services, health, welfare, and education.

We have already mentioned the succession issue, and it now remains to discuss briefly the country's economic downturn, which, along with a fast-growing population, calls into question the feasibility of the social contract that was at the foundation of Faysal's order.

This social arrangement has been based on massive spending in the creation of a cradle-to-grave welfare system, as well as a system of subsidies, all without any form of taxation. This worked as long as oil prices were high. But low oil prices for well over a decade, combined with huge expenditures for the Gulf War, have begun to make the system wobble. Per-capita income has dropped from $17,000 in 1981 to $6,975 in 1993. Although analysts argue over how Saudi Arabia will weather this crisis, many believe that it cannot be done without serious cuts in services and subsidies and a halt to expensive projects. Moreover, developments in the 1990s signified that there were cracks undermining the foundations of Faysal's monarchical order. The absence of a personal income tax, heavy investment in wheat growing, and the absorption of large numbers of university graduates in the public sector under conditions of a fast-growing population and shrinking national income demonstrated that these underpinnings were losing their effectiveness.

In 1994 and 1995, some steps were taken in this direction, a move facilitated by temporarily higher oil prices. Yet it is unclear if those changes are temporary or structural. For the monarchy, however, it is nearly a no-win situation. Major cuts must be made in order to restore financial health, but those very cuts threatened to undermine the social contract. The question remains: If the royal family stops subsidizing the people, can it continue to demand to be the sole decisionmaker?

The new middle class is no longer able to count on a secure future in government and public-sector companies, both of which instituted hiring freezes in 1994. There were reports on the deterioration of public services (in

Jiddah, for instance, poorer neighborhoods had to receive their water by tanker truck as municipal capacity was insufficient), and in late 1994 unemployment among recent college graduates was reported at 25 percent.[19]

When the living was good, there were few complaints. But as the economic situation worsened in 1994 both the newly established Islamist Committee for the Defence of Legitimate Rights (CDLR) and others railed at royal perks, such as special medical treatment and better privileges at Jiddah's airport for royalty. Islamists picked up on this malaise and used it heavily in propaganda.[20]

Although some criticism has come from liberal-modernist members of this new middle class, the most strident and vocal rebukes have come from Islamist activists, circles close to the establishment *ulama*, and even from establishment *ulama* themselves.

Obviously, Saudi Arabia is a very traditional and Islamic country. It is natural that most opposition from dissatisfied sectors of the population would find it most appropriate to articulate their difficulties in the Islamic idiom. Moreover, over the years the monarchy has encouraged the growth of Islamic and other universities at home by providing funds for construction, as well as free tuition, in an effort to prevent youths from having to travel outside the kingdom to receive higher education. This had led to a downturn in those going overseas and a nearly threefold increase in those enrolled in Saudi universities. In what the monarchy may now perceive as a policy that has backfired, instruction in these institutions has produced radical fundamentalists, and students with similar views tend to flock there. According to one researcher, this had led to a degree of "brainwashing" of students by radicals.[21] Indeed, Saudi Arabia's radical Islamist leadership is primarily composed of lower-level *ulama* associated with the country's universities, and it is from there as well where this leadership draws its rank and file.

The turning point was the Gulf War. In April 1990, Defense Minister Sultan had proudly told a magazine that "there are no foreign troops in the Kingdom of Saudi Arabia. This is because the kingdom's policy is to rely on Allah and the arms of its sons in defending itself and its holy places."[22] A few months later, following Iraq's invasion of Kuwait on 2 August 1990, U.S.-led Coalition forces were pouring into the kingdom. Many Islamists felt humiliated at being defended by Christian powers. Leading Islamist and chair of the department of theology at al-Madinah's Umm al-Qura University, Safar al-Hawali, echoed what was to become a common refrain: "You do not say 'God will protect us,' you say 'America will protect us.' America has become your God."[23] Hawali languished in prison for several years, along with Islamist colleague Salman al-Awdah. Both were arrested in September 1994 following Sunni radical fundamentalist demonstrations in the city of Burayda.

The first signs of organized Islamist criticism of the monarchy after the Gulf War came in the form of petitions presented to the royal family by various members of the *ulama*. The first of these appeared in mid-May 1991 and was signed by 400 *ulama*, including senior ones. Heading the list of demands was the establishment of a *majlis al-shura* (consultative council). In an explanatory letter, the petitioners attacked important components of Faysal's monarchical order: they demanded an end to the economic monopoly of the royal family and other elite families and an end to nepotism and favoritism in government appointments; and they challenged the foreign and military policy of the government as un-Islamic. Moreover, these fundamentalists attacked the royal family for personal deportment not in line with the *shari'a* and hence engaging in immoral behavior—a far cry from the image presented by Faysal. Pressure from the government in June forced the Senior Ulama Council to publish a condemnation of the petition. The council announced that Muslims did not have the right to petition kings but could advise them privately.[24] This was an apology of sorts, since the leading cleric, Abd al-Aziz Bin Baz, and another top *alim*, Muhammad al-Salih al-Uthaymin, had privately associated themselves with the petition. The monarchy had put them on notice: we will hear you, but let us not air our dirty laundry in public.

The senior *ulama* continued in 1992 to issue veiled attacks on the monarchy. In March, Shaikh Abdallah bin Jibrin, a senior *alim* and member of the Directorate of Religious Rulings, Preaching, and Guidance (*da'irat al ifta, al-da'wa wal-irshad*), issued a strong attack on the newspaper *al-Sharq al-Awsat*. He castigated the daily for publishing news that humiliated Muslims, as well as stories and photographs of infidel actors and actresses, and issued a *fatwa* that forbade Muslims to purchase or distribute the paper. It was reported that the *fatwa* was widely distributed at King Saud University. *Al-Sharq al-Awsat* is owned by Prince Salman bin Abd al-Aziz, King Fahd's full brother and the governor of Riyadh.[25] Jibrin's attack thus constituted an indirect attack on the monarchy. In 1993, Jibrin was to be one of the founders of the radical Islamist CDLR.

Even the top Saudi *alim*, Bin Baz, was not beyond veiled attacks on the monarchy. For many years it has been the practice of upper-class Saudis, including members of the royal family, to send their children abroad to study. Bin Baz attacked this practice in July 1993, by issuing a *nasiha* (a piece of advice, or even an admonition) warning against travel overseas to study, particularly during the summer. Non-Muslims overseas would cause good Muslims to doubt their faith, become lax in fulfilling their duties, develop hedonistic tendencies, and be dazzled by Western culture. "I therefore warn my Muslim brothers in Saudi Arabia and other lands against journeying to these countries," stressed Bin Baz.[26]

In September 1992, a large group of more than a hundred lower-level *ulama*, including many faculty at Islamic universities, *du'at* (proselytizers), imams, and *khatib*s, published a detailed critique of the monarchy entitled "Memorandum of Advice." To a great extent, these men represented a new counterelite to the establishment *ulama*, and they were demanding to be heard. The memorandum repeated many themes from the earlier petition, such as an end to corruption and the lack of respect for individual rights. Yet it also complained that the *ulama* were not being consulted by the lay rulers in commercial, military, and economic areas. Much of the memorandum indirectly and directly challenged the most senior *ulama* for not enforcing a greater application of religion—in essence, not doing their job. They demanded more Islamic programming and greater access to the media, which itself should be overseen by a body of *ulama*, presumably of their own ilk.[27]

Although they did not engage in blatant, open criticism of the senior sages, they did point out what they regarded as contradictions in Bin Baz's *fatwa*s and his association with the royal family. In their views, these *fatwa*s had been unlawful. Sa'd al-Faqih, then director of CDLR's London office, wrote of senior *ulama* support of the al-Sauds: "There only remains in its support a group of official Ulama who make fatwas declaring what is legitimate, not out of conviction but out of the consequences of not doing so. . . . This credibility [of these *ulama*] will not prevent the regime from collapsing."[28]

In the mid-1990s, CDLR and its splinter organization, the Movement for Islamic Reform in Arabia, have best vocalized the agenda of the Islamist segment of the new middle class and have carried the banner of the Islamist challenge to Faysal's order. The CDLR announced its existence in May 1993. Four of the six founders of the organization were also signatories of the memorandum. The founding of the CDLR represented an escalation of the Islamists' struggle and an unprecedented challenge to the monarchy. First, it was a publicly constituted protest organization, something nearly unheard of in Saudi Arabia. Its very name suggested that the government and the senior *ulama* had defaulted and were not doing enough to protect the legitimate—but also, Islamic, *shari'a*—rights of Muslims. Moreover, this was an Islamist group with a difference. No longer willing to tolerate the lack of serious deliberation in the kingdom, it made a point of exporting its message. It turned openly to the Western media by fax and met with officials at the U.S. embassy in Riyadh. The government moved quickly to crush the committee and arrest its members, enlisting the help of Bin Baz to delegitimize their form of public protest.[29] The CDLR spokesman, Muhammad al-Mas'ari, escaped to Britain, from where he published CDLR material, via fax and over the Internet, as well as CDLR's AT&T and MCI calling-card numbers, with precise instructions on how to dial the organization toll-free from Saudi Arabia while avoiding Saudi intelligence.[30]

CDLR's very existence was a challenge to Faysal's order, which had determined that *ulama* could give advice, privately, in exchange for influence. The organization put forth the usual Islamist demands, but it did so with a much bigger bang. CDLR and other Islamists did not challenge the institution of the monarchy per se, only the unsuitability of the corrupt, un-Islamic al-Sauds to rule.[31] As such, CDLR propaganda made a point of drawing attention to injustices against the tribal sector in the kingdom.[32] Moreover, CDLR attacked the very foundation of the Saudi monarchical system by calling into question the age-old alliance between *ulama* (religious scholars) and *umara* (rulers). The *umara* only pretended to have respect for scholars, maintained the CDLR. "Some of their paid accomplices in the massive disruption," said CDLR, referring to establishment *ulama*, "helped to project a highly favorable image of the miscreant while suppressing the squalid reality." When the founder of the kingdom, Abd al-Aziz, was not able to get the endorsement of the scholars, wrote CDLR, he gained their silence. CDLR declared that Fahd had "antagonized the most credible of the Scholars, and the ones with the most influence in society." He had arrogantly and recklessly arrogated to himself the role of head *alim* and mufti (professional jurists) by creating the Supreme Council for Islamic Affairs (*al-Majlis al-ala lil-shuun al-islamiyya*) in October 1994.[33] In the view of CDLR, he had gone around the legitimate scholars. The council was seen by the organization as an attempt to hijack Wahhabi legitimacy and consolidate Islam according to al-Saud. CDLR protested the choice of Defense Minister Sultan bin Abd al-Aziz to head the council, because he was "renowned for his hatred and abuse of preachers and scholars."[34]

The summer of 1994 witnessed an increase in Islamist activity. Leaders were outspoken in their criticism of the regime's policies. For example, for the Saudi monarchy, as well as for many citizens, the participation of the national team in the soccer World Cup games in the United States was an occasion for national pride. The games were a royal event, attended by several princes as well as thousands of Saudi students in the United States. King Fahd telephoned the coach on the eve of the game with Belgium.[35] But the Islamists rejected the entire festival. Amid reports of the frenzy surrounding the team's 1–0 victory over Belgium, which thrust it into the final sixteen, it was announced that each player would receive $267,000 in bonuses. Islamist leader Salman al-Awda appealed to Saudis at U.S. universities to ignore the "football farce." Not only was so much money wasted on it, but attending the matches resulted in a loss of the religious way of life and the temptation to drink, take drugs, and engage in forbidden relations. Instead, students in the United States should engage in Islamic missionary work and concentrate on defeating the enemies of Islam, he concluded.[36]

On 9 September 1994, the authorities arrested the popular preacher Hawali. Assessing that he might be next, the other leading Islamist cleric, Awda, went into hiding in Riyadh. He reappeared on 11 September, at the head of twenty-car motorcade that traveled to Burayda. At his mosque there, he roused his followers to oppose the regime's efforts to stifle the opposition.

He was then called to the governor's mansion in Burayda, but—fearing arrest—arrived in a convoy that the CDLR reported contained 500 followers. Awda refused to sign a document agreeing to desist from Islamist activity and left for his mosque, where large gatherings were held throughout that day and the next. The meeting sent a petition to the Senior Ulama Council, accusing them of complicity in the regime's violation of human rights and freedom of expression and assembly. CDLR reported that there were 20,000 signatures attached to the petition. On 13 September, security forces entered the mosque and arrested Awda. More mass protests followed at the governor's mansion. "Traditional clerics" tried to persuade the people not to attend, but the more radical new-generation clerics won the day, wrote the CDLR.[37] CDLR put the number of protesters at 8,000, but foreign diplomats in Riyadh confirmed that some 500 activists had occupied the governor's quarters.[38] Protests continued for several days. CDLR reported about 1,300 arrests; the regime and the Saudi press initially made no reference to the events.[39]

Rejection of the monarchy was also evident in terrorist acts. On 13 November 1995, a bomb exploded at the headquarters of the U.S.-staffed Office of the Program Managers of SANG, killing five Americans. In May 1996 four Sunni Saudi nationals were executed for the crime. A larger bomb destroyed a housing complex used by the U.S. Air Force on 28 June 1996, killing nineteen.

The events of the 1990s seemed to have shaken the Islamic bedrock of the monarchy and lessened support among the new and, particularly, educated middle class. Objective difficulties such as the downturn in oil prices certainly were responsible for much of the complaints, but oppositionists pointedly questioned the Islamic credentials of the regime as well as favoritism, both of which were part and parcel of Faysal's order.

THE MONARCHY'S RESPONSE

While arresting vocal oppositionists the monarchy has sought to respond to the challenge by establishing the *majlis al-shura* and reorganizing the Islamic establishment in such a manner as to further co-opt the establishment *ulama*, also attempting to control the appointments and speeches of lower-level religious officials. It is still too early to determine if the monarchy was attempting to create new sources of legitimacy or defending the traditional ones.

The composition of the new sixty-member council, appointed in August 1992, was weighted toward academics; more than half held doctoral degrees.[40] The large number of people included with specific technical expertise showed that the king intended the council to spend a lot of time as a kind of scientific advisory council. In toto, the appointees presented a picture of skilled loyal subjects, none of whom could be expected to cause trouble.

Although the council represented no immediate change in the status quo, it was a further step in the formalization of rule in the kingdom. Although its role was strictly limited, its formation introduced the possibility that over time its members would become bolder and that issues debated would leak out and increase the scope of participatory discourse in Saudi Arabia. The regime must have surely realized this; thus the establishment of the council signified substantial risk-taking on the part of the monarchy in response to demands for participation.[41]

In what appeared to be another effort to co-opt the leading religious figures, Fahd announced in July 1993 that Bin Baz had been appointed general mufti (al-Mufti al-Amm) of Saudi Arabia, with the rank of minister. He was also named president of the Senior Ulama Council and of the Administration of Islamic Studies and Rulings (Idarat al-Buhuth al-Islamiyya wal-Ifta).[42]

These moves signified the increasing importance Fahd attached to legitimation by the religious establishment, considering the ongoing threat from the Islamists. Bin Baz was the leading alim in the country and was often called upon to justify actions of the government. He was now part of the government and would share responsibility for its actions.

The senior, high-level ulama defended the royal family and the monarchy. Bin Baz, wrote the weekly al-Majalla, always called for obeying the rulers; theoretically, even if they were evil, evil could not be removed by a more evil thing.[43] He justified the arrest of those "who departed (kharaju) from the proper path . . . until they return to it."[44] Three prominent establishment ulama—Bin Baz, Muhammad bin Salih al-Uthaymin, and Jibrin—condemned the CDLR faxes dispatched to the kingdom as seditious. Bin Baz warned Saudis "not to read them or look at them." "A Muslim . . . should not cause unrest but should try to unite people with advice, guidance and benign words," he said. Uthaymin said that such publications were slanderous and that it was a sin to slander rulers; Jibrin, a cofounder of the CDLR who later denounced the group—issued a lukewarm condemnation of Mas'ari's faxes, which, he said, should not be distributed or published "regardless if they are true or not." Most important to the monarchy, both Bin Baz and Uthaymin's statements were supportive of the royal family, emphasizing unity and respect for authority.[45]

CONCLUSION

The Saudi monarchy is struggling to maintain its functions as a ruling institution, as royal family, and as primary representative of Wahhabi Islam. As the ruling institution, the monarchy is finding it more difficult to keep its paramount leadership in Saudi society in the face of demands for changes in the social contract and for greater participation by liberal and Islamist elites.

Although there are signs of a willingness to bring others into the policymaking circle, as witnessed by the establishment of the Consultative Council, much remains to be done. Moreover, its role as a provider of economic welfare and security has been eroded as calls for new economic reforms are being made.

In its role as the royal family, the al-Saud monarchy faces the challenge of maintaining the balance between kinship groups established by Faysal. Opening up the kingship candidate pool to include the grandsons of Abd al-Aziz may offer some opportunities to strike a new balance, but that remains to be seen.

The Saudi monarchy's function as carrier of the message of Wahhabism seems to be the most threatened of all its functions. As the government continues to have difficulty, in light of lower oil prices, to keep up its end of the social contract, many young people are moved to take a second look at the religious primacy of the al-Saud leaders. A culture of opposition has developed around younger *ulama*, in the universities, and among Saudis who have fought in Afghanistan, which raises serious questions about the Islamic legitimacy of the Saudi monarchy.

Faysal's order thus hangs in the balance. The possibility exists, however, that a new, third-generation prince might be able to restore that balance or, more likely, create an entirely new one. The path chosen by that as yet unknown prince will determine the future of the Saudi monarchy as it enters the twenty-first century.

NOTES

1. Ghassan Salame, "Political Power and the Saudi State," in Albert Hourani, Philip Khouri, and Mary Wilson (eds.), *The Modern Middle East* (London: Tauris, 1993), pp. 579–600.

2. Ayman al-Yassini, *Religion and State in the Kingdom of Saudi Arabia* (Boulder: Westview Press, 1985), pp. 83–96.

3. Gabriel Ben-Dor, *State and Conflict in the Middle East* (New York: Praeger, 1983), following J. P. Nettl's thesis.

4. Yassini, *Religion and the State,* pp. 81–106.

5. Ibid., pp. 22–34.

6. Joseph Kostiner, *The Making of Saudi Arabia: From Chieftaincy to Monarchical State* (New York: Oxford University Press, 1993). The Ikhwan were zealous tribal groups from Najd who were instrumental in the Saudi state's territorial expansion but rejected the subsequent introduction of regional calm and internal centralization.

7. Summer Huyette, *Political Adaptation in Saudi Arabia: A Study of the Council of Ministers* (Boulder: Westview Press, 1985), pp. 65–134; Helen Lackner, *A House Built on Sand: A Political Economy of Saudi Arabia* (London: Ithaca, 1978), pp. 57–88, 137–214; Nazih Ayubi, *Overstating the Arab State: Politics and Society in the Middle East* (London: Tauris, 1995), pp. 244–255.

8. For the best treatment of the current succession issue, see Simon Henderson, *After King Fahd: Succession in Saudi Arabia* (Washington, D.C.: Washington Institute for Near East Policy, Policy Paper No. 37, 1994).

9. Ibid., p. 22.

10. Leonid Brezhnev died in November 1982. He was succeeded as the leader of the Soviet Union by Yury Andropov until the latter's death fifteen months later. Andropov was succeeded by Konstantin Chernenko, who died in 1985.

11. Joseph Kostiner, "State-Building and Radical Islam in Saudi Arabia: The Decline of Faysal's Order," unpublished paper.

12. Saudi Press Agency, 1 January 1996—Foreign Broadcast Information Service Daily Report (DR), 1 January 1996.

13. *Foreign Report*, 1 February 1996.

14. Saudi Press Agency, 22 February 1996—Saudi Embassy, Washington, D.C.

15. On "Wahhabification," see Joshua Teitelbaum, "The Saudis and the *Hajj*, 1916–1933: A Religious Institution in Turbulent Times," unpublished M.A. thesis, Tel Aviv University, 1988; G. de Gaury, *Faisal: King of Arabia* (London: Barker, 1966), pp. 45–49.

16. Kostiner, "The Decline of "Faysal's Order.'"

17. Mark Heller and Nadav Safran, *The New Middle Class and Regime Stability in Saudi Arabia* (Cambridge: Center for Middle East Studies, Harvard University, Harvard Middle East Papers, No. 1, 1985).

18. By defensive modernization we mean structural, industrial, economic, and educational reforms undertaken not to revolutionize society but rather to take advantage of oil wealth to preserve and strengthen traditional values and modes of government. Faysal used these steps to make an unwritten social contract with the Saudi people: The monarchy would use oil wealth to provide for most everyone's needs; in exchange, the people would accept the al-Saud leaders and refrain from demanding political participation.

19. *Washington Post*, 18 December 1994.

20. Ibid.

21. F. Gregory Gause III, *Oil Monarchies: Domestic and Security Challenges in the Arab Gulf States* (New York: Council on Foreign Relations, 1994), pp. 54–64; Mordechai Abir, *Saudi Arabia: Government, Society, and the Gulf Crises* (London: Routledge, 1991), p. 191.

22. Interview to *al-Hawadith*, 27 April 1990, quoted in Jacob Goldberg, "Saudi Arabia," *Middle East Contemporary Survey (MECS)*, vol. 14 (1990), p. 590.

23. Ibid., p. 617.

24. J. Kostiner, "Saudi Arabia," *MECS*, vol. 15 (1991), pp. 613–640; Gause, *Oil Monarchies*, pp. 96–97; Abir, *Saudi Arabia*, pp. 189–190.

25. *Al-Muharrir*, 29 March 1993; Teitelbaum, *MECS (*1993), p. 577; see also Teitelbaum's piece on the Saudi-controlled media in *Jerusalem Report*, 16 November 1995. Jibrin earned notoriety in 1991 for his *fatwa* proclaiming the apostasy of the Shi'ite and calling for their death (see *al-Jazira al-Arabiyya*, December 1991).

26. *Al-Hayat*, 14 July 1993; Teitelbaum, *MECS* (1993), p. 577.

27. On the "Memorandum of Advice," see Teitelbaum, *MECS* (1992), pp. 676–677; Gause, *Oil Monarchies*, pp. 35–36. A text of the memorandum, with the signatories and their occupations, may be found in *al-Way*, January 1993.

28. *Middle East Dialogue*, 10 May 1994.

29. On the founding of the CDLR, see Joshua Teitelbaum, *MECS (*1993), pp. 577–579.

30. "*Kayfiyyat al-Ittisal al-Amn bil-Lajnah*," CDLR announcement, London, undated.

31. See most issues of *CDLR Monitor* and its Arabic sister publication, *al-Huquq*.

32. CDLR communiqué, no. 8, 8 May; no. 14, 21 August; CDLR press release, 2 October 1994.

33. *CDLR Monitor*, no. 20, 4 November 1994.

34. *CDLR Monitor*, no. 17, 14 October 1994.

35. *Daily Telegraph*, 27 June; *Washington Post*, 30 June 1994.

36. Letter from Salman bin Fahd al-Awda, carried by MSANEWS, 3 July 1994.

37. CDLR communiqué, no. 17, 11 September; CDLR press release, 14 September 1994.

38. *New York Times*, 22 September 1994.

39. CDLR press release, 19 September 1994. In March 1996, the CDLR split, and a new group, the Movement for Islamic Reform in Arabia (MIRA), was formed by the director of the CDLR's London office, Sa'd al-Faqih.

40. For some representatives no biographical details were available.

41. Teitelbaum, *MECS* (1993), pp. 582–583.

42. R. Riyadh, 10 July—DR, 12 July; *Financial Times*, 12 July; *Le Monde*, 13 July; *al-Hayat*, 14 July 1993. Bin Baz, who is blind, was born in Riyadh in 1910. He had held several religious positions.

43. *Al-Majalla*, 25–31 July 1993.

44. *Al-Watan al-Arabi*, 25 November 1994.

45. Uthaymin, quoted in *al-Hayat*, 18 November; Jibrin in *al-Hayat*, 3 October; Bin Baz in the Saudi Press Agency, 10 November—BBC, SWB, 12 November, and Reuters, 11 November 1994. The CDLR contended that Bin Baz had been blackmailed into condemning it: Interior Minister Na'if bin Abd al-Aziz had promised "the naive Shaikh" that he would release prisoners if he condemned the CDLR (*CDLR Monitor*, no. 23, 25 November 1994).

10

The Kuwaiti Royal Family in the Postliberation Period: Reinstitutionalizing the "First Among Equals" System in Kuwait

Uzi Rabi

If the al-Sabah had not existed, it would have been necessary to invent them.
—*Economist*, 21 January 1967

In all the countries of the Persian Gulf region, the emirate of Kuwait included, the state is ruled by a "traditional" monarchical leadership. The titles may vary—*kingdom, sultanate, emirate*, and so on—but the Gulf governments are all in essence hereditary and patriarchal. Any student of the region becomes aware of the extensive and complex relationship between the ruling families and the states they control.

In Kuwait, the al-Sabah dynasty has been in power continuously since the eighteenth century. Little is known about the origins of the al-Sabah family except that it originates from the Utbi[1] section of the major Anaza tribe, which dwelled in Najd, in central Arabia. The al-Sabah family is reported to include at present more than 12,000 members.[2] It is currently led by Shaikh Jabir al-Ahmad al-Sabah, the current emir of Kuwait, and consists of all the living descendants in the male line of the dynasty's founder, Sabah I (r. 1752–1756).[3] In practice, only male descendants of Shaikh Mubarak al-Sabah (Mubarak the Great, r. 1896–1915) are eligible to become emir, or supreme leader; two main branches of Shaikh Mubarak's lineage were important in this respect, named after his two sons: al-Jabir and al-Salim. Emir Jabir is of the al-Jabir branch and the designated successor; Prime Minister Sa'd al-Abdullah is of the al-Salim branch. The authority to appoint an heir apparent and prime minister rests with the emir, following consultations with his relatives, especially senior members of al-Sabah who form the Ruling Family Committee.

151

As head of state, the emir is also the supreme commander of the armed forces. He rules through his prime minister and cabinet ministers. Important ministerial portfolios, such as foreign affairs, information, interior, defense, oil, justice, and legal and administrative affairs, are held by members of the ruling family and their entourages. In 1988, for instance, the sixteen-member government included six princes of the al-Sabah family holding important portfolios.[4] Not all members of the al-Sabah family are engaged in politics. Many of them have opted for careers in government administration, business, and other occupations for which they have trained at universities in the United States and Western Europe.

Before expanding further on how to view Kuwait for analytical purposes, it is essential to stress that unlike other ruling families in the region the al-Sabahs did not establish their dynasty by the sword, and they could not claim descent from the Prophet, as could the imam of Yemen or the sharif of Mecca. Although there are a number of common characteristics among the Persian Gulf littoral states, generalization is impossible. Kuwait (and to a large extent Bahrain and Dubai) evolved from city-states, drawing on the traditional political practices of the Arabian Desert and the Persian Gulf. By this tradition, the dominant tribal group or clan ruled the city and the state. The ruler's main responsibility was to secure the peaceful environment crucial for both profitable trading and the maintenance of the ruler's own supremacy. Before oil, the ruler's income was derived from licenses for trade and pearl-fishing, customs duties, and taxation on commodities such as date palms, all of which together were sometimes secondary in importance to the profits he made as a result of his own commercial transactions.[5] Since the 1940s, oil revenues served to preserve continuity at the apex of the political system, despite the social changes they brought.

The al-Sabahs have acquired the right to rule through a voluntary division of responsibilities between themselves and other notable Utb families with whom they emigrated to Kuwait during the eighteenth century.[6] Although their rule was autocratic, decisions were made after consultation with senior families within the Kuwaiti community. Merchant families in particular were consulted, because of the al-Sabah dependence on trade taxes. Prominent among them were the al-Ghanim, al-Saqr, al-Badr, al-Shimlan, and al-Qatami families. Tribal leaders were also consulted periodically when the emir held *diwaniyya*,[7] gatherings at which influential members of the Kuwaiti community could make appeals before the leadership. One can therefore characterize the ruling family as "first among equals" in the Kuwaiti oligarchy. Put differently, there was an unwritten social contract whereby the al-Sabahs were allowed to remain politically preeminent through consultation as long as security, internal peaceful conditions, and trade flows were provided.[8]

Salient events throughout the twentieth century served to test the durability of that social contract and the ways in which it has influenced relations between state and society in view of the changing political configurations between ruler and elites.

The question of the autocratic power of the al-Sabahs vis-à-vis the merchant community first arose in 1921, after the death of Salim al-Mubarak and just before the accession of his successor. Actually, since Mubarak's accession to power in 1896 the al-Sabah family had tended to centralize power in their hands, seeking ways to increase their wealth. It was best reflected in their ability to arbitrarily levy taxes, which was understood by the merchant families as a breach of the social contract. In 1921, this prompted some of the heads of Kuwait's most influential merchant families to form a twelve-member *al-Majlis al-Istishari* (consultative council), headed by a leading merchant.[9] The merchants informed members of the al-Sabah family that they would accept as a ruler only a candidate who would assent to their conditions, in particular to the formation of a *majlis* (council) by which they would establish their authority in the administration of the country for the long term.[10] Ahmad al-Jabir (r. 1921–1950), who succeeded to the throne unchallenged, pledged himself to work in tandem with the *majlis* in administering Kuwait's affairs.

Subsequently, the interwar period was marked by great economic hardship. A Saudi economic blockade that brought Kuwaiti trade to a halt and the collapse of the pearling industry—two side-effects of the world economic depression—adversely affected most Kuwaitis. Bankruptcy, poor government administration, and renewed attempts by the al-Sabahs to monopolize state power and economic life, which contrasted with the declining economy, resulted in antigovernment agitation and growing demands for reforms. The merchants emerged as the moderate but main leaders of this movement. Having lost much of their economic strength, they opted for an alliance with dissident branches of the ruling family in order to facilitate access to decision-making mechanisms. In 1938 they formed a secret society, the National Bloc (*al-Qutla al-Wataniyya*), which stood behind a wave of protests, and petitioned the emir to fulfill his 1921 pledge. This led to the establishment of the fourteen-member Legislative Council.[11] Although it was dissolved by Emir Ahmad al-Jabir barely six months after its creation, that move produced a highly active and articulate opposition.[12] Debate within the assembly gave a special flavor to Kuwait's political culture, characterized by an element of openness and a willingness to publicly air antigovernment claims. This growing outspokenness contributed to the rise of a privately owned and independent Kuwaiti press.

Before the advent of oil production, the Kuwaiti political arena was dominated by a ruling coalition comprised of the emir, the trading families, and

other notable tribal and religious figures; it was characterized by tense relations on one hand and the social contract on the other.[13] The al-Sabah princes'
ruling style enabled them to survive the years in which less adaptable dynasties were swept from power in Egypt (1952–1953) and Iraq (1958). They thus
intermittently opted to extend centralized power and sought ways to increase
their wealth, thereby presenting their willingness to breach the first-among-
equals system. They were, however, willing to revert to a compromise with
Kuwait's elites in keeping with the social contract.

No wonder that with Kuwait's independence in June 1961, and in view
of Iraq's subsequent threat of invasion, Kuwait's political elite—the al-Sabah
family, the merchant upper class, and the opposition forces—moved to establish legitimacy through a constitution and an elected national assembly, reinforcing the prevailing social contract. Implicit in this arrangement was an assumption envisioning the assembly as working in tandem with the executive
branch dominated by the al-Sabahs, protecting and promoting the traditional
pattern of rule. The ruling family in Kuwait took the view that the citizens
could have a national assembly—provided that political power and control remained in the hands of the ruling family.

With the arrival of the oil age, the Kuwaiti political system was restruc-
tured, resulting in a real expansion of the political role of al-Sabah authority.
The new revenues spared al-Sabah rulers the need to extract resources
through taxation and repression, which would harm their relations with
Kuwait's trading families and other tribal and religious networks. This is not
to say that during the 1950s and 1960s the ruling family ignored the members
of the old coalition; but now the merchants (as well as tribal and religious
leaders) were bought off by the state. It was easier for the state to subsidize
them rather than repress them. Oil funds have cemented the state system so
that as long as funds have provided for the welfare of all citizens—even after
the needs of the royal family and the "state" have been met—order and apparent sociopolitical peace were maintained. Nationals were entitled to free education, free health care, and a variety of other subsidized services, including
housing. The al-Sabah regime opted to develop the social contract by making
new allies among the Kuwaiti community through wealth distribution and development.[14] The bulk of the population benefited materially from the new
welfare state that rapidly expanded in its role and size.

The political functions of the al-Sabah family now grew. It gained the
ability to provide economic security through welfare and employment, dis-
pose of a public bureaucracy, and manipulate the elite. It is no wonder that the
emir cultivated family networks as recruitment reservoirs for the increasingly
large and bureaucratic government.

Under these circumstances, the role of constitutional arrangements was
doubtful. The constitution was drafted by a partly elected constituent assembly (al-Majlis al-Ta'sisi) and made effective on 16 November 1962. Among

the elected were people like opposition leader Ahmad al-Khatib, a representative of the intelligentsia and the would-be leader of the pan-Arab nationalists, who became vice chairman of the assembly, and Thunayyan al-Ghanim, who had been a leader of the 1938 reform movement and had been imprisoned for several years after its suppression.[15] Those activists were generally prominent businessmen, high-ranking officials, and professionals; some of them were Nasserites and pan-Arab nationalists (*Qawmiyyun al-Arab* adherents). Ghanim became chairman of the founding assembly. Political leaders such as then Defense Minister Sa'd al-Abdullah (prime minister and crown prince since 1977), and Jabir al-Ahmad, then minister of finance (emir since 1976), were part of the assembly that drafted the Kuwaiti constitution.[16] Among other provisions, the 183-article constitution called for the elected, fifty-seat National Assembly; in January 1963 Kuwait held its first assembly elections.

To be sure, Kuwait did not aspire to turn into a Western-style democracy, nor did it do so. Only adult men who can trace the origins of their families in the emirate back to 1919, and therefore qualify as Kuwaiti citizens, were allowed to vote. Women were then and are now excluded, regardless of their status as citizens.[17] Also, whenever the National Assembly has mounted a coherent opposition to the government, it has been suspended. The first dissolution was in 1976 and lasted for five years. Four articles of the constitution (concerning the dissolution of the legislature and freedom of the press) were also suspended. They were reinstated four years later. In the 1980s, Kuwaiti politics witnessed dramatic upheavals effected mainly by Islamic radicals. For example, the *al-Mujtama*, the weekly magazine of the Social Reform Society, which advocated gradual adoption of an Islamic lifestyle, became politicized. The strength of the Islamic movement, notably that of the Social Reform Society, was evident during the parliamentary elections of 1981, the first to be held following the dissolution of the parliament in 1976.[18] During the 1981–1984 Kuwaiti parliament, religious groups were represented by four deputies, including two members of the Muslim Brotherhood.[19]

The Islamic revolution in Iran during 1978–1979, reflected in the religious revival and awareness of Kuwaiti Islamists, combined with the decline in oil revenues in the 1980s and the subsequent cut in the welfare budget, produced a climate of dissent. There were two pressing items on the opposition agenda, relating to economic conditions and security. Foremost was the 1982 collapse of the unofficial stock market (*Suk al-Manah*), which impoverished many businessmen, saddling Kuwaiti banks with investors' debts amounting to 2.2 billion dinars (U.S.$7.5 billion). Kuwait subsequently lost its position as the Gulf's major business center to Abu Dhabi.[20] The opposition held the al-Sabah family responsible for the economic decline. Second, a series of bomb attacks brought home a sense of vulnerability. Deputies laid blame on the al-Sabah government for seriously attenuating Kuwait's economy. With oil revenues further declining and with increasing threats of subversion in 1986, the emir reacted swiftly, suspending the National Assembly for the second time.[21]

THE RESTORATION MOVEMENT: 1986–1990

There are no political parties in Kuwait, and politics, especially after the dissolution of the National Assembly, was played out by several main opposition groups. Moderate Sunnis were aligned under two main groups: the first, the Islamic Constitutional Movement (*al-Haraka al-Islamiyya al-Dusturiyya*), advocated gradual, moderate changes toward an Islamic lifestyle. Among their leaders were people like Ismail al-Shatti, editor of the newspaper *al-Mujtama*. The second, known as the People's Islamic Bloc (*al-Tajammu al-Islami al-Sha'bi*), sought to turn Kuwait into a Shari state. Shi'ite fundamentalists acted mainly as independent candidates and were not affiliated with political parties.

There were also leftist groups, consisting of the Nasserite–pan-Arab nationalist *Qawmiyyun al-Arab,* led by veterans such as Ahmad al-Khatib and Jasim al-Qatami, both leaders of the would-be *al-Minbar al-Dimuqrati* (Democratic Forum). These groups, which stood at the center of opposition activity during the 1960s and 1970s, were most vociferous in criticizing the al-Sabah government and carried the banner of restoring parliamentary activity. Accordingly, they held a number of *diwaniyya* gatherings, arguing that "the thousands of educated Kuwaitis with a tradition of democracy deserve more than rule by decree." Some of them went as far as to suggest that the status of the royal family should be reduced to that of a constitutional monarchy, as in Britain.[22]

But the most significant opposition group consisted of prominent businessmen, high-ranking officials, and professionals, such as Ahmad al-Sa'dun and Hamid al-Ja'wan, whose strengths stemmed from wealth, established connections with the al-Sabahs, and public respectability. As part of Kuwait's traditional elite, they sought to reform the system, not to ruin it. They did not have an extremist ideological platform or a revolutionary agenda; they were interested in a dialogue with the regime. Their demands for reasonable and moderate change won broad support, notably from the press that despite censorship openly identified with their ideas. The radical Arab nationalists and the Muslim fundamentalists, whose revolutionary platforms attracted only modest support, were aware of their limitations and decided to join the parliamentary reformists. Thus, the leaders who set the tone for the entire opposition movement were in fact business elites and educated professionals.[23]

The goal of this group was not full-fledged democracy but rather the restoration of parliamentary activity such as had existed prior to the 1986 dissolution of the assembly. Regarding the al-Sabahs as first among equals, they had secured from them in 1921 and 1938 the privilege of consulting the rulers along with avenues for economic prosperity in return for their loyalty. These achievements were reflected in the National Assembly and in the sociopolitical structure of the country ever since. From the perspectives of business elites and educated professionals the dissolution of the assembly in 1986 was a breach of the social contract they had with the regime, evident in their loss of power and status, which enabled the al-Sabahs to run the country without the checks and balances provided by their involvement.

Their demand to reinstate the assembly was aimed at regaining their "lawful rights" to have input on laws, policies, and budgets and to be able to criticize the regime. Accordingly, the opposition made three demands: revitalization of the 1962 constitution, restoration of parliamentary life, and retention of the election law that divided the country into twenty-five electoral zones and symbolized the election arrangements. The al-Sabahs, for their part, feared that the deputies would interfere with Kuwait's foreign policy and turn the assembly into an opposition center for reform-oriented members, fundamentalist and Nasserite alike. Above all, the al-Sabahs doubted that the constitution provided them with sufficient means to control the assembly. They perceived its reinstitution as an invitation to repeat the upheaval that had developed in the assembly of the early 1980s. The crown prince, Sa'd al-Abdullah, warned that the authorities would crack down on rallies in which "demonstrators' targets went beyond restoring parliamentary life and threaten[ed] to undermine Kuwait's security."[24] Instead, the al-Sabah rulers spoke about "a new democratic formula for assembly-government relations."[25]

Clearly, the regime and the opposition were pursuing two different policies. The al-Sabahs wanted to ensure ex ante that they would retain power over a new assembly, whereas the opposition insisted on the reinstitution of the National Assembly prior to any changes. When the two camps failed to reach an agreement, the al-Sabahs acted unilaterally, announcing elections for a provisional assembly that would determine the fate of constitutionalism. Al-Sabah control over the assembly was to be retained through twenty-five appointed deputies and a pro–al-Sabah majority among the fifty others who would be elected from twenty-five constituencies. On 22 April 1990 Emir Jabir announced the formation of a transitional National Assembly, with elections to be held on 10 June. There were 350 candidates, selected from a total of 563 who had registered for the elections.

The seventy-five-member National Assembly convened on 9 July with the emir having appointed twenty-five of its members, including five ministers, thereby securing a large degree of control over its activities. Although the assembly had fifty elected and twenty-five appointed members, the 50 percent quorum rule enabled the government to ensure a majority easily. The number of ministers in the new cabinet that was installed on 20 June 1990 increased from eighteen to twenty-two. All the al-Sabah ministers stayed on.[26]

Articulating the opposition's view of the new assembly, Ahmad Sadun pointed out that the new body could propose legislation, but it would have to be approved by the cabinet and the emir; it could question ministers but not force them to take any action; it could debate the budget, but the government could implement it as it chose.[27]

EFFECTS OF THE IRAQI INVASION

The Gulf War shattered the confidence of Kuwaiti society and replaced it with nightmarish reality: invasion, conquest, loss of independence, and exile of the ruling family and more than half of its population. The Iraqi invasion on 2 August 1990 occurred amid a political process whereby the al-Sabahs were trying to mend fences with Kuwait's elite and its parliamentary opposition and develop new plans based on the improved economy. Even before the Iraqi invasion there had been opposition to the al-Sabah government. No wonder that the Kuwaiti government-in-exile, seeking to display a united front against Iraq, strove beginning in early September 1990 to demonstrate that the "parliamentary movement" did not challenge the legitimacy of al-Sabah rule. Accordingly, it held a national convention in Taif, Saudi Arabia, in October 1990, attended by more than 1,000 delegates representing the Kuwaiti elite. There, the al-Sabah rulers complied with the opposition's demands, agreeing to "consolidate democracy under the 1962 constitution"; nullify the June 1990 elections; hold new elections according to the provisions of the constitution; allow women to vote and "to have a say in politics"; and lower the voting age from twenty-one to eighteen.[28] In the postliberation period (April 1991), the opposition groups submitted to Jabir a declaration, signed by eighty-nine notables, calling on the government to fulfill its promises.[29] Their demands focused on earlier concerns that had characterized the previous four years (1986–1990): the restoration of the National Assembly and the elections called for in the 1962 constitution. The petition also called for the appointment of capable individuals to the cabinet; freedom of the press and of assembly; reform of the civil service; and an independent judiciary.[30] They were quick to accuse the ruling family of continuing their preinvasion practices. It was argued that the al-Sabah rulers neither changed their thinking nor adopted a new mechanism of sharing responsibility with the people. Indeed, Kuwaiti leaders did not fulfill their promises to restore the National Assembly that had been suspended in 1986.[31]

The opposition also held the al-Sabahs responsible for failing to prepare for the Iraqi invasion. The manner in which Kuwait had been defeated by Iraq and the quick surrender led the opposition to accuse the rulers of mismanagement. It was argued that while members of the Kuwaiti resistance movement stayed to fight most members of the Kuwaiti royal house had fled the country.

The late return of the crown prince and the even later return of the emir (who arrived three weeks after liberation) added to the grievances.[32] Regardless of their ideology, the Kuwaitis who had remained in the country during the occupation, fought the Iraqis, and acquired a taste of power and self-rule were to become vociferous critics of the regime.

The opposition further questioned the government's economic conduct, specifically the misguided investment policies of the London-based Kuwaiti Investment Office during the war and the massive public spending spree initiated by the government in early 1992. In the light of Kuwait's defeat by Iraq, and the difficulties experienced after liberation, many questioned whether the al-Sabah family was fit to rule and demanded changes in the nature of Kuwaiti government. "How can there be," asked one opposition leader, "a change in management and in government when the authorities are still relying on the same persons, advisers, and aides who held those positions previously and who are responsible for the disaster of the invasion and occupation of Kuwait?"[33]

Criticism of the government focused not only on specific policies but also on the entire system. For the first time, Kuwait was witnessing a possible weakening of the power of the al-Sabah ruling family. What had started in 1989 as an elite movement to restore the National Assembly had in 1992 become a broad-based movement, critical of all aspects of al-Sabah policy. Opposition was nurtured by the difficulties in reactivating economic enterprise, in particular Kuwait's oil industry, and by a declining population. Initially, the regime achieved its goal of reducing the number of foreigners to less than that of the Kuwaitis—but at a high price to the state bureaucracy and private businesses.[34] The al-Sabah rulers' qualifications to guide Kuwait's defense and economic policy were widely questioned, leading to growing popular protest against the rulers' lack of accountability to the Kuwaiti public and to demands for wider political participation.

But this somewhat contradictory picture needs some balance. Although such demands demonstrated how critical the opposition was of the ruling family, they also demonstrated that the opposition was reluctant to topple al-Sabah rule and wished mainly to reform it. The people who traditionally struggled for political participation and had led the opposition after the liberation were mostly notables—wealthy and well-educated businessmen who shared their social origins and interest in stability under the al-Sabahs and who did not question the family's inherent right to rule. Indeed, the business community wanted a stronger say in the decisionmaking process; a merit-based government; and more opportunities for the private sector—but not at the price of ruining the al-Sabah regime.

To be sure, Kuwait's political factions were deeply divided over Kuwait's future course of state-building. The Islamic fundamentalist groups differed in their ideological convictions, offered divergent remedies to the country's specific problems, and differing opinions as to whether Kuwait should develop as a secular- or as a *shari'a*-dominated polity. But all the opposition groups—Islamic fundamentalists, leftists, and middle-of-the-road reformists—did have a common denominator, namely, the desire to guarantee constitutionally the existence of a political opposition, free expression, the right to advise the government, and even, if possible, the right to share power with it. Fearing an internal rift, the opposition was unwilling to confront the U.S.-supported al-Sabah government after liberation. Consequently, all groups put forward several major demands for change in the Kuwaiti regime by establishing a common interest in a parliamentary monarchy.

The al-Sabah leaders, for their part, advocated the status quo, that is, a regime led by the al-Sabah princes and governing through patron-client contacts and tribal and familial values. After all, the family had for two centuries enjoyed widespread support among Kuwaitis. Such paternalism was reflected by Sa'd al-Abdullah's assertion that "it [would be] a gross mistake to believe that it would be better for Kuwaitis if my family were relieved of its state of responsibility."[35] The al-Sabahs apparently wanted to regain popular support first by providing reasonable living conditions and bringing back exiled Kuwaitis who would back their compatriots—the al-Sabahs—vis-à-vis the Kuwaitis who had remained behind during the invasion. They also gave high priority to the reconstruction of services, administration, and internal security that were essential to ensure minimal living conditions and to bolster the regime's popularity. In parallel, the authorities chose to establish a new al-Sabah–led government that would also include representatives of the main political groups and appear to be a "national salvation" government focused on immediate reconstruction problems.[36] It was best reflected in the new government, formed in April 1991, as the number of al-Sabah members were reduced from seven to five while nine non–al-Sabah newcomers were brought in. The regime's success in restoring basic services and returning many Kuwaiti prisoners of war from Iraq, as well as the al-Sabahs' continued dominance, seemed to prevent a transfer of power to the opposition and ensured the government's supremacy.

But subsequent political developments, especially the October 1992 elections, have demonstrated that the al-Sabahs could no longer fully rely on patronage and tribal loyalty. Political groups felt encouraged to take positions on public issues and to intensify their antigovernment campaign. The Kuwaiti electorate, although relatively small (less than 82,000 in the October 1992 elections),[37] was politically aware and outspoken and did not hesitate to criticize the al-Sabah family on account of Kuwait's difficulties. Seeking to preserve their regime, the al-Sabah rulers tried to pacify opposition groups by initiating political change that would accommodate opposition demands but still preserve their dominance. With no way out, the reinstitution of the National Assembly became a viable goal not only for the opposition but for the ruling family as well.

The results of the October 1992 ballots took observers by surprise. The vote led to the election of a majority of thirty-four (out of fifty) opposition and independent deputies.[38] The free elections, which took place without allegations of major irregularities, marked a change in Kuwaiti political life as the electorate registered open opposition to its rulers. The election of deputies such as the Democratic Forum's Nibari and Khatib, and the Sunni fundamentalist editor of the journal *al-Mujtama*, Isma'il al-Shatti—all veteran antigovernment agitators—signaled tension and anti–al-Sabah parliamentary activity. The question was whether the new assembly and the al-Sabah–dominated government would embark on a confrontation course or, in keeping with Kuwait's time-honored tradition, would develop avenues of cooperation to cope with Kuwait's problems with a measure of consensus.

Although the atmosphere was strained, with the al-Sabah–led government and the political groups suspecting other activities and probing one another's positions, all sides were careful to avoid an open clash. The deputies quickly reached a modus vivendi with the al-Sabah princes through cooperation and compromise in forming a new government and selecting a Speaker for the assembly, thereby preventing an immediate political crisis. The al-Sabahs kept trying, intermittently, to manipulate and favor the various elites, new ones and old alike. Anxious to enlist popular support among business elites and the middle class, the government was quick to satisfy the ambitions of business elites and the professional middle class by incorporating their representatives in an elected parliamentary body authorized to scrutinize the activities of the government.

Iraq's invasion and occupation of Kuwait accelerated a shift in Kuwaiti public opinion. Kuwaitis regarded the National Assembly's attempts to oversee government policy as a primary sign of democratization. The assembly attempted to live up to popular expectations for democratization, mainly by investigating financial misdeeds committed by Kuwaiti authorities. One aspect of the investigation concerned high-ranking officials of the Kuwaiti Oil Tanker Company (among them members of the al-Sabah family) suspected of embezzling more than U.S.$1 billion in public funds in a transaction involving the purchase and sale of oil tankers.[39] The assembly also enacted new financial laws and procedures that embarrassed the authorities and resulted in the resignations of several senior officials and army officers. In early 1993, the assembly turned its attention to another formerly taboo issue, namely, Kuwait's role in the collapse of oil prices that stood as background to the August 1990 Iraqi invasion. The National Assembly's investigation of the government's failure to prevent the Iraqi occupation served to indicate that the assembly also took great interest in security affairs. One major outcome of the investigation was the resignation, in March, of General Jabir al-Khalid al-Sabah, the chief of staff, probably in an attempt to avoid further questioning by the assembly about the military's ineffectiveness and lack of preparedness.[40]

Notwithstanding the National Assembly's criticism of the government, relations between the two bodies remained sound. The restoration of parliamentary democracy in Kuwait after the 1992 elections has opened the door to a renewed partnership between the ruling family and prominent members of the new parliament, especially in fields that constituted a major concern for most Kuwaitis, such as national security. Government members and deputies were eager to work with the United States to craft a joint strategy that would contain the threats posed by Iran and Iraq, assure U.S. access to Gulf oil, and provide basic welfare. Despite the deputies' criticism, most of them cooperated with government members.

Developments shortly after liberation have shown that an altered political system emerged, based on the Kuwaiti constitution of 1962, which clearly embodies a somewhat different power-sharing arrangement between the al-Sabah family and the people of Kuwait. To be sure, the composition of the government remained essentially unchanged, and the government remained dominated by the al-Sabahs. Although key ministries stayed in the hands of members of the ruling family, there were some significant changes in the power of opposition groups. Most meaningful was a renewed ascendancy of Kuwait's merchant families. Interested in privatization and broad economic ventures and opposed to the National Assembly's restriction of such initiatives, the merchant elite class was the main beneficiary of the April 1994 government reshuffling. A prominent member of a major merchant family, Ali Hilal al-Mutayri, was appointed minister of commerce and industry. The rulers thereby gradually weakened the Islamist ministers who, despite their ministerial position, kept an anti–al-Sabah attitude. These ministers were removed from the government and lost much of their influence.[41]

Beyond the activities of the National Assembly, the al-Sabahs nurtured other institutions that signified public political participation, such as the *diwaniyya*. In contrast to late 1989 and early 1990, when the al-Sabah regime disrupted opposition *diwaniyyas*, in the postliberation period the government monitored large opposition *diwaniyyas* but did not interfere with them. *Diwaniyyas* and active voluntary societies—clubs, guilds, and professional associations—have been effective in articulating positions opposed to state policies and the extension of al-Sabah power.[42] It should be noted that campaigning can become intensely personal in a country where only some 100,000 people are eligible to vote. No wonder that government officials, their supporters, and their opponents hold a plenitude of *diwaniyyas* each evening after the last prayer. At times, opponents of the ruling family's authoritarianism used their formal positions in the state to resist government control in the name of civic values. All these gatherings have contributed to the formation of flexible and pragmatic coalitions that became a vibrant framework for Kuwaiti political discourse.[43] It was best reflected in the ruling family's support for women's rights (albeit as a counter to the rising power of Islamic groups), one of the hottest issues in discussion within the National Assembly during the postliberation period. Until the 1992 elections, most *diwaniyyas* had excluded women.[44] Such bodies—the National Assembly and *diwaniyyas* alike—helped to increase political activities of different social groups and diversify the political arena. It thus helped to reinstate the first-among-equals system in Kuwait.

The results of the October 1996 ballots indicate that the opposition that developed during the postliberation period has receded somewhat. Disputes within some of the political groupings, such as the Islamic Constitutional Movement, that had contributed to the defeat of one of its candidates, Isma'il al-Shatti, in the elections suggested that the al-Sabah–led government has strengthened its position. The results showed a decline in power of the Islamists. The new National Assembly had only twenty-four Islamist deputies, as compared to the thirty-five opposition deputies elected in 1992. Government supporters won an overall majority.[45] Most of the progovernment deputies— wealthy businessmen, tribal leaders, and educated professionals—were regarded as "service" deputies, interested in the fulfillment of government promises for better roads, housing, jobs, and drainage facilities.[46] In this respect, the significance of tribal descent, clientelism, organization, and service-oriented campaigning proved superior to ideological incentives for voting.

However, the pendulum of Kuwaiti politics has kept swinging. The July 1999 elections to the National Assembly resulted in a sharp increase in the representation of Kuwaiti liberals, who now hold around sixteen out of fifty seats in the assembly. The results also showed that Islamists of various groups taken together gained the same number as the liberals.[47] Among the main losers were the "service MPs" who were elected in 1996 on a platform of securing improved services, housing, and jobs. While the liberals who have increased their representation were being portrayed as part of the opposition, the greatest advances were made by the National Democratic Groupings, a new liberal grouping established after the 1996 election. Its supporters tended to be younger and more closely connected with Kuwaiti business and old merchant families than those of the more veteran Democratic Forum, which is rooted in an older, somewhat pan-Arab Nasserist tradition.

These two main factions of the liberal and Islamist groups compete in straining the government, criticizing its policies and demanding to cross-examine cabinet ministers. The rivalry between Islamist and liberal values over dominance in Kuwaiti society, and between the National Assembly and the government over power, is far from terminating. The ruling al-Sabah family has thereby become more accustomed to scrutiny, and the National Assembly has grown used to the al-Sabahs' endurance in power. An uneasy cooperation has been evolving. Government and opposition have to learn to work together far more effectively. An important step in this direction became evident when Foreign Minister Shaikh Sabah al-Ahmad served as a coordinator between the government and the National Assembly. This dynamic indicates the reinstitution, albeit in a somewhat different, modern, and limited shape, of the classic social contract by which the ruling family is viewed as first among equals.

CONCLUSION

The Kuwaiti system reflects a unique amalgam in which two allegedly contradictory concepts—"Kuwait for the Kuwaitis" and "Shaikh Jabir, the father of the Kuwaiti family"—could live together. Tribal paternalistic rule seemed to have been somewhat attenuated and influenced by business and educated elites, but the al-Sabah ruling family remained in power and was able to maneuver and even to manipulate the various elites, new ones and old alike. As one Kuwaiti observer has illustrated: "Unlike other Gulf countries where kings and Emirs seized power by force, Kuwaitis have chosen their ruling family by their own free will. We could have easily abandoned them during the Iraqi occupation; instead, the people asked the ruling family to return. This creates obligations on both sides."[48]

NOTES

1. The name Utb comes from the Arabic word for wander (*atab*). In 1744 sections of that tribe "wandered" out of the desert and into the Gulf area and became the utb.

2. The family was said to have 12,000 members toward the end of the 1980s; see Alan Rush, *Al-Sabah: History and Genealogy of Kuwait's Ruling Family, 1752–1987* (London: Ithaca Press, 1987), pp. 1, 2.

3. They are officially registered as members of the ruling family and are distinguished from other Kuwaitis by the title *shaikh* (f. *shaikha*).

4. Kuwait News Agency (KUNA), 26 January—Foreign Broadcasting Information Service (FBIS), 26 January 1988.

5. Rosemary S. Zahlan, *The Making of the Modern Gulf States* (London: Unwin Hyman, 1989), pp. 24–27.

6. Jill Crystal, "Coalitions in Oil Monarchies: Kuwait and Qatar," *Comparative Politics*, 21–22 (1989), pp. 427–429.

7. The term *diwaniyya* is used for a room in the house where family and friends meet regularly for discussing social and political issues. The gathering itself is also called a *diwaniyya*.

8. Crystal, "Coalitions in Oil Monarchies," pp. 429–433.

9. Jaqueline S. Ismail, *Kuwait* (New York: Syracuse University Press, 1982), p. 71.

10. Salim al-Jabir al-Sabah, *Les Emirats du Golfe: Histoire d'un People* (Paris, 1980), p. 181, as quoted by Zahlan, *The Making of the Modern Gulf States*, p. 26.

11. Ismail, *Kuwait*, p. 73.

12. For a full account on the 1938 events, see M. al-Rumaihi, "Harakat 1938 al-Islahiyya fi al-Kuwayt wa al-Bahrayn wa Dubay," *Journal of the Gulf and Arabian Peninsula Studies*, 1 (1975).

13. Ismail, *Kuwait*, pp. 71–77.

14. Crystal, "Coalitions in Oil Monarchies," pp. 433–435.

15. Zahlan, *The Making of the Modern Gulf States*, p. 26.

16. Rush, *Al-Sabah*, pp. 15–18.

17. M. A. Tetreault, "Civil Society in Kuwait: Protected Spaces and Women's Rights," *Middle East Journal,* 47 (1993).

18. *Sawt al-Khalij*, 5 March 1981.

19. Zahlan, *The Making of the Modern Gulf States*, p. 43.

20. *Financial Times (FT)*, 13 March 1990.

21. Radio Kuwait, 3 July—FBIS, 7 July 1986.

22. *New York Times (NYT)*, 11 March 1990.

23. *Al-Watan al-Arabi*, 23 February 1990.

24. Crown Prince Sa'd al-Abdullah's interview with *Arab Times*, 17 January 1990.

25. *Al-Watan al-Arabi*, 2 March 1990.

26. *Al-Anba* (Kuwait), 21 June 1990.

27. *Economic Intelligence Unit, Country Reports (CR)*, Kuwait, no. 2 (1990), p. 6.

28. *Al-Qabas, International Herald Tribune (IHT)*, 15 October 1990.

29. *CR*, Kuwait, no. 2 (1991), p. 9.

30. *NYT*, 25, 28 February; *IHT*, 8 March 1991.

31. *IHT*, 2 August, 31 December 1991.

32. Abdallah K. Alshayeji, "Kuwait at Crossroads: The Quest for Democratization," *Middle East Insight*, 8 (1992), pp. 41–46.

33. *Al-Watan al-Arabi*, 19 May 1991.

34. *Al-Watan al-Arabi*, 29 March 1991.

35. Agence France Press, 22 January—FBIS, 24 January 1992.

36. J. Kostiner, "Kuwait," in A. Ayalon (ed.), *Middle East Contemporary Survey*, vol. 15 (Boulder and Tel Aviv: Westview Press and the Moshe Dayan Center for Middle Eastern and African Studies, Tel Aviv University, 1993), pp. 528–530.

37. According to the Ministry of Information, the election on 5 October, in which some 81,400 Kuwaiti males over the age of twenty-one were eligible to vote, brought out 85 percent of the electorate. See *FT*, 7 October 1992.

38. *Sawt al-Kuwait al-Duwali*, 7–8 October 1992.

39. *Al-Sharq al-Awsat*, 8 January; *al-Hayat* (London), 9 March 1993.

40. *Al-Hayat* (London), 9 March 1993.

41. *CR,* Kuwait, no. 2 (1994), pp. 6–10.

42. See Shafeeq Ghabra, "Voluntary Associations in Kuwait: The Foundation of a New System?" *Middle East Journal*, 45 (1991).

43. *Al-Musawwar*, 30 October 1992.

44. Tetreault, "Civil Society in Kuwait," pp. 275–291.

45. *Al-Siyasa*, 10 October 1996; *al-Wasat*, 19 October 1996.

46. *FT*, 12 December 1996.

47. *CR*, Kuwait, no. 3 (1999), pp. 10–15.

48. Kenneth R. Timmerman, "Kuwait's Real Elections," *Middle East Quarterly* (December 1996), pp. 53–58.

11

The Persistence of Monarchy
in the Arabian Peninsula:
A Comparative Analysis

F. Gregory Gause III

Nowhere in the Middle East has monarchy as a regime type been more successful in perpetuating itself than in the Arabian Peninsula. Of the eight remaining ruling monarchs in the Arab world, six (Saudi Arabia, Kuwait, Bahrain, Qatar, the United Arab Emirates, and Oman) inhabit the Arabian Peninsula, and one (Jordan) is a close neighbor. This fact has led some analysts, whose views will be discussed below, to attribute the longevity of Arabian monarchies to some peninsular cultural distinctiveness, be it tribalism, "traditionalism," or Islam. The problem with such sweeping explanations is that monarchical institutions in Yemen, a country as tribal, traditional, and Islamic as its neighbors, were swept away during the 1960s. The imamate of North Yemen was overthrown in 1962 and, despite a long civil war, was unable to restore its rule. The agglomeration of chiefdoms that British colonial authorities melded with Aden to form the Federation of South Arabia in 1962 was defeated by the National Front in 1967, and Britain turned over power to the only avowedly Marxist regime in the Arab world.

Therefore monarchical successes in Arabia cannot be attributed simply to cultural traits associated with Arabian society. Two factors stand out distinguishing successful Arabian monarchies from failed ones. First, the surviving Arabian monarchies have enjoyed political and military support from powerful allies, particularly during times of crisis; those that fell did not have great-power patrons willing to protect them from their enemies, and their domestic opponents had considerable support from Egypt, then the most powerful regional state. Second, the surviving Arabian monarchies have had, in most cases since the 1950s and commonly since the 1970s, substantial revenue with which to bolster domestic rule over relatively small populations. That oil revenue came directly to the ruling families from the international economy, and the families were able to use it to build extended patronage networks without incurring limiting political obligations to domestic groups or alienating any powerful domestic constituency through taxation. Simply put, they had the money to buy off potential opponents. The failed monarchies of Yemen were very poor and could not build such extensive rentier welfare states.

Neither of these two factors is a sufficient condition for monarchical survival. The shah of Iran had strong U.S. support yet was overthrown. King Idriss of Libya had oil revenues and governed a small population yet lost his throne. Domestic politics are also important. The surviving monarchies in Arabia used their externally generated financial and political assets to very good effect domestically to solidify regime stability. These international assets had to be mediated by the regimes into their own domestic contexts, and therefore regime strategy cannot be ignored in explaining the difference between continuing and failed monarchies. Choice does matter. Much of the discussion in this book revolves around such regime strategies.

However, even the most skilled cardplayer cannot dominate the table without some chips in her pile. Likewise, the most sagacious monarch might find himself in trouble if he does not have resources at his disposal to co-opt or destroy internal enemies and fend off outside challengers. It is oil money and external political-military support that provided the chips to the successful Arabian monarchies. The failed Arabian monarchies did not have those chips. The success and failure of monarchy in the Arabian Peninsula in the twentieth century had more to do with the position of Arabian countries in the regional security picture and the international political economy than with their particular domestic characteristics.

THEORETICAL PERSPECTIVES ON MONARCHY IN THE MIDDLE EAST

The academic analysis of monarchy in the Middle East, specifically in Arabia, has taken some interesting twists and turns since 1970. But one thread has knitted the varied analyses together: the centrality of domestic political and cultural factors in explaining either the obsolescence or the persistence of monarchy in the region. The starting assumption for analysts of the 1950s and 1960s was that monarchies were anachronisms, their days numbered. Daniel Lerner's influential book *The Passing of Traditional Society* foretold a steady advance of "modernization" that would sweep away the "traditional" regimes in the region.[1] Manfred Halpern saw only two paths for royal survival in the region: to become "the principal force for modernization" or to become a constitutional monarchy. "Modern Middle Eastern kings seem especially prone, however, to fall repeatedly between these two stools, finally never to rise again."[2] Neither spent much time discussing monarchy as a regime type, an indication of how irrelevant they thought it was and how soon it would disappear.

The definitive statement in the social-science literature on the waning days of monarchy was given by Samuel Huntington in his classic *Political Order in Changing Societies* (1968). Echoing, but with much greater detail and logical force, ideas advanced by Halpern in the Middle East context, Huntington argued that the "king's dilemma" left what he called "traditional monarchies" little choice but to promote social and economic reforms and centralize power to do so. But that process of change and centralization would lose them their traditional bases of support (like large landowners), whereas their unwillingness to share power would alienate the groups and classes produced by social and economic change. "The future of existing traditional monarchies is bleak," concluded Huntington. "The key questions concern simply the scope of the violence of their demise and who wields the violence."[3]

The academic consensus on the fading of monarchy seemed, of course, to be borne out by events in the region. In the twenty-five years after World War II monarchies collapsed in Libya, Egypt, Yemen, and Iraq. The late Kings Hussein in Jordan and Hasan in Morocco seemed to be holding on by their fingernails. But hold on they did, as did the remaining monarchs in Arabia. During the 1970s the academic question shifted from explaining the disappearance of monarchy in the Middle East to explaining its perdurance, but the emphasis on domestic factors remained. Michael Hudson, in his influential 1977 study, *Arab Politics: The Search for Legitimacy*, saw the monarchies of the Arabian Peninsula as being able to maintain their legitimacy, and thus their stability, because they maintained a "traditional political culture." Hudson wrote: "The ideal Arab monarchy, perfectly legitimized, entirely congruent with the values of the traditional political culture, would be an Islamic theocracy governed by the ablest leaders of a tribe tracing its lineage to the Prophet. . . . The kingdoms of the Arabian peninsula are in reality not far removed from this ideal, and Saudi Arabia perhaps comes closest of all to it."[4]

One could argue with Hudson's characterization of the Arabian monarchies (none of which, for example, claim descent from the Prophet), but his logic is clear. These monarchies survive because they remain close to the traditions of Arabia. Much like the earlier explicators of monarchy's demise, he explained its longevity by looking exclusively at domestic factors, in this case his notion of political culture. This theme was taken up by other analysts trying to explain the stability of the Arabian monarchies after the fall of the shah of Iran. The ability of Saudi Arabia and its neighbors to avoid the pitfalls of the shah was attributed to the fact that the Arabian monarchies had not tried to "modernize" as aggressively as did Pahlavi Iran. They remained "traditional," "tribal," and "less developed"—and thus more in tune with their societies.[5]

The argument from "tradition" described above has recently been repackaged in Marxist wrappings by Hisham Sharabi. Sharabi does not focus exclusively on the Arabian monarchies; instead he questions just how different monarchical regimes are from other forms of government in the Arab world. His contention is that Arab political culture is "neopatriarchal," where the "central psychosocial feature . . . is the dominance of the Father (patriarch), the center around which the national as well as the natural family are organized. . . . In both settings the paternal will is the absolute will, mediated in both the society and the family by a forced consensus based on ritual and coercion."[6] For Sharabi, the Arabian monarchies are just one variant of the neopatriarchal state that dominates the Arab world. In his analysis, we should not be surprised by the persistence of monarchy in Arabia or anywhere else in the Arab world. It fits perfectly with the political culture of the region.

Another variation on the argument that monarchy fits the Middle East was recently made by Lisa Anderson. Although she explicitly criticizes cultural explanations for monarchy's resilience, she sees it as a regime type "compatible with (though not, obviously, required by)" the imperatives of state-building. Like Sharabi, though from a functionalist rather than a cultural-Marxist perspective, she does not see that much difference between monarchies and the "presidential monarchies" masquerading as republics in the region. Both are "centralized, personalistic" and "actually or potentially coercive," much like the regimes that built states in Europe centuries ago. Monarchies might be even better suited to the task of state-formation than are republics, since monarchs "are relatively well equipped to reassure the previously privileged, a stratum often of particular importance in the early stages of national transformation." In facing the task of building a new state, Anderson argues, "the advantages of legitimated absolutism are considerable."[7]

Anderson's functional explanation of monarchy's persistence is a considerable advance on the argument from tradition. However, it suffers from the same central flaw: concentrating exclusively on domestic political factors. Moreover, by emphasizing the similarities between Middle Eastern monarchies and "presidential monarchies," both Sharabi and Anderson are less able to account for monarchical stability. The collapse of Arabia's monarchies would not falsify their arguments, since the successor republics would be just as "neopatriarchal" or just as "centralized, personalistic, and coercive" as their monarchical predecessors. Monarchy fits the domestic realities of Middle Eastern states, but other regime types do so equally well. We must look elsewhere for an explanation of why monarchy survives in Arabia, that is, to external rather than domestic factors.

Few analysts have recognized the importance of international relations and exogenous revenues in explaining the longevity of Arabia's surviving monarchs.[8] It is to that task that I now turn. First, I critique arguments from "tradition," the most prevalent and long-lasting of the explanations for monarchy in Arabia, through a comparison of the successful and failed monarchical regimes of the Arabian Peninsula. I then present my preferred alternative explanation, which is based on the location of the Arabian monarchies in the matrix of regional security and international political economy.

"TRADITIONALISM" AND MONARCHY IN ARABIA

The arguments that monarchy in Arabia is buttressed by an Arabian tradition of absolute and patriarchal rule—a tradition based upon some mixture of history, tribalism, and Islam—ignore a number of important facts about twentieth-century Arabian monarchy. First, as the monarchical states have developed during the second half of the century, they have accrued power and taken on social tasks far beyond the imaginings of tribal shaikhs and the *umara* of settled areas of past Arabian eras. Although the monarchs themselves self-consciously cloak their rule in the symbols of Arabian tradition (a point that will be taken up below), their style of government is something totally new in the region. They control vastly more revenue, distribute it increasingly through rational-bureaucratic methods, and exercise broader and deeper control over their subjects' lives, more so than any of their Arabian predecessors could have dreamed. State-society relations have altered dramatically, with the power balance tilting drastically to the former. The family names of the rulers might have stayed the same, but the Arabian monarchical states qua states are very new.[9]

In some cases the geographical reach of the state is new. The modern state of Saudi Arabia in its current borders is a product of the 1930s—not even a century old. It contains areas that historically had been separate and fractionated political entities—Hijaz, Asir, Hasa—that accepted Najdi–Wahhabi–al-Saud rule reluctantly and under duress. Most observers of Arabia, basing their judgments on Arabian historical experience, expected the kingdom to fall apart after the death of its charismatic founder.[10] To this day it is difficult to speak of a unified Saudi political culture, given the continued tensions among Hijazis, Najdis, and Shi'ite Hasawis and the new political cleavages between neo-Wahhabis and technocratic modernizers. Even in Najd itself Saudi rule has been fiercely contested. It took Abd al-Aziz more than twenty years to finally vanquish his Rashidi competitors for political supremacy there, and Najd has been the center of Islamic opposition to "backsliding" Saudi rule—both in the 1920s and today.[11] Saudi Arabia is not a "naturally" or "traditionally" unified country: it is a recent political achievement.

The sultanate of Oman is similarly a new construction. Although the al-Bu Said rulers of Muscat extended their control to Inner Oman and Dhufar in the past, that control was never secure, sometimes nominal, and frequently of short duration. The Ibadi imamate provided an alternative locus for political leadership in Inner Oman; tribal autonomy in Dhufar was jealously guarded. The ability of the sultan of Muscat to claim effective rule over the territories that now compose Oman dates only to the 1950s, with the British military campaign in Inner Oman, and to the 1970s, when British and Jordanian advisers and Iranian soldiers helped the Omani army put down the Dhufar Rebellion.[12]

The families of the smaller monarchies of the Gulf have a longer history of continuous rule in their city-states. However, their stability from the mid-nineteenth century up to independence in the latter half of the twentieth century has as much to do with British guarantees of their rule as it does with their own traditional roles as leaders. The British protected the shaikhdoms from outside threats (Saudi Arabia, the Ottomans, Iraq, and Iran), from each other (the Bahraini-Qatari dispute), and, at times, from their own people (radical Arab-nationalist agitation in the 1950s and 1960s). Britain drew their borders, provided their defense, subsidized their governments, and arbitrated intrafamily disputes over succession.[13]

So none of the existing Arabian monarchs can claim a long historical pedigree of unfettered independent rule in their states. Moreover, the nature of their rule—their relations with citizens—has changed drastically as a result of oil wealth. Rule in Arabia has historically meant limited rule. There was never enough wealth to build large distributive states and maintain substantial standing armed forces. Rulers had to negotiate with merchants for money and with tribes for military support. The personal skills of the ruler—in battle, in diplomacy, in mediation among contending tribes and other social groups—were key to the maintenance of his rule. That is why so many Arabian states did not long outlast their founders. The reach of the state never extended very far geographically or very deep in terms of the aspects of its members' lives that it controlled and affected.

Oil changed all that. For the six surviving monarchies of the Arabian Peninsula, oil has allowed the ruling families to bring the state into direct contact with its citizens and to affect a vast array of aspects of their daily lives. In these six states citizens more likely than not work for the state. The state provides or heavily subsidizes housing, education, and medical care. Consumer necessities—food, electricity, gasoline, telephone service—are substantially subsidized. Citizens in the private sector rely on state contracts, licenses, and financing. Oil wealth has also provided the state with the wherewithal to build large coercive apparati, control the media, and dominate or eliminate organizations (labor unions, professional syndicates, sports and social clubs, religious institutions) that in the past provided space for autonomous social and political organization. In all, the state can affect the daily lives of its citizens, for good and for ill, to an extent undreamed of by previous Arabian rulers. In terms of their relations with their societies, the six surviving monarchies of the Arabian Peninsula are new states.[14]

Conversely, the overthrown imams, sultans, and shaikhs of Yemen governed in a way that would have been very familiar to their grandfathers: playing balance-of-power politics among quasi-independent tribes, enjoying very limited sources of revenue, presiding over bureaucracies that were no more than household staffs. The imamate of Yemen was, in its geographical extent, in the first half of the twentieth century as new a state as Saudi Arabia. The Zaydi imams had provided (at times no more than nominal) central authority in the northern highlands for centuries, but their control over the southern areas of geographic Yemen, where Shafii Sunnis are the vast majority of the population, was historically intermittent. With the collapse of the Ottoman Empire, Imam Yahya claimed sovereignty over the territory down to the British-Ottoman border demarcation (and beyond, too), and that claim was recognized by the European powers. But Yahya and his son Ahmad never succeeded in building institutions of control and distribution. In crises they depended upon their ability to rally the support of the autonomous Zaydi tribes of the Hashid and Bakil confederations. They ruled as mediators and judges, in the tradition of Zaydi imams, more than as administrators or state-builders. When the one-month reign of Imam Badr was ended by military coup in September 1962, the imamate state had little if any role in the daily lives of its citizens.[15]

The various sultans, shaikhs, and sharifs of British-protected South Arabia made the imams of Yemen look like the Weberian ideal of rational-bureaucratic rulers. They presided over small and poor statelets, not governing as much as mediating among their subjects. British efforts to impose "good government" on Aden's hinterland in the last two decades of its rule weakened the rulers by taking away the few sources of power that they possessed. By organizing tribal levies into British-officered regular forces, the British colonial authorities denied the rulers their ability to purchase tribal loyalty by distributing firearms. By eliminating tribal tolls and instituting bureaucratic budgetary processes in the Federation of South Arabia, Britain weakened the tribes economically and took from the rulers the ability to make cash payments to tribal leaders. Once Britain made it clear that it would no longer provide military protection to the hinterland rulers, they soon fell to the National Liberation Front, which made good use of tribal discontent in fomenting rebellion in South Arabia. Britain took from these leaders the means they had historically used to maintain their precarious rule yet provided no alternative sources of power whereby they could sustain themselves after the British withdrawal.[16]

The successful monarchies remade themselves, thanks largely to oil revenues, into new kinds of states, different from any that had preceded them in Arabian history in the depth and extent of their influence on citizens' lives. The failed monarchies in Yemen did not have the means to build the kind of welfare states that their neighbors did. Their halfhearted efforts to adopt rational-bureaucratic state structures never went far enough to establish for them a new basis for authority and control. They therefore continued to rely on the means they had used to maintain their rule in the past—playing tribal balance-of-power politics, that is, distributing guns and money to the tribes. But their very efforts at reform undercut their ability to use effectively the tried and true mechanisms of divide and rule. Lacking substantial outside revenues and governing poor societies, they could not reinvent themselves. Their problem was not that they became too modern but that they could not become modern enough. So the maintenance of traditional forms of rule cannot explain the longevity of Arabian monarchy.

Likewise, the prevalence of tribalism in the Peninsula cannot provide a satisfactory explanation for monarchy's success as a regime type. Autonomous tribal forces have been the bane of peninsular monarchical rule for centuries. They were resistant to centralized authority and provided an alternative locus of political loyalty to their members. The history of Arabia is replete with examples, dating back to the time of the first *khalifa*, of tribal rebellion against centralizing rulers.[17] Even in the twentieth century tribal autonomy has been the biggest challenge to Arabian state-builders. Keeping the tribes in line was a never-ending task for King Abd al-Aziz, and tribally based Ikhwan forces posed the most serious military threat to his state-building efforts during the late 1920s.[18] The resistance to the extension of Muscat's authority in both Inner Oman and in Dhufar was organized along tribal lines.[19] In Yemen, tribal autonomy—exacerbated by the civil war in the north from 1962 to 1970—has frustrated the development of centralized rule.[20]

The successful monarchies have been those that have tamed tribalism: rallying tribal support when necessary but, once established in power, breaking the autonomy of the tribes. Saudi Arabia is the model here. Since the time of King Abd al-Aziz, Riyadh has sought to settle the nomadic tribes and make them economically dependent upon the state. Oil wealth has provided the means to achieve those goals. Probably less than 10 percent of the Saudi population now practice the pastoral nomadic lifestyle that was characteristic of so many Arabian tribes at the beginning of the twentieth century.[21] The Saudis have denied the tribes independent access to arms and channeled tribal military power into the national guard, where units are organized along tribal lines but are under the control of the ruling family. Like the Saudis, the rulers of Kuwait used economic inducements to gain the loyalty and break the autonomy of Bedouins in their state. They offered housing and jobs (primarily in the police and military) to the Bedouins in exchange for political support. This tactic succeeded in both settling the tribes and making them economically dependent upon the al-Sabah ruling family.[22] In Oman, Sultans Sa'id and Qabus relied on foreign assistance to subdue the tribes militarily, and then Qabus used the new oil wealth of the state to build his own force (channeling tribal military power into it) and to provide economic incentives to the tribes to pledge loyalty to his rule.

All the Peninsula monarchies have encouraged the maintenance of tribalism as an important personal identity marker. They have provided financial support and an honored social place to tribal shaikhs. They celebrate tribalism in official representations of national culture. But they have all successfully accomplished what their predecessors had failed to do: deny the tribes any autonomous political and military role in their societies.

In Yemen the monarchical regimes failed to bring the tribes to heel, largely because they could neither build independent military forces to confront them nor provide the extensive economic benefits that would have attenuated tribal loyalty and linked tribesmen directly to the state. Having failed to tame tribalism, the southern Arabian monarchs found that autonomous tribal power, far from being a support for their rule, was an important element in their downfall. Imam Ahmad in Yemen alienated large sections of the Hashid tribal confederation by killing their paramount shaikh in 1959.[23] When his son Badr was overthrown in the 1962 military coup, many of the Hashid tribes fought effectively on the side of the new republican regime. Shaikh Abdallah al-Ahmar, the son and successor of the murdered Hashid paramount shaikh, has remained since the early 1960s a prominent member of the Yemeni republican regime and today is a leader of a major political party, the Yemeni Reform Grouping, and served as Speaker of parliament. Even tribal shaikhs who fought on the side of the imam in the Yemeni civil war accepted the 1970 settlement, which guaranteed a large amount of tribal autonomy in exchange for recognition of the republican system.[24]

In South Arabia, the National Liberation Front was able to exploit tribal discontent at British measures that challenged their livelihood and autonomy to make the tribes the military backbone of their conquest of the countryside. As sultanate after shaikhdom collapsed in the countryside during the fall of 1967, not only could the hereditary rulers not count on tribal support; they saw tribal forces go over to a movement that once in power brutally suppressed tribal power and autonomy.[25] Far from being a support for monarchical regimes, tribes in Arabia have had no larger ideology than autonomy and self-interest and have been willing to both support and to oppose rulers of republican and monarchical stripes depending on the circumstances. What unites the successful state-builders of Arabia is their ability to tame tribalism by disarming, settling, and integrating tribes into the larger state. Autonomous and politicized tribal groups are not necessarily a support for monarchy, but they are certainly an opponent to centralized states.

The third panel of the fanciful cultural triptych of Arabian monarchy is religion. By melding together religious and political authority, it is argued, Arabian monarchs have been able to use the symbols and discourse of Islam to buttress their rule. The preeminent case for this argument is, of course, Saudi Arabia. Without a doubt the revival of the Wahhabi *da'wa* allowed Abd al-Aziz to marshal greater forces for his conquests and to unite the fractious elements of Najdi politics.[26] It is also true that the Saudi state has built an extensive religious bureaucracy meant to legitimate its rule and serve the state's purposes.[27] However, there are two problems with the argument that Arabian Islam is conducive to monarchical systems of government in general.

The first problem is that other religious-political governing institutions in Arabia have collapsed. The imamate of Yemen had a centuries-long history of melding sectarian leadership of the Zaydi community with political power.[28] It fell to a secular Arab nationalist coup in 1962. The Ibadi imamate in Inner Oman was defeated by the sultan of Muscat, who claimed no particular religious dignity, and Inner Oman has been ruled from Muscat since the mid-1950s. It is useful to notice also that the rulers of Kuwait, Bahrain, Abu Dhabi, and Dubai have never made the claim to represent some special religious authority yet have been as successful at maintaining rule as their professedly Wahhabi neighboring rulers in Qatar and Sharja (al-Shariqa).

The second problem with the argument that Arabian Islam is hospitable to monarchy as a form of government is that the most serious opposition to the Saudi regime in the 1920s and the most serious opposition today both pointed to an Islamic justification for opposition. The question of whether opposition to particular Saudi rulers has meant for such groups opposition to monarchy per se—along Khomeinist lines—is an interesting but unsettled question in the scholarship. There can be no doubt, however, that Islamic-inspired opposition has been, and continues to be, a major headache for even the most self-consciously Islamic regime on the Peninsula.[29]

The persistence of the belief that Arabian culture—tradition, tribalism, and Islam—are conducive to monarchical forms of rule, in the face of serious evidence to the contrary, is at least partially explainable by the policies of the monarchical regimes themselves. They want their citizens, and the rest of the world, to think that they are in fact embodiments of centuries-old Arabian traditions and deeply held cultural beliefs. This is the core of the ideological legitimation strategies of all the Gulf monarchs. The state-supported efforts to reconstruct Arabian and Gulf *turath* (heritage) symbolize the desire of the rulers to connect themselves and their states to a tame and idealized view of their pasts. Thus "tribalism" in the state's cultural lexicon becomes not a threat to centralized authority but rather a combination of folklore (sword-dancing, crafts, camel-raising) and the justification for a hierarchical pyramid of political authority.[30] Peninsular monarchs, particularly in Saudi Arabia and Oman, like to present to their publics, mostly through the medium of television, the picture of themselves as *shaikh al-mashayikh* for the country as a whole, receiving the obeisance of tribal shaikhs.

The connection of the smaller monarchical states to the sea—pearling, boat-building, and long-distance trade—is celebrated in their national museums as a unifying element of state identity rather than as a class-based—and frequently exploitative—economic enterprise. Even in dress, by eschewing the suit coats and ties of their republican (and monarchical) colleagues elsewhere in the Middle East and appearing in public only in *dishdasha* and *abaya*, the Peninsula monarchs want to emphasize their ties to their countries' histories and cultures, as they interpret them.[31] Saudi Arabia goes farther than the other monarchies in making Islam an integral part of its legitimation formula, but all take care to make sure that religious institutions buttress the authority of the state. That is harder in Bahrain, where Sunni rulers govern a Shi'ite majority, than in the other states, but all make an effort to, at minimum, supervise and control the way religion and politics mix.

These efforts to invent traditions, or to interpret traditions in ways that support the ruling regimes, are neither unusual nor unique to the Arabian Peninsula monarchies. They are also undoubtedly, to some measure, successful. Some proportion of their citizens (it is hard to tell how many, or even if they are a majority) accept the idea that their rulers rule because they are authentic representations of local political, social, and cultural norms. But the depictions of their place in local culture that the rulers provide must be recognized as interpretations, not "facts," and open to challenge and reinterpretation by opponents. Like anywhere else, the Peninsula monarchies' depiction of their own history has to be taken with more than a few grains of salt.

REGIONAL SECURITY, OIL, AND THE FATE OF ARABIAN MONARCHIES

The survival of monarchy as a regime type in Arabia cannot be attributable to domestic political-cultural factors, because the most important of those factors—tribalism and Islam—are shared by countries where monarchy has survived and where it has collapsed. What set the fallen monarchies in Yemen apart from their Peninsula neighbors were their lack of strong outside-power support when they faced crises (and strong outside-power support for their enemies) as well as lack of oil revenues. Those two factors best explain why monarchs continue to rule in some parts of Arabia but not in others.

The Yemeni imamate had faced other serious internal challenges in the years following World War II, but the military coup of 1962 was different. In this case a powerful regional actor—the Egypt of Abd al-Nasir—was actively supporting the new republican government. It is clear now that Abd al-Nasir's government had prior knowledge of the coup and helped to organize it.[32] Immediately after the coup Cairo sent combat troops to San'a to protect the new regime. By February 1963 20,000 Egyptian troops were in North Yemen under the personal command of Abd al-Hakim Amr, the highest-ranking Egyptian military commander. Between that point and the Egyptian withdrawal at the end of 1967, there were never fewer than 20,000 Egyptian troops in Yemen protecting the new republic, and during some periods their numbers reached as high as 70,000.[33]

The royalist forces that opposed the new republican regime did have help from foreign patrons. Saudi Arabia provided material and logistical support and safe haven for the royalists in Saudi territory. Great Britain, fearing Egyptian influence in Aden colony and its South Arabian protectorates, also assisted the royalists.[34] However, neither had the military power nor the diplomatic strength to force an Egyptian withdrawal. The only outside power that might have been able to accomplish that goal was the United States. The John F. Kennedy administration was attempting to woo Nasir away from his ties with the Soviet Union and rejected appeals from Saudi Arabia to help it counter Egyptian influence in North Yemen. In December 1962, Washington extended diplomatic recognition to the republican regime in Sana.[35] At the crucial stage in the Yemeni civil war—when the imamate could possibly have been restored—the United States sympathized with the republicans.

After the Egyptian withdrawal from North Yemen at the end of 1967, foreign support for the royalists also disappeared. Great Britain, which had left South Arabia at about the same time (see discussion below), no longer had an interest in or base for helping the royalists. Saudi Arabia did support a renewed royalist offensive, which reached the outskirts of the capital itself. The apparently imminent fall of the regime, however, brought new sources of outside support to the beleaguered republicans. The new government in South Yemen sent "volunteers" to aid the city's defenders. Syrian pilots flying Soviet planes joined the republican forces.[36] The royalists' offensive was broken, and Saudi support for them began to dry up. By 1970 the republican government reached an agreement with Saudi Arabia and tribal supporters of the imam to end the civil war.[37] Muhammad al-Badr, the last imam of Yemen, retired to Great Britain, where he died in 1996.

A similar story unfolded in South Yemen. Great Britain entered into protectorate treaties with the various shaikhs and sultans outside Aden around the turn of the century to provide a buffer between its colony and both the Ottomans and the Zaydi imam in North Yemen. However, it was only after World War II that the British began to take a more active role in governance in Aden's hinterland. New treaties with the local rulers obligated Britain to increase revenues and to organize the military forces. In an effort to prepare the region for eventual independence, Britain in 1959 cobbled the various chiefdoms together into the Federation of Arab Emirates. When, under heavy British pressure, Aden joined the group it became known as the Federation of South Arabia. The Federation as a whole relied heavily on

British financial and military backing, as increasingly did the individual rulers in their states.[38]

The crisis for the Federation and the chieftains of the hinterland began in 1963, when a tribal revolt in a remote area drew the attention of the Egyptians, now ensconced across the border in North Yemen. Its leadership was soon taken over by a radical nationalist group called the National Front for the Liberation of South Yemen, its core being the local chapter of the Arab Nationalist Movement. British troops eventually subdued that particular revolt, but the National Liberation Front continued to agitate, both in the countryside and in Aden, against British rule and to challenge other South Yemeni political groups for leadership of the independence struggle. Violence escalated through 1965 and 1966, as the Federation began to rely increasingly on British forces for its security.

The death warrant of the Federation was the February 1966 announcement by the cash-strapped Labor government that Britain would abandon its base in Aden by the beginning of 1968 and terminate its treaties of protection with the local rulers. Earlier promises of a defense treaty with the Federation of South Arabia were also withdrawn. As British forces withdrew from the countryside during the summer and fall of 1967, the protected chiefdoms fell one by one to the National Liberation Front. A full-scale civil war raged in Aden during September-October 1967 between the National Liberation Front and other South Yemeni groups while Britain stood aside. In November 1967 the British-created South Arabian Army declared its loyalty to the National Liberation Front, and that is how Britain formally turned over power to the first Marxist regime in the Arab world.[39]

Outside-power support for the monarchies in Saudi Arabia and the smaller Gulf states is vastly different. Whereas Britain abandoned the sultans and shaikhs of South Arabia to their fate in 1967, it reacted very differently when Iraq threatened its former protectorate of Kuwait in 1961. At that time Britain sent troops to deter an Iraqi attack, keeping them there until the crisis had passed and an Arab League force arrived in replacement.[40] And though the United States recognized the Yemen Arab Republic in 1962—despite the presence of Egyptian troops in the country—it made it very clear to Cairo that it would tolerate no Egyptian threat to Saudi Arabia. President Kennedy told the Saudi leadership that despite his differences with them on Yemen the United States would guarantee Saudi security itself against Egypt. When the Egyptian air force attacked border areas in the kingdom, U.S. combat planes stationed at Dhahran flew demonstrative sorties over Saudi cities.[41] British forces played a key role in Oman's successful campaign in the early 1970s to suppress the South Yemeni–supported revolt in Dhufar.[42]

The regional atmosphere for the smaller monarchies of the lower Gulf region was also much different than that faced by the Yemeni monarchical states. Because of the coincidence of Kuwaiti independence and the Iraqi threat to it occurring while Abd al-Nasir was feuding with President Abd al-Karim Qasim of Iraq, the man who did so much to destabilize monarchical rule in Yemen was a staunch defender of Kuwait.[43] During the height of Nasirist pan-Arabism, Bahrain, Qatar, and the Emirates continued to be under direct British protection. When they became independent in 1971, Abd al-Nasir had passed from the scene. The dominant regional powers then—the shah's Iran and Saudi Arabia—were staunch supporters of their internal stability. Egypt, in pursuit of better relations with both of those states, had ceased to play a major role in the Peninsula.

The early and tangible expressions of great-power support for Kuwait and Saudi Arabia became even more explicit and more tangible in the subsequent decades. In the wake of the Iranian Revolution, and despite serious strains in the U.S.-Saudi relationship over U.S. policy on Arab-Israeli (Camp David) and other issues, the United States sent a carrier task force to the region and AWACS planes to Saudi Arabia. In the wake of the Soviet invasion of Afghanistan and the Iranian Revolution, President Jimmy Carter declared that any effort by a hostile power to dominate the Persian Gulf would be viewed as a direct threat to U.S. interests.[44] The Carter doctrine was a direct security guarantee for Saudi Arabia, the only U.S. ally in the Gulf after the fall of the shah. President Ronald Reagan announced in 1981 that the United States would not allow Saudi Arabia to become "another Iran" and authorized the sale of AWACS to the kingdom despite significant opposition in Congress.[45]

There is little need to rehearse the military commitment that the United States and other great powers made to the Gulf monarchies during 1987–1988, with the reflagging of Kuwaiti oil tankers and the provision of naval protection to the shipping of the Gulf Cooperation Council states. That military commitment was then dwarfed by the Coalition forces assembled for Operations Desert Shield and Desert Storm.[46] Unlike with the monarchical systems in Yemen, when the other Arabian monarchs faced threats from outside their borders the great powers proved willing to come to their assistance.

The other factor differentiating monarchical regimes in Yemen from Peninsula neighbors was oil. Neither the imam of Yemen nor the rulers of the Federation of South Arabia had any oil revenues. The imams lived hand to mouth. Since imamate Yemen lacked a formal budgeting process, it is impossible to clarify the revenue situation that existed. But we do know that the last imams had hardly enough money to keep a very small regular army (around 10,000 men) together, and they had little after that to build a bureaucracy, provide social welfare benefits, or even adequately police the country.[47] The Federation rulers were almost completely dependent upon British subventions to maintain themselves, subventions that were set to disappear after British withdrawal. They had little state revenue to speak of, certainly not enough to create an effective distributive state that would have vested the economic interests of important social groups in the stability of their regimes.[48] Put more simply, the monarchical rulers in Yemen by the early 1960s were broke; being broke, they could not buy any friends.

It hardly needs to be mentioned that the surviving monarchs in Arabia *did* have enough money to buy quite a few friends. The smaller emirates of the lower Gulf region became independent at a time when oil prices were on the rise, just two years before the oil-price revolution of 1973–1974. But even before the boom years of the 1970s, oil provided a secure financial base for the monarchies that were independent before then. In the 1930s, before the development of oil resources, King Abd al-Aziz reportedly said to his British adviser, H. St. John Philby, "If anyone offers me a million pounds now, he would be welcome to all the concessions he wants in my country."[49] By the 1950s, when both regional and internal pressures against Arabia's monarchs began to mount, his successors had a steady and, after 1960, increasingly large source of revenue in the proceeds of oil sales. In 1950 the Saudi government realized U.S.\$57 million from oil sales; in 1955, \$341 million; in 1965, \$663 million; and in 1970, \$1.214 billion.[50] There were some tight financial years in the late 1950s, but the Saudis, even before the oil boom of the 1970s, always had enough money to sustain their military, provide for their network of tribal clients, and begin to build a bureaucratic state.

The Kuwaitis were, comparatively, even better off than the Saudis, given their much smaller population. During the 1950s and the 1960s Kuwaiti oil production was equal to or greater than Saudi production, and its oil revenues were roughly equal.[51] The Kuwaiti rulers used that revenue to neutralize the political power of the large ruling family and the merchant class, providing both with financial support in return for political loyalty; they began to build the Kuwaiti welfare state.[52]

Of course, after 1973 the Peninsula monarchies had what appeared at the time to be unlimited revenues. The oil revolution particularly strengthened their hold on power, because those enormous amounts of money came directly into the rulers' hands from the international economy. They were not mediated through the domestic economy, and therefore domestic groups could obtain the benefits of oil money only if the government chose to provide such benefits. The oil revolution allowed the Gulf monarchies to become the dominant players in their economies, with even the private sector (nominally "private" as it was) dependent upon government spending, contracts, licenses, and capital. It further allowed the governments to provide an array of services—including a practical guarantee of government jobs—directly to citizens. The economic interests of almost everyone in these states became vested in the stability of the regimes. Oil revenues also gave the monarchs the wherewithall to build large coercive apparati to police their populations and assure that opponents had neither the time nor the space to build support.[53]

The heady days of seemingly limitless revenues are now over for the Gulf monarchs, with unforeseen consequences for the future. But there can be no doubt that oil revenues have played a major role in getting them to the present circumstances.

CONCLUSION

If Arabian culture can be understood as the combined effects of "tradition," tribalism, and Islam, then the fate of monarchy on the Arabian Peninsula cannot be attributed to cultural factors. Successful and failed monarchs partook in similar measures of those cultural attributes. The most important difference between success and failure has been their place in the regional and global strategic-economic picture. Because they had oil, the successful monarchies could bolster themselves domestically and attract powerful foreign patrons to protect them. That set them apart from the failed monarchical institutions in southern Arabia.

This argument does not negate the importance of domestic political factors in explaining the persistence of monarchy in Arabia. Oil and foreign protection gave the perduring Arabian monarchies the resources and breathing space to build and solidify their rules during the second half of the twentieth century, when other monarchies were falling. Those monarchs could have chosen other paths, squandering resources and losing foreign friends. That they did not is a credit to their political skills and, in some cases, their luck. But these international factors of oil and outside-power protection gave the leaders of Saudi Arabia and the smaller monarchical states a much greater margin of error domestically than that enjoyed by the imams of Yemen and the rulers of the Federation of South Arabia.

Oil and international protection together explain the persistence of Peninsula monarchies in the twentieth century. They are not an ironclad guarantee of stability in the twenty-first century. Foreign protection is something the monarchs have little control over. In a future crisis, world powers might not see them as important enough to save or be able to intervene on the monarchs' behalf for their own reasons. Increased dependence on foreign military support might excite domestic opposition to the monarchs, as it has in other parts of the Middle East. Oil is also no guarantor, as the shah of Iran and the king of Libya discovered. The monarchies of the Peninsula now face the difficult challenge of adjusting the welfare systems they built during the 1970s, a time of very small populations and seemingly endless resources, to a future of rising populations, established high expectations, and relatively flat oil prices. How skillfully they renegotiate the rentier bargain with their own societies will go a long way to determining whether another book on the persistence of Middle East monarchies can be written in the future.

NOTES

1. Daniel Lerner, *The Passing of Traditional Society* (Glencoe, Ill.: Free Press, 1958).

2. Manfred Halpern, *The Politics of Social Change in the Middle East and North Africa* (Princeton: Princeton University Press, 1963), pp. 41–43.

3. Samuel Huntington, *Political Order in Changing Societies* (New Haven: Yale University Press, 1968), pp. 177–191; quotes from p. 191.

4. Michael Hudson, *Arab Politics: The Search for Legitimacy* (New Haven: Yale University Press, 1977), p. 167.

5. See Fouad Ajami, "Iran: The Impossible Revolution," *Foreign Affairs*, 67 (1988/89), p. 138; and James A. Bill, "Resurgent Islam in the Persian Gulf," *Foreign Affairs*, 63 (1984), p. 122.

6. Hisham Sharabi, *Neopatriarchy: A Theory of Distorted Change in Arab Society* (New York: Oxford University Press, 1988), p. 7.

7. Lisa Anderson, "Absolutism and the Resilience of Monarchy in the Middle East," *Political Science Quarterly*, 106 (1991), quotes from pp. 12, 13, 15.

8. Two of the exceptions, who focus as I do on the importance of oil revenues and outside power protection, are Mary Ann Tetreault, "Autonomy, Necessity, and the Small State: Ruling Kuwait in the Twentieth Century," *International Organization*, 45 (1991), pp. 565–591; and Nazih N. Ayubi, *Overstating the Arab State* (London: I. B. Tauris, 1995), chapter 7.

9. This point is emphasized by a number of analysts of politics in Arabia. Jill Crystal wrote of Kuwait and Qatar that the "apparent stability on the system's surface has been accompanied by powerful transformations in the distribution of power just below the surface." *Oil and Politics in the Gulf: Rulers and Merchants in Kuwait and Qatar* (New York: Cambridge Univresity Press, 1990), p. 1. Khaldun Hasan al-Naqib emphasized the dramatic economic and social changes that occurred in the region from the pre-nineteenth-century period through the 150 years of British dominance of the area and the recent shift from the "rentier state" to the "authoritarian state" in the Gulf monarchies. *al-mujtama' wa al-dawla fi al-khalij wa al-jazira al-arabiyya* (Beirut: markaz dirasat al-Wahda al-arabiyya, 1987), particularly chapters 5 and 6. Anderson, "Absolutism and the Resilience of Monarchy," also emphasizes the important changes of the twentieth century, pp. 6–11.

10. This was the prediction of Abd al-Aziz's British confidant and English-language court historian, Harry Philby. See H. St. John B. Philby, "The New Reign in Saudi Arabia," *Foreign Affairs*, 32 (1954).

11. On the formation of the kingdom, see Joseph Kostiner, *From Chieftaincy to Monarchical State: The Making of Saudi Arabi, 1916–1936* (New York: Oxford University Press, 1993), chapters 1 and 2; and Nadav Safran, *Saudi Arabia: The Ceaseless Quest for Security* (Cambridge: Harvard University Press, 1985), chapter 2. On the recent Islamic opposition to the regime, centered in Najd, see F. Gregory Gause III, "The Gulf Conundrum: Economic Change, Population Growth, and Political Stability in the GCC States," *Washington Quarterly*, 20 (1997).

12. On Omani history, see Calvin Allen, *Oman: The Modernization of the Sultanate* (Boulder: Westview Press, 1987); and John Wilkinson, *The Imamate Tradition of Oman* (New York: Cambridge University Press, 1987).

13. On the political history of the smaller Gulf monarchies, and the British role therein, see Crystal, *Oil and Politics in the Gulf;* Fu'ad Khuri, *Tribe and State in Bahrain* (Chicago: University of Chicago Press, 1980); Fred H. Lawson, *Bahrain: The Modernization of Autocracy* (Boulder: Westview Press, 1989); Frauke Heard-Bey,

From Trucial States to United Arab Emirates (New York: Longman, 1982); Rosemarie Said Zahlan, *The Making of the Modern Gulf States* (London: Unwin Hyman, 1989).

14. For an extended discussion of the rentier state phenomenon on the Arabian Peninsula, see F. Gregory Gause III, *Oil Monarchies: Domestic and Security Challenges in the Arab Gulf States* (New York: Council on Foreign Relations Press, 1994), chapter 3, and the sources cited therein. For a fascinating anthropological study of the changes oil wealth brought to one central Arabian town, see Soraya Altorki and Donald Cole, *Arabian Oasis City: The Transformation of Unayzah* (Austin: University of Texas Press, 1989).

15. The best account of Yemeni political history remains Robert W. Stookey, *Yemen: The Politics of the Yemen Arab Republic* (Boulder: Westview Press, 1978). On the very low level of state capacity in the twentieth century imamate, see J. E. Peterson, *Yemen: The Search for the Modern State* (Baltimore: Johns Hopkins University Press, 1982), chapter 2; Robert D. Burrowes, *The Yemen Arab Republic: The Politics of Development, 1962–1986* (Boulder: Westview Press, 1987), chapter 2.

16. This argument is demonstrated at greater length in F. Gregory Gause III, *Saudi-Yemeni Relations: Domestic Structures and Foreign Influence* (New York: Columbia University Press, 1990), pp. 31–48.

17. Ira Lapidus, *A History of Islamic Societies* (New York: Cambridge University Press, 1988), p. 38.

18. Joseph Kostiner, "Transforming Dualities: Tribe and State Formation in Saudi Arabie," in Philip Khoury and Joseph Kostiner (eds.), *Tribes and State Formation in the Middle East* (Berkeley: University of California Press, 1990); Christine Moss Helms, *The Cohesion of Saudi Arabia* (Baltimore: Johns Hopkins University Press, 1981), p. 113, Tim Niblock, "Social Structure and the Development of the Saudi Arabian Political System," in T. Niblock (ed.), *State, Society, and Economy in Saudi Arabia* (London: Croom Helm, 1982); Henry Rosenfeld, "The Social Composition of the Military in the Process of State Formation in the Arabian Desert," *Journal of the Royal Anthropological Institute*, 95 (1965); and Henri Rosenfeld, "The Military Forces Used to Achieve and Maintain Power and the Meaning of Its Social Composition: Slaves, Mercenaries, and Townsmen," *Journal of the Royal Anthropological Institute*, 95 (1965).

19. J. E. Peterson, *Oman in the Twentieth Century* (London: Croom Helm, 1978), chapter 7.

20. Gause, *Saudi-Yemeni Relations*, chapter 2. Paul Dresch, in his outstanding anthropological study of Yemeni tribalism, writes that "in the years around 1980 the tribes were often as little subject to direct governmental control as they had been in, say, the mid-nineteenth century." Dresch, *Tribes, Government, and History in Yemen* (New York: Oxford University Press, 1993), p. 361.

21. Dale F. Eickelman, *The Middle East: An Anthropological Approach*, 2nd ed. (Englewood Cliffs, N.J.: Prentice Hall, 1989), p. 78. An excellent account of sedentarization in one of the most isolated of the Arabian tribes can be found in Donald P. Cole, *Nomads of the Nomads: The Al Murrah Bedouin of the Empty Quarter* (Arlington Heights, Ill.: AHM Publishing, 1975).

22. Crystal, *Oil and Politics in the Gulf*, pp. 88–89.

23. Manfred W. Wenner, *Modern Yemen, 1918–1966* (Baltimore: Johns Hopkins University Press, 1967), pp. 125–126.

24. Gause, *Saudi-Yemeni Relations*, pp. 24–25.

25. Ibid., pp. 41–48.

26. Turki al-Hamad, "tawhid al-jazira al-arabiyya: dawr al-idiulujiyya wal-tantim fi tahtim al-bunya al-ijtima'iyya al-iqtisadiyya al-mu'iqa lil-wahda," *al-mustaqbal al-arabi*, 93 (1986); Helms, *The Cohesion of Saudi Arabia*, chapters 1–3.

27. Ayman al-Yassini, *Religion and State in the Kingdom of Saudi Arabia* (Boulder: Westview Press, 1985), chapter 4.

28. The most complete account of the imamate's history in English is Stookey, *Yemen*, chapters 4–6.

29. R. Hrair Dekmejian, "The Rise of Political Islamism in Saudi Arabia," *Middle East Journal*, 48 (1994); Gause, *Oil Monarchies*, pp. 31–39.

30. Eric Davis, "Theorizing Statecraft and Social Change in Arab Oil Producing Countries," and Muhammad Rajab al-Najjar, "Contemporary Trends in the Study of Folklore in the Arab Gulf States," in Eric Davis and Nicolas Gavrielides (eds.), *Statecraft in the Middle East: Oil, Historical Memory, and Popular Culture* (Miami: Florida International University Press, 1991), pp. 176–201.

31. Crystal, *Oil and Politics in the Gulf*, pp. 161–164; Gause, *Oil Monarchies*, pp. 26–28.

32. This is admitted by Yemenis who were involved. See Abd al-Rahman al-Baydani, *azmat al-umma al-arabiyya wa thawrat al-yaman* (n.p., 1983), pp. 149–150, 260–266; Abdallah al-Juzaylan, *al-Tarikh al-Sirri lil-Thawra al-Yamaniyya* (Cairo: Madbuli Bookstore, 1979), pp. 79–80, 89–90; Lajna min Tanzim al-Dubat al-Ahrar, *Asrar wa Watha'iq al-Thawra al-Yamaniyya* (Beirut: Dar al-awda, 1978), pp. 103–105. The best account of Egyptian policy in Yemen makes this point clear also. Ahmad Yusif Ahmad, *al-dawr al-masri fi al-yaman* (Cairo: al-Hay'a al-Misriyya al-Amma lil-Kitab, 1981), pp. 108–111.

33. Gause, *Saudi-Yemeni Relations*, chapter 4.

34. Ibid.

35. Fawaz Gerges, *The Superpowers and the Middle East: Regional and International Politics, 1955–1967* (Boulder: Westview Press, 1994), pp. 154–157.

36. Gause, *Saudi-Yemeni Relations*, pp. 76–77.

37. Ibid., pp. 79–82.

38. The most recent account of British policy in South Arabia, by one who helped to implement it, can be found in Glen Balfour-Paul, *The End of Empire in the Middle East: Britain's Relinquishment of Power in Her Last Three Arab Dependencies* (New York: Cambridge University Press, 1991), chapter 3.

39. Ibid., chapter 3; Gause, *Saudi-Yemeni Relations*, pp. 41–48; Joseph Kostiner, *The Struggle for South Yemen* (New York: St. Martin's Press, 1984).

40. A full account of the 1961 crisis can be found in Abdul-Reda Assiri, *Kuwait's Foreign Policy: City-State in World Politics* (Boulder: Westview Press, 1990).

41. Safran, *Saudi Arabia*, p. 96; Fawwaz Gerges, "The Kennedy Administration and the Egyptian-Saudi Conflict in Yemen: Co-opting Arab Nationalism," *Middle East Journal*, 49, no. 2 (1995), p. 305.

42. Allen, *Oman*, pp. 73–74; Peterson, *Oman in the Twentieth Century*, pp. 191–194.

43. Malcolm Kerr, *The Arab Cold War,* 3rd ed. (New York: Oxford University Press, 1971), p. 20.

44. Safran, *Saudi Arabia*, pp. 304, 319.

45. *New York Times*, 2 October 1981, pp. A1, A28.

46. For a summary of these incidents, see F. Gregory Gause III, "Gulf Regional Politics: Revolution, War, and Rivalry," in W. Howard Wriggins (ed.), *The Dynamics*

of Regional Politics: Four Systems on the Indian Ocean Rim (New York: Columbia University Press, 1992).

47. Peterson, *Yemen*, p. 57: "Consequently, the [imamate] state provided few services and exercised only a modicum of control over the countryside."

48. As late as 1966, Britain provided 61 percent of the Federation's budget; only 7.5 percent was raised in direct taxes, and almost all of that in the city of Aden. Great Britain, Central Office of Information, Reference Division, *Aden and South Arabia*, No. R5671/66, June 1966, p. 27.

49. Quoted in Robert Lacey, *The Kingdom: Arabia and the House of Saud* (New York: Avon Books, 1981), p. 229.

50. Richard F. Nyrop et al., *Area Handbook for Saudi Arabia*, 3rd ed. (Washington, D.C.: U.S. Government Printing Office, 1977), p. 265.

51. Keith McLachlan, "Oil in the Persian Gulf Area," in Alvin J. Cottrell (ed.), *The Persian Gulf States: A General Survey* (Baltimore: Johns Hopkins University Press, 1980), pp. 212–213, 218.

52. Crystal, *Oil and Politics in the Gulf*, pp. 62–93.

53. For an extensive discussion of how oil strengthened the regimes in the Gulf monarchies, see Gause, *Oil Monarchies*, chapter 3.

12

The Throne in the Sultanate
of Oman

Joseph A. Kechichian

> I have undertaken the action against my father in an effort to place the country along the path of reconstruction and development.
> —Majid Khadduri, *Arab Personalities in Politics*, 1981

Sultan Qabus bin Sa'id was heir not just to the throne he inherited from his father but also to a dynasty that provided Oman with impressive leaders. It was men like Ahmad bin Sa'id (r. 1744–1783), Sultan bin Ahmad (r. 1792–1804), Sa'id bin Sultan (r. 1807–1856), and Turki bin Sa'id (r. 1871–1888) who shaped the country's history and who gave its policies an overall direction. To Qabus's credit, this rich legacy was not abandoned for foreign imitations and short-term revolutionary rhetoric. Following in his predecessors' footsteps, some of whom at different times acted in similar fashion, the sultan acceded to the throne on 23 July 1970 with little save his determination to open the country to the world. His decision to rejuvenate Omani society, as well as the policy of *infitah* (openness), were both daunting tasks for what was then a rather fragmented country "struggling to achieve unity and modernization."[1]

Much like Charles de Gaulle, who had "a certain idea of France," Qabus set out to reinvent Oman.[2] His greatest challenge was to end the sultanate's isolation from the Gulf region, the Arab community, and the world at large. Since he was an unknown personality to most regional leaders, it was necessary for Qabus to prove his independence without reneging on commitments made by his predecessors to Britain. His "idea of Oman," which relied on age-old and proven principles, would mold much of his internal and foreign policies. Aiming to achieve lofty goals—maintaining the country's integrity and the population's dignity—Qabus recalled how Omani empires fared and, without wishing to reconstitute them, imagined a renaissance that would ensure a better life for his people. He would draw inspiration from the past, work diligently in the present, and look forward to the future, making sure that Omanis shared in those same aspirations. Two hundred years earlier, Ahmad bin Saʿid adopted similar policies and, despite many problems along the way, Oman survived.[3]

THE AL-BU SAʿID IN POWER

Although modern sultans emerged from the al-Bu Saʿid dynasty, the family was more stratified than is commonly assumed. There was, for example, a tribal affiliation rooted in central Oman, chiefly around the towns of Adam, Izki, and Nizwa. Al-Bu Saʿid rulers, however, were the descendants of Ahmad bin Saʿid, the first al-Bu Saʿid ruler of Oman. The two men—Ahmad bin Saʿid and Qabus bin Saʿid—are often compared even though that is the result of similarities in surname rather than authority. Because Arab names carry the father's surname, the distinction between al-Bu Saʿid and al-Saʿid descendants is not always understood. The latter are the descendants of Saʿid bin Sultan. Al-Bu Saʿid tribal leaders won the right to rule over Oman in 1744, because they actively participated in the political life of the Yaribah dynasty (1625–1737), which allowed a considerable number to gain useful leadership experience.[4] Al-Bu Saʿid governors, mostly in remote areas of Oman, were effective and proved to many that they could be trusted, even if members of the family jockeyed for power.[5] Consequently, the extent of each ruler's success was determined by the level of family harmony, as well as by internal opposition groups and outside powers who put limitations to his authority. Yet because the sultanate was not truly united under the authority of a central government, relatives of the ruler acted as semiautonomous leaders in their respective fiefdoms. The city of Rustaq, for example, was almost continuously held by the descendants of Azzan bin Qays, a grandson of Ahmad bin Saʿid. This collateral branch of the family controlled Rustaq until 1955 even after losing power in 1917. Other important cities, including Sohar, did not formally join Muscat until 1929, when Saʿid bin Taymur extended his authority over it. The need to buttress power, which required the display of strong leadership, created a level of internal opposition to the sultan's influence throughout the years. As this factionalism was widely known, foreign powers positioned their resources to influence Muscat as best as possible. Several rulers fell victim to outside interferences, and, when they attempted to play one against another, the course of Omani affairs changed for good.

When Sayyid Sultan died in 1804, Muscat was thrown into turmoil as his two young sons, Saʿid and Salim, faced opposition from within the family as well as from the al-Sauds in Najd (who eventually united the many tribes of the Arabian Peninsula into the kingdom of Saudi Arabia). Badr bin Sayf, Sayyid Sultan's nephew, rushed to the rescue of his two cousins and, because of his privileged ties with the Saudis, helped diminish Riyadh's threat to Muscati independence. Unfortunately, Badr's ambitious policies proved disastrous, because fighting broke out in the north, where the Qawasim tribal groups in Sharjah and Ras al-Khaymah captured Hormuz and Bandar Abbas. Although Badr regained authority over Bandar Abbas, Sayyid Sa'id ousted his uncle in 1807 and assumed control over Muscati affairs, reflecting cultural traditions in which competence was highly valued and failure seldom tolerated.

Sayyid Sa'id became the new ruler of Muscat at age seventeen. What he inherited was far less palatable than is generally assumed. First, the phenomenal Omani influence in the Gulf, so carefully put in place by Sayyid Sultan bin Ahmad, was virtually gone. Only the cities of Qawadar and Bandar Abbas remained. The Qawasim were left the freedom to do as they pleased—and they took full advantage of this freedom.

To be sure, Riyadh was disturbed that one of its allies in Muscat was murdered, but Sa'id quickly informed the Sa'udis that he would uphold Badr's numerous pledges to them. The annual tribute, set at MT$50,000 (Maria Theresa dollars, the Portuguese currency in use at the time throughout the Persian Gulf region), would be honored, which proved amply satisfactory to the al-Saud. Sa'id faced an equally daunting challenge as the French, unhappy with the rising influence of the British political agent in Muscat, started attacking his ships in the Indian Ocean. Sayyid Sa'id had to make peace with Paris and, to that end, dispatched an envoy to Mauritius to restore friendly relations and establish commercial links. As expected, that visit was interpreted negatively by the British, who perceived any Omani-Franco contacts as a potential threat to their interests: London would simply not tolerate a French presence in the Gulf. It informed Sayyid Sa'id of its decision in most direct terms, which included unabashed threats. Sa'id, challenged by both Paris and London, faced his first foreign crisis in 1807 but chose to take a neutral stance. A French consular agent was invited to set up residence in Muscat, even if London, through its influential India Office, refused to acknowledge the move. Unfortunately for Sa'id, the French did not offer commercial concessions, which in part caused Muscat to enter a period of economic strangulation.

As difficult a challenge as the Franco-British rivalry represented, it paled in comparison to the many other challenges Oman faced in the Persian Gulf region. By early 1808, the Qawasim had established a respectable flotilla (sixty-three large vessels and 19,000 men) in the Gulf, where they ruled with impunity. Their control extended along the entire Shamaliyyah coast, the strategic Strait of Hormuz, and the numerous islands across from Persia. For Sa'id, the path was clear: regain ground lost to the Qawasim before they permanently destroyed Omani business interests.

In the period following 1808, Sayyid Sa'id mounted several raids on coastal areas held by the Qawasim, which triggered a fierce response by the

Wahhabi Saudis. In 1810, with the help of the Utb tribal families, Sa'id was able to block a Saudi war campaign against Oman. Sa'id was also able to extend his authority over Sharja and to improve his relations with the Qasimi rulers of Ras al-Khayma. But when Britain agreed with the Trucial coast shaikhs in 1820 to abolish piracy in the Gulf, the Omani influence along the Gulf coastline attenuated.

After forty years of warfare with the Utb and Qawasim, Muscat's Persian Gulf policy—that is, control of Gulf commerce—came to a halt. Not only were Bahrain and Ras al-Khaymah entrenched in new fiefdoms, and not only were the al-Sauds weakened and the British strengthened in the area; Muscati commercial interests declined markedly as well. Although British objectives were not met to the extent hoped for by London, "Muscat was no longer free to follow an independent policy in the Gulf."[6] Sayyid Sa'id bin Sultan needed to look elsewhere for commercial expansion. In time, he and his successor would turn to Zanzibar.

Other Omani rulers fell prey to foreign interferences in the sultanate's internal and regional affairs. Sultan Faysal bin Turki (1888–1913), for example, was a clear victim of circumstances and British overbearance. Seeking to balance and possibly attenuate British predominance over Oman, Faysal's preference was for the French, not merely to replace one colonial power with another but also to benefit from Paris's financial promises. He consented to French proposals to open a coaling station at Bandar Jissa, near Muscat, and agreed to fly the French flag on his fleet. The British, however, failed Faysal's plan and ordered him aboard their flagship to witness his palace and capital city bombarded. In 1899, he surrendered "and was subsequently forced to renounce the Bandar Jissa action in a public speech."[7] Unable to achieve his objective (i.e., reduce British influence), Faysal's rule lapsed into oblivion. He died in October 1913 as the British reestablished their influence in Oman, the reconstituted imamate threatened the authority of the ruler in Muscat, and the government lay in shambles.

The rule of Faysal's successor, Taymur bin Faysal (1913–1931), was marked not only by struggles against British influence but also by unassertive attempts to centralize his rule. He strived to extend the sultan's authority over the entire country as well as improve his administration. With his son Sa'id appointed president of the newly created Council of Ministers, Taymur introduced a number of basic administrative improvements between 1921 and 1929. In time, and with British assistance, he regained firm control over the land and replenished the treasury. His successes were not free of controversy, however. He was continuously challenged by feuds and assassination attempts within the family, nurtured by intertribal fighting and decisive British interference in internal politics. It had been one thing for London to manage Oman's foreign policy, but now Britain took interest in domestic politics as well. London concluded that a peace treaty would solve most of the problems plaguing the sultanate and brokered the 1920 Treaty of Sib that recognized the reality that two chiefdom-states existed in Oman—his and that of the Ibadi imam. A line separating the two was drawn between the coast and the interior, which left scars for several generations.

After that imposed peace, Taymur ruled by title only and spent most of his time in India, attending to Oman's needs sparingly. He preferred life in India because of Bombay's more sophisticated environment. Disinterested in Omani affairs, he abdicated in 1932 when his son Sa'id acceded to the throne, thereby opening one of the most difficult chapters in Omani history.

SAYYID SA'ID BIN TAYMUR

Sayyid Sa'id bin Taymur (r. 1932–1970) had three advantages when he became ruler in 1932: he was educated, had government experience, and did not excessively annoy the British. London, however, extricated the same humiliating "letter of accession" that drew the parameters of the ruler's real power and defined the limits of his potential political objectives.

Seeking to reform Oman and motivated by impressions from visits he made to the Far East in 1937 and to the United States, Britain, France, Italy, India, and, a few years later, to Egypt and Palestine, Sayyid Sa'id bin Taymur concluded that Oman needed to achieve two objectives. First, Oman had to regain both economic and political independence from Britain. Second, the nation had to unify and thereby end the divisive environment that had stifled its meager resources and prevented its development. Both of these objectives required additional resources that were buried under the Rub al-Khali Desert, a region he did not control. Not surprisingly, the sultan's plans coincided with those of Britain; seeking to limit Saudi Arabia's influence over the Arabian Peninsula, Britain had abandoned its long-held policy of divide and rule in favor of establishing a strong central authority in Oman. A dormant dispute over the Buraymi Oasis was rekindled in 1952 as Saudi influence spread into Oman and as Imam Muhammad bin Abdallah al-Khalili and a number of tribal leaders came to welcome Saudi financial largesse. This Saudi money, flowing into the coffers of influential Omanis, achieved little for the Omani state, but such were the rules and ways of the desert. Sa'id bin Taymur was nevertheless on the verge of defeating the Saudis when Britain, acting under strong U.S. pressure, prevented a victory. Because Sa'id was not allowed to expel the Saudis from Oman, his popularity among his own population diminished considerably. At least one commentator concluded that the British advice was "unwise," speculating that a victorious Sa'id would have unified the country and "would probably have . . . spared the civil war that broke out in 1955."[8] Demoralized and humiliated by the British action, Sa'id depended on London to stabilize his monarchical rule by restoring a semblance of law and order and was, after his swift victory over his own people, beholden to that valuable assistance.[9]

Sa'id's rule was thereafter marred by conflicting interests. On the one hand, Oman was united by a sultan who owed his throne to the British. Instead of becoming independent, Sa'id bin Taymur became ever more dependent on London for the minimal economic, political, and military assistance the country received at the time. On the other hand, the awakening of radical Arab nationalism, which was galvanizing the masses from Cairo to Baghdad and Algiers to Damascus, threatened to sway dissatisfied tribal groups against the sultan. Unfortunately for Sa'id, and despite his pronouncements to the contrary, Oman became the cause célèbre for the Arab radicals. The deposed imam and his supporters received Arab League backing to put the "question of Oman" before the United Nations. No matter how hard London tried, few were dissuaded that the sultanate was indeed an independent state, its leaders masters of their own destinies, the British benign guests.

Under these conflicting pressures, Sa'id apparently was reluctant to extend his reliance on Britain. He rather preferred to spend on British credit. Since London could not force the sultan from borrowing, and since Sa'id refused to spend what he did not have, Oman's economic outlook suffered considerably. In hindsight, nothing could exonerate Sa'id from the impossible conditions his inaction created, but the theory that he was using the only available means at his disposal to distance Oman from Britain cannot be dismissed out of hand.[10] If this interpretation was corroborated, the unfortunate implication would be that Sa'id bin Taymur was ready to sacrifice a large part of his population and, sadly, that few British officials worried or cared about Oman. Although London did, of course, look after its own interests, Sa'id's decision to leave Muscat in 1959 buttressed the thesis. Salala, in the Dhufar area, would be more peaceful. His self-exile isolated him from most of his family and many of his British advisers and postponed Omani development considerably.

Sa'id embarked on a tightfisted financial management that enabled Oman to pay its debts but also encouraged chaos and disturbances. Opponents rallied around the former imam or the Marxist-inspired, Yemeni-financed People's Liberation Front. Even if his well-meaning efforts to gain his people's independence could succeed in the long run, Sa'id became an albatross with clipped wings.[11] Still, because of Sa'id's reliance on the British to conduct Omani foreign policy, other Gulf leaders scorned him. With the exception of Shaikh Zayid of Abu Dhabi, who visited Sa'id in Salala in 1968, Oman had no Arab allies.[12] The country was physically and politically isolated, threatened by a secessionist movement in the south, dependent on London for its survival, and, more ominously, had few prospects for a disenfranchised population eager to throw the country's doors wide open to Arab nationalism.

Sa'id was deposed on 23 July 1970 after thirty-eight years on the throne. His main aim—uniting Oman—was only partially achieved because the Dhufar area remained isolated and, increasingly, threatened with secession.

SULTAN QABUS

Three decades after Sultan Qabus assumed power, the way he acceded to the throne remains a sensitive subject. There was, to be sure, widespread disenchantment with Sa'id bin Taymur's rule as well as his inability to control rebel activities in Dhufar. Qabus, who was under virtual house arrest in Salalah, became the center of opposition within the ruling family and, with the assistance of several influential members of the household as well as senior British officials (including the consul-general in Muscat, David C. Crawford), plotted to overthrow his father.[13] Understandably, Qabus was bitter toward his father and in an early interview stated that his father "knew five languages, but he wasn't cultured. Knowledge is one thing and culture is something else. He adopted a policy and would not agree to give it up, because he believed that his policy was the best one. He was headstrong and bigoted. He didn't believe in change. His thinking went back to an age which is not this present age. So he had to fall from power, and this is what happened."[14]

Qabus inherited a government vacuum, a civil war in the south, meager finances, and no regional allies. Myriad challenges faced the young ruler, who committed himself to rebuilding the Omani nation-state. To his credit, he quickly realized that his popularity was the result of the new openness policy, not of ingrained adulation, and that he needed to rapidly prove himself in the eyes of his subjects. Rather than shy away from his father's legacy, he distanced himself publicly from Sa'id bin Taymur by declaring: "In the past, I had marked with mounting concern and intense dissatisfaction the inability of my father to control affairs. Now my family and my armed forces have shown their allegiance to me. The old Sultan has left the country and I promise that the first thing I shall dedicate myself to will be the speedy establishment of a modern government."[15]

Qabus flew to Muscat, where he committed himself to change by stating: "Oh people, I shall work with despatch to make your life happier and your future better. Every one of you must help in this task."[16] He appointed his uncle, Sayyid Tariq bin Taymur, prime minister, removed from power key figures associated with the old regime, dismissed Major Leslie Chauncy (then British consul-general) for incompetence, declared slaves and prisoners free, inaugurated a weekly newspaper, the *Al-Watan*, and authorized the establishment of two radio stations, one each in Muscat and Salala.[17] He also granted amnesty to Omanis in exile for plotting against Sayyid Sa'id, appealed to them to return and contribute to a reinvigorated society, and pledged to invest in an Omanization program that would take over from "guests" serving Muscat. Within months, Qabus changed the name of the country to the Sultanate of Oman, adopted a new flag, and devoted a great deal of attention to the Dhufar Rebellion.

Qabus was thirty years old when he first laid eyes on Muscat. He quickly summoned the manager of the Muscat branch of the British Bank of the Middle East, as well as the director of Petroleum Development (Oman) (PDO) and the defense secretary, to brief him on the state of his nation. These officials told Qabus the truth: Oman was financially sound even if in dire straits with regard to national development. Despite such challenges, the young ruler heartened the enthusiastic crowds gathered to welcome him, promising them a prosperous future. The genuine expression of support that many displayed toward the new ruler when so few individuals actually knew him or had seen him before was remarkable. Expectations were high among the population, but government officials had no idea what would or should happen next. Coup leaders, in fact, had barely planned for the day after.

Despite such uncertainty, Qabus realized that a national vision was essential. For without such a vision—shared by the majority of Omanis—it would simply be impossible to establish national unity. The time was right for a radical change in internal Omani affairs. The socioeconomic transformation of the Persian Gulf was proceeding much faster elsewhere than in Muscat, and fear that the sultanate's self-imposed retrenchment might ruin its chances for success ran high. Moreover, Oman's modest oil revenues after 1964 were not devoted to sorely needed development requirements. Tension in Dhufar also meant that the sultanate's entanglement in the south was draining its meager resources and that Sa'id bin Taymur had not been capable of defeating the rebels who challenged his authority. The British were also concerned with the old sultan's archconservatism and intransigence in opening up the sultanate to outside investments. London did not want to leave the area, as plans for precisely such a withdrawal were announced in 1968, leaving behind a dark spot. It was a British responsibility to bring the conflict in Dhufar to an end.

Lacking the experience that his father had when he acceded to the throne, Qabus was ill prepared to take a firm lead and impose his authority. As he knew few Omanis, he was surrounded by British advisers—"alternatively fawning and patronizing"—upon whom he depended for the truth. The young ruler knew that he "could make no positive policy decision without their support, and indeed, without their strength to ensure its implementation." What he lacked were Omani friends and contacts in Muscat and among the tribes of the Batinah coast. His British-led army "controlled communications throughout the country, and through Cable and Wireless Limited, between Oman and the outside world." One astute commentator concluded that "he had escaped from one situation where he had no power into another."[18] Without experience, and lacking the means to achieve independence from his British advisers, Qabus nevertheless set out to tackle the sultanate's many problems on several fronts. He entrusted the establishment of a new government to his uncle and, having drawn one fundamental lesson from his father's legacy, set out to gain economic independence. Because the ruler understood that he needed to prove himself, he addressed the problems of his government head-on and tackled the Dhufar Rebellion without reservation. Determined to bring that festering problem to an end, he vowed to settle the conflict at whatever cost, even with British assistance if need be. His fierce determination demonstrated that Qabus would not shy away from difficulty despite the lack of experience and his isolation in his own country. It also demonstrated that the young ruler was confident in his abilities to introduce change and, above all, trusted his subjects to assume their share of responsibilities.

THE MONARCHY AND THE MODERN STATE

It was first imperative to fill the vacuum in Oman's central political process. Proclaiming his intentions to modernize the country and to abolish unnecessary governmental restrictions imposed by his father, Qabus called on his uncle, Tariq bin Taymur, then in exile, to become prime minister on 9 August 1970 and form the sultanate's first government. Sayyid Tariq, a younger brother of the deposed Sa'id bin Taymur, was educated in Germany and was married to a German woman (his own mother was a Christian Circassian); he was a bon vivant of Beirut society and was well versed in the business world. His command of Arabic, Turkish, English, and German as well as his keen awareness of developments in the Gulf region—the result of his extensive business representations—made him an ideal candidate for the newly created post. To be sure, the ruler was keenly aware that Oman had very limited political capacity. Tariq's savvy was a desperately needed commodity in Muscat. Well informed and intelligent, Tariq was a natural ally of his nephew as both lamented Sultan Sa'id's regressions and lack of trust in the Omani population to lead a developed life. Unlike his brother, Tariq was liked and respected in Oman as well as among the large Omani exiled community throughout the Middle East. For those reasons, members of the British planning committee advised the ruler to bring in his uncle in part to neutralize his enormous potential power. Perhaps this prompted the appointment, but a more logical explanation centers around Qabus's desire to benefit from his uncle's experiences in world affairs.

Both men realized that Oman's internal needs could not be satisfactorily met while the country remained isolated. Qabus charged Tariq with the immense task of securing diplomatic recognition around the world even if regional disputes prevented accelerated resolutions and, in doing so, preserving and developing monarchic rule in the sultanate.

THE POSTCOUP GOVERNMENT: TRANSFORMING MONARCHICAL AUTHORITY

Few really know what caused Tariq bin Taymur's appointment as prime minister. One commentator maintained that "Tariq was invited back personally by the Defense Secretary, and it is not certain whether he made the invitation before or after seeking the Sultan's permission."[19] The evidence buttressing this assertion came from the new prime minister himself, who complained that his responsibilities were left undefined. Since no precedent existed on how responsibilities would be divided, the distribution of authority hinged upon a mix of modern ministerial tasks and traditional, chiefdomlike arrangements and on an entente between the sultan and his prime minister. This lack of clarity regarding burden-sharing may have cast the die against a successful alliance between the two men. The situation was made more difficult because of the hovering British presence, which neither man trusted. It was finally agreed that the sultan would maintain oversight over all financial matters, as well as issues related to the country's petroleum capabilities, defense, and internal security. The prime minister's primary responsibility would be to develop northern Oman. Foreign affairs was left in a vague area, with each of the two men assuming that it fell within his prerogative. It may be useful to add at this juncture that the relationship between the two was a great deal more complex than is generally assumed. To a certain extent, the sultan deferred to his uncle because of the prime minister's age and family relationship, whereas Tariq deferred to Qabus as his sovereign. Whether the pair ever transcended the difficult family pressures imposed on such a relationship is impossible to assess. What is certain, however, was that neither was truly governing the sultanate. That luxury was reserved to the Interim Advisory Council chaired by a retired British colonel—the defense secretary—that behaved in a particularly cavalier fashion. With the prime minister out of the country, the Council reached several decisions that were placed in front of the ruler for ratification.

The position of secretary for financial affairs was first offered to the manager of the British Bank of the Middle East; but when he declined an accountant who had served in Zambia was produced, and Tariq understood that his sole role would be to advise rather than run the department.

Because the sultan maintained oversight over all financial affairs, the Interim Advisory Council assumed that Tariq need not be consulted. In this respect, Qabus behaved like his father, who prevented any Omani from having details of the sultanate's real income. As "over 95 percent of revenue at this time came from oil, and as the oil concession was in the name of the Sultan, this too was kept from Omani eyes."[20] Oil revenues were deposited into a special account from which the sultan would make deposits to the exchequer. This procedure did not change until 1975, when Qabus appointed an Omani to manage the country's finances. Over the years, however, the bulk of oil income went straight to the exchequer, with a modest portion left for the ruler's needs.

The Arab world's political rumor mills, which publicized in the press that Tariq returned to Oman under British coaxing, did little to help bolster the confidence of the fledgling government. Understandably, the prime minister was quite angry with the rumors and resented the undue influence that the sultan's British advisers possessed. He often complained that senior British expatriate officials were making decisions for Oman without anyone's authority, especially in the crucial petroleum, finance, and defense sectors. The best evidence to buttress this assertion was the lack of trust placed by Britain in Omanis to make decisions for themselves. These well-meaning but naive middle-management bureaucrats were too proud to even fathom that Omanis could shoulder basic responsibilities on their own. Tariq was concerned that the ruler's advisers were slick and so persuasive that the options presented were not exclusively aimed at serving Oman's best interests. Often, the prime minister would voice his views so openly that they filtered back, naturally, to the palace. The prime minister thus blamed British advice and interference for a substantial part of Oman's problems in the early 1970s. This anomalous situation attested to the difficulties in determining policymaking and the authority to implement policies. Had the ruler and the prime minister achieved more agreement, had the British advisers provided more sound advice, and had more appraisals and analyses been provided, improvement would have emerged sooner than it actually did.

Moreover, the government was handicapped by a lack of trained personnel who could assume the reins of responsibility at a multitude of bureaucratic levels. To be sure, Tariq did not move to rapidly staff his government with qualified Omanis. Even the basic reorganization of the prime minister's office, whereby a chief of staff would supervise a highly motivated group of specialists, was rejected on the basis that such a realignment interfered in the sensitive relationship between the ruler and his prime minister. When Tariq resigned at the end of 1971, "he still had no staff, not even anyone to type a letter for him, and devoted friends had the unenviable task of opening and actioning some hundreds of letters that had come for him and had been left untouched during his term of office."[21] The introduction of change notwithstanding, mismanagement—overspending, corruption, inappropriate staffing of manpower, financial largesse—accompanied the rush to bring the sultanate into the modern world.

To his credit, Tariq realized the need for planning precisely to help avoid the mistakes associated with the indiscriminate use of the country's natural resources. In November 1970, he instructed his advisers to draw up a five-year plan that unfortunately was conveyed "in the form of a single sentence."[22] What the national priorities and objectives of this plan would be were left unclear; what kind of society the plan envisioned was also left vague. The only guidance was that the plan ought to provide, in its fourth year, a survey of Nizwa with the goal of moving the capital to the interior. Such guidance illustrated how Tariq foresaw the need to heal old wounds and, in this case, unite the country by eliminating perceptions of separation imbedded in the "Muscat and Oman" concepts. Still, nothing came of this, as no plan was ever produced under Tariq.

Although Tariq fared poorly on domestic matters, his diplomatic achievements were substantial. Since Sultan Sa'id bin Taymur had chosen to conduct foreign relations through London, there were no Omani diplomatic representations anywhere in the world in 1970. The extent of foreign representations in Muscat were the British and Indian consulates and the yearly (sometimes twice-yearly) visits of a U.S. consular agent from Saudi Arabia. Sultan Qabus and Sayyid Tariq set out to immediately establish diplomatic relations with Arab and leading non-Arab states. Tariq's numerous contacts with influential leaders in the Arab world facilitated that task immeasurably, and Oman was quickly admitted into the League of Arab States in 1971 against, ironically, the opposition of Iraq and the People's Democratic Republic of Yemen. Membership in the United Nations followed in October 1971. The fact that Tariq spent much of 1971 out of Oman—pleading the sultanate's case on the world stage—in some ways explains his lack of attention to internal matters.

Still, several nonpolitical ministries were quickly set up in 1970. One of the most effective was the Ministry of Health, which was headed by a qualified Omani physician who earned degrees in Pakistan and Britain. Almost immediately, dramatic progress was witnessed in the establishment of hospitals and other health-care facilities. A capable Omani administrator from Zanzibar as well as an experienced Dutch physician, recruited by the Netherlands government as director of medical services, provided sorely needed supervision in setting up the ministry and defining its priorities. Other energy was devoted to the Ministries of Education, Economy, and Labor.

The diversification of authority and the establishment of ministries were innovations. Indeed, the pace of change was so rapid that Muscat was often caught off-guard by internal developments. On 1 September 1971, Omani laborers working for foreign contractors staged a strike, protesting the increasing number of semiskilled foreign workers in the country, mostly Indian and Pakistani. The main target for their criticism—and the target of professional agitators trained outside Oman—was neither the sultan nor the prime minister. The strikers directed their anger toward the minister of labor, quickly highlighting the disharmony that existed within the government and creating a public "awareness that the Sultan and the government were not necessarily always the same entity."[23]

Faced with the dilemma of balancing his own expectations from the prime minister and the contradictory advice he was receiving, Qabus had to consider that a break in his relationship with Tariq was inevitable.[24] Qabus's haphazard decisions to grant oil concessions in the Ras-Minji area to a U.S.-based oil broker, Wendell Philips, in March 1971, and then to withdraw it in December of that year[25] on the advice of an Arab entrepreneur group, was the last straw.

Under the circumstances, as Tariq heard of these developments from newspaper reports and as his relations with Qabus were suffering, Tariq concluded that the British were undermining his position and that the new intelligence services were probably watching him.[26] Disappointed by his own lackluster performance, Tariq bin Taymur left for Germany in December 1971 and resigned in January 1972. Tariq was impeded as well by his own lack of ability and experience in public administration and political development. Eventually, the two men were reconciled, and "uncle and nephew developed a close relationship that was cemented in March 1976 by the marriage of the Sultan to one of Tariq's daughters."[27]

Irrespective of the family's legacy, why did the experiment of a monarchical institution with a prime minister fail in the early 1970s?

First, there was no precedent for any division of power. In earlier reigns, ministers served the sultan with a clear separation of authority. The hastily devised office of prime minister did not allow for a clear division of power, and whether Oman was ready for a modern government was, of course, highly debatable. Unmistakable, however, was the sultan's unwillingness to dilute his power. For his part, Tariq was not prepared to accept a simple administrative role. Ironically, no one other than Tariq was qualified to assume governmental responsibilities, and in the event the need to replace him with another prime minister was not considered.

Second, British interference did a great deal to ensure the failure of the prime ministership, as even a partial shift of authority into the hands of someone they did not trust constituted an unacceptable threat to their influence with the sultan.

Third, despite all their public support for Tariq, regional leaders loathed the establishment of such a precedent. The rulers on the Arabian Peninsula reminded Qabus of the need to maintain a form of government that was well suited for their tribally based societies. Many, if not all, viewed the prime ministership as the first step in the establishment of a constitutional government in which the role of the ruler would not be paramount.

What emerged was a three-pronged pressure cooker that threatened the stability of the young country. Under the circumstances, Qabus made several key decisions to streamline his fledgling government. Over British objections he brought in Arab advisers to recommend appropriate development projects. He also appointed Tariq as his senior adviser while asking several British advisers to leave. Simply stated, Qabus gradually concluded that they were not politically qualified. Finally, although Tariq contemplated the idea of a constitutional monarchy in Oman, neither he nor the sultan were ready for political experimentation. The sultan told a Lebanese journalist that "it was not possible to follow the Western tradition of democratic systems. We are not yet ready to embark upon this stage. We have no constitution. We have no chamber of deputies."[28]

Critics had concluded that Qabus rejected the establishment of a popularly elected constituent assembly. To be sure, a rival organization with effective power would have created a potentially threatening environment for Qabus, especially in the early 1970s. This criticism, however, was proven shallow, as the sultan encouraged the gradual development of a semiparticipatory form of government, with additional steps anticipated over a period of time.

Qabus's Arab advisers reduced his reliance on British support and introduced him to the Egyptian, Jordanian, and Saudi leadership; increased opportunities to receive financial support from alternative sources and coordinate intelligence and surveillance activities; and recruited development experts. Such developments produced two interesting results. First, there was a noticeable change in the country's outlook; second, Qabus grew in the position. While his enemies continued to label him a "British puppet," his authority at home rose steadily. A strong foundation of trust was laid by this ruler, who did not flinch from taking difficult, sometimes painful, decisions and was no longer relying on British advisers alone. When the sultan lost his trust in an individual, including the British secretary of defense, he removed that individual, and that, too, was publicly noted. Within a matter of a few years, British political clout evaporated as the sultan came to rule in toto.

To be sure, Sa'id bin Taymur's policy of looking to the Indian subcontinent for services that the British failed to provide was rapidly amended. The vast Arab world was tapped for whatever Oman needed, thereby ending the sultanate's three centuries of isolation. This was, after all, an Arab country with deep roots in the Muslim world and was not a natural part of the West. Of course, Muscat was keen not to import the Arab world's perennial problems, ranging from the repercussions of the Arab-Israeli conflict to a confrontation with Western powers. Rather, a subtle effort was made to place the country within the larger Arab orbit while reserving the right to alter course as needed. Moreover, the change in outlook did not mean that Muscat was distancing itself from Islamabad in favor of Cairo—geography dictated that the Pakistani capital was closer than the Egyptian capital—but that it was involved in a period of serious reassessment.

By the mid-1970s, a number of ministries were created and portfolios assigned to prominent individuals, and the sultan retained for himself the key

posts of internal security, defense, finance, and oil affairs. Still, this all attested to a privatization of cabinet positions and to the elusive way in which
the sultan conducted his government's defense and foreign affairs, which created major obstacles in coordinating activities within and among the ministries.

Between 21 January 1973 and 14 December 1979, the Omani cabinet
was reshuffled eleven times as the number of ministerial departments grew
from eight to twenty-three. A number of specialized bodies were set up, including the National Defense Council, established on 11 March 1973 to act as
a consultative branch to the sultan, the Interim Planning Council, established
on 7 March 1972[29] and chaired by Thuwayni bin Shihab, and the Central
Bank of Oman, established in December 1974 and under the governorship of
Tariq bin Taymur.[30] To be sure, these changes illustrated the economic
progress under way.

By 1975, however, few political steps were taken to give Oman a written
constitution or a parliament; political parties were not allowed. The scarcity
of such institutions raised serious questions about Oman's political future.
Nevertheless, Qabus was persuaded that an effective parliamentary system
could only exist when Omanis matured politically and exercised their freedom of speech in a more responsible way. According to Qabus, "a parliament
whose members we will choose can be created; we can create a phony parliament to give the impression of a semblance of democracy in our country. All
this is possible, but does it correspond to the aim for which a parliament is
supposed to exist? We need more time to reach this stage."[31] There was more
than an element of truth in his declaration. With few trained Omanis and a
high level of illiteracy (65–70 percent) among its population, the sultanate
was not ready to experiment with political systems in the late 1970s and early
1980s.

By the late 1980s, social development and rapid modernization increased
the demand for legislation on such issues as labor regulations, banking, investment, and exploration of natural resources, among others. As economic
activity picked up in the sultanate, the burdensome task of drafting legislation
by decree took its toll on the ruler and his Council of Ministers. In as much as
the arbitrary decisionmaking process created some resentment among merchants and members of the small intelligentsia, Muscat opted for added participatory steps, in part to alleviate some of the political burdens that over-
whelmed it.

Several government officials proposed to enlarge popular participation
through the Council on Agriculture, Fisheries, and Industry (CAFI). Until
that time, the purpose of the twelve-member, appointed council was to encourage citizen participation in identifying priorities pertaining to basic sub-
sistence. CAFI meetings led a number of participants to speculate on potential economic and political developments. Because multilevel conversations

were encouraged, discussions of "democracy," and how it could be applied to Oman, were routinely held. Those developments led Sultan Qabus to issue a series of royal decrees on 18 November 1981 abolishing CAFI and establishing a State Consultative Council (SCC; al-Majlis al-Istishari lil-Dawla) in its place.[32]

At the SCC's first session, Qabus defined it as "a continuation of [his] policy aimed at achieving a greater scope for citizens to participate in the efforts of the government to implement its economic and social projects [through] the task of formulating opinion and advice" on the country's economic and social development.[33] Despite such lofty goals, the SCC's fifty-four delegates could only advise the ruler, since the SCC was not a parliament and therefore did not possess legislative powers.[34] Few Omanis were aware of what the SCC was supposed to be and do, because the government failed to explain its functions and because each delegate represented "all" of Oman rather than any particular region. Given the sultanate's complex tribal relations, this is understandable, as it is difficult to classify each delegate's constituency. Furthermore, in the absence of an official census, proportional representation remained impractical in the early 1980s. A lack of communications between Omanis further hampered potential progress within the SCC. Because of its limited scope, the SCC was not meant to be a permanent fixture on the political scene. Rather, it was another step in the critical institution-building process, so essential to a state lacking so much. Whether Qabus envisioned a complete set of institutions at this early stage was far less important than his willingness to pursue policies that gradually introduced them. This much is certain: his early mistakes prompted him to adopt more failproof measures to build institutions for and by Omanis.

THE SULTANATE'S EMERGING INSTITUTIONAL FRAMEWORK

Although the sultanate of Oman may be described as an absolute hereditary monarchy, with the ruler in direct control over government, significant political changes have been introduced in recent years.

Another immediate concern was the status of the state itself. Qabus knew firsthand that he was ruling over a divided country. Consequently, he took measures to unify the sultanate, first by changing the name of the country—from "Muscat and Oman" to the "Sultanate of Oman"—and second by amending the Municipality Department. The latter dealt with local affairs up and down the coast, although an earlier statute (Law 1369 [1952]) provided that the Municipality Department had the "power to acquire and hold property both movable and immovable" and the authority to issue "by-laws for the security and good administration of the towns and impos[e] necessary taxes approved by the Sultan."[35] Still, the Municipality Department proved insufficient to run a unified country. Muscat was keenly aware of the need to set up specialized organs that would assume responsibility for specific tasks, carry them out, and, in a rather innovative step, be accountable for whatever activities they conducted.

Qabus formed a Council of Ministers and convened *walis* (regional governors) for a thorough overview of his intentions and plans. The governors maintained law and order throughout the sultanate and reported directly to the minister of interior, who in turn was responsible to the sultan. (It must be emphasized nevertheless that in the interior of Oman real authority was exercised by tribal and religious leaders for the better part of the 1970s.) In addition to the minister of interior, Qabus appointed a minister of justice in 1970. The two were amalgamated into the Ministry of Interior and Justice on 1 January 1972. Although the establishment of the Ministry of Justice did not signify any change in the judicial organization that existed prior to 1970, Qabus displayed a unique acumen for the need to develop an effective—even impeccable—judicial system. In fact, the relationship between political and religious authorities in Oman had been firmly established since the eighth century C.E., when a majority of Omanis embraced Ibadism and "defiantly held fast to their faith and their political independence."[36] He also kept tight control over the armed forces through a deputy minister of defense and on finance through another adviser.

THE MAJLIS AL-SHURA

"With the setting up of this council, a new era and a new experiment start in Oman," declared Sultan Qabus of Oman as he inaugurated the Consultative Council (*Majlis al-Shura*) on 21 December 1991.[37] It was unprecedented in its scope and substance, and Qabus called upon Omanis to assume nation-building burdens. The Majlis, declared the ruler, was intended to bridge the gap between citizen and government. It was, in comparative terms, a concordance. In many respects, the 21 December announcement was the fulfillment of the sultan's earlier pledge to establish a reinvigorated institution in which all *wilayats* (provinces) would be represented.[38] Qabus drew broad outlines for the kind of Majlis he envisaged, calling on the government to submit to the peoples' will and be responsible to its representatives. The Majlis, he declared, will be a "step on the road of participation that will serve the aspirations and ambitions of the citizens throughout Oman."[39] Made at the height of the 1990 crisis in the Persian Gulf when Oman—under United Nations mandate—was poised for war against Iraq, the pledge raised many eyebrows throughout the region. In time, however, others emulated his forward-looking mandate. Still, for Oman, the establishment of the Majlis was nothing short of a giant step forward on the road to full political participation. To be sure, Qabus's frank assessment may well have been dictated by events in the area. Nevertheless, his policies were building on the legacy of the 1980s.[40]

Many compared the Majlis-SCC bodies to the Kuwaiti and Bahraini assemblies (both of which came under strong pressure and were, eventually, abolished), even if the SCC was only meant to act in an advisory capacity.[41] Unlike the Kuwaiti and Bahraini examples, the SCC's deliberations were held in camera, and all of its appointed members were part of the government. Although some deliberative freedoms were allowed, deliberations were mostly rather technical and principally affected the country's economic sector. By and large the debates were cautious, if not bland. As the secretary-general of the Majlis, Abdal-Qadir al-Dhahab, confided: "We were learning how to deliberate." "Even the notion of representation," continued the secretary-general, "was difficult to assess since no precedents existed for us to understand how to articulate positions and act responsibly toward our constituents. Besides we had no idea who our constituents were!"[42] By all accounts, the SCC's forty-five appointed members, of whom seventeen represented cabinet officers, stumbled for the better part of the decade. It was, as Al-Dhahab underlined, a "learning process." Oman's move toward a wider public participation proved to be a slow and complex process.

Yet in that process the new Majlis served as an important state-building institution. Although thirty of its delegates lived in the Muscat region,[43] the fifty-nine members represented the sultanate's fifty-nine provinces. In April 1991, prominent religious and secular members of each province were asked to name three candidates for their respective areas. In turn, each community actively sought candidates to fill the three vacancies. This, in and of itself, required some doing. In fact, since all candidates knew ahead of time that only a single person would represent a province, at least two others would have to accept public defeat and embarrassment. It was only the participatory feature that allowed for a full commitment as many realized that higher interests were at stake. The mere opportunity to be part of Omani history was considered glorious by most. The government did not participate in this initial phase of public deliberation, much of which was held in open forums to encourage participation. In an environment in which honor is paramount, this was a major accomplishment. In the end, a list of 177 candidates was drawn up and submitted to the government in September 1991. After a security screening, the names were submitted to Sultan Qabus for final selection. The sultan then chose a third of the candidates to compose the first Majlis in November 1991. In making his choices, however, he ran the risk of alienating 118 other prominent Omanis whose participation in the process indicated, at the very least, a commitment to the institution. The process moved rapidly after the initial pledge. Qabus appointed Shaikh Abdallah bin Ali al-Qa'tabi Speaker of the new Majlis. Al-Qa'tabi, a former Interior Ministry undersecretary and the

SCC's last president, held forward-looking views, much like those of Qabus. The Majlis would be different from the SCC. Al-Qa'tabi informed his associates that he was ready to shoulder new responsibilities.

Al-Qa'tabi closed the first Majlis session by saying that its establishment was a "curtain raiser for a new era of joint national action," hinting that further political reforms were likely before the completion of the assembly's first three-year term.[44] Others were equally confident that permanent changes were imminent. The deputy prime minister for legal affairs, Sayyid Fahd bin Mahmud al-Sa'id, remarked that more was expected from the Majlis and that it "was only coincidental that there were no women members [in the first Majlis]."[45] This was a clear indication that Oman was not just experimenting with participatory government but that it was taking appropriate measures to stay well ahead of changing circumstances. Women would be called upon to assume their rightful roles in society not for superficial reasons but because it was in the best interests of Oman. The sultan himself took the country's pulse on the issue in the course of his annual tour of the interior.

In informal settings, he heard firsthand his people's grievances, complaints, and suggestions that often belied the picture painted by close advisers regarding the state of affairs in the country. When a grievance had merit, the sultan almost always summoned the responsible minister or officer and instructed him to deal with the matter immediately. It was the sum total of such interactions that most probably persuaded Qabus to call upon his people to take a more active part in the political process.

Unlike with the purely advisory SCC, the sultani decree establishing the Majlis called on its members to assume "responsibilities." In fact, the Majlis's bylaws were quite specific and, at least by Omani standards, nothing short of revolutionary. Article 78, for example, specifically stated that members may question cabinet officers, a privilege that was rapidly exercised.[46] Affirming its new role, the Majlis obtained broader authority in many fields, including the enactment of legislation, participation in the preparation of the country's development plans, and making citizens aware of development goals and priorities. Moreover, the Majlis included in its authority periodic evaluations of the state's efforts in implementing policies, assistance in efforts to preserve the environment and protect it from pollution, and the development of the role of the citizen through feelings of collective responsibility. Such authority was accompanied by a major change in how the Majlis's various organizations operated. It also laid the foundation that determined how duties and responsibilities were carried out to assume continuous coordination and constructive cooperation between the Majlis and the government. The Speaker also affirmed that one of the first duties of Majlis members was to preserve the gains that the Omani revival had achieved in bringing out the innate capabilities of the Omani people, developing their talents, and preparing them for a better future.[47]

It is still too early to determine whether the role of the new Majlis will expand to cover more than economic and social issues; still, it represents a substantial concession to political participation. But for all the progress, the Majlis remains an advisory body—at least for now. The reviewing of social and economic laws, before they become finalized, as well as members' rights to question cabinet ministers, indicate that such activities may eventually translate into a legislative role if the institution were allowed to evolve into an assembly deemed orderly and responsible by the sultan. Its current conservative composition almost guarantees that it will not follow the paths of its Kuwaiti and Bahraini counterparts, which were shut down for embarrassing their respective regimes. In the immediate future, many more sensitive issues will be discussed in public, including most notably the state's strategy for diversifying its income so that oil will not be the only source of national wealth. The thorny subject of self-sufficiency in national work will also receive careful scrutiny. Establishing a national cadre of qualified administrators, and training them within the framework of the "Omanization" plan, is sure to preoccupy many officials as well. Although less enticing than foreign policy or security issues, they are indeed the questions that concern and affect citizens most directly. Discussion of those issues will contribute to the healthy debate under way that, in turn, stands as the precursor to larger and more effective political participation.

TRENDS

Less than three decades ago, the only form of communication between the ruler and his subjects was through the irregular notices posted on Muscat's main gates. Mostly related to "customs" issues, they resembled school bulletin boards, announcing "edicts" from the "bursar and the headmaster."[48] Qabus has brought the country a long way and, in 1994, announced that the membership of the Majlis would be adjusted to eighty to reflect the country's latest census results.[49]

In what was one of his most important pronouncements, the sultan also announced that the first two women members of the Majlis, Shakur bint Muhammad bin Salim Al-Ghammari and Ta'iba bint Muhammad bin Rashid al-Mawwali, would join the institution.[50] Qabus underlined the role that women must play in Omani society, drawing on Islamic teachings to emphasize his points. He chastised those who relegated women to subservient positions and those who belittled women's status in Islam. "Women and men are companions," declared the sultan, and "the Prophet, praise and peace be upon him, has instructed us to the role of women." He called on every Omani woman to shoulder her responsibilities in ensuring that the sultanate benefited from the input of women. Qabus also sought their cooperation to teach children "the habit of saving as a contribution to the national economy" and, more important, to be "frugal and to distance themselves from the extravagance . . . appearing among developing countries."[51]

The ruler called on Omanis to welcome this momentous decision, declaring that the participation of women candidates "will not be confined . . . to the Muscat Governorate, but will gradually be extended in accordance with circumstances in other Governorates and Wilayats." By launching forward on this path, Oman further highlighted its difference from the other conservative Arab Gulf monarchies, even as it drew attention to this critical issue: Muscat understood that the burden of a large and growing expatriate community could only be alleviated by galvanizing the indigenous female population. In a candid interview, the ruler acknowledged that he had "long held the belief that to exclude women from playing a meaningful role in the life of their country amount[ed], in essence, to excluding 50 percent of that country's potential."[52] Squarely addressing the question, Qabus embarked on this epoch-making path. It was a form of accountability that acknowledged the need to draw on internal strengths. For Oman to prosper and succeed in conducting its affairs, as well as to retain its monarchic system of government, it will be essential to maintain domestic harmony, and that is the ruler's primary objective.

Nevertheless, the al-Bu Sa'id dynasty did not promote intercourse with its subjects. By establishing the SCC and the Majlis, Sultan Qabus began a turnaround involving the educated elite in the country's policymaking apparatus. Still, it seems that liberalization of the political system has remained slow as Sultan Qabus has struggled to balance the more conservative tribal elements of society with those of the younger, educated Omanis.

In 1996 Qabus issued the "Basic Law of the State" (*al-Nizam al-Asasi lil-Dawla*)—Oman's first constitution. Such a move can be viewed as yet another step toward wider public participation, but it was mainly aimed to formalize rule in the sultanate at a time when the country was staking its economic future on foreign investments and localization of the workforce. The Basic Law codified much of the existing practice. It defined the type of governance as *sultani* and enshrined the sultanship as hereditary among the male descendants of al-Sa'id.

Elsewhere in the region succession tends to pass from father to son, although the process depends on the assent of the family as a whole. The problem in Oman is that the sultan is childless, and for the first time in more than a century there is no obvious successor. The Basic Law provides a formula for the al-Sa'id royal family to select a new sultan when necessary, namely, within three days of the throne falling vacant. If they fail to reach an agreement, then they must turn to a letter left behind by Sultan Qabus that names his preference. Unlike other Gulf states, Oman's al-Sa'id family is relatively small, numbering fewer than 100 male members, and so speculation about contenders focuses on a limited circle. Although there is no explicitly designated crown prince, some of the ambiguity related to the issue lessened.

Oman has been reaching a new phase, in which the high standard of living enjoyed by its citizens, based on oil revenues, may become difficult to maintain. The oil boom of the 1970s made a high level of prosperity possible. However, neither the oil prices nor the export earnings were sustainable for long, and by 1986 both started dropping. The carefree period, for all practical purposes, was reaching a close.

NOTES

1. Majid Khadduri, *Arab Personalities in Politics,* Washington, D.C.: The Middle East Institute, 1981, p. 242.

2. The comparison with the French leader is appropriate because of similarities in style. De Gaulle referred to his "idea of France" and Qabus aimed to "restore the past glories" of the sultanate. See, for example, Charles de Gaulle, *Memoires de Guerre: L'Appel, 1940–1942)* (Paris: Plon, 1954), p. 1; and "Speech of His Majesty Sultan Qabus bin Sa'id on the Occasion of the 2nd National Day, 18 November 1972," in Muscat, Ministry of Information, *The Speeches of H. M. Sultan Qabus bin Sa'id, Sultan of Oman, 1970–1990,* 1991, p. 19.

3. The historical legacy of Oman is discussed in Nur al-Din Abdallah bin Humayd al-Salimi, *Tuhfat al-Ayam Bi Sirat Ahl Uman* (Cairo, 1966); see also Hamid bin Muhammad bin Ruzayq, *al-Fath al-Mubin fi Sirat ul-Sada Al Bu Saidiyyin* (Cairo, 1977); and Robert G. Landen, *Oman Since 1856: Disruptive Modernization in a Traditional Arab Society* (Princeton: Princeton University Press, 1967).

4. The year 1744, ironically, also saw the rise of the al-Sauds to power in Riyadh. See David Holden and Richard Johns, *The House of Saud: The Rise and Rule of the Most Powerful Dynasty in the Arab World* (New York: Holt, Rinehart, and Winston, 1981).

5. J. E. Peterson, *Oman in the Twentieth Century: Political Foundation of an Emerging State* (London: Croom Helm and Barnes and Noble Books, 1978), pp. 59–60.

6. Ibid., p. 61.

7. Ibid., p. 47.

8. John Townsend, *Oman: The Making of the Modern State* (London: Croom Helm, 1977), pp. 50–51.

9. The 1955 campaign is discussed in James Morris, *Sultan in Oman: Venture into the Middle East* (New York: Pantheon, 1957).

10. In the course of several conversations with Omani officials, this alternative interpretation of Sayyid Sa'id bin Taymur's behavior was amply clarified, with widely divergent conclusions. Some of my interviewees believed that Sa'id bin Taymur was doing what the British told told him to at all times, whereas others entertained the possibility that the ruler was indeed plotting against the British. Without solid evidence to conclude one way or the other, the *possibility* that the ruler may have entertained this option should not be dismissed.

11. Sa'id bin Taymur analyzed the situation rather clearly in 1968 when he stated that he meant to achieve precisely such an independence. See "The Word of Sultan Sa'id bin Taymur, Sultan of Muscat and Oman, About the History of the Financial Po-

sition of the Sultanate in the Past and the Hopes for the Future, After the Export of Oil," in Townsend, *Oman*, pp. 192–198.

12. The invitation to Shaikh Zayid was one of the few foreign policy measures taken by Sa'id bin Taymur. Zayid accepted and the two men discussed proposals to join in the Federation of Trucial States, then under debate in the lower Gulf region. Both men discussed the creation of a greater Oman but that was not to be. See Ian Skeet, *Muscat and Oman: The End of an Era* (London: Faber and Faber, 1974), p. 202.

13. Born on 18 November 1940 and raised in Salalah, the future ruler's confinement was excessively harsh, even if it allowed Qabus to study Islamic Law. In 1958 Sa'id bin Taymur consented to send him to Britain, where Qabus earned a degree from the Royal Military Academy at Sandhurst (1960). Following that, he served a tour of operational duty with a British infantry battalion (the Cameronians) in Germany. Subsequently, he returned to Britain to study municipal government and went on a world tour before returning to Salalah in 1964. Eager to contribute in whatever capacity his father saw most appropriate, Qabus asked senior members of the ruling family to intercede with Sa'id bin Taymur, to no avail. This refusal embittered the young prince, "and by 1970 the Heir Apparent had reached the conclusion that Sa'id should be overthrown." Despite his forced isolation, it must be emphasized that Qabus knew of dramatic changes occurring elsewhere in the world, especially within the Arab arena, and was keenly aware of nationalist sentiments in his own country. News of developments in the Dhufar reached him regularly through a network of Omani and British visitors. See Peterson, *Oman in the Twentieth Century*, pp. 201–202.

14. *Al-Watan*, 6 April 1972, in Townsend, *Oman,* pp. 78–79, n. 1.

15. Sultanate of Oman, *Oman: A Modern State* (Muscat: Ministry of Information, 1988), p. 7.

16. Quoted in Mohammed Ali Masoud Al-Hinai, *The Dynamics of Omani Foreign Policy: Omani-Gulf Relations, 1971–1985*, unpublished doctoral dissertation, University of Kent at Canterbury (UK), 1991, p. 58.

17. Because there were no printing presses in Muscat, *Al-Watan* (The Nation) was printed in Beirut, then flown to the sultanate.

18. Townsend, *Oman*, p. 78.

19. Ibid., p. 79.

20. Ibid., p. 81.

21. Ibid., pp. 83–84.

22. Ibid., p. 85.

23. Ibid., pp. 90–91.

24. Ibid., p. 90.

25. Ibid.; see also Peterson, *Oman in the Twentieth Century,* p. 197, n. 36.

26. Townsend, *Oman,* p. 91.

27. Ibid., p. 92; see also Frank A. Clements, *Oman: The Reborn Land* (London: Longman, 1980), pp. 65–75.

28. *Al-Watan* (Muscat), 6 April 1972, p. 1.

29. This body was replaced in September 1972 with a Supreme Council for Economic Planning and Development—later the Ministry of Development.

30. Clements, *Reborn Land,* pp. 75–90.

31. Attia Adel Moneim Attia, "Oman," in Albert P. Blaustein and Gisbert H. Flanz (eds.), *Constitutions of the Countries of the World* (Dobbs Ferry, N.Y.: Oceana, 1974), p. 3.

32. Dale F. Eickelman, "Kings and People: Oman's State Consultative Council," *Middle East Journal,* 38 (1984), pp. 61–71. The first president of the SCC was Khal-

fan Nasir al-Wahaybi, followed on 28 October 1983 by Hamud Abdallah al-Harthi, an Omani of East African origin educated at Baghdad University.

33. Ibid., p. 56.

34. The SCC was not intended to limit Sultan Qabus's authority; while 9 "cabinet officers" sat on the SCC, the minister of petroleum and mineral resources did not, further indicating the ruler's policies regarding the extent to which participation would be implemented. On 28 October 1983, the SCC membership was increased from 45 to 54. Fifteen of the original members remained in office as 30 new members were appointed by Qabus. Furthermore, while the SCC may have had a semblance of balanced representation from its inception with respect to its members' regional, ethnic, religious, and educational backgrounds (of the original 44 SCC delegates, 18 were from the interior representing tribal leaders, 18 from the capital of Muscat and the Batinah, and 8 represented East African and Musandam officials), it was hard pressed to speak openly about thorny internal matters. The religious breakdown was as follows: 24 Ibadis (54.5 percent), 13 Sunnis (29.5 percent), and 7 Shias (16 percent). SCC members' educational levels were: 17 traditional/basic (39 percent), 5 traditional/advanced (11 percent), 6 primary modern (13 percent), 6 intermediate (13 percent), 4 secondary (9 percent) and 6 university (13 percent). None of the original 45 members were from among the "university-educated Omanis who ha[d] completed the major part of their schooling since the beginning of the 'new era' in 1970." See ibid., pp. 61–67.

35. Text of Omani Nationality Law No. 1 of 1972, published in *The Compilation of Operational Laws*, assented to by the sultan on 13 December 1972 in Husain M. Al-Baharna, *The Arabian Gulf States: Their Legal and Political Status and Their International Problems* (Beirut: Librairie du Liban, 1975), p. lxi. It is instructive to note that Oman was one of the few countries on the Arabian Peninsula to grant citizenship through naturalization.

36. In this respect, the young sultan's training in Britain (where he observed the workings of local government) proved very useful. Nabil M. Kaylani, "Politics and Religion in Uman: A Historical Overview," *International Journal of Middle East Studies,* 4 (1979).

37. "Nas al-Khitab al-Sami li-Hadrat Sahib al-Jalalat al-Sultan Qabus bin Sa'id al-Mu'azam bimunasabat iftitah al-fitrat al-ula li-Majlis al-Shura" (Text of His Majesty Sultan Qabus' Inaugural Address to the First Session of the Majlis Al-Shura), in *Al-Watha'iq Al-Khasat Bi-Majlis al-Shura, al-Fatrah al-Ula* (Private Documents of the Majlis Al-Shura, First Session; hereafter Wathaiq 1991), Muscat: Majlis Al-Shura, 21 December 1991, p. 1.

38. The sultan made this pledge in November 1990. See "Speech of His Majesty Sultan Qabus bin Sa'id on the Occasion of the 20th National Day, 18 November 1990," in *The Speeches of H. M. Sultan Qabus bin Sa'id, Sultan of Oman, 1970–1990* (Muscat: Ministry of Information, 1991), pp. 215–216; see also "Oman Planning Democratic Step, Will Form Consultative Assembly," *Los Angeles Times*, 19 November 1990, p. A14.

39. *The Speeches of H. M. Sultan Qabus bin Sa'id,* p. 215.

40. *Al-Majlis al-Ishtishari lil-Dawla: Abr Aq Min al-Zaman, 1981–1991* (The State Consultative Council: A Decade in Time, 1981–1991) (Muscat: Dar Jaridat Uman, n.d.).

41. Jalal Shams, "Al-Fikr al-Idari fi Majlis al-Istishari li-dawlat Uman" (The Modern Administrative Idea in the Majlis al-Istishari in Oman), *Al-Idari* (1982), parts I–III. On the Kuwaiti and Bahraini assemblies, see John E. Peterson, *The Arab Gulf*

States: Steps Toward Political Participation (New York: Praeger for The Center for Strategic and International Studies, Washington, D.C., 1988), pp. 27–83.

42. Interview with Secretary-General Abd al-Qadir al-Dhahab at Majlis Headquarters in Sib, 29 April 1992.

43. Eickelman, "Kings and People," p. 61.

44. Interview with Speaker Abdallah bin Ali al-Qa'tabi at Majlis Headquarters in Sib, 13 October 1993.

45. Interview with His Highness Sayyid Fahd bin Mahmud Al-Bu Sa'id, Deputy Prime Minister for Legal Affairs in Muscat, 14 October 1992.

46. Wathaiq 1991, p. 48.

47. "Nas Kalimat al-Rad ala Khitab al-Sami alati alqaha al-Shaikh Abdallah bin Ali al-Qa'tabi" (Shaikh Abdallah bin Ali al-Qa'tabi's Response to the Sultani Speech), 21 December 1991, in Wathaiq 1991, pp. 12–17.

48. Skeet, *Muscat and Oman*, p. 29.

49. Husayn Abd al-Ghani, "Al-Sultan Qabus u'linu tadwir Majlis al-Shura wa-yad'u ilal-saytarat ala al-nimu al-sukani" (Sultan Qabus Announces Changes in the Majlis al-Shura's Membership Based on Census Results), *Al-Hayat*, 14 January 1994, p. 6.

50. Husayn Abd al-Ghani, "Qabus iftataha dawrat Majlis al-Shura biltashdid ala dawr al-mara'at" (Qabus Opened the Majlis Session by Stressing a Role for Women), *Al-Hayat*, 27 December 1994, p. 4.

51. "Speech by His Majesty Sultan Qabus bin Sa'id Al-Bu Sa'id on the Occasion of the Opening of the Second Term of the Majlis al-Shura," December 1994.

52. Ann Joyce, "Interview with Sultan Qabus bin Sa'id Al Sa'id," *Middle East Policy*, 3 (1995).

13

The Persian Monarchy and the Islamic Republic

David Menashri

The fall of the shah of Iran in 1979 stands in striking contrast to the manner in which other Middle Eastern monarchies have been toppled. Most were new regimes, toppled mainly by army officers who sought popular support for themselves and their new ideology only after seizing power. By contrast, the Iranian Revolution was a mass movement, led primarily by clerics who enjoyed popular support before seizing power. Moreover, the "new" ideology of the Islamic Revolution was in many ways the return to the glorious heritage of the past and to the ideology—Islam—most familiar to Iranians, which also prescribed their attitudes toward the monarchy and political system.

For all the salient differences distinguishing it from other Middle Eastern coups, the Islamic Revolution was, nevertheless, basically consistent with earlier opposition movements in modern Iran: the Tobacco Movement (1891–1892); the Constitutional Revolution (1905–1911); and the national movement headed by Mohammad Mosaddeq (1951–1953). Those movements had their origins in reactions against the reigning shah's policies, which caused diverse forces to unite around a common cause. In all of them, mass action played a decisive role; their differences notwithstanding, in each movement various groups rallied around one major symbol that proved powerful in unifying them all: tobacco and the concessions in general in the late nineteenth century; constitutionalism and the concept of freedom at the turn of the century; nationalism, oil, and nationalization of oil in the early 1950s; and Islam and an Islamic Republic in 1979.

Although all these movements were successful in attaining their initial goals, the earlier eruptions had set limited objectives. The Islamic Revolution, by contrast, set out—and was able—to change the regime, that is, revolutionaries now claimed that the monarchy's politics—indeed the very nature of its rule—were un-Islamic. "Neither the East nor the West, but the Islamic Republic" (*na Sharqi na Gharbi, Jomhuri-ye Islami*) was one of their most powerful slogans. Put simply, an Islamic republican system was to replace the old monarchical reign.

This chapter will discuss the approach of the revolutionary movement toward the Iranian kingship and the genesis of Khomeini's antimonarchical creed. It would thus also seek to explain the movement's rejection of the monarchy, and review the initial experience in replacing the monarchy by an Islamic-republican system, led by the clergy.

THE LEGACY OF THE PAST: THE SAFAVIDS
AND QAJAR HERITAGE

The Iranian state, since the pre-Islamic era, was essentially based on the twin powers of religion and kingship. A tract on rulership and statecraft (probably from the sixth century) attributed to Ardeshir illustrates the delicate nature of such an interrelationship. He advised his successors that kingship and religion are "twin brothers":

> There is no strength for one of them except through its companion, because religion is the foundation of kingship, and kingship the protector of religion. . . . Be attentive to the teaching of religion. . . . You will be carried by the glory of kingship to [display] disdain towards religion. . . . There will arise within religion leaders lying hidden among the lowly from the populace and the subjects and the bulk of the masses—those whom you have wronged, tyrannized, deprived and humiliated. And know that *a clandestine leader in religion and an official leader in kingship can never coexist within a single kingdom, except that the leader in religion expropriates what is in the hands of the leader of kingship.* [This is so] because religion is the foundation and kingship the pillar, and the lord of the foundation has prior potency over the entire office as against the lord of the pillar.[1]

In fact, since the growing of clerical power that followed the victory of the *usuli* over the *akhbari* doctrine and the decline of the power of the Qajar Dynasty, the Iranian-Shiʿite clerics occasionally led popular movements against the central regime. Already at the outset of the nineteenth century, John Malcolm was struck by the power that Iranian clerics had mastered. These men of religion,

> who fill no office, receive no appointment, who have no specific duties, but who are called—from their superior learning, piety and virtues—by the silent but unanimous suffrage of the inhabitants . . . to be their guides in religion and their protectors against the violence and oppression of their rulers, and who receive from those by whose feeling they are elevated a respect and duty *that lead the proudest of kings to join a popular voice.*[2]

Even though "the theoretical negation" of the legitimacy of temporal powers has been "always kept in reserve" as an "effective weapon against rulers who dared to overrule," the clerical will, in reality that of the *ulama*, more often than not, tended to cooperate with the rulers rather than to negate them or to disclaim their right to rule. Authorities such as Abu Ja'far Muhammad Ibn Hasan Ibn Ali al-Tusi (d. 1068) and Abu Abdallah Muhammad Ibn Idris (d. 1202), recognized the possibility of the existence of "righteous, just rulers" (*al-sultan al-haqq al-adil*) and the permissibility of working for them under certain conditions in the absence of the imam. This recognition received further refinement under the Safavids. To quote Molla Mohammad Baqer (Mohaqqeq Sabzavari; d. 1679), "If there is no just and judicious king to administer and rule this world, the affairs will end in chaos and disintegration." It is therefore "inevitable, and imperative, for people [to be ruled by] a king who will rule with justice and follow the practice and tradition of the Imam."[3]

The Ithna Ashari creed had become the official religion in Iran (early sixteenth century) and "was bound to pose a challenge to the legitimacy of the shah." If the *mujtahids* were the only legitimate rulers of a Shi'ite state, was not the shah a usurper? In terms of their theory, Roger Savory concludes, "he was." But should he be overthrown? "No, said the majority of the ulama . . . [realizing that] even if they conceded the right to govern to the shah, their power in a Shi'i state *without* sovereign control was still greater than it would be in a Sunni state in which they would be in a minority position with no political power at all."[4] Thus, in fact, under the Safavids "the religious institution was incorporated into the organization of the state and subjected to a greater measure of control than herefore and . . . subordinated to the political institution." Ann Lambton adds: "By admitting the need for a king to wield the sword in the exercise of justice, the Shi'is accepted, like the Sunnis before them, the interdependence of religion and kingship."[5]

Jean Chardin, who was in Iran at the time of the coronation of Shah Suleyman (1666), put the situation in a nutshell:

The clerics consider that the rule by laymen was established by force and usurpation, and that civil government belongs by the right to the *sadr* [head of the religious establishment] and to the Church . . . but the more generally held opinion is that royalty, albeit in the hands of laymen, derives its institution and its authority from God; that the king takes the place of God and the prophets in the government of the People; that the *sadr* and all other practitioners of the religious law, should not interfere with the political institution; that their authority is subject to that of the king even in matters of religion. This latter opinion prevails; the former opinion is held only by the clergy and those whom they supervise; the king and his ministers close the mouths of the clergy as it pleases them, and force the clergy to obey them in everything. In this way, the spiritual is at the moment completely subordinate to the temporal.[6]

The *ulama* "continued to uphold the theoretical position, if only in private."[7] Such claims, as Nikki Keddie suggests, may have been expressed more strongly and more often orally and in close circles.[8] Yet eventually the majority of *ulama* then "generally preferred a more acquiescent position toward the monarchy." They even referred to the governance of monarchy as the "Shadow of God on the Earth" (*zil allah ala al-arz*) and viewed the shah as someone who acts "like lieutenant of God" (*shabih janshin-e khoda*)—as did Mirza Abul-Qasem Gilani Qomi during the early Qajar period. Some even alluded to monarchy and clergy as complementing each other in securing faith and the current affairs of the people.[9] They have often stressed, however, that in the absence of the Hidden Imam, the "King's rule is a trial" and did not carry any divine legitimacy.[10]

The Safavid collapse put an end to whatever "religious pretensions" the rulers had, and—to borrow Said Arjomand's terminology—"caesaropapist-monism" gave way to a "hierarchy-state dualism." Shi'ite jurists legitimized this division, "stressing the independence of religion and kingship," acknowledging the importance of their collaboration.[11] Once the separation has been established, and "given the indisputable superiority of God over earthy powers, theocratic monism is but further logical step that could theoretically be taken at any time."[12] Yet even then there has been no such direct claims under the Qajars. The *ulama* seemed content with the prevalent division of political and religious authority and acknowledged the autonomy and power of the kingship.[13]

Khomeini's predecessors in the Constitutional Revolution did not negate the monarchy as such but mostly wished to limit its power and force the shah to follow the counsels of the *mujtahids*. With the independence and survival of the country at stake, out of love for the country rather than loyalty to the monarchy, they felt that "illegitimate or irreligious monarchy" (*saltanat-e gheir-e mashrue*) had to be tolerated, even if temporarily. Some thought this was necessary even to protect Islam.[14] In the conflict between the *mellat* (nation) and the *doulat* (state), the *ulama* supported constitutionalism for the strengthening of an "Islamic kingship."[15] Even the activist clerics then had held "the rule of the infallible Imam" as "presently impossible" and supported a temporal constitutional regime, provided it "corresponds with religion and limits the king's dictatorship."[16] Moreover, the idea of republicanism was generally unknown and often not fully perceived by most Iranians. Thus, Mehdi Qoli Hedayat, for example, though greatly impressed by the ideas of freedom and fraternity of the French Revolution, still regarded the republic as an ineffectual system of rulership. He viewed it as "a school without a headmaster."[17]

For a while in 1924, Reza Khan seemed to entertain the idea of republicanism. Although his actions make his sincerity about such an idea "seriously questionable," the leading *ulama* then set against the idea on the basis of its incompatibility with Islam.[18] Ayatollah Hasan Modarres led the campaign. Again, it was due not only to strict doctrinal devotion but also to pragmatic calculation—the nature of the "republic" Reza was about to establish and its links with imperialism.[19] What the *ulama* feared most were probably the secularizing policies of Kemal Ataturk's republicanism. Moreover, according to his own testimony, Modarres was not necessarily against a "true republic" (*jomhuri-ye vaqei*). In fact, he said, the rulership at the outset of Islam was, in a way "a kind of republican government," (*taqriban va balke tahqqiqan*). Yet the "kind of republic" that Reza Khan and the supporters of republicanism "want to impose on us," he added, "is not based on the will of people" but only reflects Britain's schemes.[20] Be that as it may, when the bill was presented to the Majlis on 20 March, Modarres and his group formed a coalition with the antirepublican faction in the Majlis to oppose it. Those opposing republicanism alluded even then that an attack on the monarchy was tantamount to an attack on Islam. Demonstrators in the Majlis Square shouted: "Down with the republic!" (*morde-bad jomhuri*) and "We want the Prophet's faith, we don't want a republic!" Reza backed off, submitting—he said—to the will of the nation.[21] Visiting Qom, he went on to promise to safeguard Islam. Consequently, a telegram sent by the leading religious authorities (Ayatollahs Abul-Hasan Isfahani, Mohammad Hosein Na'ini, and Abdul-Karim Ha'iri) confirmed: "There have been expressed certain ideas concerning a republican form of government that are not to the satisfaction of the masses and inappropriate to the needs of the country." Having been asked by the signatories to "eliminate" such an idea, Reza Khan did conform. They, therefore, commended him: "May God grant that all people appreciate the extent of this act and give full thanks for this concern."[22] In 1924, thus, many of the mainstream *ulama* still seemed to view the monarchy as a suitable form of government for Iran,[23] and some were convinced that monarchy and Islam were interdependent.[24]

In December 1925, Reza Khan—then adopting the surname Pahlavi— "with a view toward reviving the imperial glory of pre-Islamic Iran"—was appointed by the Majlis to be the shah of Iran.[25] Reza Shah, in turn, pledged to safeguard Islam. In his oath before the Majlis, he swore "on the Word of God and on all that is revered in the eyes of God" to "defend the territorial integrity of the kingdom and the rights of the nation" and to "strive for the propagation" of Ithna-Ashari Shiism.[26] Yet his actual policy proved quite distinct from such confessed devotion. In practice, he conformed to what Pio Filippani-Ronconi called "the traditional pattern of the *Shahanshahi-ye Iran*, viz., the sacral royalty of Iran."[27] His son Mohammad Reza Pahlavi took this notion even farther, both in his practical politics and his ideological perceptions of the nature and role of the monarchy.

KHOMEINI'S EARLY THOUGHT: OPPOSITION TO THE SHAH

In his early writings, Khomeini did not demand the concentration of political authority in the clergy. In a way, his views during the 1940s and 1950s were generally in keeping with the attitudes current among the mainstream *ulama* of the time. In fact, by 1953 many of them supported the shah against Mosaddeq.[28] Although part "of the sullen opposition of the Pahlavis," Khomeini politically followed Ayatollah Mohammad Hosein Burujerdi, the leading religious authority of the time, who out of fear of anarchism and leftists cooperated with the monarchy to preserve law and order.[29] Burujerdi rejected clerical involvement in politics, viewed monarchy and Islam as fundamental to Iranian nationalism,[30] and even expressed "admiration for the Shah in warm and friendly terms." He said in 1960: "I pray day and night for the person of the Shah-in-Shah, for whom I entertain sincere regard."[31]

In his discussion of governance in *Kashf al-Asrar* (Revealing of the Secrets; first published in the early 1940s), Khomeini undertook a mild defense of the monarchical system, in keeping with Burujerdi and the "traditional" clerical view. He then wrote: "We do not claim that the government [*hokumat*] should be in the hands of the theologian [*faqih*]" but that the government should act "according to the divine law," as is in the best interest of the state and the people. The religious leadership should have "supervision [*nezarat*] over the legislative and the executive branches of the Islamic state." The shah should follow the law and view himself as part of the state and be committed to serve the people and not transgress the boundaries of the divine law.[32] True, "the form of monarchy then regarded as acceptable by Imam Khomeini bore little resemblance to the actual state of the Iranian monarchy" in the 1970s,[33] but the point remains that at that time Khomeini still ascribed to the "traditionalist" idea that the *ulama* should advise rulers rather than replace them.[34]

Even in the early 1960s, while forcefully attacking the shah and his reform program (during the White Revolution), Khomeini still stopped short of labeling the monarchy as un-Islamic.[35] In 1963, referring to the shah's father's exile, he turned to Mohammad Reza Pahlavi and stated: "Shah, I don't wish the same to happen to you; I don't want you to become like your father. Listen to my advice. Listen to the ulama of Islam."[36] Upon being released from arrest (April 1964), Khomeini made a similar statement: "Do we say the government should go? We say the government should stay. But it should respect the laws of Islam, or at least the constitution." Khomeini, thus, seemed then "to hold out the hand of compromise" and "to suggest there would be grounds for reconciliation," if the government "accepted the guidance of the religious community, and allowed the ulama a share in administration."[37] Even in his initial years in Najaf, he still seemed to uphold a similar attitude.[38] Eventually, in the late 1960s, Khomeini formed his antimonarchical conceptions. But even so, until just before the revolutionary takeover, he remained careful not to demand the overthrow of the monarchy.[39]

Since the Islamic Revolution, public attention in the region and beyond has been focused on Khomeini to the point of equating his vision with Islam, or at least with Shiism. But, then, as before, Shiism has not been monolithic, with the Shi'ite concepts of *ijtihad* and *taqlid* virtually guaranteeing pluralism. In fact, Khomeini's revolutionary doctrine—and his rejection of the monarchy—have not been supported by the *ayatollah uzam* (grand ayatollahs) of his time.

The most profound differences were visible between Khomeini's revolutionary creed and the thought of Ayatollah Mohammad Kazem Shari'atmadari, the most prominent cleric in Iran in the 1970s. For Shari'atmadari the main goal of the revolution was to establish a democracy based on the will of the people in the light of Islamic law.[40] Even during the revolutionary upheaval of 1978, he still seemed to view the establishment of a true Islamic government as unattainable. Moreover, for him, the change of government was not an end but rather a means: the replacement of the monarchy by a republic, he stressed, would be meaningless, unless complemented by democratization.[41] Just prior to the shah's exile he still maintained: "It is not the form of government that is important, but the way it behaves."[42] The Islamic republic, he acknowledged after Khomeini's triumphant return to Iran, would be very different from the times of the Prophet and Imam Ali. "They were God's appointed representatives," he said, whereas now "no Prophet and Imam exists"; the leader of the Islamic state will be "an ordinary man elected and dismissed by other men."[43]

Like Khomeini, Shari'atmadari regarded lawmaking as the prerogative of God and legal interpretation as the prerogative of the *ulama*. Yet, Shari'atmadari, coming closer to the Western concept of republicanism, offered wider responsibility to the people in deciding their path. In his view, an Islamic regime is "based on the people's will. It is the government of the people, for the people and against dictatorship and despotism."[44] Even after the revolutionary success, he said: "In Islam there is no provision that the clergy must absolutely intervene in matters [of state]."[45] Clerical involvement in day-to-day politics should be limited, in his view, to functions of guidance, instruction, and supervision.[46] In a March 1979 referendum to determine the fate of the regime, he demanded a free choice: instead of asking "Are you in favor of an Islamic republic?" he suggested leaving the question open to "What kind of political system would you prefer?"[47] He scorned the articles in the constitution vesting undiluted powers in the clerics, claiming that they expropriated people's sovereignty. Explaining his decision to ultimately boycott the plebiscite to approve the constitution (December 1979), he said: "It is inadmissible for an article of the constitution to enshrine the principle that the power is embodied in the nation [Articles 5 and 56] . . . and for others [Articles 4, 5, and 110] to take the power from the people and entrust it to a few individuals."[48] Although Khomeini's creed might have been more loyal to the theoretical philosophy of the early days of Islam, Shari'atmadari's traditionalist vision was in greater conformity with the mainstream views of recent centuries' *ulama*.

Another prominent cleric, Ayatollah Mahmud Taleqani, a leading figure in Khomeini's revolutionary camp, published in 1955 Mohammad Hossein Na'ini's essay "Hokumat az nazar-e Islam" (Rulership from an Islamic Point of View; orig. 1909), in defense of the constitutional movement against detractors who had declared it un-Islamic. In his introduction, Taleqani hailed the essay, which he viewed as "not only a means to provide the constitution with an Islamic basis, but, more importantly, as a source for the study of Islamic social and political principles."[49] In a debate in the early 1960s on the selection and function of the *marja-e taqlid* (source of imitation) he further elaborated against the conception that a single individual could be the *marja* and proposed to form a central council of clerics instead. Such "decentralization," he then said, would lessen the chances of dangerous intervention in politics on the part of the *marja*.[50] After the victory of the revolution, he still believed that clerics' political activity should be reserved for exceptional circumstances only and appealed to the clerics to return to the mosques in view of the chaos that the revolutionary committees had wreaked on Iranian society immediately after the takeover. He declared in June 1979 that acceptance of political office by clerics would only "increase existing problems."[51]

KHOMEINI'S REVOLUTIONARY APPROACH: *VELAYAT-E FAQIH*

Since 1970, Khomeini denounced the monarchical system, arguing that its basic principles (dynastic succession and ceremonial trappings) contradict the principles of government and political organization of Islam. In his book *Al-Hukumah al-Islamiyyah*, he elaborated on this new-old vision. God, he then wrote, "has no partner" and is "the True Monarch." Therefore, Islam "proclaims monarchy" as a "wrong and invalid" system of rulership. It represents the "evil system of government" that prompted Imam Hussein "to rise up in revolt and seek martyrdom in an effort to prevent its establishment" in the seventh century.[52] He stated that Islam "is fundamentally opposed to the pillar of monarchy"[53] and cited the Quranic verse *Lahul-mulk* to sustain this claim.[54] In his view, "the greatest disaster that befell Islam" was the usurpation of rule by Mu'awiya from Ali, "which caused the system of rule to lose its Islamic character entirely and to be replaced by a monarchical regime." The shahs' crimes "have blackened the pages of history." Even those monarchs who were reputed as "good" were "vile and cruel"; the "deeds of the evil monarchs one can scarcely comprehend." He quoted the Prophet that "the title of King of Kings [Shahanshah] . . . is the most hated of all titles in the sight of God. . . . Monarchy is one of the most shameful and disgraceful reactionary manifestations."[55] In the absence of the imam, therefore, the clerics are the only legitimate source of authority. The ideal system is an Islamic republic.

In this philosophy, however, the term *republic* does not necessarily contain the Western democratic associations of sovereignty of the people. In fact, it seems to reflect mainly antimonarchist intentions. The terms *velayat-e faqih* and *hokumat-e Islami* express his innermost thoughts better than *Jomhuri-ye Islami*. Interestingly, Arjomand stresses in his book *Al-Hukumah al-Islamiyyah* that "there is no mention of an Islamic *republic*." Certainly, the "delegitimization of monarchy" occurred prior to the legitimization of "Islamic government" and "was a far more important factor in contributing to the demise of the Pahlavi regime." The idea of republicanism did gain some currency in Iran following World War I and even more so in the 1940s (with the formation of the Kurdish Republic of Mahabad and the establishment of the independent Republic of Azerbaijan), but "it remained in the background" and began to be espoused openly only on the eve of the revolution.[56]

There seemed thus to be a "remarkable consensus" among Shi'ite jurists throughout the centuries regarding the interpretation of the "authority verse" of the Quran (IV:59): "Obey God, His Prophet, and those who command authority." According to their idealistic vision, those in authority (*ulu'l-amr*) are neither the rulers (emirs) nor the *ulama*—neither of whom is immune from error and sin—but rather the infallible (*ma'sum*) imams.[57] In the imam's absence, however, kingship enjoyed some legitimacy as an acceptable tool of governance. The "shaking of the foundations of the legitimacy of monarchy" began "with the erosion of the traditional conceptions of kingship resulting from the introduction of democratic theories in Iran."[58] But, taking it all in all, there has been "no concrete exposition or justification of active political authority for the jurisconsult."[59] This continued, says Arjomand, up to Khomeini's "formulation of a new Shi'ite political theory."[60] Khomeini's claims that monarchy is un-Islamic and that the *fuqaha* should rule directly, adds Nikki Keddie, "were new to the mainstream of Shi'i thought."[61]

In modern Iranian history, few prominent figures have in fact advocated, "with varying degree of elaboration," the prerogative of the *faqih* to assume political power: al-Karaki (mid-sixteenth century), Molla Ahmad Naraqi (1771–1829), and Khomeini.[62] Khomeini refers mainly to the legal work of Naraqi (*awa'id al-ayam*)[63] but "extends" such early *usuli* arguments, "which were designed to establish the legal authority of the Shi'ite doctors, to eliminate the duality of hierocratic and temporal authority altogether."[64] It was "a political struggle," and Khomeini's motives had "little to do with theological traditions." He "instituted political innovation in the garb of traditional religion," Bayat maintains. He has, in fact, "effectively revolutionized Shi'i Islam."[65]

In a way, ideologically speaking, Khomeini's doctrine thus constitutes a revolution in Shi'ite theology no less than an Islamic revolution. He proposed new interpretations and gained his support mainly from low-level clerics, over the heads of the leading theologians. Yet he made his "new" creed the ideology of the Islamic republic and the philosophy of the Islamic regime in power. It was, thus, a revolution that led to the formation of an Islamic regime.

THE ORIGINS OF REVOLUTIONARY THOUGHT

How can one then account for the profound change in Khomeini's concepts in the 1970s? Why did he combine opposition to the shah with total rejection of the monarchy?

Clearly, Khomeini's ideology had its roots in early Islam. The functional and doctrinal changes in Shi'ite Islam of the last two centuries—the victory of the *usuli* creed, the decline of the power of the Qajar Dynasty throughout the nineteenth century, and the previous popular movements against the regime—further contributed to shaking the bases of monarchy and helped to prepare the ground for such a change. The more activist-revolutionary atmosphere in Najaf may have similarly influenced his vision. It was there that radical neofundamentalism was first developed to some degree by Ayatollah Muhsin al-Hakim (the *marja-'e taqlid* in the 1960s) and later by Ayatollah Muhammad Baqir al-Sadr.[66] The new generation of Iranian lay Shi'ite political thinkers in the 1960s (i.e., Jallal Al-e Ahmad, Ali Shari'ati, Abul-Hasan Bani Sadr, and Mehdi Bazargan) had had their share, too, in weakening the legitimacy of the monarchy and proposing an alternative system. The call of lay intellectuals for struggle (*moqavemat*) against the shah, their criticism of the West, and their appeal to Islam to arouse the masses and as the cure for the problems facing Iran were in keeping with Khomeini's general thinking during his years in Najaf. He maintained ties with Iranian intellectuals and encouraged them.[67] It seems that they, in turn, encouraged him. Antimonarchical thought and support for republicanism could be more easily found in their vision than in his own Islamic perceptions.

But whatever possible intellectual antecedents we can cite, Khomeini's ideology was still mainly a response to the realities in Iran as they emerged since the 1963 White Revolution. The social, economic, and political roots of the Islamic Revolution have been already discussed by numerous scholars. Here, reference will be made only to the possible causes for antimonarchy sentiments and thoughts.

In modern Iran, a clear correlation can be seen between the strength of the shahs and their policy toward the *ulama*. When the shah was weak, he usually accommodated them. When he felt strong, as was the case during the years of the White Revolution, he often acted against them. Mohammad Reza Pahlavi went much farther, not only in the measures taken to suppress Islam but also in proposing alternatives, which—viewed from the *ulama* perspective—were tantamount to blasphemy and constituted a threat to faith. Khomeini's creed was, in a way, "a belated political reaction to the *ulama*s' loss of influence in a rapidly changing society."[68] And, in fact, the claim that the responsibility of the *faqih* to rule "is primarily a political manifesto and not a jurisprudent proposition."[69] In his bid to overthrow the shah from his place of exile in Iraq, "Khomeini took a bold step" by asserting that the *ulama*—and only they—possessed the "right to rule."[70]

While advancing secularization and offending the religious establishment, the shah also worked to exploit religious sentiments to reinforce the monarchy and his rule. He wished to make the monarchy, not Islam, appear as the cohesive element of Iranian society. In his words: "We have always had differences of race, color, creed . . . but under the monarchy, the divergencies have been sublimated into one larger whole symbolized in the person of the Shah."[71] In fact, he worked to limit the role of Islam in the country and to make the person of the shah the symbol of the Iranian state. While proclaiming the White Revolution, the shah still appealed for a triangular loyalty to God (*Khoda*), shah, and homeland (*mihan*). Twelve years later, when he formed the Rastakhiz (Resurrection) Party, he demanded instead loyalty to the monarchy, the constitution, and the White Revolution.[72] God no longer figured in the list. The shah made the exclusion of Islam from Iran's official life clear and loud on the fiftieth anniversary of Pahlavi rule. He declared: "We, the Pahlavi dynasty, nurse no love but that of Iran, and no zeal but for the dignity of Iranians; recognize no duty but that of serving our state and our nation."[73]

Yet he reaffirmed his faith in Islam[74] and used religious terms to legitimize his reforms. He often related the stories of how Imam Ali, Imam Reza, and the Hidden Imam appeared to him in his youth: "From the time I was six or seven, I have felt that perhaps there is a supreme being who is guiding me. . . . I am convinced that I have been able to accomplish things that, unaided by some unseen hand, I could never have done."[75] He attributed his achievements to his being "guided by an unseen hand, and watched over by the mystical force." Throughout his life, he added "this divine spark has guided me, helped, protected, and saved me."[76] God "had ordained me to do certain things for the service of my nation," he said; "I consider myself merely an agent of the will of God."[77] And again: "My reign has saved the country, and it has done so because God was on my side."[78] After the countercoup in 1953, he added: "Once again the mysterious divine power came to my rescue, made my people revolt against Mossadeq . . . brought me back to my country and restored to me my crown and kingdom."[79] His exile in 1953, he said, "reminded me, as a good Muslim, of Mohamed's Hegira . . . who 'fled' only to dramatize his situation. I could do the same."[80] In fact, he once said that he viewed as one of his objectives "to rebuild the faith in the way the prophet really meant the religion to be."[81]

In 1967, he crowned himself. "I represent the people of Iran," he reasoned. "Through my hands, it is they who crown me."[82] The 1971 celebrations to commemorate the twenty-fifth anniversary of the monarchy were in fact also part of a policy aimed at eliminating Islam as the main element of social cohesion, to be replaced by loyalty to the monarchy and the nation-state; to place the monarchy and the shah above religion and the clerics. To Western critics the shah then replied: "You Westerners don't know the philosophy behind my power. The Iranians think of their sovereign as a father. What you call 'my celebration' was to them the celebration of Iran's father. The monarchy is the cement of our unity."[83]

An even more blatant step in the same direction occurred in 1976, when the Muslim calendar was replaced by an "imperial" one, counting the years from the accession of Cyrus the Great, rather than from the Prophet's Hijra. The calendar issue antagonized religious and nonreligious people alike. The decision was taken only a few days before the Persian New Year, without any public debate. Furthermore, the new year was declared to be the year 2535, even though the 2,500th anniversary had been celebrated only five years previously. Ironically, Marvin Zonis noted, "the highwater mark of the grandiosity of the Pahlavi system was reached only three years before the Shah's fall." Thus, "the grandiosity and fall" were linked.[84]

It was the shah who had equated the monarchy, nationalism, and the reform "revolution" and made them identical with his rule. The shah found further comfort in the scholarly glorification of the monarchy in Iranian history.[85] His adoption of the title *aryamehr* (leader of the Aryan race) "reaffirmed this primordial spirit of Iran fostered by a monarchy whose aim was to combine the continuity of the ancient principles with modern transformation." Filippani-Ronconi added: "The concept of sacral kingship" thus appeared to be "consciously cultivated in Iran twenty-five centuries after the foundation of the Achaemenian Empire," and the "figure of the Eternal King" was "further personalized."[86] As Prime Minister Emir Abbas Hoveyda wished to portray it, Iran and the monarchic system "are so closely interwoven" that they "represent one concept."[87] Likewise, Khomeini, in his opposition to the shah, anathematized them all: throwing the "baby" (Iranian nationalism, monarchy) out with the "bathwater" (the shah and his policies). Sacral kingship, thus, was replaced by an Islamic republic.

THE AYATOLLAHS IN ACTION

Perhaps the most profound achievement of the Islamic Revolution was the unification of religion and state and the transfer of all powers—religious and secular—to the highest religious authority: the *marja-e taqlid*. Yet it was in this realm that the revolution probably faced its most crucial challenge and its dogma experienced the most devastating retreat. The problem was twofold yet interrelated. First was the need to reconcile the philosophy of the Islamic Revolution and the interests of the Iranian state and to define the limits of government authority under an Islamic rule; second was a political and personal challenge, relating to succession, the power structure, and the struggle for power following the death (in 1989) of the founding father—Ayatollah Khomeini.

In contrast to the revolutionary creed, power was gradually moved from theologians to religio-politicians.[88] Khomeini himself sanctioned the supremacy of the pragmatic interests of the state over the philosophy of the revolution. The decisions of 1987–1988 "in favor of state paramountcy in society's affairs" gave "dramatic new power to the state" and sanctioned its dominance.[89] Hashem Rafsanjani then interpreted Khomeini's guidelines, stating: "In our country, the law should follow Islamic doctrine. However, if necessary, priority will be given to government decision over doctrine."[90] Khomeini's succession promoted a similarly blatant deviation from the *velayat-e faqih* vision. According to the Shi'ite tradition embodied in the 1979 constitution, Khomeini's successor was supposed to be the most learned and righteous (*a'lam wa-asdaq*) *faqih*. But the prominent theologians of the postrevolutionary era did not fit politically, as none of them fully identified with his revolutionary creed, and the religio-politicians lacked the scholarly credentials for succession. That no single ayatollah was recognized as a sole *marja* and that theological rifts persisted among the top clerics was not exceptional in Shi'ite history.[91] But then, with actual power vested with the shahs, their differences "existed in books" only.[92] With civil power assumed by the clerics, such disagreements have severely disturbed the proper functioning of the government.

The constitutional changes of 1989 gave official blessing to the eventual separation of *marja'iyya* from *velayya*, to allow any *faqih* with "scholastic qualifications for issuing religious decrees" to assume leadership. Moreover, it was then decided that preference should be given to those who are better versed in topics of "political and social issues." Although the level of religious scholarship for the position of the *Rahbar* (Supreme Leader) was deemphasized, political experience was given greater weight. The selection of Ayatollah Ali Khamene'i for succession (then only a Hojjat ul-Islam), and the eventual separation of *marja'iyya* from *velayya*, were blows to one of the most basic revolutionary creeds. Clerics (albeit of lesser ranks) were still in charge; but authority was not exercised by the *maraje'* (sources of authority). Khamenei had never been considered one of the prominent *mujtahids* qualified to give an independent opinion.[93] And even now, "no mullah or religious student, nor any ordinary Iranian" would "seek a *fatwa* from him."[94] Such a separation "is a major blow to the regime's conception of itself as an Islamic state."[95] This was a "divorce" between the supreme religious and political functions.[96]

No less devastating were the realities established under the Islamic rule. The newspaper *Salam* (published in Tehran) wondered whether, given the prevalent economic crisis and the poverty and sufferings of the masses, it was at all possible "to term Iranian society an Islamic society?"[97] Referring to a renowned *hadith*—"*Al-mulk yabqa maa al-kufr wala yabqa ma'a al-Zulm*" (a regime can survive under circumstances of blasphemy but it can not survive in a reality of injustice) one reader asked *Jahan-e Islam*: "Isn't all this discrimination, favoritism, overcharging, . . . nepotism . . . shortages . . . and the existing social gaps" a clear sign of injustice?[98] Moreover, some members of the ruling elite abused their "power and amassed great wealth, which contributed to the growing chasm between themselves and the traditional clergy." Even more disturbing for the latter, the clerics in power were "debasing the spiritual values" by their "corrupt behavior."[99] The contradiction of the regime—wealthy *mullah*-bureaucrats preaching virtue to the poor—had further "engendered rampant anger and cynicism" in the views of some observers.[100] The clergy's image, in the views of many, was thus "deeply tarnished."[101] Clearly, the Iranian Revolution has shown that Islam can serve as "a powerful ideology of resistance," with an "immense capability for mass mobilization," but as the hegemonic ideology of a modern bureaucratic state, it is "no less susceptible to the corrupting influence of power and privilege than other ideologies."[102]

Combining the multiple distress, Hashim thus concludes: Iran in the early 1990s has been "ideologically bankrupt, economically and morally exhausted . . . increasingly unpopular domestically." It faced "acute pressures and threats" to its political legitimacy and domestic stability.[103] Abbas Abdi (one of the mentors of the 1979 hostage-taking) noted that the revolution "has failed to change the political structure of the country."[104] More than that, politics and Islam "are now clearly separated in the minds of many who not long ago would have used religious vocabulary to describe their political aspirations."[105]

Given clerical control on one hand and harsh reality on the other, one could also attribute the government's failures to Islam. Seyyed Mohammad Qomi, giving vent to such concerns, challenged the doctrine of *velayat-e faqih* altogether. By nature, he claimed, state and religion—not monarchy and Islam—"are incompatible" and "must be separated." Since governments inevitably commit violations, it is counter to the interests of Islam that clerics run the state. The clerical rule, he maintained, had already disgraced Islam.[106] Some clerics have thus become "just as cautious about becoming too involved in politics as their nineteenth century predecessors had been."[107]

Many Iranians express the fear that in the long run the Iranian-Islamic experience may prove harmful for Islam. One foreign journalist challenged Rafsanjani. Although Iranian policy is based on Islam, he said, the situation in Iran is no better than in other developing countries. How is it then possible to regard "the rules of Islam" as "the best" guide to solving "the country's problems"?[108] Former Prime Minister Medhi Bazargan warned that the new realities were "the main threat" to "Islam as a faith."[109] Mohammad Khatami (the former minister of Islamic Guidance who was elected president in May 1997), expressed fear—well before his election to the presidency—that such realities even "endangers Islam."[110] Tehran University philosopher Abdul-Karim Sorush, making a distinction between religion and ideology, pointed to the dangers of turning Islam into a governing political ideology.[111] So did some prominent clerics, such as Ayatollah Hosein Ali Montazeri and Ayatollah Ahmad Azeri-Qomi (d. 1999), as well as intellectuals like Hojjat ul-Islam Mohammad Mojtahed Shebastari and Hojjat ul-Islam (and professor) Mohsen Kadivar in Iran today.[112]

In addition, many Iranians openly question the very basic concept of *velayat-e faqih* and its conformity with the initial concept of the Islamic Republic. Thus, for example, Heshmatollah Tabarzadi, one of the leaders of the Iranian students, said in an interview in 1999 that the Islamic republic has turned into *velayat-e faqih* that gradually turned into *velayat-e faqih motlaqe* (an absolute) and eventually became now *velayat-e faqih motlaqe fardi* (an absolute *velayat-e faqih* ruled by one person), who is regarded as standing above the law and the constitution. Was all the bloodshed meant only to replace the shah with someone with even wider authority? he asked. Tabarzadi went on to say that in fact an Islamic republic does not exist any more in Iran, that the rule of one supreme authority stands against the law and the constitution, which negates the very concept of republicanism and is, in fact, anti-Islamic.[113]

No less important, Islam is now seen as the "official ideology; and the clergy, no longer as the savior of the people but as the state's agents." The gap has widened "between the imposed Islamic culture and the evolving Iranian society."[114] Many Iranians are "questioning the very notion of clerical rule" and claiming that the practices of the Islamic rule "are giving Islam a bad name."[115] A "growing array of political interest groups, intellectuals, and even some mullahs argue that it's time for the clergy to begin sharing power or stepping aside." Many clerics now "think it was a mistake to take government office."[116] Ayatollah Mohammad Reza Mahdavi-Kani, upon resigning his post as the head of the Tehran Militant Clergy Association, urged that the next president should not be a cleric but someone with proven management ability and political and economic experience.[117] The next president, some suggested, should wear a tie rather than turban. After centuries of struggle between the turban and the crown—as Arjomand put it—and after the former has emerged triumphant, there are calls to replace the turban with a necktie. As things turned out, the new president, Mohammad Khatami, is a Hojjat ul-Islam. But his election clearly demonstrated the desire for change and the Iranians' opting for practical solutions.

CONCLUSION

On every count, Khomeini's ideology prescribed the opposite to what the shah's philosophy prescribed: the separation of religion and state was to be done away with, spiritual and temporal power united, nationalism replaced by supranational aspiration, and monarchy replaced by a republic. The shah and Khomeini were thus moving Iran to entirely different directions, upsetting— each in his own way—the traditional equilibrium between religion and state.

The shah had thus bluntly ignored Aedeshir's advice and upset the balance between religion and kingship. It was its "complete neglect" by the Pahlavis, "rather than any tendency within Shi'ism," that aggravated the rift between the Shi'ite hierocracy and the Pahlavi state.[118] In fact, the delegitimization of the monarchy preceded the legitimization of the velayat-e faqih.

Khomeini, upon assuming power, moved to the other extreme. Revolutionary leaders even came to regard him as of equal rank with the Prophet himself or with Imam Ali. Characteristic of this was Rafsanjani's argument, in 1982, that the Muslim community of revolutionary Iran was "functioning" even much better than that of the days of the Prophet. Whereas Prophet Muhammad complained about his people's laxity, Khomeini delighted in their Islamic bearing; whereas the Prophet's advice was often ignored, everybody accepted Khomeini's guidance, he said.[119] Just as the shah identified himself with Iranian nationalism and the institution of the monarchy, many revolutionaries in Iran tend to equate its rule with true Islam.

Thus, in its search for a response to the challenge of modernity, Iran over the last two centuries has been fluctuating between extremes: from total detachment from the West to an enthusiastic emulation, and then back to animosity and hatred toward it: from rapid Westernization to total Islamization. No less important, the Islamic Revolution focused attention on the centrality of religion to the fabric of Iranian society, and as a result the doctrine of Khomeini was often taken as representing Islam. However, an analysis of the views of leading ulama reveals a divergence of attitudes on almost every question, including the very concept of velayat-e faqih. Moreover, the experience of the revolutionary regime so far reveals that one cannot detach Iran altogether from the influence of its encounter with the West or from its attachment to its cultural and national traditions. This became even more evident in the circumstances that led Khatami to the presidency and the views expressed by the new president since then.

It appears, then, that Iran will continue to shift between the various poles until it finds the proper equilibrium between its Islamic heritage and its Iranian pre-Islamic tradition, between the legacy of Cyrus and the tradition of Imam Ali, between Islam and the West, and between religion and state.

NOTES

1. Said Amir Arjomand, *The Turban for the Crown: The Islamic Revolution in Iran* (New York: Oxford University Press, 1988), p. 76; quoted from M. Grinaschi, "Quelques specimens de la litterature sassanide conserves dans les bibliotheques d'Istanbul," *Journal Asiatique*, 254 (emphasis added).

2. Sir John Malcolm, *History of Persia* (London: 1815), 2, p. 443 (emphasis added).

3. Hamid Enayat, *Modern Islamic Political Thought* (Austin: University of Texas Press, 1988), pp. 12, 173.

4. Roger Savory, "The Export of Ithna Ashari Shi'ism: Historical and Ideological Background," in David Menashri (ed.), *The Iranian Revolution and the Muslim World* (Boulder: Westview Press, 1990), pp. 23–24.

5. Ann K. S. Lambton, *Qajar Persia* (Austin: University of Texas Press, 1987), pp. 279–280.

6. Jean Chardin, *Voyage du Chevalier Chardin* (Amsterdam: 1711), 6, pp. 7–94. Translation by Savory, "The Export," pp. 23–24.

7. Ibid., pp. 23–24.

8. Nikki Keddie, "Religion, Society, and Revolution in Modern Iran," in Michael Bonine and Nikki Keddie (eds.), *Continuity and Change in Modern Iran* (Albany: SUNY Press, 1981), p. 21.

9. Mohsen Kadivar, *Nazariye-haye Doulat dar Fiqh-e Shi'e* (Views on Government in Shi'i Jurisprudence) (Tehran: Nashr-e Ney, 1376 [1997–1998]), pp. 70–71. See also Said Amir Arjomand, *The Shadow of God and the Hidden Imam* (Chicago: University of Chicago Press, 1984), p. 223.

10. Hamid Algar, *Religion and State in Iran, 1785–1906: The Role of Ulama in the Qajar Period* (Berkeley: University of California Press, 1969), p. 22; Arjomand, *The Shadow of God*, p. 223.

11. Arjomand, *The Turban for the Crown*, pp. 12–55; Said Arjomand, "The State and Khomeini's Islamic Order," *Iranian Studies*, 13 (1980), p. 149; Arjomand, "The Shi'ite Hierarchy and the State in Pre-Modern Iran: 1785–1890," *European Journal of Sociology*, 22 (1981), pp. 40–78.

12. Arjomand, *The Turban for the Crown*, p. 75.

13. Arjomand, "The State and Khomeini's Islamic Order," p. 149; Arjomand, "The Shi'ite Hierarchy and the State," pp. 40–78; Arjomand, *The Turban for the Crown*, pp. 12–55.

14. Enayat, *Modern Islamic Political Thought*, p. 174.

15. Arjomand, *The Turban for the Crown*, p. 80.

16. A. H. Hairi, *Shi'ism and Constitutionalism in Iran: A Study of the Role Played by the Persian Residents of Iraq in Iranian Politics* (Leiden: Brill, 1977), pp. 102, 235–237.

17. Mehdi Qoli Hedayat, *Khaterat va Khatarat* (Tehran: Rangin, 1950–1951), p. 21.

18. Mohammad Faghfoori, "The Ulama-State Relations: 1921–1941," *International Journal of Middle Eastern Studies*, 19 (1987), p. 418.

19. For a detailed discussion of the controversy over republicanism then, see Hosein Makki, *Tarikh-e bist Saleh-e Iran* (Tehran: Ilmi, 1374/1995), 2, pp. 470–618.

20. Ibid., p. 495.

21. Ibid., p. 498.

22. Abdollah Mostowfi, *Sharh-e Zendegani-ye Man, ya Tarikh-e Ejtema'i va Edari Dowre-ye Qajariye* (Tehran: Zaddar, 1964), 3, p. 601; Shahrough Akhavi, *Religion and Politics in Contemporary Iran: Clergy-State Relations in the Pahlavi Period* (Albany: SUNY Press, 1980), p. 29; Mehdi Qoli Hedayat, *Khaterat va Khatarat*.

23. Akhavi, *Religion and Politics,* p. 29.

24. Ervand Abrahamian, "The Crowd in Iranian Politics, 1905–1953," in H. Afshar (ed.), *Iran: A Revolution in Turmoil* (London: Macmillan, 1985), p. 136.

25. Arjomand, *The Turban for the Crown*, p. 62.

26. L. P. Elwell Sutton, "Reza Shah the Great: Founder of the Pahlavi Dynasty," in George Lenczowski (ed.), *Iran Under the Pahlavis* (Stanford: Hoover Institution Press, 1978), pp. 27–28.

27. Pio Filippani-Ronconi, "The Tradition of Sacred Kingship in Iran," in George Lenczowski (ed.), *Iran Under the Pahlavis*, pp. 79–83.

28. Willem Floor, "The Revolutionary Character of Ulama: Wishful Thinking or Reality?" in Nikki Keddie (ed.), *Religion and Politics in Iran: Shi'ism: From Quietism to Revolution* (New Haven: Yale University Press, 1983), p. 93.

29. Michael Fischer, "Imam Khomeini: Four Levels of Understanding," in John Esposito (ed.), *Voices of Resurgent Islam* (Oxford: Oxford University Press, 1983), p. 152.

30. Akhavi, *Religion and Politics,* p. 78.

31. Ibid., p. 22, quoting from *Kayhan*, 2 August 1960.

32. Ayatollah Ruhollah Khomeini, *Kashf al-Asrar* (Tehran: Zaffar, 1979), pp. 232–233. See more in Akhavi, *Religion and Politics*, pp. 163–164; Afshar, *Iran*, p. 222; Hamid Algar, "Imam Khomeini, 1902–1962: The Pre-Revolutionary Years," in Edmund Burke and Ira Lapidus (eds.), *Islam, Politics, and Social Movements* (Berkeley: University of California Press, 1988), p. 276.

33. Algar, *The Pre-Revolutionary Years*, pp. 276–277.

34. Keddie, *Islam in Change*, p. 536. See also Nikki Keddie, *Roots of Revolution: An Interpretive History of Modern Iran* (New Haven: Yale University Press, 1981), p. 206.

35. Imam Khomeini, *Islam and Revolution: Writings and Declarations* (translated and annotated by Hamid Algar) (London: KPI, 1985), pp. 174–176.

36. Khomeini, *Islam and Revolution*, pp. 177–180; see also Floor, "The Revolutionary Character of Ulama," p. 91.

37. Shaul Bakhash, *The Reign of the Ayatollahs: Iran and the Islamic Revolution* (New York: Basic Books, 1986), p. 32. William Millward argues that Khomeini defended constitutional monarchy at least until 1963; see "The Islamic Political Theory and Vocabulary of Ayatollah Khomeini, 1941–1963," paper for Middle East Studies Association Conference, Salt Lake City, Utah, 1970, as cited in Keddie, *Islam in Change*, p. 541.

38. See Khomeini's letter to Prime Minister Amir Abbas Hoveyda in 1967, in Khomeini, *Islam and Revolution*, pp. 189–192.

39. Akhavi, *Religion and Politics*, p. 167.

40. *Kayhan*, 24 February 1979; Agence France Presse (AFP), 28 January 1979—Foreign Broadcasting Information Service, Daily Report (DR), 30 January 1979. See my article, "Shi'ite Leadership: In the Shadow of Conflicting Ideologies," *Iranian Studies*, 13, nos. 1–4 (1980), pp. 119–145.

41. *Der Spiegel*, 27 August 1978; *Ettela'at*, 29 and 31 August, 1 and 3 September 1978; *International Herald Tribune*, 31 October 1978; AFP, 28 October 1978—DR, 31 October 1978.

42. *Kayhan International*, 31 October 1978.

43. *Kayhan International*, 3 February 1979.

44. *Kayhan International*, 24 January 1979; see similarly, *Ettela'at*, 31 August 1978, 28 January 1979, and 31 May 1979.

45. Akhavi, *Religion and Politics*, p. 174, quoting *Iran Times*, 25 May 1979.

46. Radio Tehran, 30 July 1979—British Broadcasting Corporation, Summary of World Broadcasts (SWB), the Middle East and Africa, 1 August 1979. Similar views are expressed in an interview with Shari'atmadari in: *Ettela'at*, 28 January, 1 and 5 February, 19 May 1979; *Kayhan International*, 19 May 1979; *al-Watan* (Kuwait), 25 May 1979.

47. Akhavi, *Religion and Politics*, p. 175; Menashri, "Shi'ite Leadership," pp. 125, 134; *Cumhuriyet*, 16 March 1979.

48. *Cambio 16* (Madrid), 23 December 1979—DR, 28 December 1979. See also *Bamdad*, 8 December 1979; *Middle East*, 63 (January 1980), pp. 32–33.

49. Mangol Bayat, "Mahmud Taleqani and the Iranian Revolution," in Martin Kramer (ed.), *Shi'ism, Resistance, and Revolution* (Boulder: Westview Press, 1987), pp. 70–72.

50. Ann Lambton, "A Reconsideration of the Position of the Marja' al Taqlid and the Religious Institution," *Studia Islamica* (1964), pp. 125–126.

51. David Menashri, *Iran: A Decade of War and Revolution* (New York: Holmes and Meier, 1990), pp. 92–93. Akhavi, *Religion and Politics*, p. 174; *Iran Times*, 8 June 1979.

52. Khomeini, *Islam and Revolution*, p. 31.

53. Akhavi, *Religion and Politics*, p. 163.

54. Arjomand, *Traditionalism in Twentieth-Century Iran*, pp. 223–224.

55. From a speech on 31 October 1971, in Khomeini, *Islam and Revolution*, pp. 200–202.

56. Arjomand, *The Turban for the Crown*, pp. 147–149.

57. Ibid., pp.177–178, and the sources quoted in n. 1, p. 242.

58. Ibid., p. 147.

59. Seyyed Hossein Nasr, Hamid Dabbashi, and Seyyed Vali Reza Nasr (eds.), *Expectation of the Millennium: Shi'ism in History* (Albany: SUNY Press, 1989), pp. 296–297.

60. Arjomand, *The Turban for the Crown*, p. 177.

61. Nikki Keddie, "Religion, Society, and Revolution in Modern Iran," in Michael Bonine and Nikki Keddie (eds.), *Continuity and Change in Modern Iran* (Albany: SUNY, 1981), p. 31.

62. Hossein Nasr, Dabbashi, and Vali Reza Nasr, *Expectation of the Millennium*, p. 299.

63. Khomeini, *Islam and Revolution*, pp. 100, 107, 124.

64. Said Arjomand, *Traditionalism in Twentieth-Century Iran*, pp. 222–223.

65. Bayat, *Taleqani and the Iranian Revolution*, pp. 67–68.

66. In a paper for the Middle East Studies Association (Boston, 1986), for example, Hrair Dekmejian claimed that the concept of *velayat-e faqih* was in fact originally thought of by Ayatollah Baqir al-Sadr. See also Amatzia Baram, "The Radical Shi'ite Movement in Iraq," in Emanuel Sivan and Menachem Friedman (eds.), *Religious Radicalism and Politics in the Middle East* (New York: SUNY Press, 1990), pp. 112–119.

67. Speaking of young Iranians active in antishah campaigns abroad, Khomeini wrote in *Velayat-e Faqih:* They are "enjoining the good upon us; they say to us: We have organized Islamic Associations; now help us." Khomeini, *Islam and Revolution*, p. 129. For a brief discussion of their thought, see David Menashri, *Iran in Revolution* (in Hebrew; Tel Aviv: Hakibutz Hameuhad, 1988), pp. 66–72; Keddie, *Roots of Revolution*, pp. 213–230.

68. Bayat, *Taleqani and the Iranian Revolution*, pp. 67–68.

69. Hossein Nasr, Dabbashi, and Vali Reza Nasr, *Expectation of the Millennium*, p. 299.

70. Arjomand, *The Turban for the Crown*, pp. 178–179.

71. Mohammad Reza (Shah) Pahlavi, *Mission for My Country* (London: Hutchinson, 1961), p. 327.

72. *Ettela'at*, 3 March 1975.

73. *Kayhan International*, 23 March 1976, as quoted in Marvin Zonis, *Majestic Failure: The Fall of the Shah* (Chicago: University of Chicago Press, 1991), p. 82.

74. Mohammad Reza Pahlavi, *Mission for My Country*, pp. 54–58; R. K. Karanjia, *The Mind of a Monarch* (London: Allen and Unwin, 1977); *Kayhan*, 7 November 1976.

75. Mohammad Reza Pahlavi, *Mission for My Country*, pp. 54–58. See also *Kayhan*, 7 November 1976; Oriana Fallaci's interview with the shah, *New Republic*, 1 December 1973, pp. 15–21; Karanjia, *The Mind of a Monarch,* pp. 97–100.

76. Karanjia, *The Mind of a Monarch*, p. 100.

77. Mohammad Reza Pahlavi, *Enqelab-e Sefid*, p. 16.

78. Fallaci interview with the shah.

79. Karanjia, *The Mind of a Monarch*, p. 98.

80. Zonis, *Majestic Failure*, p. 101.

81. E. A. Bayne, *Persian Kingship in Transition* (New York: American Universities Field Staff, 1968), p. 50.

82. Farah Pahlavi, *My Thousand and One Days: An Autobiography* (London: W. H. Allen, 1978), p. 62, as quoted in Zonis, *Majestic Failure*, pp. 94–95.

83. Gerard de Villier, *The Imperial Shah: An Informal Biography* (Boston: 1976), p. 284.

84. Zonis, *Majestic Failure*, p. 61.

85. Mohammad Reza Pahlavi, *Mission for my Country*, pp. 19–20.

86. Pio Filippani-Ronconi,"The Tradition of Sacred Kingship in Iran," pp. 73, 82, 85.

87. *Kayhan International*, 15 March 1975, as quoted in Zonis, *Majestic Failure*, p. 82.

88. The distinction between "theologians" and religio-politicians is complex, inasmuch as leading politicians (such as Ali Akbar Rafsanjani, Mohammad Khatami, and Ali Akbar Nateq Nuri) had certain religious credentials, whereas leading clerics often engaged in politics. In this context, however, persons who gained prominence due to their religious scholarship and in recognition of their religious authority are termed "theologians," whereas those who exercised authority as a result of their political power are referred to as "politician-clerics." For an elaborate discussion of such

distinctions, see David Menashri, *Revolution at a Crossroads: Iran's Domestic Politics and Regional Ambitions* (Washington, D.C.: Washington Institute for Near East Policy, 1997).

89. Farhad Kazemi, "Civil Society and Iranian Politics," in Augustus R. Norton (ed.), *Civil Society in the Middle East* (Leiden: Brill, 1996), vol. 2, pp. 123–124; Ervand Abrahamian, *Khomeinism: Essays on the Islamic Republic* (Berkeley: University of California Press, 1993), p. 57. See also Ahmad Ashraf, "Theocracy and Charisma: New Men of Power in Iran," *International Journal of Politics, Culture, and Society*, 4 (1990), p. 139.

90. NHK Television, Tokyo, 1 February—SWB, 3 February 1988.

91. See words of Khomeini in this regard: *Jomhuri-ye Islami*, 7 November; *Kayhan* (Tehran), 26 November 1988.

92. See words of Khomeini: Radio Tehran, 11 November—BBC, SWB, 14 November 1988.

93. Roy P. Mottahedeh, "The Islamic Movement: The Case of Democratic Inclusion," *Contention*, 4 (Spring 1995), pp. 114–115.

94. Edward G. Shirley [pseudonym], "Fundamentalism in Power: Is Iran's Present Algeria's Future?" *Foreign Affairs*, 74 (1995), p. 38.

95. Ahmed Hashim, *The Crisis of the Iranian State* (London: Adelphi Papers 296, 1995), pp. 5, 23. See, similarly, Laurent Lamote [pseudonym], "Domestic Politics and Strategic Intentions," in Patrick Clawson (ed.), *Iran's Strategic Intentions and Capabilities* (Washington, D.C.: National Defense University, 1994), pp. 5, 10–12; Abdulaziz Sachedina, "Who Will Lead the Shi'a? Is the Crisis of Religious Leadership in Shi'ism Imagined or Real?" *Middle East Insight*, 11 (1995), p. 25.

96. Olivier Roy, *The Failure of Political Islam* (Cambridge: Harvard University Press, 1994), p. 179. See also Menashri, *Revolution at a Crossroads*, pp. 83–86.

97. *Salam*, 31 January 1995.

98. *Jahan-e Islam*, 31 January 1995.

99. Hashim, *The Crisis of the Iranian State*, pp. 7, 24.

100. Shirley, *Fundamentalism in Power*, p. 39.

101. Lamote, "Domestic Politics and Strategic Intentions," p. 12.

102. Ali Banuazizi, "Iran's Revolutionary Impasse: Political Factionalism and Societal Resistance," *Middle East Report* (November-December 1994), p. 5.

103. Hashim, *The Crisis of the Iranian State*, p. 3. In the words of Banuazizi: it is becoming "ideologically rigid, economically unstable, politically repressive and internationally isolated": Banuazizi, "Iran's Revolutionary Impasse," p. 2. See similarly, Lamote, "Domestic Politics and Strategic Intentions," pp. 6–8, 24; Shirley, *Fundamentalism in Power*, pp. 35, 39.

104. *Christian Science Monitor*, 20 April 1995.

105. Shirley, "The Iran Policy Trap," *Foreign Affairs*, 74 (1995), p. 87.

106. *Kayhan* (London), 15 December 1994—DR, 20 January 1995.

107. Mottahedeh, "The Islamic Movement," pp. 126–127.

108. *Ettela'at*, 8 June 1994.

109. Bazargan's interview with *Kiyan*, 11 (March-May, 1993).

110. Lamote, "Domestic Politics and Strategic Intentions," p. 12.

111. Abdul-Karim Sorush, *Farbetar az Ideolojy* (Tehran: Sarat, 1993). See also his speech in the ceremonies honoring Bazargan, 26 January 1995, at Hoseini-ye Ershad: Abdul-Karim Sorush, "He Who Was Bazargan by Name and Not by Attribute," *Kiyan*, 4, no. 23 (February-March 1995), pp. 2–36; translated in DR, 21 July 1995. See also Menashri, *Revolution at a Crossroads*, pp. 17–19.

112. David Menashri, "Whither Iranian Politics? The Khatami Factor," in Patrick Clawson et al., *Iran Under Khatami: A Political, Economic, and Military Assessment* (Washington, D.C.: Washington Institute for Near East Policy, 1998), pp. 13–51.

113. An interview with Tabarzadi broadcast over Radio Israel (in Persian), 6 and 7 April 1999.

114. Lamote "Domestic Politics and Strategic Intentions," pp. 7–9.

115. Gary Sick, "A Sensitive Policy Toward Iran," *Middle East Insight*, 11 (1995), pp. 21–22.

116. *Los Angeles Times*, 6 June 1995.

117. *Kayhan* (London), 3 August—DR, 31 August 1995.

118. Arjomand, *The Turban for the Crown*, p. 80.

119. *Ettela'at*, 18 December 1982. On another occasion he compared Khomeini to Imam Ali: *Kayhan*, 4 June 1983. See similarly, Menashri, *A Decade of War and Revolution*, pp. 264–265.

PART THREE

Challenges

14

Gulf Monarchies as Rentier States: The Nationalization Policies of the Labor Force

Onn Winckler

Following the 16 October 1973 announcement by the ministers of the Organization of Petroleum Exporting Countries (OPEC) of their decision to double the prices of all types of crude oil, it was widely felt that a profound social and economic change was about to occur. A surge in economic power was predicted based on the sharp rise in revenues from the export of crude oil, natural gas, and petroleum products. Income from oil exports by the seven Middle Eastern members of OPEC rose from U.S.$10 billion in 1972 to a peak of $217 billion in 1980 (current prices).[1] Those revenues transformed the major oil-exporting countries of the Persian Gulf into the wealthiest countries in the Arab world.

The huge oil revenues also transformed the Gulf monarchies into rentier states par excellence. A *rentier state* is one in which the government's revenues consist largely of external rent, such as oil and gas revenues, foreign aid, and other kinds of direct payments. After October 1973, oil revenues in the oil-exporting Gulf countries represented more than 80 percent of governmental revenues and about 95 percent of total exports. Although only a few percent of the labor force in those countries was directly engaged in the oil industry, their entire populations were able to enjoy the oil wealth. Thus, citizenship in one of the Gulf monarchies became a welfare ticket and even an economic profit. The rentier attitude that consequently evolved among Gulf citizens has had an evident effect on the structure and composition of the labor force. Hazen Beblawi described this situation: "It is important to add that the rentier nature of the new state is magnified by the tribal origins of these states. A long tribal tradition of buying loyalty and allegiance is now confirmed by an *etat providence*, distributing favours and benefits to its population."[2]

According to the standard model for industrialized countries, taxation and government go hand in hand. Put simply, governments cannot exist without taxation. There has been no need for taxation in the Gulf monarchies since the oil boom. The governmental budgets of these states are still based almost solely on oil revenues, which renders the main role of governments to be that of managing the distribution of oil wealth among national populations. Because oil is a national asset in these countries, the state is the major player in the economy. Even the private sector is heavily dependent upon government contracts and public spending. By exercising such a large role in the economy, the government can extend privileges to its allies, even in the private sector, and thereby increase the support and stability of the current political system.[3]

This chapter focuses on Gulf states' attempts to nationalize their labor forces, set against the general processes of socioeconomic development, and the role of the monarchical regimes in shaping this policy.

STRATEGY FOR SOCIOECONOMIC DEVELOPMENT IN THE GULF OIL MONARCHIES

At the beginning of the 1970s, the authorities of the Gulf oil monarchies had to deal with the complicated dilemma of what to do with the suddenly massive revenues from oil exports. As oil is a depletable resource, its price fluctuating substantially, the development of alternative sources of income and employment through economic diversification became a major target. The Gulf monarchies decided to invest in three major fields.

First was the development of the infrastructure system. The Gulf states allocated large sums to everything from roads, highways, airports, and railroads, to telecommunications systems and power stations, to the building of governmental ministries and services. This was an essential step in the transformation from a developing into a developed country.

Second was investment in the industrial sector. Due to the instability of oil prices, the leaders of the Gulf monarchies realized that in order to ensure a long-term, high level of per capita income and gross domestic product (GDP) it was necessary to develop the industrial sector and, to a lesser extent, the agricultural sector.

Finally, the Gulf states made substantial improvements in the area of social services, including health care and education, as well as housing facilities. Kuwait was the first among the Gulf monarchies to introduce the concept of the welfare state by distributing part of its oil revenues to the indigenous population through a series of comprehensive social services, most of which were provided free. Thus, the role of the government was primarily that of a distributor of a portion of national oil revenues among the population.[4] During the 1960s and the 1970s, the remaining Gulf monarchies adopted similar policies to broadly distribute the windfall.

These large-scale development plans required an extensive workforce of a size and quality that could not be supplied by local sources due to small national populations. In 1975, the total national populations of the six Gulf countries were estimated to be little more than 6 million, with about 4.6 million in Saudi Arabia alone.[5] Furthermore, high illiteracy rates rendered the labor forces of the Gulf monarchies unprepared to meet the challenge of ambitious socioeconomic development plans. In Bahrain, for example, in 1971, the illiteracy rate of the population fifteen years and older was slightly more than 50 percent among males and 72 percent among females. In Saudi Arabia, with the largest population, the illiteracy rate of those fifteen years and older in 1974 was estimated to be 65 percent among males and 98 percent among females. In addition, the Gulf states were plagued by low rates of labor-force participation, caused mainly by the high natural increase rates.[6]

As a result of such basic labor limitations, the Gulf oil monarchies elected, in the short run, to import large numbers of temporary foreign workers, mainly from neighboring Arab countries, as well as from Southeast Asia, Europe, and North America, in order to implement the various socioeconomic development plans. Their long-run strategy was to supply the necessary workforce from local sources by providing comprehensive educational and health services for the national populations, while adopting pronatalist policies, which encourage higher birth and fertility rates, in order to substantially and rapidly increase the size of the national populations. It is important to emphasize that the Gulf oil monarchies never considered addressing their labor shortage with a policy of mass naturalization for foreign workers.

IMPLEMENTATION OF THE STRATEGY: IMPORTING FOREIGN WORKERS

In accordance with this strategy, the authorities of the Gulf monarchies implemented liberal immigration policies during the 1970s and early 1980s. Economic, demographic, and political factors converged on a single objective: liberalizing entry in order to generate a large supply of labor. This goal took priority over security issues or consideration of the long-term dangers inherent in the growth of a large proportion of foreign workers and their accompanying family members.[7]

The new liberal immigration policy, coupled with the extensive requirements of the workforce, resulted in a rapid increase in the number of foreign workers during the second half of the 1970s and early 1980s. By 1975, the total number of foreign workers in the six Gulf monarchies was 1.4 million, or 51 percent of the total workforce. Ten years later, in 1985, the number had in-

Table 14.1　Gulf Monarchies: National and Nonnational Workforce, 1975–1990 (in thousands)

	1975				1980			
	National	Nonnational	Total	Percentage of nonnational to total	National	Nonnational	Total	Percentage of nonnational to total
Saudi Arabia	1,026.5	773.4	1,799.9	43.0	1,220.0	1,734.1	2,954.1	58.7
Kuwait	91.8	212.7	304.5	69.9	107.8	383.7	491.5	78.1
Bahrain	45.8	30.0	75.8	39.6	61.2	81.2	142.4[a]	57.0
Oman	137.0	70.7	207.7	34.0	119.4	170.5	289.9	58.8
Qatar	12.5	53.8	66.3	81.1	14.7	106.3	121.0	87.9
UAE	45.0	251.5	296.5	84.8	53.9	470.8	524.7	89.7
Total GCC	1,358.6	1,392.1	2,750.7	50.6	1,577.0	2,946.6	4,532.6	65.0

	1985				1990			
	National	Nonnational	Total	Percentage of nonnational to total	National	Nonnational	Total	Percentage of nonnational to total
Saudi Arabia	1,440.1	2,661.8	4,101.9	64.9	1,934.0	2,878.0	4,812.0	59.8
Kuwait	126.4	544.0	670.4	81.1	118.0	731.0	849.0	86.1
Bahrain	72.8	100.5	173.3	58.0	127.0	132.0	259.0	51.0
Oman	167.0	300.0	467.0[b]	64.2	189.0	442.0	631.0	70.0
Qatar	17.7	155.6	173.3	89.8	21.0	230.0	251.0	91.6
UAE	71.8	612.0	683.8	89.5	96.0	805.0	901.0	89.3
Total GCC	1,895.8	4,373.9	6,269.7	69.8	2,485.0	5,218.0	7,703.0	67.7

Sources: ESCWA, *Survey of Economic and Social Developments in the ESCWA Region—1992* (Amman, October 1993); State of Kuwait, Ministry of Planning, Central Statistical Office, *Annual Statistical Abstract 1981–1989,* various issues (Kuwait); State of Bahrain, Central Statistical Organization, Directorate of Statistics, *Statistical Abstract—1992* (Manama); Birks and Sinclair, *International Migration;* EIU, *Country Profile, Oman, Yemen, 1992–1993;* EIU, *Country Profile, Bahrain, Qatar, 1991–1992.*
　　Notes: a: Related to 1981.
　　　　　b: Related to 1986.

creased to 4.4 million, almost 70 percent of the total workforce (see Table 14.1).

　　The import of labor on a large scale did not require any special effort, as the economic incentives were more than sufficient. The wages offered to foreign workers were several times higher than those paid at home for the same work. For example, according to a survey conducted in 1977, wages in the construction sector of the Gulf oil monarchies were 780–1,130 percent higher than those paid in Egypt.[8]

　　Compared to other waves of labor migration, the movement to the Gulf oil monarchies during the 1970s and 1980s had several other unusual and significant features. The first was that it involved, unlike the import of Mediterranean workers into Western European countries during the 1960s, many

Table 14.2   Gulf Monarchies: Population per Physician, 1960–1994

	1960	1970	1980	1988	1994
Saudi Arabia	16,370	7,460	1,640[c]	719[d]	576
Kuwait	1,210	1,050	590	782	601
Bahrain	2,330	2,340	1,220	1,077	1,164
Oman	31,120	8,640	1,730	1,160	878
Qatar	1,950[a]	1,9660	1,180[c]	664	790
UAE	—	1,250[b]	900	863	720[e]

Sources: World Bank, *World Tables,* 3rd ed.; ESCWA, *Statistical Abstract,* Sixteenth Issue, 1996.
  Notes: a. Related to 1965.
       b. Related to 1971.
       c. Related to 1978.
       d. Related to 1989.
       e. Related to 1993.

technicians and other professional workers, not just unskilled and semiskilled workers. Second, the huge influx of foreign workers and their accompanying family members meant that since the early 1980s the majority of the workforce was constituted by foreigners—a unique phenomenon.[9]

INCREASING AND IMPROVING THE NATIONAL WORKFORCES: HEALTH SERVICES

National health services in the Gulf monarchies are among the world's most modern, with health services either highly subsidized or provided free to all citizens. Within one generation, the health systems in these countries advanced tremendously. One of the major indicators for this improvement is the ratio between physicians and the population. Although in Saudi Arabia in 1960 there was one physician for every 16,370 inhabitants, that ratio had decreased to 1,640 in 1980 and again to only 576 in 1994. In Oman, the ratio decreased from 31,120 to 878 during the same period. This trend was evident in the other Gulf oil monarchies as well (see Table 14.2).

This substantial improvement in health facilities contributed to a marked reduction of crude death rates. In Saudi Arabia, the rate dropped from 22.5 per 1,000 inhabitants in 1960 to 3.8 in 1996; in Qatar, from 18.1 to 4.7; and in Oman, from 27.8 to 5.1 (see Table 14.3). There were two main factors for the sharp decrease in crude death rates. The first was a dramatic drop in infant mortality rates. The infant mortality rate in Saudi Arabia, for example, dropped from 184.5 per 1,000 live births in 1960 to 22.2 in 1996. In Qatar and the United Arab Emirates (UAE), the decrease was from 135.0 to 16.7 and 16.0, respectively, during the same period. The second factor was an

Table 14.3   Gulf Monarchies: Natural Increase Rates, 1960–1996

	1960				1970			
	CBR	CDR	NI	TFR	CBR	CDR	NI	TFR
Saudi Arabia	48.9	22.5	2.6	7.2	47.9	18.1	3.0	7.3
Kuwait	44.4	9.7	3.5	7.3	48.2	57.7	4.3	7.2
Bahrain	46.3	14.8	3.2	7.1	39.7	8.8	3.1	6.5
Oman	50.5	27.8	2.3	7.2	49.8	21.6	2.8	7.2
Qatar	42.3	18.1	2.4	7.0	34.2	12.9	2.1	6.9
UAE	46.5	19.0	2.8	6.9	35.8	11.1	2.5	6.8

	1988				1996			
	CBR	CDR	NI	TFR	CBR	CDR	NI	TFR
Saudi Arabia	44.1	7.0	3.7	6.7	44.6	3.8	4.1	7.3
Kuwait	42.2	2.6	4.0	6.2	24.7	2.3	2.5	3.4
Bahrain	39.5	4.5	3.5	5.8	27.5	5.8	2.2	3.7
Oman	47.3	9.0	3.8	6.5	41.3	5.1	3.6	6.7
Qatar	37.6	4.3	3.3	5.4	37.3	4.9	3.2	3.6
UAE	39.6	3.4	3.6	6.7	25.1	5.3	2.0	4.3

Sources: The World Bank, *World Tables,* 3rd ed., Vol. 2—*Social Data from the Data Files of the World Bank* (Baltimore: Johns Hopkins University Press, 1984); ESCWA, *Population Situation—1990;* ESCWA, *Demographic Data Sheets,* No. 9 (1997).

Notes: CBR: Crude birth rate per 1,000 people; CDR: Crude death rate per 1,000 people; NI: Natural increase (%); TFR: Total fertility rate.

unprecedented increase in life expectancy. The life expectancy at birth for men and women in Saudi Arabia increased from 43.0 years in 1960 to 72.0 in 1996. In Bahrain, the increase was from 55.5 years to 70.4 years, and in Oman, from 38.5 years to 70.1 years during the same period (see Table 14.4).

PRONATALIST POLICIES

The small national populations of the Gulf oil monarchies relative to their political aspirations and economic needs led authorities to adopt various pronatalist measures following the oil boom. The main objective of such policies was to rapidly increase the number of citizens in order to reduce the percentage of foreigners within the total population in the short run and to diminish the demand for foreign workers in the long run.[10]

The Bahraini government, for example, in its reply to the Third United Nations Population Inquiry of 1976, noted that its high rates of natural increase made a positive contribution to the achievement of its targets for so-

Table 14.4   Gulf Monarchies: Infant Mortality Rates and Life Expectancy at Birth, 1960–1996

	1960		1970		1980		1988		1996	
	IMR	LE	IMR	LE	IMR	LE	IMR	LE	IMR	LE
Saudi Arabia	184.5	43.0	145.5	48.5	113.8	54.1	63.5	66.7	22.2	72.0
Kuwait	89.0	59.5	49.2	65.8	33.9	70.1	13.6	75.3	14.1	76.9
Bahrain	127.5	55.5	74.0	61.8	53.3	66.7	33.1	71.1	23.2	70.4
Oman	193.3	38.5	158.3	43.6	128.4	48.5	65.6	61.4	34.2	70.1
Qatar	135.0	46.3	76.5	52.0	53.3	57.7	24.4	70.3	16.7	72.3[a]
UAE	135.0	46.5	76.5	55.0	53.3	62.6	27.8	72.7	16.0	75.2

Sources: World Bank, World Tables, 3rd ed.; ESCWA, Population Situation—1990; ECWA/ ESCWA, Demographic Data Sheets, various issues, 1982–1997.
   Notes: a. related to 1994.
      IMR: Infant mortality per 1,000 live births; LE: Life expectancy (years).

cioeconomic development by ensuring a sufficient supply of labor for future economic development.[11]

   Since the early 1970s, several measures have been adopted by the Gulf oil monarchies, with the aim of encouraging high crude birth and fertility rates.

   The strictest measure, taken by the Saudi authorities as a result of the disappointingly small numbers of Saudi nationals revealed in the 1974 population census, was that contraceptives were pronounced as contrary to the teaching of Islam; their import was banned in 1975.[12] Another measure, aimed at raising the fertility rate among nationals, was the initiation of government housing projects. In all the Gulf monarchies, with some small variation, the government sold housing at cost or provided plots of land for building. The governments also offered long-term loans for housing with very low interest rates.[13] The Qatari government, for example, was responsible for the construction of many popular housing projects for Qatari nationals with low incomes. According to the law (Law 1/64), the beneficiaries of these houses must pay back 60 percent of the cost over twenty to twenty-five years. In addition, disabled nationals are provided free housing.[14] However, besides encouraging high fertility rates, the distribution of land to the population also had a political purpose: to increase support for regimes. In Kuwait during the 1950s, such a policy constituted one of the major channels used by the government to distribute oil revenues to the merchant elite and tribal notables. The regimes of Qatar and the UAE adopted a similar policy, and in Saudi Arabia the system of land gifts has been in force since the beginning of Abd al-Aziz Ibn Saud's reign.[15]

   Third, the encouragement of early marriage was taken to be the norm. Since the 1980s, the Kuwaiti government has granted a marriage allowance of

KD2,000 (Kuwaiti dinar; KD0.29 = U.S.$1 as of 1985) to citizens marrying for the first time, with an additional KD1,000 as a soft loan. The allowance was designed to compensate men for the expenses incurred by the custom of *mahr* (bride's dowry), which the groom gives to the bride's father.[16] Despite the severe damage caused to the Kuwaiti economy as a result of the Iraqi invasion, a large increase in the marriage grant to Kuwaiti nationals was approved by the Council of Ministers at the beginning of 1992. According to that decision, eligible Kuwaiti males were entitled to receive U.S.$14,000 (half as a grant and half as a loan) for their marriage to Kuwaiti women, twice the previous sum. The reason for such a large increase, according to then Kuwaiti minister of finance, Nasir Abdallah Al-Rawdan, was "to encourage Kuwaiti youths to marry."[17] And finally, full subsidies for education (including books, clothing, etc.) were provided from first grade through the university level.

Such measures were, undoubtedly, effective in accomplishing the aim of maintaining high fertility rates. During the last twenty-five years, the populations of the Gulf oil monarchies increased by some of the highest rates in the entire world. By 1996, the total national populations of the six Gulf monarchies numbered 17.5 million,[18] compared to little more than 6 million in 1975—representing an almost threefold increase during two decades.

EXPANSION AND IMPROVEMENT OF EDUCATIONAL FACILITIES

In addition to ensuring the expansion of the indigenous populations, the Gulf states took measures to improve their educational systems as well. They spent impressive sums on educational objectives. Funds were allocated not only for the construction of schools and universities but also for the import of teachers from neighboring Arab countries. Likewise, the governments fully subsidized nationals who were studying at universities in Western Europe and North America. The high priority for education was part of the "rapid growth" strategy adopted by the Gulf monarchies, once they committed themselves to modernizing their economy and society.[19]

The results of this strategy were soon evident. The number of students per 100,000 inhabitants in Saudi Arabia increased from 364 in 1975 to 1,455 in 1996. In Qatar, the corresponding increase was from 455 to more than 1,500 (see Table 14.5). By the 1993/94 academic year, there were almost 200,000 students in various institutions of higher education in the Gulf monarchies, more than 155,000 in Saudi Arabia alone.[20]

However, it seems that beyond the economic and social aims of these educational policies there was a political objective as well. The Gulf monarchies hoped to convince their populations that personal economic and social prosperity rested upon the existing regimes and that the continuation of the current

Table 14.5   Gulf Monarchies: Number of Students per 100,000 Inhabitants, 1975–1996 (selected years)

		1975	1980	1985	1996
Saudi Arabia	MF	364	662	917	1,455
Kuwait	MF	804	991	1,377	2,247[a]
Bahrain	MF	259	550	974	1,445[b]
Oman	MF	—	2	78	532
Qatar	MF	455	991	1,493	1,518
UAE	MF	—	282	576	804

Sources: UNESCO, *Statistical Yearbook,* various issues, 1980–1998.
Notes: MF: Males and females.
    a. Related to 1995.
    b. Related to 1994.

high standard of living depended upon the regimes' survival. In addition, extending the public educational system throughout the country, from the first grade to higher education, enabled the regimes to control the curriculum and the teachers, something that was used to increase students' identification with regimes and their values. Moreover, by controlling the educational system, the governments were able, at least partially, to prevent opposition elements from entering educational institutions, particularly universities.

NATIONALIZATION POLICY OF THE LABOR FORCE

During the first half of the 1980s, the authorities of the Gulf monarchies started to implement a policy of nationalizing the labor force, whereby they hoped to gradually reduce the numbers and percentages of foreign workers within the total labor force and replace them with local manpower. Their primary assumption focused on limiting the number of work permits issued to foreign workers while increasing and improving the available national workforce, which would eventually bring about the replacement of foreign workers with national workers. Although this basic assumption was shared by all the Gulf states, each country implemented a slightly different policy.

Several factors converged to promote such nationalization policies. The first was the economic slowdown that occurred after 1982, and even more markedly since 1986, when oil prices dropped dramatically. The second factor was the substantial increase in unemployment and underemployment within the national workforces. The third was the high cost of providing wages and subsidizing public services for foreign workers and accompanying family members. However, it seems that the most important factor was political: the authorities feared that large numbers of foreigners might bring about unwanted social and even political changes. Nationalization policies were thus perceived as an essential means to secure the future of the existing regimes of the Gulf monarchies.

The main aim of the Kuwaiti nationalization policy was to equalize the sizes of the national and foreign populations by the year 2000, if not earlier. Kuwait hoped to accomplish that aim by reducing the need for foreign workers with the introduction of advanced technology in construction projects and services and by scaling down labor-intensive projects that made little contribution to overall economic development. The plan also contained an incentive for the private sector to employ nationals by imposing the welfare-services costs for foreign employees (such as health care and education for accompanying family members) on the employers rather than on the government. It was assumed that if employers were made to bear these costs then they would be forced to reduce the number of foreign workers they employed.[21]

In August 1989, the Bahraini government initiated an intensive five-year "Bahrainization" program whereby it hoped to replace one-third of all jobs held by foreign workers with locals. Letters were sent to most private-sector companies directing them to increase the number of nationals they employed by 5 percent annually. Specific job categories were singled out by the government for takeover by nationals, including senior administrative personnel, supervisors, engineers, technicians, computer operators, nurses, clerks, accountants, secretaries, sales and marketing personnel, and hotel and restaurant workers. The goal was that some 400 companies, employing approximately 60,000 foreign workers, would lay off 20,000 such employees by 1994 and replace them with nationals.[22]

Likewise, one of the major goals of the Saudis' Fourth Five-Year Development Plan (1985–1990) was to reduce the number of foreigners in the kingdom by 1.2 million (of whom about 600,000 were workers) by the end of 1989.[23] In addition, from the mid-1980s, senior foreign workers were expected to provide professional training to nationals as an integral part of their jobs in order to facilitate their being replaced in the future by nationals.[24] In April 1987, the Omani minister of labor, Mustahil Ibn Ahmad al-Mashani, stated that foreign workers could no longer be hired in eleven job categories, including public-relations personnel, Arabic typists, security officers, apprentices, drivers, fishermen, and shepherds.[25] The UAE's Federal Labor Law, enacted in 1980, imposed strict limitations on the mobility of foreign workers from one job to another, requiring them to leave the country for at least six months before changing employment. In addition, inspection campaigns were initiated in order to crack down on illegal immigration and violation of the labor laws and regulations.[26]

Thus, during the mid-1980s, there was a general sense, among politicians as well as labor and economic experts, that the number of foreign workers would decline gradually in the coming years due to a combination of several factors. First, by that time most of the major infrastructure projects, which employed a large share of the foreign workers, would be completed. Henry Azzam, the chief economist of the Gulf International Bank, claimed in 1987 that: "The largest and most vulnerable part of the foreign work-force in the Gulf has been the unskilled and semi-skilled Asian construction workers. The exodus of this group is expected to continue in the coming few years."[27] Second was the sharp decrease in oil prices during 1986–1987. According to projections from the mid-1980s, the drop in the oil prices, which led to substantial cuts in governmental budgets and economic development plans, would result in a net loss of approximately 2 million foreign workers by 1991.[28] These two factors, combined with the nationalization policy, led to the assumption that in the coming years the number of foreign workers would be significantly reduced.

Indeed, during 1984–1987 there was a reduction in the number of foreign workers, though not as much as expected. In the UAE, 600 out of 10,000 foreigners working in the banking sector lost their jobs in 1985. An economic expert in Kuwait claimed that about 50,000 out of 1 million foreigners left the country during 1984–1985.[29] In Saudi Arabia, the number of work permits issued for foreign workers in 1984 fell by nearly 5 percent compared to previous years. In Bahrain, the number of work permits issued in 1986 was 21 percent less than those issued in 1984.[30] According to official Omani figures, approximately 100,000 foreign workers left the country during 1986–1987. In 1986, for the first time, a net drop of more than 27,000 foreign workers was recorded, almost entirely from the private sector.[31]

However, the decreases were short-lived. Overall, during the second half of the 1980s, the number of foreign workers did not decrease, and by 1988–1989, with the recovery of oil prices, the number of foreign workers had actually increased. By mid-1990, on the eve of the Iraqi invasion of Kuwait, the total number of foreign workers in the six Gulf monarchies was estimated to be more than 5.2 million, compared to 4.4 million in 1985—an increase of almost 20 percent. Such figures demonstrate that nationalization policies did not achieve the goal of overall reduction—in absolute numbers or percentage—of foreign workers. Moreover, in each of the Gulf states the number of foreign workers even increased during the second half of the 1980s (see Table 14.1).

OBSTACLES TO THE IMPLEMENTATION OF THE NATIONALIZATION POLICY

The main obstacles to successful implementation of the nationalization policy in the Gulf oil monarchies can be estimated.

First is the unwillingness of nationals to accept jobs that they considered to be socially undesirable. Robert E. Looney noted this in regard to Saudi Arabia:

> Labor theory suggests that the unwillingness to accept socially undesirable jobs can be overcome by payment of higher wages than in desirable jobs. It appears, however, that in Saudi Arabia the social factors are so strong that, given the limited size of the labor markets, and the inefficiency of labor and capital in the modern industrial sector, the wide gap is not large enough to draw Saudi workers into the formal sector. The extended family, subsidized loans, and the existence of the informal sector, enabling occasional work to supplement other income, allow Saudi workers to set a high reservation wage.[32]

Furthermore, the government provides general subsidies to the population by supporting costs of electricity, gasoline, water, telephone, and the like. Given that health care and education are also free, the national population can afford to be very selective regarding their employment decisions.

Second is the preference of nationals for public-sector rather than private-sector employment, as government work provides more convenient working hours, job security, and attractive wages.[33] A third obstacle is that local employers prefer foreign workers over local workers. There are several reasons for that, notably that the wages demanded by foreign workers are generally much lower than those demanded by nationals. In Saudi Arabia, for example, a survey of the manufacturing industry revealed that Saudi workers' wages were more than twice as high as those of foreign workers.[34]

In an interview with managers and supervisors of the Kuwait Petroleum Corporation, Mary Ann Tétreault noted that "most [of the above-mentioned] deplored their inability to fill entry and midlevel positions with qualified Kuwaitis, who can get easier jobs working fewer hours for the same pay in other government agencies."[35] In fact, private-sector employers' concern is that the authorities will enforce a Kuwaitization policy, obliging them to employ nationals instead of foreign workers. One company director said that "this would be disastrous. We have already cut our margins. If we had to pay the wages Kuwaitis demand, we would not be competitive."[36] According to a survey held by the Saudi daily newspaper *Ukaz* regarding the implementation of the Saudization policy, many young Saudis viewed it as a "mere slogan." One Saudi graduate told the paper that the advertisements were "nothing more than a meaningless routine. . . . In fact, the positions went to expatriates." A Saudi governmental official commented: "The private sector demands from workers some qualities like patience and hard work while Saudi youths are often running after comfort and salary increases. If they want to work at all in the private sector, they do so only until they get a government job."[37] Despite the alienation of foreigners from the local population, both foreigners and nationals continue to benefit from the situation.[38]

Lack of skilled workers and graduates in technical occupations presents a fourth obstacle to nationalization. Employers blame the educational system for failing to produce the kind of quality needed in the labor market. They would like to see more emphasis put on vocational and technical training and education. The employers also claim that universities should devote more resources to the teaching of exact sciences, computers, and finance rather than to the arts, social sciences, and Islamic studies.[39]

Indeed, during the 1993/94 academic year there were 153,780 students in the various institutions of higher education in Saudi Arabia; only 25,266 (16.4 percent) were enrolled in engineering, exact sciences, agriculture, and medicine faculties while the rest were studying arts and literature, education, shari'a, and religion. In Qatar, during the 1995/96 academic year there were 8,271 students, of whom only 1,627, or less than 20 percent, were enrolled in science, engineering, and technology programs.[40] This pattern persists in the other Gulf oil monarchies as well.

The fifth and perhaps the most critical obstacle to nationalization of labor markets is represented by the political systems as well as the relationships between the governments and their citizens. Despite the tremendous economic and social changes the Gulf monarchies underwent as a result of the oil boom, the political power is still concentrated in the hands of the ruling families that continue to perform traditional, deeply rooted roles. Birks and Rimmer comment:

> Much of the modern development [of the Gulf monarchies] is an extension of the traditional obligations between Shiekhs and their tributary populations, translated into modern form: thus it has become the obligation of the rulers to provide employment for their national populations, who accept it as a right in exchange for their loyalty and upholding of the social norms. Employment of nationals in these states, especially in government, [is] therefore seen as a means of spreading, rather than generating, income.[41]

The expanded state bureaucracy also provides the authorities with more levers to use in controlling the society, as well as in distributing part of the oil wealth among the national populations. In this regard, Beblawi noted: "Though utterly free enterprise oriented, the number of government employees in the oil states is only matched by socialist-oriented states."[42]

In addition, the "sponsorship system" encourages the exploitation of foreign workers, who are in some cases required to pay part of their income to their initial sponsor, even when they are actually working for someone else. This system not only encourages the expansion of the rentier mentality among the citizens but also becomes conducive to the importation of additional foreign workers.[43] In the UAE, for example, nationals have been known to earn money by supplying visas and sponsorship, but not employment, to foreign workers who were prepared to pay about AED5,000 (Arab Emirates dirham; AED3.67 = U.S.$1 as of 1996) only for the privilege of obtaining the necessary work permits.[44]

THE NEW STAGE: THE NATIONALIZATION POLICY IN THE 1990S

After the second Gulf crisis, the oil-exporting countries implemented new labor laws and regulations designed to substantially and rapidly reduce the scale of the foreign workforce. Such laws and labor regulations were prompted by the failure to implement the nationalization policy during the second half of the 1980s, the economic damage caused by the Gulf crisis, the prolonged low oil prices, and the increasing unemployment rates among nationals.

In the aftermath of the Gulf crisis, Saudi Arabia and Kuwait, the largest labor importers, preferred workers from countries that had supported the international coalition against Iraq, mainly Egyptians and Syrians, rather than workers from countries that supported Iraq, mostly Jordanian Palestinians and Yemenites. During the first few months after the crisis, as many as 800,000–900,000 Yemenites were ousted from Saudi Arabia and returned to Yemen;[45] about 350,000 Jordanian Palestinians, most of them from Kuwait, had to return to Jordan.[46]

The Saudi government's new strategy for tackling the problem of increasing numbers of foreign workers involves imposing quotas for nationals in the private sector, something that came into force in December 1995. The quotas are intended not only to reduce the foreign population in the kingdom but also to reduce the huge sums of money they transfer home every year. As part of the government's new strategy, the authorities have stopped issuing visas for a growing list of job categories while increasing the cost of employing foreigners by raising costs for visas and health insurance.[47]

A main goal of the Saudis' Sixth Five-Year Development Plan (1995–2000) is to encourage Saudi firms to employ local workers by devoting more emphasis and resources to the quality of their education and to the skilled training needed by the private sector, by developing policies for replacing expatriate manpower with national labor, and by stimulating the private sector to provide employment opportunities for Saudi nationals.[48]

The approach taken by the Bahraini Ministry of Labor regarding high unemployment rates among nationals involves a training fee levied on employers, up to 75 percent of which can be recouped for the cost of any recognized training, in addition to the establishment of an employment services bureau that aims to assist the unemployed by matching their qualifications with available work opportunities. In addition, the government has set legal Bahrainization requirements for the private sector.[49]

In his national speech on 18 November 1992, Sultan Qabus of Oman said: "Omani youth must demonstrate a serious desire to work, to make use of the many opportunities that are open to them in the private sector and not waste their time waiting for vacancies in government employment."[50] The Omanization drive has designated quotas for both the private and public sectors. The Fourth Omani Five-Year Development Plan (1991–1995) aimed to create 180,000 new jobs, of which 120,000 were reserved for nationals.[51]

It seems that the strictest policy regarding foreign workers was put into effect by the UAE. At the end of June 1996, the Ministry of the Interior announced that illegal immigrants would be given a three-month amnesty period in which to leave the country before a new entry and residency law was adopted in the autumn. The new law contained heavy fines and long prison sentences for violating the law. By early November 1996, the mood in the UAE had indeed changed. According to official figures, by the final 31 October 1996 deadline, approximately 167,000 illegal immigrants had left the country voluntarily.[52]

Many of the laws and regulations that have characterized the second stage of the nationalization policies are, in fact, not new: most of them were in force in some form during the second half of the 1980s as well. However, the difference between the two periods is in the emphasis placed on enforcement of those laws and regulations, which has been much more vigorous in the 1990s than previously.

The baby (oil) boom generation of the 1970s, at least partially a result of pronatalist government policies, has been entering the labor market since the early 1990s and has raised unemployment rates among nationals. In the UAE, for example, according to official figures, there were 15,600 unemployed nationals, comprising more than 15 percent of the local workforce at the beginning of 1996.[53] Likewise, in Bahrain, Minister of Labor Shaikh Khalifa bin Sultan al-Khalifa stated that the unemployment rate among nationals had reached 15 percent by the beginning of 1993.[54]

At the same time, the number of foreign workers continued, nevertheless, to increase during the early 1990s. In Saudi Arabia, for example, in 1995 there were 6.2 million foreign workers and accompanying family members, representing a 47 percent increase over the number at the beginning of the decade.[55] The same trend also occurred in Kuwait. By mid-1996, the number of foreign workers was higher than 900,000,[56] as compared to 731,000 prior to the Iraqi invasion. In the other Gulf monarchies, the number of foreign workers did not decrease during the 1990s, except in the UAE after the measures taken in late 1996. It seems that so far these countries have not succeeded in accomplishing the targets of nationalization policy regarding labor forces.

CONCLUSION

The Gulf oil monarchies have experienced unprecedented rates of population growth since the early 1970s. This baby boom has created a wholly new demographic structure, and by the mid-1990s more than 40 percent of the indigenous populations were under the age of fifteen. This generation's entry into the labor force will place great stress on the economies of the Gulf oil monarchies. According to the various projections, by the year 2000 the total population of the six Gulf oil monarchies will reach almost 20 million. However, much more important is the growing number of youngsters who will enter the labor market in the coming years as a result of the wide-based age pyramid.[57]

Although all of the Gulf monarchies are labor-importing countries, unemployment among nationals is steadily rising with rapid population growth and the preference of local laborers to work in the public sector. At the same time, work opportunities in the public sector are becoming scarcer as governments attempt to reduce their involvement in the economy.[58]

For many years, the authorities guaranteed full employment for citizens by using huge oil revenues to create jobs in the public sector while employing foreign workers to perform the manual or specialized work that their own citizens were either unwilling or unqualified to do.[59] Along with the free provision of comprehensive social services, the employment of nationals in the public sector was one of the major tools used to allow the oil wealth to percolate among the citizens. Thus, the ability of Gulf governments to cut their budgets due to the economic recession seems to be very limited by the salaries of nationals already employed by the public sector, which constitute a large proportion of the budgets. In Bahrain, for example, salaries for public-sector employees constitute about 50 percent of budget outlays, and another 30 percent is allocated to various recurrent costs, resulting in a growing budget deficit.[60]

A similar situation exists in Kuwait and Saudi Arabia. In fiscal year 1994/95, the Kuwaiti budget deficit was predicted to be U.S.$5.4 billion, representing about 10 percent of total GDP.[61] The budget deficit of the Saudi government for fiscal year 1992 was $10.5 billion.[62] Since 1988, the Saudi government has been financing its budget deficits with long-term bonds. As a result, by mid-1994, the total Saudi government debt was about $55 billion and rising, all of it incurred since 1983, after the end of the "oil decade."[63] The most prominent expression of the sharp recession in the Saudi economy during the first half of the 1990s was the steady decline in per capita income, which dipped as low as $7,000 in 1995.

Moreover, there is concern in Saudi Arabia that high rates of unemployment among nationals could one day lead to social problems and even political unrest.[64] The rulers of the Gulf oil monarchies can no longer afford prolonged high unemployment rates among nationals (which, for example, had reached about 15 percent in Bahrain and the UAE by 1995/96)[65] because of the political implications that might result. Yet from an economic point of view they cannot continue to employ almost the entire national labor force in the governmental sector, especially in light of the rapid population growth and the rising number of nationals entering the labor market every year.

More than twenty years after the oil boom of October 1973, the rulers of the Gulf oil monarchies face a complicated dilemma. On the one hand, narrowing the subsidies for social services, and possibly even imposing personal income taxes, would substantially reduce the standard of living of their populations and would create the potential for the kind of social and political unrest that could threaten the existing regimes. The political unrest in Bahrain a few years ago, which was partially a response to the high unemployment rates among nationals, is only one example of the close connection between high unemployment, a decline in the standard of living, and increased political unrest.[66] On the other hand, continuing to supply free comprehensive social services, without implementing personal taxes, while continuing to employ almost the entire national workforce in the public sector will increase the budgetary deficit. This severe dilemma has yet to be resolved, and it seems that it will continue to constitute one of the most pressing issues for the Gulf oil monarchies in coming years.

NOTES

1. Gad G. Gilbar, *The Middle East Oil Decade and Beyond* (London: Frank Cass, 1997), p. 1.

2. Hazem Beblawi, "The Rentier State in the Arab World," in Giacomo Luciani (ed.), *The Arab State* (London: Routledge, 1990), p. 89. See also Nazih N. Ayubi, *Over-Stating the Arab State: Politics and Society in the Middle East* (London: I. B. Tauris Publishers, 1995), pp. 224–240.

3. F. Gregory Gause III, *Oil Monarchies: Domestic and Security Challenges in the Arab Gulf States* (New York: Council on Foreign Relations, 1994), pp. 42–43. See also Kiren Aziz Chaudhry, "The Price of Wealth: Business and State in Labor Remittance and Oil Economies," *International Organization*, 43 (1989), pp. 123–125.

4. Beblawi, "The Rentier State," p. 90. See also United Nations (UN), Department of International Economic and Social Affairs, *Case Studies in Population Policy: Kuwait*, Population Policy Paper, No. 15 (New York, 1988), p. 8.

5. J. S. Birks and C. A. Sinclair, *International Migration and Development in the Arab Region* (Geneva: ILO, 1980), p. 131, table 6.

6. UN, ECWA (Economic Commission for Western Asia), *Demographic and Related Socio-Economic Data Sheets for the Countries of the ECWA*, No. 2 (Beirut, 1978), country pages.

7. See Sharon Stanton Russell, "Politics and Ideology in Migration Policy Formulation: The Case of Kuwait," *International Migration Review,* 23 (1989), p. 36.

8. Bent Hansen and Samir Radwan, *Employment Opportunities and Equity in a Changing Economy: Egypt in the 1980s—A Labour Market Approach* (Geneva: ILO, 1982), pp. 91–92. See also Industrial Bank of Kuwait (IBK), by Issa al-Quisi, "Discrimination and Earning Differentials in the Kuwait Labor Market," IBK Papers, No. 29 (September 1988).

9. Roger Owen, *Migrant Workers in the Gulf* (London: Minority Rights Group, 1985), p. 4.

10. See Muhammad Faour, "Fertility Policy and Family Planning in the Arab Countries," *Studies In Family Planning,* 20 (September-October 1989), p. 261.

11. The Population Division of the UN Department of International Economic and Social Affairs and the UN Fund for Population Activities (UNFPA), *Population Policy Compendium: Bahrain* (New York, 1980), p. 3; see also Lee L. Bean and A. G. Zofiry, "Marriage and Fertility in the Gulf Region: The Impact of Pro-Family, Pro-Natal Policies," Cairo Demographic Center, Working Papers, No. 36 (Cairo, 1994); Onn Winckler, "Demographic Developments and Population Policies in Bahrain," *Middle East Contemporary Survey (MECS)*, vol. 20 (1996), pp. 200–201.

12. Allan G. Hill, "Population Growth in the Middle East and North Africa: Selected Policy Issues," in A. L. Udovich (ed.), *The Middle East: Oil, Conflict, and Hope* (Lexington: Lexington Books, 1976), p. 36; James Allman, "The Demography Transition in the Middle East and North Africa," in James Allman (ed.), *Women's Status and Fertility in the Muslim World* (New York: Praeger Publishers, 1978), pp. 24–25.

13. Baquer Salman al-Najjar, "Population Policies in the Countries of the Gulf Cooperation Council: Politics and Society," *Immigrants and Minorities*, 12, no. 2 (1993), p. 212.

14. Zuhair Ahmed Nafi, *Economic and Social Development in Qatar* (London: Frances Pinter Publishers, 1983), p. 41.

15. Gause, *Oil Monarchies*, p. 54.

16. UN, *Kuwait*, pp. 33–34; ESCWA, *Population Situation in the ESCWA Region—1990* (Amman, 1992), p. 119.

17. *Gulf States Newsletter,* 6 April 1992, p. 5.

18. ESCWA, *Demographic Data Sheets*, No. 9 (1997).

19. Gilbar, *The Middle East Oil Decade*, pp. 5–8.

20. ESCWA, *Statistical Abstract of the ESCWA Region,* No. 16 (New York: UN Publications, 1996), pp. 117–128.

21. A. L. Kohli and Musa'ad al-Omaim, "Changing Patterns of Migration in Kuwait," *Population Bulletin of ESCWA*, No. 32 (June 1988), p. 92; UN, *Kuwait*, p. 51.

22. *Gulf States Newsletter,* 21 August 1989, p. 13.

23. *Arab Times*, 16 July 1987, 15 October 1988.

24. *Middle East Economic Digest (MEED)*, 30 (29 March 1986), p. 8.

25. *Middle East Newsletters, Gulf States,* 20 April 1987, pp. 11–12.

26. MERI Report, *United Arab Emirates* (London, 1985), pp. 99–100; "Growing Concern over Dependence on Foreign Workers," *Arab Oil* (September 1983), pp. 27–28.

27. *Middle East Newsletters, Gulf States*, 15 June 1987, p. 6.

28. *Middle East Newsletters, Gulf States,* 30 June 1986, p. 6.

29. *Al-Bayan* (Dubai), 16 December 1985.

30. J. S. Birks, I. J. Seccombe, and C. A. Sinclair, "Labour Migration in the Arab Gulf States: Patterns, Trends, and Prospects," *International Migration,* 26 (1988), p. 269 and p. 277, table 3.2.

31. The Economist Intelligence Unit (EIU), *Country Profile, Oman, Yemen,* 1992/1993, p. 13.

32. Robert E. Looney, *The Economic Development of Saudi Arabia: Consequences of the Oil Prices Decline* (Greenwich: JAI Press, 1990), p. 80.

33. *Gulf States Newsletter,* 20 November 1995, p. 10; see also Rob Franklin, "Migrant Labor and the Politics of Development in Bahrain," *Merip Reports,* 15, no. 4 (May 1985), p. 10.

34. M. Endo, "Saudization: Development in the Early 1990's and Prospects for the Rest of the Decade," *JIME REVIEW* (Winter 1996), p. 79; see also *The NCB (National Comercial Bank) Economist,* 5 (June/July 1995), p. 8.

35. Mary Ann Tetreault, "Kuwait's Economic Prospects," *MEED* (January 1993), p. 12.

36. *MEED,* 40 (23 February 1996), p. 8.

37. *Gulf States Newsletter,* 9 July 1990, pp. 14–15; see also *MEED,* 37 (12 March 1993), p. 46.

38. *Gulf States Newsletter,* 4 October 1993, p. 10.

39. *The NCB Economist,* June/July 1995, p. 7; *Gulf States Newsletter,* 20 November 1995, p. 10.

40. ESCWA, *Statistical Abstract,* No. 16, pp. 145–146.

41. J. S. Birks and J. A. Rimmer, *Developing Education Systems in the Oil States of Arabia: Conflicts of Purpose and Focus* (Durham: Centre for Middle Eastern and Islamic Studies, 1984), p. 4.

42. Beblawi, "The Rentier State," p. 91.

43. *The NCB Economist,* June/July 1995, p. 10.

44. *MEED,* 40 (6 December 1996), p. 34.

45. J. Addleton, "The Impact of the Gulf War on Migration and Remittances in Asia and the Middle East," *International Migration,* 29 (1991), p. 514; "Asian Expatriates—Coming Back," *Middle East* (October 1991), p. 36; *MEED,* 35 (4 October 1991), p. 6.

46. *MEED,* 35 (4 October 1991), p. 6; 36 (14 August 1992), p. 19; ESCWA, *Expert Group Meeting on the Absorption of Returnees in the ESCWA Region with Special Emphasis on Opportunities in the Industrial Sector,* Amman, 16–17 December 1991 (Amman, October 1992), p. 3. See also Nicholas Van Hear, *New Diasporas: The Mass Exodus, Dispersal, and Regrouping of Migrant Communities* (London: UCL Press, 1998), pp. 81–93.

47. *MEED,* 40 (5 April 1996), p. 30.

48. *MEED,* 38 (11 November 1994), p. 30.

49. *MEED,* 40 (22 November 1996), pp. 9–10.

50. *MEED,* 37 (6 August 1993), p. 10.

51. *Gulf States Newsletter,* 23 September 1991, p. 7.

52. *MEED,* 40 (4 October 1996), pp. 2–3; 40 (6 December 1996), p. 34; *Gulf States Newsletter,* 21 October 1996, p. 6.

53. *Gulf States Newsletter,* 8 April 1996, p. 13; *Jordan Times* (Amman), 23 March 1996.

54. *MEED,* 37 (12 March 1993), p. 8.

55. *MEED,* 40 (5 April 1996), p. 55.

56. EIU, *Country Report—Kuwait,* No. 3 (1996), p. 12.

57. *Gulf States Newsletter*, 20 November 1995, pp. 8–9.

58. ESCWA, *Survey of Economic and Social Developments in the ESCWA Region—1995* (New York: UN Publications, 1996), p. 41.

59. *Jordan Times*, 3 January 1996.

60. *MEED*, 39 (24 November 1995), p. 26.

61. *MEED,* 38 (8 July 1994), p. 4.

62. "Saudi Arabia: Spendthrift No More," *Middle East* (February 1994), p. 24.

63. "Saudi Arabia Faces Maturity," *Middle East* (July/August 1994), p. 20.

64. *MEED,* 40 (5 April 1996), p. 28.

65. See *Ha'aretz* (Tel Aviv), 24 December 1997.

66. Regarding the political unrest in Bahrain see EIU, *Country Report—Bahrain*, No. 4 (1995), p. 14.

15

Good Counsel to the King: The Islamist Opposition in Saudi Arabia, Jordan, and Morocco

Gudrun Krämer

Do Islamists react differently to monarchies, and if so, is that reaction related to the rulers' legitimacy, specifically Islamic legitimacy? Does such legitimacy offer rulers better protection against the "challenge of political Islam" than is available to their republican neighbors and rivals of differing ideological outlooks? Until the 1980s, Islamic movements in Middle Eastern monarchies appeared to be marginal and received little notice. As Islamism, or fundamentalism, was widely interpreted as a "revolt against modernity," and as the monarchies, particularly the Arab monarchies, were thought to be more "traditional" and less modern(ized) than most of the republics, there appeared to be less of an incentive, or need, to revolt against them in the name of Islam, traditional values, and "authenticity." And indeed, with the exception of the Iranian Revolution in the spring of 1979 and the occupation of the Great Mosque in Mecca in November of the same year, none of the monarchies has so far been faced with the insurgent, militant Islam that has shaken modernizing authoritarian regimes like those in Egypt, Syria, and, more recently, Algeria.

This is not to say that there aren't any Islamists in those countries who make themselves heard and felt in the streets, in the universities, and in cultural and intellectual circles. Their presence has been brought out in the course of political liberalization that several monarchies have engaged in, like many of the republics. In virtually all instances where, during the last two decades, Arab regimes have initiated a policy of controlled political liberalization, loosening the restrictions on free speech and association, Islamic movements, parties, and activists have emerged as the strongest force of opposition. Whenever they have been allowed to participate in local and national elections that were not too openly manipulated, Islamist candidates obtained 12–20 percent of the vote. Important exceptions to this trend include

Algeria, united Yemen, and Kuwait, where Islamists gained a higher share of the vote without, however, winning a majority. In the Palestinian territories, in contrast, they obtained a minor share only, and in Morocco they played no significant role in electoral politics. Jordan conformed well to the overall pattern, whereas Saudi Arabia has so far not held any elections.[1] Monarchies, then, were found all across the board, from typical ones, such as Jordan, to exceptional ones, such as Kuwait, with a higher share of Islamist votes, or Morocco, with a significantly lower one.

The three monarchies to be surveyed here have very different histories, and their rulers use different kinds of legitimation. Indeed, they do not seem to have much in common apart from the very fact of being monarchies (none, incidentally, is very traditional).[2] Jordan fits the ideal type of the artificial state created by the colonial powers after the dissolution of the Ottoman Empire.[3] Saudi Arabia came into being as a result of conquest—not much different from the many European states that are not considered artificial. Morocco, by contrast, though deeply marked by French colonial rule and influence, has strong roots in history (in this respect similar to Oman or Kuwait) and a relatively well defined sense of national identity, based on Arabism and Sunni Islam of the Malikite rite. "Artificiality," then, seems to be largely unrelated to stability. Regarding their political economy, Saudi Arabia is the quintessential rentier state, and Jordan is generally classified as a semi-rentier.[4] Interestingly, the concept has not yet been systematically applied to Morocco.

There are also significant differences in regime legitimation and the role of Islam therein, which are widely assumed to matter to the Islamists. Here it might be useful to distinguish between several aspects of "Islamic" legitimation, or legitimacy. The three main aspects are: lineage (descendance from the family of the Prophet Muhammad); function (the protection and propagation of the faith, the application of the *shari'a*, protection of the holy places of Islam, etc.); and religious authority proper (authority to decide on dogmatic or legal questions, to give legal opinions, and to exert independent legal reasoning, or *ijtihad*)—all of which may or may not be linked to religious charisma (*baraka*). Function more than the other aspects makes the ruler dependent on performance—and his subjects' evaluation of it. Religious prestige can flow from any one of those elements or from a combination of them. The only contemporary Middle Eastern monarch to enjoy undisputed religious prestige and authority is the Moroccan king, who in his person unites all four elements: lineage, charisma, function, and authority. Neither his Saudi nor his Jordanian counterpart can claim any religious authority in a narrow sense. Their legitimation is essentially dynastic. Incidentally, Saudi Arabia and Hashemite Jordan are the only modern Middle Eastern states to bear the name of the ruling dynasty, and only the Hashemites are descended from the

Prophet. The ascendancy and power of the Saudi dynasty, by contrast, was originally based on its alliance with the religious reform movement of Muhammad Ibn Abd al-Wahhab (d. 1791), to compensate, in part, for its lack of religiously significant lineage.

With respect to society, the differences among the opposition and, more particularly, the Islamists, are equally marked. Although in Morocco intellectual, political, and associational pluralism has for a long time been recognized and "civil society" been given some space, this is a much more recent phenomenon in Jordan; in Saudi Arabia, pluralism is neither recognized nor institutionalized. The religious space, or *champ religieux*, is again most highly diversified in Morocco, ranging from saints to scholars, as well as from religious brotherhoods to the institutions of "official Islam" that include the king himself. It is less diverse in Jordan and much less so in Saudi Arabia, where expressions of Islam that are deemed unorthodox by the Wahhabi establishment, ranging from the Shi'ites to most Sufis, are not tolerated (and, it might be added, hardly studied and known).

In spite of these differences, the three monarchies have a few traits in common. All three have projected an image of respect for Islam, often ostentatiously so, and for "tradition," variously defined. None has played a prominent role in Arab nationalism, and none has adopted "socialist" policies. Clientelism and personalistic ties to the ruler or the royal family, respectively (best known as *wasta* in Jordan), are crucial to system maintenance, and though the army and security services may be indispensable for keeping the king/ruling family in power, they do not act as the locus of autonomous decisionmaking in the political and economic spheres. They are the instruments of power, not its source. In all three cases, the king is the single most important player and the ultimate arbiter among domestic actors, interests, and ideologies. The kings, or the ruling families, portray themselves as the indispensable unifying element in a plural society otherwise threatened by internal division based on ethnicity, tribalism, and political conflict—the supreme symbol of national unity. It is the ruler or the ruling dynasty who, according to this view, serves to guarantee order against the threat of chaos, anarchy, and civic strife, all included in the highly evocative *fitna*, or disturbance of a moral and social order divinely sanctioned, a temptation to the believers, or instability (*tout court*). Yet the importance of dynastic-religious legitimacy for system maintenance ought not to be overrated. When it comes to political stability and royal succession in Jordan, Morocco, and Saudi Arabia, the same anxious questions are usually asked as regards the Syria of Hafiz al-Asad and the Iraq of Saddam Hussein, both of whom have worked at setting up dynasties.

What then is the impact of regime legitimization on the content form and expression of Islamist opposition?[5] What are its core demands, and what is its social base? Is it any different from opposition to various republics?

CASE STUDIES: SAUDI ARABIA

The Gulf crisis of 1990–1991 created fresh interest in Saudi society and renewed demands for reform and political participation following in its wake,
an interest that continued to be firmly focused on the stability of the system.
In the 1970s, Michael Hudson compared the Saudi monarchy to one-party
rule: the royal family controlled the country, which it regarded as its *mulk*
(property, or seized power), and the population; emphasized Islam to legitimize its control and justify its policies; and used the regular police, the army,
the national guard, the intelligence services, and the religious police to control the public and private behavior of its subjects.[6] His analysis still seemed
to be valid in the mid-1990s. The dynasty's claims to religious prestige and
legitimacy were entirely based on function and, hence, at least theoretically,
predicated on their ability to deliver and to conform to expectations of the relevant public. Claims to religious authority were still made by Abd al-Aziz,
generally known as Ibn Saud, in his capacity as imam of the Wahhabi community (which referred to themselves as *muwahhidun*, that is, "believers in
God's Oneness," or *tawhid*), a title he took over from his father in 1915 and
discarded in favor of various nonreligious titles such as sultan of Najd (1921),
king of the Hijaz (1926), and, finally, king of Saudi Arabia (1932). Despite its
negative connotations (see Quran 27:34), which must have been perfectly familiar to his Wahhabi followers, the title *malik* (king) may have been more
acceptable to outsiders: non-Wahhabi Muslims on one hand who otherwise
might have thought he assumed caliphal authority, and Europeans to whom it
suggested political power and prestige on the other. The title *imam* seems to
have been abandoned by his successors, and in the 1990s it was not publicly
used anymore.[7] Within the framework of *siyasa shari'yya* (political authority
defined by the *shar'ia* denoting enforcement of Islamic law and conduct), the
Saudi monarch is accorded wide-ranging authority to organize justice and
even to issue decrees in areas not regulated by Islamic law (*fiqh*).[8] But he is
no longer considered a religious scholar himself: his role is that of guardian
of the faith, the content of which is determined by the *ulama* who are, as the
famous saying has it, the "heirs to the prophets." The search for a religious
role was expressed differently when, in 1986, King Fahd assumed the title of
"custodian [literally: servant] of the two holy shrines" (*khadim al-haramayn
al-sharifayn*). As custodian of the holy places in Mecca and Medina, patron
of the pilgrimage, and promoter of Islamic causes throughout the world, the
king, though lacking in religious authority, acquired religious prestige and influence at home and abroad that, however, needed to be continuously confirmed by proper conduct and policies.

According to official doctrine, formalized in the Basic Law of Governance of March 1992, the Quran and the Sunna serve as the constitution of
the land—a condition that, the problematic content of the claim aside, should

give the *ulama* a central place in state and society. In fact, their role and influence have become closely circumscribed and largely restricted to the field of law proper. Since the defeat of the Ikhwan in 1929–1930 and the establishment of the Saudi state in 1932, the *ulama* have been subjected to government control and converted into state employees.[9] The establishment, in 1970, of the Ministry of Justice clearly marked this tendency. This was followed, in 1971, by the Council of Senior Scholars (*hay'at kibar al-ulama*) made up of some fifteen to twenty senior scholars who are all appointed by the king.[10] One result was that the *ulama*, in contradistinction to other groups in society, built up a proper hierarchy headed by Shaikh Abd al-Aziz Bin Baz, until his death in spring 1999, secretary general of the Administration of Religious Studies, Legal Opinion, Mission, and Guidance (*idarat al-buhuth al-ilmiyya wal-ifta wal-dawa wal-irshad*), head of the Council of Senior Scholars, and paramount *mufti* (professional jurist) of the kingdom who, in 1993, was given ministerial rank. The *ulama* were consulted when the ruler saw fit (see, e.g., the decisions to bring in foreigners to end the occupation of the Great Mosque in 1979 and to defend the kingdom in 1991, which were legitimized by *fatwa*s issued by the highest religious authorities). But they do not seem to be involved in the formulation of policies and strategic decisions in foreign and security affairs, socioeconomic development, and political organization. Even their highest-ranking members are not part of the inner circle of power. Their function is essentially to legitimize policies and strategies that have been debated and determined elsewhere. The lack of independence and influence, strongly resented among religious scholars and officials, was clearly expressed in the opposition's "Memorandum of Advice" of July 1992.

The activities of the religious police, whose intrusions into public and private life seem to have intensified since the Gulf War of 1991, have equally given rise to resentment, even among Islamist circles. The religious police, or the Association for the Propagation of Virtue and the Suppression of Vice (*hay'at al-amr bil-maruf wal-nahi an al-munkar*), whose members are generally known as *mutawwa*, was probably formed in 1903 and headed by Shaikh Abdallah Ibn Abd al-Latif al-Shaikh, one of the descendants of Muhammad Ibn Abd al-Wahhab, to enforce Wahhabi doctrines and modes of conduct in the newly conquered Saudi domains.[11] They had already been integrated into the police force before the foundation of the kingdom in 1932, turning them, like the *ulama*, into agents of the government.[12] (As the spheres of virtue and vice, good and evil, *maruf* and *munkar* are vague and ill-defined, and as there were no laws restricting the field of legitimate intervention of the *mutawwa*, at least until the promulgation of the Basic Law of Governance, their scope for action is wide. To join their ranks, no qualification is needed beyond a basic knowledge of Islam and the *shari'a*. They have their own headquarters and branches in the major towns in the country, they can make their own arrests, and there is no legal appeal against their actions.[13]) During and after the

Gulf War, even the Islamist opposition criticized their unwarranted encroach-
ments on privacy, emphasizing the fact that according to Islam private homes
are inviolate and spying is illegal.[14] Both principles were confirmed in the
Basic Law of Governance of March 1992 (Article 37).

Opposition, even violent opposition, to Saudi rule is by no means new.
During the 1960s there had been riots against the introduction of what tradi-
tionalists considered to be illicit technological innovations (*bida, munkar*). In
1969, a coup attempt by air force officers aiming to establish the "Republic of
the Arabian Peninsula" was aborted. Since then, the composition and orientation of domestic political opposition have changed considerably. As in most
Middle Eastern countries, left-wing, liberal, and nationalist thought and
movements—their appeal seeming to have been limited even in the 1950s and
1960s—have been eclipsed by Islamist activism.[15] Extreme restrictions on
political expression and association in a country where professional syndicates, labor unions, and political parties are illegal and the press is scrupu-
lously censored have left the private and the religious spheres as virtually the
only ones where people could meet, debate, and voice criticism. Yet until the
Gulf crisis, there was little interest in, and even less knowledge of, the Islamic
opposition inside the kingdom. Knowledge is still very limited and highly
fragmentary.[16] The seizure of the Great Mosque in Mecca, the most sensitive
public space in the kingdom, by the followers of Juhayman Ibn Muhammad
Ibn Sayf al-Utaybi (b. 1936), a former colonel in the national guard and erst-
while student at the Islamic University at Medina, attracted widespread attention.[17] Juhayman's ideas appear to have been consciously modeled on those
of the Ikhwan, and the uprising seems in part to have been motivated by the
desire to revenge their defeat at the hands of the Saudis. The idea of a *mahdi*,
however, who was to appear on the turn of the fourteenth-century *hijra* (corresponding to November 1979) and whom Juhayman identified with his
brother-in-law, Muhammad bin Abdallah al-Qahtani, was clearly alien to the
Wahhabi tradition. The rebels, at any rate, condemned in vibrant, messianic
tones the royal family's practices and claims to Islamic legitimacy. They also
attacked the *ulama*, including Shaikh Abd al-Aziz Ibn Baz himself, who subsequently denounced them as Kharijite heretics and classified their insurrec-
tion as *hiraba*, one of the crimes punishable by death.[18] The revolt coincided
with Shi'ite unrest in the Eastern Province that was in part inspired by the
Iranian Revolution. The two movements, however, do not appear to have been
coordinated or to have shared common demands and aspirations beyond the
most basic ones of justice and reform. Thanks to the help of French security
experts, the uprising was eventually put down, and sixty-three of its leaders
and members were executed, without trial, in 1980.

During the 1980s, there was some indication of religious protest among
Saudi youths, university students, and teachers who did not, however, engage
in open criticism of the king, the monarchy, or the public order.[19] Although

Islamist publications, bookstores, and clandestine audiotapes proliferated, there were few signs of organized activity. By the mid-1980s, some of the factors had accumulated that elsewhere had contributed to the rise of Islamist protest and activities: declining oil revenue and living standards; intensified urbanization; the spread and visibility of Western influence; growing social disparities, inequity, and corruption in high places; and blatant contradictions between official rhetoric and actual policies coinciding with the rise and increasing assertiveness of Islamist movements in other parts of the Arab world. The two Gulf Wars were to expose the weakness of the Saudi kingdom, its vulnerability to external threats, and its dependence on the West that many Saudis continued to see not only as un-Islamic but as positively anti-Islamic. In certain ways similar to the self-criticism that had been provoked in other parts of the Arab world by the defeat in the 1967 June War against Israel, the Gulf crisis of 1990–1991 gave rise to serious soul-searching in Saudi society and intensified criticism of official practices and policies. The novelty was not that there should have been criticism of the social, moral, and political order at all but that it should be voiced publicly, overriding the concern for, if not the obsession with, maintaining the facade of unity, calm, and self-assurance. If the accusation of *fitna*, disturbance of the religiously sanctioned social order, was to be risked, it was apparently considered a lesser evil than to continue pretending that all was well in the kingdom of Saudi Arabia.

A first indication of unrest was given when, in early November 1990, some fifty women, most of them highly educated professionals, drove through Riyadh in open defiance of an unwritten ban on women's driving, provoking an outcry in religious circles outraged by this act of *fitna*. The government reacted quickly, using the incident to demonstrate its unswerving loyalty to, and implementation of, Wahhabi principles. The women were arrested, dismissed from their jobs, and stripped of their passports. In December, the interior minister formally issued a ban on women's driving. Though some of the measures were subsequently reversed, the ban remained, and the point had been forcefully made: there were to be no concessions on the highly symbolic issue of women's place in an Islamic society. The "public invisibility of women had become a visible symbol of the monarch's piety."[20]

In December 1990, at the height of tension preceding war with Iraq, forty-three academics, writers, businessmen, and government officials of religious as well as "liberal" leanings circulated a petition to the king asking for a thorough revision of the kingdom's political and legal institutions, including notably the systemization of *fatawi* (religious opinions); the issuing of a basic law of governance; establishment of a consultative council (*majlis al-shura*); revival of municipal councils; reform of the judicial system; limitations on the activities of the Association for the Propagation of Virtue; and greater freedom, within the framework of the *shari'a*, for women.[21] These "liberals," however, lacked an efficient network to enforce their views and demands. A few months later, in May 1991, leading *ulama*, academics, and professionals, including Abd al-Aziz Ibn Baz himself, took the unprecedented initiative of handing an open letter to the king, which had been circulated widely in mosques throughout the kingdom, demanding extensive reform of the political and judicial systems, beginning with the establishment of a consultative council, and calling for the strict application of Islamic norms and values in public life as well as in economic and foreign policies. Going beyond their liberal colleagues, they also called for the buildup of a strong army and for a foreign policy based on national interest "without relying on alliances not sanctioned by the *shari'a*"—a not-so-veiled attack on the alliance with the United States. Throughout, the emphasis was on justice, equity, and full accountability of government officials—no criticism of the al-Sauds or the institution of the monarchy, yet a clear enough condemnation of the corruption and injustice rampant under their rule.[22] Again, its significance lay not so much in the fact that there was criticism at all but that it was made public and that the code of silence was broken.

The petition was followed by the Memorandum of Advice (*mudhakkirat al-nasiha*) dated July 1992 and sent to Ibn Baz in August, which elaborated on the points raised previously.[23] Again, criticism was not directed against the institution of the monarchy or the person of the king but against specific "deviations" that were thought nonetheless to be amenable to reform. The memorandum attacked corruption (*fasad*) in its widest sense—economic, moral, and political; nepotism and favoritism; growing inequality and the degradation of public services; the denial of freedom of expression (for Islamic preachers, teachers, and activists); and the close cooperation with and dependence on Western powers at the expense of an exclusively Islamic orientation of Saudi foreign and security policies. It called for justice and equality of all Saudi citizens (*muwatinun*) before the law;[24] the establishment of a Shura Council; the strict and exclusive application of the *shari'a* (requiring, for example, the abolition of all un-Islamic laws and decrees, dues, and taxes, as well as the revision of treaties with non-Muslim and un-Islamic governments and agencies); the independence of the judiciary and respect of the legitimate (*shar'i*) rights of all citizens, that is, rights conforming to the *shari'a*, not necessarily to the international standards of human rights;[25] the cleansing of society in general, and of government and the administration in particular; and the promotion of a strong economy built on self-sufficiency and the ban on interest; as well as, lastly, foreign and security policies oriented toward Muslim states and Muslim interest. The demand for complete supervision over all aspects of public policies by the *ulama*, and the strict conformance of all public and private life to the *shari'a* as interpreted by them, implied a vision of an Islamic state that, in that respect at least, would come close to the Iranian model. Such would even enhance the power and influence of the "clerics," since they would not be subordinated to one supreme jurisconsult (*faqih*) and leader (Persian: *rahbar*) but, in theory at least, follow their conscience only. It would replace strict state censorship as exercised by a number of government agencies, such as the General Directorate of Publications and the Supreme Information Council, by another.[26] With all its emphasis on strict Islamic values, norms, and conduct, the document contained some interesting innovations. Although it emphasized throughout the need to return to a comprehensive, and exclusive, application of the *shari'a*, it called for the presence of defense lawyers (*muhamin*) in all lawsuits. That is an institution that is not part of the Islamic legal tradition, which only speaks of representatives of the parties (*Wakil, Wukala*), though it is already selectively used in Saudi *shari'a* courts, albeit in civil cases only and not criminal ones.[27]

Although openly critical of nepotism, favoritism, and clientelism, the memorandum never once mentioned the king or the Saudi royal family—in contradistinction to Juhayman al-Utaybi and independent Islamists who had openly criticized the royals and the principle of hereditary rule.[28] It did not condone or advocate the use of force or armed rebellion. The vocabulary of radical and militant Islam (*hakimiyyat allah, jahiliyya, jihad, takfir*, etc.) was entirely absent from the memorandum, as was the tone of religious fervor characteristic of Juhayman's letters. Instead, its authors used the sober vocabulary of Islamic theology and jurisprudence (*al-amr bil-ma'ruf wal-nahi an al-munkar, al-din al-nasiha, hisba*, etc.) still thoroughly familiar to them, which emphasizes the joint responsibility of the ruler (*wali al-amr*) and the *ulama* to establish and maintain an Islamic order. The ruler, exerting his powers within the framework of *siyasa shari'yya*, and the *ulama*, giving good counsel to the prince (*nasiha*), complement each other. As long as the ruler does nothing to openly contradict the Quran and Sunna, or the *shari'a*, thereby committing an explicit act of unbelief (*kufr bawah*), it is unlawful to rebel against him. The weapon of *takfir*, or exclusion from the community of Muslim believers, so freely used by Wahhabi forebears against anyone not of them, was not turned against the prince. Their terminology and deep respect for the *ulama* clearly distinguished the Saudi authors of the memorandum from Islamist thinkers and activists in Egypt, Algeria, Tunisia, and even Jordan and Morocco.

As in most Middle Eastern states and societies, the government response to criticism combined intimidation and repression with concessions. Although the letter of May 1991 had been widely distributed and debated in mosques and private meetings (*majalis*), the lengthy memorandum seems to have had a limited readership only. Still, the memorandum or, more precisely, the way it was made public, was swiftly denounced by the Council of Senior Scholars presided over by Ibn Baz, who, it will be remembered, had been one of the signatories of the open letter. Seven out of seventeen council members, however, whose absence was explained by "health reasons," actually refused to sign the condemnation. They were dismissed by the king in December

1992 and replaced by loyal *ulama*.[29] At the same time, King Fahd responded by promising constitutional reform, which had been announced, with beautiful regularity, in times of crisis or intrafamily power struggles (1932, 1962, 1964, 1980, November 1990), never to materialize once the demands had died down.[30] The tactics had worked after the attack on the Great Mosque, when his predecessor had appointed a committee to draft a constitution; that task, however, was never completed. On 1 March 1992, King Fahd issued by royal decree (*marsum*) the Basic Law of Governance (*al-nizam al-asasi lil-hukm*), which for the first time made the rules of government and the rights of individual citizens explicit. Yet it also confirmed the monarchical system, strengthened the power of the king, and continued to deny the citizens the freedoms of information, expression, and association. It was accompanied by the Law of Provinces and the Consultative Council Law, which met at least some of the demands made in the various petitions and memoranda.[31] In September 1992, the king named the chairman of the consultative council (*majlis al-shura*), Muhammad Ibn Ibrahim Ibn Jubayr. The council itself still failed to take shape. It was only in August 1993 that the king finally announced the names of its sixty members, who were to advise him on policy matters without, however, having any formal say in decisionmaking.[32]

The Saudi Islamist opposition still seemed to lack organization and leadership; it was apparently as informal as other intellectual and political circles in modern Saudi society, where, as will be recalled, most autonomous associations are illegal.[33] The one attempt to create an independent organization was promptly crushed. In May 1993, six prominent religious scholars and academics formed the Committee for the Defence of Legitimate Rights (CDLR, *lajnat al-difa an al-huquq al-shar'iyya*) to defend the rights of the "oppressed" (a term strongly reminiscent of the *mustadafun* invoked by Shi'ite leaders from Imam Musa al-Sadr to Imam Khomeini).[34] It was declared un-Islamic by the Council of Senior Scholars and disbanded by the authorities two weeks later. They jailed its spokesman, Muhammad Abdallah al-Mas'ari, a professor of physics who, like his father, Abdallah Ibn Sulayman al-Mas'ari, had been one of the signatories of the Memorandum of Advice, and dismissed other members from government service. Al-Mas'ari was released in November 1993, secretly went to London via Yemen, and in April 1994 refounded the organization there. Using the latest technology in telecommunications, the committee adopted a much more outspoken tone, openly denouncing the royal family as corrupt and unfit to rule and calling for an elected and accountable government.

Like the Wahhabi *ulama* in general, the Sunni Islamists are vaguely known and described as *salafiyyun*, or those who follow the ways of the exemplary first two generations of Muslims (*al-salaf al-salih*).[35] They range from establishment figures critical of certain deviations of a system that they essentially wish to see preserved to younger shaikhs and activists demanding a return to what they consider to be a truly Islamic order. They operate essentially through family and social networks of friends, colleagues, and associates. They are mostly young, middle-class urbanites led by teachers, preachers, and students, mostly from the three religious universities, al-Imam Muhammad Ibn Saud Islamic University in Riyadh, Umm al-Qura in Mecca, and the Islamic University in Medina, whose graduates have increasingly been faced with unemployment. Religious scholars and preachers play a larger role than in any other Middle Eastern Islamic movement, Iran excluded. According to R. H. Dekmejian, recently urbanized Bedouins constitute one source of mass support (in certain ways similar to recent migrants from the countryside in other Muslim countries). There is little information on tribal links and solidarities, though, or of the impact of tribal solidarities on their aims and activities.[36] The Islamists of the early 1990s are altogether more concerned with sociopolitical reform and are more articulate, more numerous, and less isolated from society than were their 1970s predecessors. Based on (some of) the signatures on the May 1991 letter and Memorandum of Advice, with fifty-two and 107 names, respectively, Dekmejian concluded that they present a relatively homogeneous profile. Some two thirds are from Najd, the heartland of Wahhabism and origin of the Saudi family; most of them are well educated, with the Riyadh universities being strongly represented; and *ulama* figure prominently among them.[37]

There is little information on radical and militant preachers and activists. In January 1992, some fifty members of a group vaguely referred to as *al-nahda al-islamiyya* (Islamic Awakening), were arrested; most of them were university students and young religious leaders who had apparently protested the Saudi family's monopoly of power.[38] In April 1994, the authorities took the unprecedented step of depriving Usama Ibn Ladin—scion of a great Saudi merchant family, a wealthy entrepreneur, and one of the most prominent supporters of the Islamic struggle in Afghanistan, Algeria, Yemen, and other parts of the Islamic world—of his Saudi citizenship. Ibn Ladin, who in 1992 had settled in Sudan, moved to London in April 1994, founded his own Association for Advice and Reform (*hay'at al-nasiha wal-islah*), issued a circular called *al-Shula*, but also declared his support for Mas'ari's CDLR.[39] In September 1994, several prominent shaikhs were arrested in Burayda, the capital of Qasim Province and known for its Islamist activism, among them Salman Ibn Fahd al-Awda (b. 1955), a lecturer at the al-Qasim branch of Imam Muhammad Ibn Saud Islamic University who had already been arrested a number of times in 1991.[40] The authorities also arrested Safar Ibn Abd al-Rahman al-Hawali (b. 1950), dean of Islamic Studies (*al-aqida*) at Umm al-Qura University in Mecca. Both were known for their attacks on the U.S. presence in the country and normalization of relations with Israel that were widely circulated on audiotapes and videos. The Ministry of the Interior procured from the Council of Senior Scholars a *fatwa* denouncing the shaikhs as

Kharijites and, after a period of silence and denial, justified the arrests as measures to safeguard the unity of the Muslim community (al-jama'a). The arrests provoked angry protest in the city of Burayda, to which the police responded with more arrests. A hitherto unknown group, the Brigades of the Faith (kata'ib al-iman), issued threats against foreigners in the country—a tactic employed previously in Egypt and Algeria—as well as against members of the royal family.[41] Yet for the time being there were no further signs of organized activity transcending local groups and activists.

There also appeared to be no links between the Sunni and the Shi'ite opposition in the country that, by and large, had lost the importance it enjoyed during the late 1970s and early 1980s. It did not at any rate show a high profile during or after the Gulf crisis. Ever since 1913, when the Eastern Hasa (al-Ahsa) region was included in the Saudi domains, the Shi'ites suffered from exclusion and oppression for what were essentially religious motives.[42] In spite of the fact that in 1959 the al-Azhar Supreme School issued a fatwa recognizing the Shi'ites as the fifth school of Islamic law (madhhab), the Wahhabi establishment, including Shaikhs Ibn Baz and Ibn Jibrin (the latter incidentally a signatory to CDLR's founding manifesto), continued to regard them as heretics (rafidun), and so did Sunni Islamists.[43] Shi'ites, whose numbers were in the 1990s estimated at some 400,000, about 8 percent of the Saudi population, were concentrated in the Eastern Province, Asir, and Medina. They were effectively barred from positions of authority in the educational system, the judiciary, the government, the army, and Aramco; intermarriage between Sunnis and Shi'ites was not permitted, and meat slaughtered by Shi'ites was considered haram. Repression increased during and after the Iranian Revolution, in which the Shi'ites were suspected of forming a fifth column within the kingdom, all the more dangerous because of their concentration in the oil-rich eastern regions. In 1979–1980, several demonstrations and strikes to celebrate the revolution, later known as the "uprising of the Eastern region" (intifadat al-mintaqa al-sharqiyya) were brutally repressed.[44] The Organization for the Islamic Revolution (munazzamat al-thawra al-islamiyya) started to broadcast from Iran, publishing a monthly, al-Jazira al-Arabiyya (which was discontinued in late 1993 following an agreement between Shi'ite exiles and the Saudi government). In 1988, an unarmed Shi'ite demonstration against the monarchy was dispersed forcefully. By and large, however, the government policy of carrots and sticks seems to have worked. Increased investment in the Eastern Province did help toward alleviating Shi'ite grievances; and the Shi'ite opposition abroad seems to have gradually moved away from revolutionary discourse inspired by the Iranian model to adopt demands for participation, pluralism, and democracy voiced by Islamist movements and activists in other parts of the Middle East.[45]

JORDAN

In most respects, Jordan offers a very different picture from Saudi Arabia. The state of Jordan, widely seen as the very epitome of artificiality in the region, has been successfully consolidated. A clear sense, however, of Jordanian national identity, uniting Bedouins and urbanites as well as citizens of Palestinian and of East Bank origins, has still not evolved.[46] Much has been made of the religious legitimation of the king. Yet Hashemite claims to leadership in general and to rule over Jordan in particular are not based on religious authority in a narrow sense but on descent from the Prophet. If that constitutes nobility, it is not local nobility or notability. Emir Abdallah's claim to religious prestige may have had a role to play with regard to the tribes and the small religious establishment in the country, and the same may be true for his offspring, King Hussein and King Abdallah II. Generally speaking, however, authority had to be forcefully asserted—and relations between the ruler, or the state, and society developed on the basis of function and services—and was greatly enhanced by British support.[47] Similar factors were, incidentally, at play in the emergence of Ibn Saud as the main ruler of the Arabian Peninsula. The Hashemites, too, considered themselves responsible for some of Islam's most holy places. Having lost Mecca and Medina to the Saudis in the 1920s, and Old Jerusalem to the Israelis in 1967, they still remained responsible for the Muslim holy places in Jerusalem and hundreds of religious institutions and extensive *waqf* (religious endowment) property in the West Bank, even beyond August 1988, when the king declared Jordan's administrative separation from those territories (*fakk al-irtibat*). On this score, he had to compete not only with the Palestine Liberation Organization (PLO) but also with King Hasan II of Morocco, who in 1969 was elected chairman of the newly created Committee for the Defence of Jerusalem, projecting his role as religious leader well beyond the Moroccan borders. Although King Hussein did not hesitate to make the most of his noble descent and his personal commitment to Islam, he did not exert, or claim, any religious authority or carry a religious title; he also did not use religious symbols and ceremonies as systematically as did his Moroccan and Saudi counterparts. In the case of Jordan, then, there is no reason why the monarchy in general and the rule of the Hashemites in particular should be regarded as natural, traditional, or religiously sanctioned.

Government policy has been described by one benevolent observer as combining "firmness with disruptive forces and tolerance toward all citizens who identify with the state."[48] The Islamic movement[49] has so far not acted as a disruptive force posing a threat to the cohesion of society and to the monarchy. Quite the contrary, Jordan provides one of the few examples of longtime peaceful coexistence, if not cooperation, between a Middle Eastern government and an Islamic movement.[50] Traditionally, the Muslim Brotherhood has played not so much the role of opposition than of His Majesty's loyal opposition. The reason for this policy is easy enough to see. In neighboring Egypt, the Muslim Brotherhood was persecuted by the Arab socialist regime of Abd al-Nasir, an experience later repeated in Ba'thist Syria, and to confront one of the few Arab regimes not hostile to them would have bordered on suicide. This is all the more so because the king and Muslim Brotherhood shared common interests and enemies. The argument was succinctly expressed by Yusuf al-Azm, one of the leading Muslim Brotherhood activists in Jordan, when in the late 1980s he explained the political line of his movement:

> The Muslim Brotherhood did not provoke the king. We had a truce with him, because we were unable to open fronts with all sides at one time. . . . We agreed with the king because Nasir was irrational in his attacks against him. We were skeptical about Nasir's relations with America. . . . We stood with the king in order to protect ourselves, because if Nasir's followers had risen to power, or a pro-Nasir government had been established in Jordan, the Muslim Brotherhood would have been liquidated, as they were liquidated in Egypt.[51]

Like its Egyptian mother organization, the Jordanian branch of the Brotherhood was registered under the law of charitable clubs and associations and was therefore not affected by the dissolution of political parties in 1957. In contrast to the Egyptian Ikhwan, it was able to maintain that status. For several decades the Muslim Brotherhood was in fact the only sociopolitical organization tolerated in the country that also enjoyed the privilege of being able to receive funds from abroad, notably Saudi Arabia and other Gulf states. Again unlike in Egypt, it does not seem to have established an underground organization or military wing. Shorter periods of tension excepted, the Brotherhood supported the king against his critics and opponents at home and abroad (Arab nationalists, Nasirists, Ba'thists, and the PLO). Its main objectives were to render Jordanian society fully Islamic (the "application of the *shari'a*") and to liberate Islamic Palestine. In spite of some verbal radicalism, it was basically reformist in practice, integrative, and nonviolent. Attention was directed toward education and the media, and gradualism (*tadarruj*), cooperation, and participation in the official political framework were adopted as the strategic option. Muslim Brothers participated in most elections, although they did so in their personal capacity only, without involving the organization as such, which was not registered as a political party. Even in the 1950s and 1960s, prominent Muslim Brothers had joined parliament and the cabinet as deputies and ministers, again formally acting as individuals only. Relations with militant Islamic opposition groups such as the Islamic Liberation Party (*hizb al-tahrir al-islami*) founded in 1952 by Taqi al-Din al-Nabhani (d. 1977), Islamic Jihad, and Islamic Jihad bi-Bayt al-Muqaddas (i.e.,

Jerusalem), established in 1980 by Asad al-Tamimi, were marked by tension and competition.[52]

By the time political liberalization, or "democratization," was initiated in the mid-1980s,[53] the Islamic movement in general and the Muslim Brotherhood in particular had already attracted a following among virtually all groups and strata of Jordanian society. Supporters included Palestinian youth and university students, notably at the universities of Amman and Yarmuk, in Palestinian refugee camps, as well as the urban middle class, including professional associations, corresponding closely to patterns observed in Egypt, Algeria, and Tunisia. In contrast to Saudi Arabia, therefore, the Muslim Brothers and other local Islamists were able to build up a wide-ranging social presence reaching far beyond the mosque—but also far beyond the parliament. Yet when in April 1989 riots erupted in several towns and villages of southern Jordan—hitherto considered strongholds of East Jordanian sentiment and royal support—neither the Islamists nor the Palestinians seem to have been strongly involved. Although originally provoked by sharp price increases linked to a program of structural adaptation, the protesters also raised political issues from which the king could not be totally dissociated: corruption in high places and lack of political reform and participation. In an interesting move, the king did not use the riots to intensify government control and repression; on the contrary, he tried to contain domestic protest by a policy of political liberalization.[54] The riots ushered in a new phase in the cycle of relaxation and restriction so characteristic of Jordanian domestic politics.

The parliamentary elections of November 1989, where parties were not admitted, although many candidates represented well-known political "trends," demonstrated the strength of the Islamists, who proved to be the best organized force of opposition.[55] Islamist candidates obtained thirty-two out of eighty seats, among them twenty Muslim Brothers and twelve independents, some of whom had links to the militant Islamic resistance groups in the West Bank and Gaza. Loyal government supporters gained more than thirty seats, leftists and liberals a mere eleven. The PLO did not, or could not, take part in the elections. Islamists continued to do well in municipal elections that were held in May and June 1990 in Zarqa (predominantly Palestinian, where the Muslim Brothers won nine out of ten seats) and Rusayfa (four out of nine seats). Their successes did not tempt the king to interrupt the liberalization process. On the contrary, he intensified his efforts to co-opt them, appointing prominent Islamists to the commission created in April 1990 to formulate a national charter.[56] In October 1990, at the height of the Gulf crisis, Abd al-Latif Arabiyyat, a lawyer and leading Muslim Brother, was elected Speaker of parliament, and on 1 January 1991 five Muslim Brothers joined the cabinet as ministers of education, religious affairs, justice, social development, and health (they left barely six months later when a new cabinet was formed under Tahir al-Masri), thereby marking their definitive inclusion in the Jordanian political establishment. In what may have been a move to contain the Islamic movement by creating counterweights among the nonreligious opposition, restrictions on individual liberties were further reduced, martial law "frozen," press censorship relaxed, and the ban on political parties lifted. The national charter, which was ratified in June 1991 by the National Congress of some 2,000 participants representing all major political trends in the country, finally sanctioned a multiparty system that was formally established in August 1992.[57] It also confirmed loyalty to the king and the Hashemite dynasty, obliging the signatories to solemnly endorse the monarchical system.

The Islamists benefited from the newly enhanced opportunities, using them to build up a political presence and to extend their networks of clientelism and patronage. In late 1992, the Muslim Brothers and independent Islamists, including the widely respected Layth Shubaylat, an engineer from Amman very active in the civil rights movement and the fight against corruption, established their own political party. Significantly, it was called the Islamic Action Front (IAF, *jabhat al-Amal al-islami*) rather than "party," a term loaded with negative connotations in the Islamic tradition. Internal friction soon led to the withdrawal of most independents, Shubaylat included, which left the Muslim Brothers in sole control of the IAF.[58] The parliamentary elections of November 1993, the first multiparty elections since 1957, were held in due time but arranged in such a way as to reduce Islamist representation in parliament. Although the Islamists' share of the vote increased by some 3 percent over 1989, their number of mandates was greatly reduced from thirty-two to sixteen deputies from the IAF plus a few independents.[59] In the heavily manipulated local elections of June 1995, Islamists won a mere nine out of more than 200 municipalities, though that included some of the most important towns and urban districts.

The continuation, amid dramatic regional change and conflict, of the liberalization process, which included the Islamists, was most remarkable. In Jordan, the main area of potential conflict between the king and the Islamic opposition did not so much concern domestic affairs but foreign policies or, to be more precise, relations with Israel and the United States. In Jordan, like everywhere in the Middle East (except Turkey, where such a demand would have been unconstitutional), the Muslim Brothers demanded a return to pristine Islamic values, symbolized in the call for the strict and integral application of the *shari'a* (with equal rights guaranteed to non-Muslims and women—within the framework of Islam). They advocated the fight against corruption (which risked involving them in a conflict with the ruling elite), against political repression, and for political freedom. Unlike many of their fellow Islamists, they acknowledged the existence of political diversity and pluralism, and during times of heightened crisis, such as the second Gulf War, they even cooperated with the powerless and therefore harmless Communist Party. Yet on all issues of domestic policies, accommodation and compromise between the Islamists, the government, and the nonreligious opposition seemed possible. It is foreign policy where the basic understanding between King Hussein and the Muslim Brothers was at risk. There had been tension when, during the Iraq-Iran War (1980–1988), the Muslim Brothers criticized the king's support for Iraq against the Islamic Republic of Iran, which, especially in its early years, enjoyed considerable support in Jordan, Gaza, and the West Bank.[60] But the crucial issue was, of course, policy toward Israel and the Palestinian entity. Despite the strong commitment to the liberation of Palestine conflicting with the king's policy of de facto coexistence with Israel, mutual interest in cooperation had always been strong enough to overcome latent tension.

In 1991, when the Allied victory over Iraq paved the way to the Madrid conference, conflict between King Hussein and the Islamist opposition seemed impossible to avoid.[61] During and after the elections of November 1989, the Muslim Brothers had again declared their rejection of all UN resolutions on Palestine, their refusal to recognize Israel, and their support for the Intifadah and Hamas—their sister organization on Palestinian soil. They had called for jihad to liberate all of Palestine and condemned negotiations with the Zionist enemy as unacceptable under Islamic law (*munkar sharan*). Yet their words were not followed by deeds, at least not on Jordanian territory. Restraint was also used on the other side. In a situation similar to the one faced by government and opposition in Egypt during the Camp David peace process, King Hussein might have been tempted to reverse the liberalization process in order to continue his policy of rapprochement with the United States and his conservative neighbors in the Gulf and of normalization with Israel. He did not do so, choosing more subtle ways of intimidation, manipulation, and control. Two instances serve to illustrate this approach. First, during the king's absence from the country during the summer of 1992, two prominent independent Islamists, Layth Shubaylat and Yusuf Qarrash, were arrested, charged with conspiracy, and condemned to heavy prison sentences. Upon his triumphant return to the country, the king included Shubaylat and Qarrash in a general amnesty, wresting from them a pledge to henceforth abstain from politics.[62] Second, the parliamentary elections of November 1993 were, after all, held a mere two months after the Israeli-Palestinian agreement on principles had been signed in September 1993; they were manipulated so as to produce a result deemed acceptable under the prevailing difficult circumstances.

The Muslim Brothers, for the most part, seemed to have understood the message. They made little progress in their domestic agenda, failing to "impose the *shari'a*," through parliamentary legislation, on public life.[63] They suffered grave setbacks on the electoral front. They were unable to change official policy regarding the United States and Israel. Yet even the peace treaty with Israel, signed in October 1994, apparently could not shake their conviction that, for the time being, there were no better options available either within Jordan or in the wider region. Although there were reports of internal debate and dissent, the Muslim Brotherhood organization and the Islamic Action Front continued to advocate a policy of "democratic," "civilized," nonviolent protest against normalization and peace with Israel. In a rare public statement rationalizing Islamist strategy, one of the major spokesmen of the IAF, Abdallah al-Akayla, declared at an international conference held in London in 1992:[64]

1. The Islamic Movement of Jordan understands the position of the Jordanian State and knows that its resources are very limited. The State's economy largely depends on foreign aid, and therefore there is a limit to what any Jordanian regime can do. . . .
2. The Movement realises that Jordan lacks the essential requirements for the establishment of an Islamic state,[65] and the regime is assured that the Islamic Movement does not seek to topple it or replace it with an Islamic regime.
3. The Movement, thanks to its social power and the services it renders to the public throughout Jordanian society, constitutes an element of security for the regime against any coup attempt. The Movement did play a positive role in the mid fifties in counteracting the leftist demonstrations which sought to topple the regime and replace it with a communist government.
4. The Movement regards the existing regime in Jordan to be a better alternative than all the leftist regimes which dominated other parts of the Arab World and repressed the Islamic Movements there.
5. The Movement constitutes a strong pressure group that expresses and defends the values, culture and civilisation of the Muslim community in Jordan. Its existence is thus respected and its activities are tolerated by the regime which is well aware of the Islamic nature of the people.
6. By virtue of its Hashemite descent, and contrary to what has been happening in other Arab countries, the ruling family in Jordan would never resort to brutal treatment or suppression of the Islamists.
7. The Islamic Movement in Jordan deplores violence and denounces terrorism. It does not believe in change by confrontation or revolution, but adopts a peaceful methodology based on gradual persuasion through dialogue. Such a policy is acceptable to the regime.
8. The regime and the Islamic Movement show a certain degree of flexibility in dealing with each other during crises whether the tension was initiated by the regime or by the Movement itself.
9. The Movement's methodology and approach are well balanced between its principles on the one hand and the limitations of the Jordanian situation on the other hand.
10. The demands of the Islamic Movement at most are reformatory in nature and encompass all aspects of life. However, they do not in any way threaten the regime or propose an alternative to it. Hence, the regime does not see that such demands constitute any real threat to its existence and stability.

Compared to Yusuf al-Azm's statement quoted above, little seemed to have changed over a span of three decades in the basic reading of the situation: it was not so much King Hussein's charisma or legitimation—religious or dynastic—that persuaded the Muslim Brothers to continue their policy of peaceful opposition; rather it was his policies and function and a perceived communality of interests—an assessment not shared by all Islamists in the country—and it was a reversible one. Similarly, King Abdallah II's resorting to means of expulsion from Jordan of four Palestinian-Islamist leaders in 1999 should perhaps be construed as an attempt to remove the most destructive Islamists from the kingdom in order to maintain a reasonable status quo with the others.

MOROCCO

The crucial role of the Moroccan king as the political and religious leader of his country is undisputed, and his masterful use of religious symbols and ceremonies is acknowledged even by fierce critics. Historically, the Moroccan sultan exerted religious authority in his capacity as descendant of the Prophet (sharif) who was, moreover, endowed with religious charisma (baraka), commander of the faithful (amir al-mu'minin), and supreme mujtahid, that is, a scholar qualified to use independent legal reasoning (ijtihad), even in the absence of political power or during phases of very limited political power. In contrast to, for example, the Saudi ruler, he therefore enjoyed religious prestige and authority independently of actual political control and function, rendering him at least potentially less vulnerable to criticism of his performance. King Hasan II acquired a reputation for unique mastery in handling and manipulating religious institutions, symbols, and ritual such as the baya—the oath of loyalty and obedience rooted in Islamic tradition—in order to preserve and legitimize his monopoly of power.[66] Unlike any other political actor, he was able to play on all religious registers, being a sharif with baraka (ostensibly proven when he survived the assassination attempts of 1971 and 1972) and amir al-mu'minin with the authority to decide on matters of Quranic exegesis and Islamic law. The latter role was again demonstrated in 1992–1993, when in the controversy over the revision of the Moroccan personal status law (mudawwanat al-ahwal al-shakhsiyya) radical ulama accused the women who had organized a referendum protesting against the revised version not only of fitna but also of apostasy (ridda). King Hasan, by simply invoking his supreme power and authority, brought the affair to an immediate halt.[67]

Compared to both Jordan and Saudi Arabia, Morocco's "religious field" is much more complex and diversified. Four elements, however, can be distinguished that frequently intermingle and overlap. Apart from the king himself, they include the mostly urban-based ulama; the Sufi brotherhoods with their zawiyas and marabuts that continue to be largely rural and that prior to independence often resisted the centralizing tendencies of the makhzan, the central government subordinated to the sultan,[68] and finally the Islamic movement that in Morocco appears to be particularly fissiparous, merged into society and difficult to distinguish from nonpolitical groups and activists. The French terms *mouvance* and even *nebuleuse islamique*, therefore, are more apt to seize the character of this trend. In Morocco, as in Saudi Arabia, major religious institutions such as the Qarawiyyin Mosque have been brought under government control and the *ulama* largely co-opted and ultimately made dependent on the king. Again as in Saudi Arabia, they have not been completely tamed:[69] there have always been independent religious scholars who refused to be co-opted and to ratify palace policies. In 1963, Shaikh Moulay al-Arabi al-Alawi, a member of the leftist Union Socialiste des Forces Populaires (USFP), went so far as to issue a *fatwa* condemning hereditary monarchy and calling for *shura*, that is, consultation and participation of the *umma* in public affairs.[70] This was a hazardous undertaking; according to the Moroccan constitution(s), the king's person is sacred and his words and deeds are immune to criticism from his subjects. During the second Gulf War, independent *ulama* openly condemned the king's policy vis-à-vis Iraq without, however, being able to alter his foreign and security policies.[71]

If Islam is truly central to Moroccan public life, discourse, and politics, the same cannot be said of the Islamic movement.[72] In the 1990s, Islamic opposition was by far less prominent and active than in neighboring Algeria and even Tunisia. In Morocco, ideological and political pluralism was recognized, within the framework defined by the king, since 1962; political parties, labor unions, professional syndicates, and autonomous associations were registered and elections held on local as well as national levels. Pluralism allowed the king to maintain his monopoly on power. The nonreligious opposition was either co-opted into the system or repressed. Again, the term *secular* should be avoided: the Istiqlal, Morocco's major opposition party, founded in 1943 by Allal al-Fasi, a noted nationalist and religious reformer, propagated an Islamic nationalism and advocated the application of the *shari'a* while fully acknowledging the religious legitimacy of the king. Generally speaking, social and political demands and protest were voiced by labor unions and professional, student, and women's associations ("civil society") rather than the political parties represented in parliament.[73]

Unlike in other Arab countries, in Morocco no broad Islamic movement emerged to take over from the left and nationalist opposition when, in the late 1960s, it began to gradually lose its broad appeal. In the 1970s, Islamic groups advocating a return to strict "Islamic" values and behavior, the cultivation of Islamic knowledge, the memorization of the Quran, and so on had been discreetly encouraged by the authorities in order to fight leftist and nationalist opposition on campuses and in the general public[74]—a strategy well known from other parts of the Middle East, Israel included, and so successfully played by Jordan's King Hussein. The focus of Islamic activism was on cultural, religious, and social issues, not on politics in a narrow sense. In 1979, a number of events combined to affect the domestic political climate: the Iranian Revolution; the reception of the shah, who was on his way to exile, by the king; the signing of the Camp David Accords; and finally the attack on the Great Mosque in Mecca. Yet the Islamic movement remained diffuse and heterogeneous, ranging from independent shaikhs such as al-Faqih al-Zamzami (d. 1989) of Tangier and his sons, whose main concerns were moral corruption and the deviation from strictly Islamic norms of conduct, to radical Islamic groups such as *shabiba islamiyya* (Islamic Youth). Founded by Abd al-Karim al-Muti, a former inspector in the Ministry of Education, it seems to have split into several factions after his departure from Morocco in 1975. Muti himself was reported to have been involved in the occupation of the Great Mosque in 1979.[75] Although in their journals and leaflets published abroad some Islamists openly attacked the monarchy and called for an Islamic revolution in Morocco, their impact inside the country remained limited. The clandestine Islamic groups that emerged and were active at the time remained uncoordinated and failed to find broad popular support, their appeal and social base being largely limited to student and university circles. Strict surveillance, mass arrests, and harsh repression led to their virtual extinction in the 1980s.[76]

The most notable figure of Moroccan Islamism, "Shaikh" Abd al-Salam Yasin (b. 1928), who published his first books in 1972–1973, did not lead a large movement. His followers acknowledged the fact when, in 1989, they changed the name of their association from *jami'yyat al-jama'a al-khayriyya* (Charitable Association of the Community) into the more modest *jama'at al-adl wal-ihsan* (Community/Association of Justice and Equity). It was banned by the king in January 1990, as he was not prepared to tolerate organized activity that might have turned into a focus of opposition, and its leaders were arrested.[77] Yasin nevertheless remained influential as an independent critic and warner. Neither he nor his followers advocated the use of force to end the corruption, evil, and deviation (*munkar, fitna*) they perceived and so strongly condemned in Moroccan society. Interestingly, Yasin, too, did not challenge the king's self-legitimation based on sharifian descent but claimed it for himself: he spoke to the king as an equal, as one sharif would to another.[78] In a way similar to the Saudi *ulama*, but lacking their formal qualifications, he claimed the right to survey, censor, and offer good counsel (*nasiha*) to a prince that in his eyes had strayed from the right path. And he took considerable risks to do what he saw as his duty. An open letter, published in 1974 under the title "Islam or the Flood" (*al-islam aw al-tufan, L'Islam ou le Déluge*), in which he criticized his monarch in unprecedented terms, cost him internment in a psychiatric clinic and three years in prison.[79]

Still, the challenge, or appeal, of political Islam remained limited, owing less to the religious authority and charisma of the king than to his effective use of coercion combined with co-optation, a strategy that worked as well with religious and nonreligious opposition alike. The fear of civic strife, or even civil war (*fitna*) of the kind raging in neighboring Algeria, strongly worked in his favor. According to this logic, the choice was not so much "Islam or the flood" but "the king or chaos" (*al-malik aw al-fitna*).

CONCLUSION

In his work, Mohammed Tozy has shown the subtle interactions and changes of register available to religious actors in Moroccan society that make it very difficult to distinguish the Islamist from the non-Islamist and should make one wary of generalizations concerning their social base and space.[80] The social base of the Islamist movements examined here does not differ significantly from what is known about similar movements in Egypt, Algeria, and Tunisia. They appeal primarily to semieducated youth and the intelligentsia, whether classified as socially peripheral or not. But at least in Jordan and in Saudi Arabia, their appeal reaches far beyond the disaffected youth so frequently described and deep into the urban middle classes whose social and economic positions are fragile, albeit not necessarily marginal; the latter are, to a large extent, excluded from decisionmaking in the economic as well as the political spheres. In Jordan in particular, Islamists are strongly represented in the professional associations of the educated middle class, especially those segments operating independently of the bureaucracy and public sector (lawyers, engineers, medical doctors, pharmacists, etc.). The "Islamic" banks, investment firms, cooperatives, and self-help and charitable associations, by contrast, that play such a prominent role in Egypt (though not necessarily linked to political activism) are much less prominent in Morocco and Saudi Arabia.

In Morocco and, even more so, in Saudi Arabia, *ulama* are strongly represented in the movement, giving it its special flavor. Most of the Islamists reviewed here advocate a strategy of nonviolent, gradualist reform (*tadarruj*) of individual behavior, the social order, and foreign policy, being firmly opposed to close cooperation with the United States or the West in general and to peace with Israel. But they do not practice *takfir* against fellow Muslims or propagate jihad against domestic critics and regimes in power. The pragmatic, moderate line has been most clearly articulated in Jordan. In all three countries, there are also militant Islamist factions that still seem marginal, lacking the broad appeal and social base they acquired in, for example, Egypt, Algeria, and Tunisia during the 1980s. Past trials, errors, and tribulations, if vicarious, may have had a role to play in the prevalent option for pragmatism, particularly so in the case of the Jordanian Muslim Brothers, who saw the

Egyptian and Syrian experiences played out virtually in front of their eyes. But again this is nothing specific to Islamists active in monarchies.[81]

Islamism is less a "revolt against modernity" than a revolt against specific ills and "deviations"—social, cultural, and political—that are identified with modernity as experienced in Middle Eastern societies. That makes political Islam less abstract and the Islamists better definable as one political actor among others, fighting not so much over metaphysics but for more tangible goals and against more concrete evils: for public morals and modes of conduct that they declare to be "right" (al-ma'ruf); for the preservation of the "traditional" (patriarchal) family; for justice, equity, accountability, and participation; for order and moral certainty; against corruption in its narrow economic and political as well as a broader moral sense; against atheism and "communism"; and against close links to the West and Israel that are still widely seen as being not only un-Islamic but manifestly anti-Islamic. All these ills are as prevalent in monarchies as in republics. In the monarchies—as in the republics—the Islamists view themselves as the nation's conscience, giving them the right and the duty to censor even a ruling monarch (al-din al-nasiha). Judging from the literature on the "Islamic order" (al-nizam al-is-lami) or the Islamic state emanating from Islamist authors in the broadest sense (to which, incidentally, the groups and persons presented here have made little contribution), one might have expected the Islamists of Morocco, Jordan, and Saudi Arabia to denounce the monarchy and hereditary rule, referring to the rule of the Umayyads who, according to contemporary conventional wisdom, abandoned consultation (shura) in favor of dynastic tyranny and unbridled autocracy (istibdad). This, of course, is not to say that Islam is against monarchy or that monarchy has consistently been condemned by religious scholars and the pious masses, which is evidently not the case.[82] The hereditary principle is not necessarily objectionable to Muslims, for even according to classical Sunni political thought, the imam-khalifa has to be descended from the Quraysh tribe. Descent from the Quraysh is still frequently invoked as one prerequisite for eligibility for the office of caliph or imam. Most contemporary Islamist authors nevertheless call for elections, or some symbols of election that usually include shura and the oath of allegiance (baya), to select the ablest leader from among a group of candidates who may or may not be defined by lineage. Again, there is nothing predetermined about this question, and an alternative Islamist discourse heavily critical of monarchy and autocratic rule is readily available.

But monarchy is not really the issue. According to contemporary Islamist thought, it is not so much the form of government that matters but its ethico-legal foundation and its function. Government and governance are perceived as techniques to see essential values implemented, and those values are Islamic ones—or simply Islam itself.[83] Put differently, it matters not so much whether the head of state be called emir, sultan, king, amir al-mu'minin, or president, or even whether he descended from the Prophet and the Quraysh; what matters is that he fulfills his duties as an Islamic ruler, defending the faith, implementing the *shari'a*, and guaranteeing order. Most of the Islamists inside Morocco, Jordan, and Saudi Arabia do not question the institution of the monarchy as such but call for basic reform and renewal of the state and society: the strict observance of "Islamic" modes of conduct, the practice of *shura*, respect for the law, that is, the *shari'a*, equality of all citizens before the law (women and non-Sunni Muslims excepted, at least in Saudi Arabia), the independence of the judiciary, and so on. Notable exceptions include audiotapes and videos clandestinely circulated within Saudi Arabia and books published abroad that vigorously attack hereditary rule in general and the malpractices of Saudi royalty and the Moroccan king in particular. As a rule, monarchs are treated with respect, but the Moroccan king excepted, they are not granted any religious legitimacy. The issue, then, is not so much monarchy and the political system in general but conduct—both private and public—as well as government policy.

NOTES

1. For overviews, see my "Cross-Links and Double Talk? Islamist Movements in the Political Process," in Laura Guazzone (ed.), *The Islamist Dilemma* (Reading: Ithaca Press, 1995), pp. 39–67; John L. Esposito and John O. Voll, *Islam and Democracy* (New York: Oxford University Press, 1996).

2. See Michael C. Hudson, *Arab Politics: The Search for Legitimacy* (New Haven: Yale University Press, 1977), chapter 7; Lisa Anderson, "Absolutism and the Resilience of Monarchy in the Middle East," *Political Science Quarterly*, 106 (1991), pp. 1–15; see also Salah Salim Zarnuqa, *Anmat al-istila' ala l-sulta fil-duwal al-arabiyya, 1950–1985*, 2nd ed. (Cairo: Maktabat Madbuli, 1414h/1993m).

3. On the topos of the artificiality of Middle Eastern states, see Iliya Harik, "The Origins of the Arab State System," in Giacomo Luciani (ed.), *The Arab State* (London: Routledge, 1990), pp. 1–28.

4. See Madawi al-Rasheed and Loulouwa al-Rasheed, "The Politics of Encapsulation: Saudi Policy Towards Tribal and Religious Opposition," *Middle Eastern Studies*, 32 (1996), pp. 96–119 (99), and Chapter 11 in this volume.

5. For a relevant discussion, see below, n. 34.

6. Hudson, *Arab Politics*, pp. 168–182.

7. See Christine Moss Helms, *The Cohesion of Saudi Arabia: Evolution of Political Identity* (Baltimore: Johns Hopkins University Press, 1981), esp. pp. 94 and following, 103–110; for the early period, see Ibn Ghannam, *Tar'ikh Najd* (ed. Nasir al-Din Asad), 2nd ed. (Beirut: Dar al-Shuruq, 1985), p. 129; and Frank Edward Vogel, *Islamic Law and Legal System Studies of Saudi Arabia*, unpublished Ph.D. thesis, Harvard University, 1993 (Ann Arbor U.M.I.), p. 523, n. 220, in which he assumes that the title *imam* was only adopted by the third Saudi ruler and not, as Ibn Ghannam indicates, the second and then projected onto the first two; for Ibn Saud's choice of titles, see also Hasan Abu Talib, *Man yahkum al-Sa'udiyya?* (Cairo: Sina lil-Nashr, 1990), p. 37. See also Aziz al-Azmeh, "Wahhabite Polity," in I. R. Netton (ed.), *Arabia*

and the Gulf: From Traditional Society to Modern State (Totowa, N.J., 1986), pp. 75–90 (84f). According to Mordechai Abir, King Faysal still used the title *imam* in the 1960s; "The Consolidation of the Ruling Class and the New Elites in Saudi Arabia," *Middle Eastern Studies*, 23 (1987), pp. 150–171 (161).

8. Vogel, *Islamic Law and Legal Studies*, pp. 466ff.

9. See Anwar Abdallah, *al-Ulama' wal-arsh thana'iyyat al-sulta fi l-Sa'udiyya* (London: al-Rafid, 1995); Ayman Al-Yassini, *Religion and Politics in the Kingdom of Saudi Arabia* (Boulder: Westview Press, 1985); Alexander Bligh, "The Saudi Religious Elite (Ulama) as Participant in the Political System of the Kingdom," *International Journal of Middle Eastern Studies*, 17 (1985), pp. 37–50; Joseph A. Kechichian, "The Role of the Ulama in the Politics of an Islamic State: The Case of Saudi Arabia," *International Journal of Middle Eastern Studies*, 18 (1986), pp. 53–71; Abir, "The Consolidation," passim. The complex relation between the ruler and the *ulama* is analyzed in depth by Vogel, *Islamic Law and Legal Studies*. On the judicial system, see further Aharon Layish, "Saudi Arabian Legal Reform as a Mechanism to Moderate Wahhabi Doctrine," *Journal of the American Oriental Society*, 107 (1987), pp. 279–292; Human Rights Watch, *Empty Reforms: Saudi Arabia's New Basic Laws* (New York, 1992), pp. 21–23; Rashed Aba-Namay, "Constitutional Reform: A Systemization of Saudi Politics," *Journal of South Asian and Middle Eastern Studies*, 16 (1993), pp. 43–88 (65–69), and Aba-Namay, "The Recent Constitutional Reforms in Saudi Arabia," *International and Comparative Law Quarterly*, 42 (1993), pp. 295–331 (318–323).

10. Vogel, *Islamic Law and Legal Studies*, pp. 202, 213f, 310–312.

11. Abdallah, *al-Ulama'*, p. 321; Mamoun Hamza Fandy, "State Islam and State Violence: The Case of Saudi Arabia," unpublished Ph.D. dissertation (Southern Illinois University at Carbondale, 1993; Ann Arbor: U.M.I.), pp. 84–92.

12. Al-Yassini, *Religion and State in the Kingdom of Saudi Arabia*, p. 70.

13. See Abdallah, *al-Ulama'*, pp. 285–334; Fandy, "State Islam and State Violence," p. 90; Human Rights Watch, *Empty Reforms*, pp. 28f; also Jean-Michel Foulquier, *Arabe Séoudite: La dictature protégée* (Paris: Albin Michel, 1995).

14. See, e.g., *Mudhakkirat al-nasiha*, Muharram 1413h/July 1992m, s. 1.

15. No attempt will be made here to define the Saudi political system and to analyze the political opposition in general. Studies written and published before the attack on the Great Mosque in November 1979 dealt with leftist and nationalist opposition groups only; see notably Fred Halliday, *Arabia Without Sultans* (London: Penguin Books, 1974); Helen Lackner, *A House Built on Sand—A Political Economy of Saudi Arabia* (London: Ithaca Press, 1978), chapter 5.

16. See notably, William L. Ochsenwald, "Saudi Arabia and the Islamic Revival," *International Journal of Middle Eastern Studies*, 13 (1981), pp. 271–286; James P. Piscatori, "Ideological Politics in Saudi Arabia," in Piscatori (ed.), *Islam in the Political Process* (Cambridge: Cambridge University Press, 1983), pp. 56–72; R. Hrair Dekmejian, *Islam in Revolution. Fundamentalism in the Arab WorldI* (Albany: Syracuse University Press, 1985), pp. 137–148; Dekmejian, "The Rise of Political Islamism in Saudi Arabia," *Middle East Journal*, 48 (1994), pp. 627–643; Nazih Ayubi, *Political Islam: Religion and Politics in the Arab World* (London: Routledge, 1991), pp. 99–104; Mordechai Abir, *Saudi Arabia: Government, Society, and the Gulf Crisis* (London: Routledge, 1993), chapter 11. For more general studies on the role of Islam in Saudi policies, see Al-Yassini, *Religion and State;* Ghassan Salamé, "Islam and Politics in Saudi Arabia," *Arab Studies Quarterly*, 9 (1987), pp. 306–326; and from an Islamist point of view, Muhammad Jalal Kishk, *al-Saudiyyun wa-l-hall al-Islami, masdar al-shar'iyya lil-nizam al-Saudi*, 4th ed. (Cairo: al-Matba'a al-Fanniyya, 1981).

17. See Johannes Reissner, "Die Besetzung der Grossen Moschee in Mekka," *Orient*, 21 (1980), pp. 193–203; for an eyewitness's account and documents, see Abd al-Azim al-Mutaanni, *Jarimat al-asr qissat ihtilal al-masjid al-haram* (Cairo: Dar al-Ansar bil-Qahira, 1400h/1980m). On the ideas of Juhayman and his followers, see Rifat Sayyid Ahmad, *Rasa'il Juhayman al-Utaybi qa'id al-muqtahimin lil-masjid al-haram bi-Makka* (Cairo: Maktabat Madbuli, 1988); Joseph A. Kechichian, "Islamic Revivalism and Change in Saudi Arabia: Juhayman al-Utaybi's 'Letters' to the Saudi People," *Muslim World*, 80 (1990), pp. 1–16. There is no agreement on the social affiliation of Juhayman's followers. In 1994, Dekmejian described them as by and large tribal, lower-class, and poorly educated ("The Rise," p. 629), whereas in 1985 he had classified the "new Ikhwan" value in describing those who participated in the takeover of the Great Mosques as "mostly young, educated, and to some degree urbanized" (*Islam in Revolution*, pp. 141, 143f). According to Ayubi, they were young, urban, educated, and mostly from Najd; about one-quarter came from the Utayba tribe; *Political Islam*, pp. 102f.

18. Kechichian, "Islamic," pp. 12–16.

19. Dekmejian "The Rise," pp. 137–148.

20. Eleanor Abdella Doumato, "Women and the Stability of Saudi Arabia," *Middle East Report*, no. 171 (1991), pp. 34–37 (36); Human Rights Watch, *Empty Reforms*, pp. 36f. For the Islamists, who perfectly understood what the incident was all about and who denounced the women as agents of secularism, atheism, and the West, see Mahmud al-Rifa'i, *al-Mashru al-islah fil-Saudiyya: qissat al-Hawali wal-Awda* (n.p., 1995), pp. 19ff (29).

21. See Aba-Namay, "The Recent Constitutional Reforms," p. 302; Abir, *Saudi Arabia*, chapter 11; see also Andrew Apostolou, "Stirrings of Political Debate," *Middle East*, November 1992, pp. 17f. English translation of the open letter in Human Rights Watch, *Empty Reforms*, pp. 59–61.

22. The letter was handed to King Fahd on 18 May and published in the Egyptian paper *al-Shab*, 21 May 1991; see Aba-Namay, "Constitutional Reform," p. 51; Human Rights Watch, *Empty Reforms*, pp. 6f., 61f. For the text of the open letter and an explanatory note that was later submitted to the *Hay'at kibar al-ulama*, see al-Rifa'i, *al-Mashru al-islahi*, annex 1, pp. 107–109, and annex 5, pp. 117–126.

23. For the text, see *Mudhakkirat al-nasiha*, Muharram 1413h/July 1992m, s. 1. For the concept of *nasiha,* constantly invoked by Saudi *ulama* and Islamic reformers, see Talal Asad, *Genealogies of Religion: Discipline and Reasons of Power in Christianity and Islam* (Baltimore: Johns Hopkins University Press, 1993), chapter 6; see also Vogel, *Islamic Law and Legal Studies*, pp. 455–463, 493, 526f.

24. Other statements of prominent signatories of the memorandum made it quite clear, however, that the principle of equality invoked here extended to neither women nor non-Sunni Muslims, such as the Shi'ite citizens of the kingdom.

25. See also below for the Committee for the Defence of Legitimate Rights, which was founded in May 1993 and quickly denounced by leading scholars including Ibn Baz as un-Islamic.

26. Fandy, "State Islam and State Violence," pp. 97f; Abir, "Saudi Arabia," p. 14.

27. *Mudhakkirat al-nasiha*, pp. 62f; Vogel, *Islamic Law and Legal Studies*, pp. 377–379; Human Rights Watch, *Empty Reforms*, p. 30.

28. Fandy refers to three Saudi books, all published abroad, denouncing the monarchy, which I was unable to see: Fahd al-Qahtani, *al-islam wal-wathaniyya al-sa'udiyya* (London: Munazzamat al-thawra al-islamiyya, 1985); Abul-Bara' al-Najdi (apparently the nom de plume of a former Saudi Islamic judge then resident in either Pakistan or Afghanistan), *al-kawashif al-jaliyya fi kufr al-dawla al-sa'udiyya* (Den-

mark: Al-Nur Islamic Boghandel, 1991); and the work of an anonymous author, *al-nizam al-sa'udi fi mizan al-islam* (n.p., n.d.), *State Islam*, pp. 62–65. For an illustration of this kind of criticism, see Sa'id al-Samarra'i, "Al Saud's Heresy: Their Links to Imperialism and Desecration of Mecca and Medina," *Arab Review*, 2 (1993), pp. 6–14.

29. The denunciation is included in the edition of the *mudhakkira* quoted here, pp. 122–125; also in al-Rifa'i, *al-mashru' al-islahi*, annex 6, pp. 127f; for reactions of some of the signatories, see ibid., annexes 8 and 9, pp. 131–140; see also Dekmejian, "The Rise," p. 634.

30. Human Rights Watch, *Empty Reforms*, pp. 5–7.

31. See Human Rights Watch, *Empty Reforms*, esp. pp. 9–14; Aba-Namay, "Constitutional Reform"; Aba-Namay, "The Recent Constitutional Reforms." Arabic text of the laws are in Amin al-Saati, *al-Shura fil-mamlaka al-arabiyya al-sa'udiyya min al-malik Abd al-Aziz ila al-malik Fahd bin Abd al-Aziz* (Cairo: al-Markaz al-Saudi lil-Dirasat al-Istratijiyya, 1412h/1991m); Mahmud Salih al-Adili, *al-Sa'udiyya. al-namud-haj al-afdal . . . lil-hukm al-Islami (huquq wa-wajibat al-hukkam wal-mahkumin)* (Tanta: Maktabat al-Azhar al-Haditha bi-Tanta, 1415h/1995m); English translation in John Bulloch, *The Shura Council in Saudi Arabia* (London: Gulf Center for Strategic Studies, 1993). For a conventional Saudi concept of *shura*, see also Adnan Ali Rida al-Nahwi, *Malamih al-shura fil-da'wa al-Islamiyya*, 2nd ed. (Cairo: al-Farazdaq Press, 1984).

32. According to Dekmejian, the list included some 30 percent bureaucrats, nearly 28 percent academics, 13 percent businessmen, 9.8 percent religious scholars and officials, a certain number of journalists and writers, as well as military and police generals. Most of them were urban, 41 percent came from Najd, 33 percent from the Hijaz, 9.8 percent from the south, and 6.6 percent from the Eastern Province (including two Shi'ites); about one-quarter represented notable Saudi families, and none belonged to the royal family; the majority was highly educated, most of them in the United States; "The Rise," p. 640. Also Bulloch, *The Shura Council;* names with a short identification, ibid., pp. 81–91. The Shura Council was inaugurated in December 1993, met for the first time in January 1994, and in the course of the year held some thirty meetings; *Nahost Jahrbuch 1994* (Hamburg: Deutsches Orient Institut, 1995), p. 140.

33. No effort will be made here to analyze the Saudi social structure or the rise of a new middle class; see, Abir, "The Consolidation"; also Khaldun al-Naqib, *al-Mujtama wal-dawla fil-khalij wal-jazira al-arabiyya (min manzur mukhtalaf)* (Beirut: Markaz Dirasat al-Wahda al-Arabiyya, 1987).

34. Text of the bulletin of 5 May 1993, in al-Rifa'i, *al-Mashru al-islahi*, annex 10, pp. 141f; also ibid., pp. 65ff and annex 11, pp. 143–146; on the entire affair, see also Rashed Aba-Namay, "The Dynamics of Individual Rights and Their Prospective Development Under the New Constitution of Saudi Arabia," *Journal of South Asian and Middle Eastern Studies*, 18 (1995), pp. 21–40 (33–36); Dekmejian, "The Rise," pp. 638f.

35. Vogel, *Islamic Law and Legal Studies*, p. 179, n. 42.

36. On the role of tribalism in modern Saudi society, see Joseph Kostiner, "Transforming Dualities: Tribe and State Formation in Saudi Arabia," in Philip S. Khoury and Joseph Kostiner (eds.), *Tribes and State Formation in the Middle East* (Berkeley: University of California Press, 1990), pp. 226–251.

37. Dekmejian, "The Rise," pp. 629, 635f.

38. Fandy, "State Islam and State Violence," p. 120.

39. Al-Rifa'i, *al-mashru al-islahi*, pp. 70ff; Nahost, *Yahrbuch* 1994, pp. 139ff.

40. On the following, see al-Rifa'i, *al-mashru al-islahi*, notably pp. 16–18, 30ff and annexes 16–18, and 161–170; names and affiliations of other radical shaikhs,

ibid., p. 23; also Fandy, "State Islam and State Violence," pp. 65, 120. I have not seen Safar al-Hawali's *Kashf al-ghama an ulama al-umma* (London, 1991). Salman al-Awda published a critique of the prominent Egyptian Islamist writer Muhammad al-Ghazali (d. 1996), criticizing in particular Ghazali's relatively liberal positions on the Shi'a as well as on women in Islamic society; *hiwar hadi ma'a Muhammad al-Ghazali*, 3rd ed. (al-Riyad, al-Khabr: Dar al-Hijra lil-Nashr wal-Tawzi, 1990). Awda and Hawali were released from prison in late June 1999.

41. Fandy, "State Islam and State Violence," p. 65; Dekmajian, "The Rise," pp. 624f.

42. On the following, see two Shi'ite sources, Hamza al-Hasan, *al-Shi'a fil-mamlaka al-arabiyya al-sa'udiyya, al-ahd al-sa'udi, 1913–1991m* s. 1 (Mu'assasat al-Baqi li-Ihya' al-Turath, 1413h/1993m); and Muhammad Abd al-Majid, *al-Tamyiz al-ta'ifi fil-Sa'udiyya* (London: Rabitat Umum al-Shi'a fil-Sa'udiyya, s.d.); also Jacob Goldberg, "The Shii Minority in Saudi Arabia," in Juan I. R. Cole and Nikki R. Keddie (eds.), *Shiism and Social Protest* (New Haven: Yale University Press, 1986), pp. 230–246; Joseph Kostiner, "Shii Unrest in the Gulf," in Martin Kramer (ed.), *Shiism, Resistance and Revolution* (Boulder and London: Westview Press and Mansell Publishing 1987), pp. 173–186; Human Rights Watch, *Empty Reforms*, pp. 37–39; ar-Rasheed/al-Rasheed, "The Politics of Encapsulation," pp. 109–111.

43. Al-Hasan, pp. 394–411, esp. 402–408; Abd al-Majid, pp. 151–158.

44. Fandy refers to Abd al-Rahman al-Shaikh et al., *Intifadat al-mintaqa al-sharqiyya* (London: Munazzamat al-Thawra al-Islamiyya, 1981), which I have not seen.

45. See al-Rasheed and al-Rasheed, "The Politics of Encapsulation," pp. 112–114; for 1988, see Fandy, "State Islam and State Violence," pp. 142–146.

46. See, e.g., Linda L. Layne, *Home and Homeland: The Dialogics of Tribal and National Identities in Jordan* (Princeton: Princeton University Press, 1994); Schirin H. Fathi, *Jordan: An Invented Nation?* (Hamburg: Deutsches Orient-Institut, 1994); Laurie A. Brand, "Liberalization and Changing Political Coalitions: The Bases of Jordan's 1990–1991 Gulf Crisis Policy," *Jerusalem Journal of International Relations*, 13 (1991), pp. 1–46 (31f), and the election analyses cited below.

47. Yezid Sayigh, "Jordan in the 1980s: Legitimacy, Entity, and Identity," in Rodney Wilson (ed.), *Politics and the Economy in Jordan* (London: Routledge, 1991), pp. 167–183 (174); see also Asher Susser and Aryeh Shmuelevitz (eds.), *The Hashemites in the Modern Arab World: Studies in Honour of the late Professor Uriel Dann* (London: Frank Cass, 1995); Gerald de Gaury, *Rulers of Mecca* (New York: Dorset Press, 1991). But for the continuing appeal of Hashemite descent, see also the statement of a prominent Muslim Brother, Abdallah al-Akayla, quoted below.

48. Wilson, "Introduction" to *Politics and the Economy in Jordan*, p. 1.

49. As in the case of Saudi Arabia and Morocco, the following refers primarily to those Islamic groups and movements that are openly engaged in politics, which in this text are usually referred to as "Islamists." This is not to deny the fact that even those who declare themselves to be apolitical may, under specific circumstances, have a political impact. In the Jordanian case, they include, notably, Sufi brotherhoods and charitable Islamic organizations on whose activities, however, information is scanty; see, e.g., Muhammad Salim Ubaydat, *Athar al-jama'at al-Islamiyya al-maydani khilal al-qarn al-ishrin* (Amman: Maktabat al-Risala al-Haditha, 1989); Musa Zayd al-Kaylani (ed.), *al-Harakat al-Islamiyya fil-Urdunn* (Amman: Dar al-Bashir, 1990). For a view from the village level, of a shaikh not organized politically but with opinions clearly touching on political matters, see Richard T. Antoun, *Muslim Preacher in the Modern World: A Jordanian Case Study in Comparative Perspective* (Princeton: Princeton University Press, 1989).

50. Literature on the Islamic movement in Jordan, closely related to the Palestinian one, has become quite extensive; the following is based on my "The Integration of the Integrists: A Comparative Study of Egypt, Jordan and Tunisia," in Ghassan Salamé (ed.), *Democracy Without Democrats? The Renewal of Politics in the Muslim World* (London,: I. B. Tauris, 1994), pp. 220–226; Ziyad Abu Amr, *Islamic Fundamentalism in the West Bank and Gaza: Muslim Brotherhood and Islamic Jihad* (Bloomington: Indiana University Press, 1994); Lawrence Tal, "Dealing with Radical Islam: The Case of Jordan," *Survival*, 37 (1995), pp. 139–156; Iyad Barghouti, "The Islamists in Jordan and the Palestinian Occupied Territories," in Laura Guazzone (ed.), *The Islamist Dilemma*, pp. 129–159; Hanna Y. Freij and Leonard C. Robinson, "Liberalization, the Islamists, and the Stability of the Arab State: Jordan as a Case Study," *Muslim World*, 86 (1996), pp. 1–32; Hani Hourani (ed.), *Islamic Movements in Jordan* (Amman: al-urdunn al-Jadid and Friedrich-Ebert-Stiftung, 1997); see also Amnon Cohen, *Political Parties in the West Bank Under the Jordanian Regime, 1949–1967* (Ithaca: Cornell University Press, 1982), pp. 144–229; Robert B. Satloff, *Troubles on the East Bank: Challenges to the Domestic Stability of Jordan* (New York: Praeger, 1986), pp. 34–38; Nivin Abd al-Mun'im Musa'ad, "Jadaliyyat al-istibad wal-musharaka (muqarana bayna jabhat al-inqadh al-Islamiyya fil-jaza'ir wa-jama'at al-ikhwan al-muslimin fil-urdunn," *al-Mustaqbal al-Arabi*, no. 145 (3/1991), pp. 54–74.

51. Quoted from Abu Amr, *Islamic Fundamentalism*, p. 5.

52. Apart from the literature cited above (n. 35), see Wahid Abdel Meguid, "The Islamic Movement in Jordan and Palestine: The Case of the Muslim Brothers (al-Ikhwan al-Muslimin)," in Ola A. AbouZeid (ed.), *Islamic Movements in a Changing World* (Cairo: Center for Political Research and Studies/Friedrich-Ebert-Stiftung, 1995), pp. 63–116.

53. On liberalization, see Jamal al-Sha'ir, "tajribat al-dimuqratiyya fil-urdunn," in: Markaz dirasat al-wahda al-arabiyya (ed.), *azmat al-dimuqratiyya fi l-watan al-arabi*, Beirut 1984, pp. 683–744; Peter Gubser, "Balancing Pluralism and Authoritarianism," in Peter J. Chelowski and Robert J. Pranger (eds.), *Ideology and Power in the Middle East* (Durham: Duke University Press, 1988), pp. 14–28; Brand, "Liberalization," pp. 13–40. For the period up to 1990, see Said Darwish, *al-marhala al-dimuqratiyya al-jadida fil-urdunn* (Amman, 1990).

54. On April 1989, see Brand, "Liberalization," pp. 15–18; Freij and Robinson, "Liberalization," pp. 8ff; also Renate Dieterich, *Transformation oder Stagnation? Die jordanische Demokratisierungspolitik seit 1989* (Hamburg: Deutsches Orient-Institut, 1999).

55. Several analyses give the number of elected Muslim Brothers as twenty-two rather than twenty. For details, see al-Urdunn al-Jadid Research Center, *Intikhabat 1989. haqa'iq wa-arqam* (Amman: al-Urdunn al-Jadid Research Center, 1991); Kamel S. Abu Jaber and Schirin H. Fathi, "The 1989 Jordanian Parliamentary Elections," *Orient*, 31 (1990), pp. 67–86; Abla Amawi, "Democracy Dilemmas in Jordan," *Middle East Report*, no. 174 (1992), pp. 26–29; Brand, "Liberalization," pp. 18–22.

56. Darwish, *al-marhala*, p. 256. A complete list of the committee members with their status and political affiliation is included in the English translation of the National Charter prepared by Dar al-Uruba, Amman. See also *al-Mithaq al-Watani wal-tahawwul al-dimuqrati fil-urdunn* (Amman: al-Urdunn al-Jadid and Konrad-Adenauer-Stiftung, 1997).

57. For details, see Amnesty International, *Jordan: Human Rights Protection After the State of Emergency* (London, June 1990); Brand, "Liberalization," pp. 20f. See also George Hawatmeh (ed.), *The Role of the Media in a Democracy: The Case of Jordan* (Amman: Center for Strategic Studies/Konrad-Adenauer-Foundation, 1994).

58. Freij and Robinson, "Liberalization," pp. 24ff.

59. See al-Urdunn al-Jadid Research Center, *Intikhabat 1993, dirasa tahliliyya raqamiyya* (Amman, 1994); Abla Amawi, "The 1993 Elections in Jordan," *Arab Studies Quarterly*, 16 (1994), pp. 15–21; Freij and Robinson, "Liberalization," pp. 22ff.

60. See Elie Rekhess, "The Iranian Impact on the Islamic Jihad Movement in the Gaza Strip," in David Menashri (ed.), *The Iranian Revolution and the Muslim World* (Boulder: Westview Press, 1990), pp. 189–206; for later contacts with Iran, see Jean-François Legrain, "La Conference de Tehran" (held 19–22 October 1991 to oppose the Madrid conference), *Maghreb-Machrek*, no. 134 (1991), pp. 124–127.

61. On the following, see Abdel Meguid, "The Islamic Movement"; Brand, "Liberalization," esp. pp. 34–37.

62. See Freij and Robinson, "Liberalization," p. 20. In 1988, a militant Islamist group calling itself "Muhammad's Army" (*jaysh Muhammad*) had attempted to assassinate King Hussein; in 1993, several members of the Islamic Liberation Party were charged with the same crime; ibid., p. 7.

63. See Lisa Taraki, "Jordanian Islamists and the Agenda for Women: Between Discourse and Practice," *Middle Eastern Studies*, 32 (1996), pp. 140–158; for the role of women in Jordanian public and political life, see *dalil al-mar'a al-urdunniyya fil-hay'at al-amma wal-siyasiyya* (Amman: Konrad-Adenauer-Stiftung, 1996).

64. Quoted from Azzam Tamimi (ed.), *Power-Sharing Islam?* (London: Liberty for Muslim World Publications, 1993), pp. 93–101 (98f.). Akayla reflected the major points of the IAF's 1993 election program; see Freij and Robinson, "Liberalization," p. 20, n. 78.

65. He does not explain what the prerequisites are.

66. The Moroccan monarchy, and religion and power in Morocco in general, have attracted a great deal of scholarly attention; see John Waterbury, *The Commander of the Faithful: The Moroccan Political Elite—A Study in Segmented Politics* (London: Weidenfeld and Nicolson, 1970); Mohammed Tozy, "Monopolisation de la production symbolique et hierarchisation du champ politico-religieux au Maroc," in *Annuaire de l'Afrique du Nord 1979* (Paris: Centre National de la Recherche Scientifique, 1981), pp. 219–234; Remy Leveau, *Le fellah marocain. Defenseur du trone*, 2nd enl. ed. (Paris: Presses de la Fondation Nationale des Sciences Politiques, 1985); Ahmed Benani, "Legitimite du pouvoir au Maroc, consensus et contestation," *Sou'al*, 6 (1987), pp. 95–128; John P. Entelis, *Culture and Counterculture in Moroccan Politics* (Boulder: Westview Press, 1989); Sigrid Faath, "'Le Hassanisme.' Das marokkanische Konzept von Demokratie," *Wuquf*, 4–5 (1989–1990), pp. 9–90; Henry Munson Jr., *Religion and Power in Morocco* (New Haven: Yale University Press, 1993); Abdellah Hammoudi, *Master and Disciple: The Cultural Foundations of Moroccan Authoritarianism* (Chicago: University of Chicago Press, 1997), as well as several contributions in Michel Camau (ed.), *Changements politiques au Maghreb* (Paris: Editions du Centre National de la Recherche Scientifique, 1991).

67. See M. al-Ahnaf, "Maroc. Le code du statut personnel," *Maghreb-Machrek*, no. 145 (1994), pp. 3–26 (12–21).

68. In Morocco as in other Muslim societies, differences between the *ulama* and the brotherhoods should not be exaggerated since there has always existed, and still exists, considerable overlap between the two groups; see, e.g., Jamal Benomar, "The Monarchy, the Islamist Movement, and Religious Discourse in Morocco," *Third World Quarterly*, 10 (1988), pp. 539–555 (546–548).

69. For details, see Muhammad Darif, *al-islam al-siyasi fi l-maghrib, "muqaraba watha'iqiyya,"* 3rd ed. (Casablanca: maktabat al-umma, 1991), pp. 91–122; Benomar, "The Monarchy," pp. 549–551; Mohamed Tozy, "L'islam entre le controle de l'Etat et

les debordements de la societe civile. Des nouveaux clercs aux nouveaux lieux de l'-expression religieuse," in Robert Santucci (ed.), *Le Maroc actuel* (Paris: 1992), pp. 407–423. For the pre-independence period, see also M. el-Mansour, "Les oulemas et le makhzen dans le Maroc precolonial," ibid., pp. 3–15; Ralf Elger, *Zentralismus und Autonomie: Gelehrte und Staat in Marokko, 1900–1931* (Berlin: K. Schwarz, 1994).

70. Benomar, "The Monarchy," pp. 550f.

71. Darif, *al-islam al-siyasi,* pp. 204ff.

72. See Benomar, "The Monarchy"; Francois Burgat, *L'islamisme au Maghreb. La voix du Sud* (Paris: Carthala, 1989); Abderrahim Lamchichi, *Islam et contestation au Maghreb* (Paris: L'Harmattan, 1991); Darif, *al-islam al-siyasi*; Munson, *Religion and Power in Morocco*, pp. 149–179, and Munson, "The Social Base of Islamic Militancy in Morocco," *Middle East Journal*, 40 (1986), pp. 267–284.

73. See Sonja Hegary, *Staat öffentlichkeit und Zivilgesellschaft in Marokko* (Hamburg: Deutsches Orient-Institut, 1997); also Faath, "'Le Hassanisme,'" pp. 45ff., with approximate party membership figures in n. 88; Noureddine El Aoufi (ed.), *La Societe civile au Maroc, Approches* (Rabat: SMER, 1992). For a very critical assessment of political conditions within the kingdom, see *Human Rights Watch Middle East*, 7 (1995): *Human Rights in Morocco.*

74. Lamchichi, *Islam et contestation,* pp. 177, 182.

75. Burgat, *L'islamisme au Maghreb*, p. 141.

76. Munson, *Religion*, pp. 153–162.

77. For Yasin's life and work, see Lamchichi, *Islam et Contestation*, pp. 108f., 122–126, 139 n. 68; Darif, *al-islam al-siyasi*, pp. 11–36 (publications) and 137–152; for the association, founded in 1983, see also Darif, *jama'at al-adl wal-ihsan,* new ed. (Casablanca: manshurat al-majalla al-maghribiyya li-'ilm al-ijtima' al-siyasi, 1995), pp. 45–68, 195–201.

78. Lamchichi, *Islam et contestation,* pp. 123, 163.

79. For an analysis, see Burgat, *L'islamisme au Maghreb*, and Lamchichi, *Islam et contestation,* pp. 122–126; excerpts in French translation in *Sou'al,* 5 (1985), pp. 151–157.

80. See, e.g., Mohammed Tosy and Bruno Etienne, "La Da'wa au Maroc. Prolegomenes theorico-historiques," in Olivier Carre and Paul Dumont (eds.), *Radicalismes islamiques*, vol. 2 (Paris: L'Harmattan, 1986), pp. 5–32.

81. For Islamist self-critique, see my "Die Korrektur der Irrtumer: Innerislamische Debatten um Theorie und Praxis der zeitgenössischen islamischen Bewegungen," in *Zeitschrift der Deutschen Morgenlandischen Gesellschaft*, Suppl. 10, 1994, pp. 183–191.

82. See, e.g., Yocelyne Dakhalia, *Le divan des rois, le politique et le religieux dans l'islam* (Paris: Aubier, 1998); Aziz Al-Azmeh, *Muslim Kingship* (London: I. B. Tauris, 1998); and Chapters 2 and 3 in this volume; Hamid Dabashi, *Authority in Islam,* new ed. (New Brunswick, N.J.: Transaction Publishers, 1993); Louise Marlow, "Kings, Prophets, and the 'Ulama' in Medieval Islamic Advice Literature," *Studia Islamica*, 81–82 (1995), pp. 101–120.

83. For a more detailed discussion of this point, see my "Islamist Notions of Democracy," in Joel Beinin and Joe Stork (eds.), *Political Islam: Essays from Middle East Report* (Berkeley: University of California Press, 1997), pp. 71–82, and "Techniques and Values: Contemporary Muslim Debates on Islam and Democracy," in Gema Martin Munoz (ed.), *Islam, Modernism, and the West: Cultural and Political Relations at the End of the Millennium* (London: I. B. Tauris, 1999), pp. 174–190.

16

Monarchies in the Middle East: A Concluding Appraisal

Fred Halliday

There is a story, possibly reflecting urban bias, that is told of the weeks following the Yemeni Revolution of September 1962. It is said that as news of the overthrow of the imam spread, tribesmen came flocking into the city. When asked why they had come, they said that they had heard of *jumhuriyya* (a beautiful woman) who had appeared there and they wanted to see her. The tribesmen were, in a way, right for their time. In the early 1960s and for much time before and some after, it appeared that republicanism, in the minimal sense of the end of dynastic rule, was sweeping the region. This is what the revolutionaries were saying. This is what social scientists, among them Samuel Huntington and Daniel Lerner, were suggesting. My own first book was entitled *Arabia Without Sultans;* the sultans of South Arabia had gone, as had the imam of the north, and the book gave an account of the campaign by the revolutionaries of Dhufar in eastern Oman to overthrow the sultan of Muscat, as he was then called. The aspirations of the Dhufari guerrillas did not, of course, stop there. As evening came on and the fighters gathered round their campfires they would shout slogans reflecting their political hopes: *Yasqut kul al-shuyukh wal-muluk, wal-imam, wal-salatin, wal-umara, wal-shah fi al-khalij wal-Jazira al-Arabiyya.* Imperialism, Zionism, "Arab reaction," and a generic foe termed "revisionism" were also denounced. Not much was left out.

The Yemeni tribesmen were to a considerable extent on the mark, too, for the Middle East as a whole during this century. Of the three major monarchical systems existing at the start of the twentieth century—the sultanate in Turkey, the shah in Iran, the king in Morocco—only the last survives. Of the monarchies that emerged in one way or another under colonial rule in the Arab states a considerable number have also been overthrown: in Egypt in 1952, in Iraq in 1958, in Libya in 1969. So too have long-established monarchies installed in important states that impinge on the Middle East and whose demise was to have significant consequences for them: the Romanovs went in Russia in 1917, the Indian maharajahs after 1948, the Greek monarchy in 1967, the Mohammadzai in Afghanistan in 1973, the Solomonic dynasty of Ethiopia in 1974. Monarchy is, as much as anything else, democracy or peasant revolution or a return to holy texts, legitimated and delegitimated by demonstration effects: what is happening elsewhere, or what is believed to be happening elsewhere, matters.

The shah took fright in 1958 when the Hashemites fell in Iraq. The Saudis have at times been alarmed by seemingly democratic developments elsewhere in the Arabian Peninsula, be it the tentative parliamentary openings in Kuwait and Bahrain in the 1970s—they encouraged local allies to close down both—or the Yemeni elections of 1993 and 1997. In 1981, six Arab states of the Gulf banded as the Gulf Cooperation Council (GCC); one might even say they huddled together when faced with the impacts of Saddam Hussein *and* Ayatollah Khomeini. Republicanism was, therefore, the dominant trend in the Middle East during the twentieth century, as it was in Europe. Of the twenty-five states that compose the Middle East today, eight are ruled by monarchs: roughly 15 percent of the region's population was under monarchical rule during the 1990s.

This has not, however, been the whole picture. The sultan of Oman remained, with some help from his friends, as did his royal conferrers in the smaller Gulf states and, above all, Saudi Arabia. The kings of Jordan and Morocco have also survived. Moreover, they have to a considerable extent prospered. In the case of the oil-producing GCC states they have enjoyed comparative stability and prosperity. Kings Hussein and Hasan, with much less money available, have, until their natural deaths, maneuvered and tacked in such a way as to defy their critics: they have been unseated neither by revolt from below nor by recurrent threats from military (the Palestinian challenge of 1967–1970 in Jordan is remembered if only because of the way it ended). Yet we retain only a dim memory of the military challenges of Abdallah al-Tall in 1948 and the dissident officers of 1957 in Jordan, and, in the case of Morocco, of the mass socialist challenges of Ben Barka and the UNFP in the early 1960s[1] and that of Muhammad Ufkir in 1972.

When did the tide turn? In retrospect, one can see that it began after the great defeat, and delegitimation, of 1967: monarchy, like Islamism, benefited from the failure of the secular Arab nationalist project. Significantly, others began to talk if not of restoration then of nostalgia or to engage in discursive uses of monarchy. As reality shifted, so social scientists have begun to look again at the monarchies, not as anachronisms living on borrowed time but as enduring aspects of Arab states and as objects of study. The literature on the enduring monarchies, although often hampered by opacity of object as well as state censorship, allows for a comparative discussion to take place. Lisa

Anderson's 1991 article marks one clear recognition of this shift of perspective.[2] Recognition of this topic, and reflection upon it, have come far. History and social scientists have abandoned any assumptions of a republican telos in politics: but this does not, or need not, entail its alternative—a monarchical telos. In the Middle East, as elsewhere (e.g., Europe and Asia), the establishment and survival of monarchies bears no *necessary* relation to modern politics: it is a contingent matter, established, maintained, and, when it happens, terminated by the balance of political forces.

THE ANALYTIC RECORD: POLITICAL CONSOLIDATION, INTERNATIONAL CONTEXT, AND MODERNITY

There are some broad conclusions that appear to follow from this thirty-year ebb of determinist republican orthodoxy. Obviously, and most important, monarchy is and may well remain a significant part of politics in the Arab world. The eight monarchies have endured a range of challenges and have been able to use the resources provided to them—financial and political—to consolidate their positions. The reasons for success on the internal level are various but include plentiful supplies of money, the adoption of nationalist policies, and assiduous construction of states. Monarchs also rule, however, by building coalitions—with armed forces, middle classes, clerical institutions—and, more broadly, through forms of controlled mobilization. These alliances shift—the Saudis have lessened their dependence on the descendants of Muhammad Abd al-Wahhab and on the clerical establishment, and the al-Sabahs in Kuwait have distanced themselves from the merchants. But all involve coalitions. It is easy to see what happens when oil rent and monarchical conceit combine to make rulers believe they can dispense with coalitions, as the case of Muhammad Reza Pahlavi showed all too clearly.[3]

They have, also, benefited from external support: the GCC states, Jordan, and Morocco have all been supported by the West and have pursued astute diplomacies to balance the conflicting pressures open to them. External support is not everything, but the monarchs know what happens when they get it wrong. All of the monarchies of the Arab world, and some of those that survived as long as they did, owed their survival to the intervention of external forces: Morocco was saved in 1912 and again in the early 1960s and 1970s; Jordan was saved in 1958 and again in 1970; Oman was saved in 1957 and again in the early 1970s; the same is true for Kuwait in 1961 and 1991; Saudi Arabia called on help in 1963 and again in 1990. The same applies to the others prior to their fall: had it not been for the British, the Egyptian monarchy might have ended much sooner than it did; the Iranian state was helped into being in Reza Khan's coup of 1921 and saved in 1953; the Iraqis could have foundered in 1941. Conversely, it was the inability of the British to act in Iraq in 1958 and Libya in 1969, and the inability of the Americans to do so in Iran in 1978, that spelled doom for those regimes. It is simplistic to attribute the emergence, or survival, of these regimes *solely* to external military or indirect security support, but it would be misleading in the extreme to ignore the importance of such backing, whether actual or threatened. There is no mystery here and no need to invoke religious tradition, either.

A second broad conclusion about Middle Eastern monarchy is that it is, as with other aspects of the relation of states and politics to ideology, at least as much political interest that shapes ideology as the other way around. Put more concretely, the religious, cultural, and historical reserves of Islam allow both legitimation and delegitimation of monarchy. It depends on who is doing the interpreting. As Bernard Lewis and others point out, monarchy is not an intrinsic part of the Islamic faith. The term *malik* is used in both pejorative and legitimate senses. The contrast with Christianity and other religions is clear: Christ was the king, and in the early modern period monarchs claimed divine right, if not directly then through Christ's anointed vicar, the Pope of Rome.[4] Elsewhere, farther east, divinity has until very recently been even more central: the kings of Nepal and Thailand retain semidivine status (the very term "divine" having a different shade of meaning outside the monotheistic world), whereas those of Japan, China, Vietnam, and Cambodia were to lose it during the course of the twentieth century. Muhammad and Allah (some references to the latter as *malik* in the Quran aside) were not normally characterized as kings, as that would have been to demean them. Islamic tradition has not even been able to acquire the kind of religious legitimation that was obtained by early modern European monarchs with the "divine right of kings."

Monarchy is not part of the five basic pillars (*arkan*) or anywhere near it. From the Quran, the *hadith* (codified oral traditions), and the broader traditions of law and custom, it is possible to derive a justification for monarchy, and this has been assiduously done over the centuries. Thus, the status of *sharif* (descent from the prophet) is one available mechanism, although it is the preserve of only two of the eight Arab monarchies today. Another means of deploying religion is to make the claim that monarchs preserve an Islam polity, long argued by the Ottomans and now, most obviously, by the Saudis: the easiest texts to use enjoin the good and forbid the evil and those that instruct the faithful to obey God, the Prophet, and those in authority.[5] Another legitimate argument is that other forms of rule, including republicanism and democracy, are anti-Islamic. The history of the term *malakiyya*, Arabic for "monarchy," illustrates that process, whereby a secular term is given, when deemed appropriate, religious sanction.[6] The title *imam*, associated in modern times with religious authority, was distinct from the *ulama* (religious clergy) in the case of eighteenth-century Oman. Equally, monarchs can be delegitimated: the terms *uzorption, zulm,* and *istibdad* (arbitrary absolutism) are there from tradition, as are the figures of the Pharaoh and Croesus. In the campaigns against the imams of Yemen during the 1930s and 1940s, the Free Yemenis opposition movement (*al-yamaniyyin al-ahrar*) used this traditional Islamic vocabulary to challenge the imams,[7] and Khomeini used *yazid*, a term of significance for Shi'ites, and the all-purpose *taghut*.[8] One of the most potent cultural dimensions of the Iranian Revolution was the resonance of the slogan that came to dominate in the latter part of 1978—*marg bar shah*, or "death to the shah." The fact it could be enunciated and called for was itself a powerful element in the delegitimation of the monarch in a country with more than two thousand years of monarchy.

It is possible to make a cultural account of monarchy in the Muslim world from the seventh century on that derives monarchy from the texts of the religion, but it is equally possible to make a different, less doctrinal story of how political and social power molded and used the texts. One could even say that the greatest exponents of secularism were the Muslim monarchies of the past fourteen centuries. Studies of kingship in earlier Islamic periods, and of particular Islamic states, do not suggest that the monarchs and their ideologists were confused on this issue.[9] Islam may provide a necessary part of the legitimation of monarchical rule; it cannot provide an explanation for it. When, in the twentieth century, it came to formulating official titles for these monarchs, the terms used reflected, again, contemporary concerns: the Saudi title *khadim al-haramayn* (custodian of the holy places), the Iranian title *aryamehr* (leader of the Aryan people), and so forth. Such choices often reflected not only the wish to appropriate some earlier symbol of legitimacy but also the desire to assert who one is *not*. Thus, the Pahlavi assertion of the Sassainian dynasty's titles was designed to contrast them to the Safavi and Qajar Dynasties that preceded them. The counterpoints of Jordanian and Saudi nomenclature need no elaboration.

A third issue that arises from the literature on monarchy is the *modernity* of the institution. By this we mean the recent origin of most monarchies and, more important, the way in which the constraints and influence of the modern world (in addition to direct political and military support from abroad) explain the emergence and endurance of these monarchies. The historical record is clear enough: of the eight Arab monarchies, only two—in Oman and Morocco—predate the twentieth century. Their survival has, moreover, much to do with the use of violence, political calculation, and foreign support. For example, the sultanate of Morocco nearly fell to internal revolt and financial crisis in 1912 and survived only because the ruler, Mula'i Hafiz, invited in French troops and agreed to a protectorate. Later it owed its survival to the way in which Muhammad V adapted to and used the national confrontation with the French to consolidate his position and then, under Hasan II, with the Spanish over Sahara. At the same time Hasan II inherited from the French a state, and an external support, that allowed him to confirm his power.

The symbols may appear continuous, but even here memory can mislead. Morocco only acquired a king, as distinct from a sultan, in 1957. Egypt's *khedive* became a king only in 1922. Even more so, the state system, the economic and social foundations, and the international context are very different. Elsewhere we see the emergence of monarchies in the context of state-building and state consolidation in the broader Middle East context after World War I: the imposition of the Hashemites on Jordan by the British, the victory of the Saudi-led tribal coalition in Arabia in the 1920s, and the evolution under British tutelage of Persian Gulf rulers from being emirs of small coastal chiefdoms into rulers, endowed with oil, of modern states. Oman is a story apart: the longest surviving Arab state (along with Egypt), it saw the conflict between two rulers, the imam of the interior and the sultan of the coast, resolved by British intervention in the 1950s. Here again, however, an apparent continuity masks major changes: the administrative and military system, the territory controlled, the relation with the tribes of the interior, even the name (from "sultan of Muscat" up to 1970 to "sultan of Oman" thereafter) involved change. The shortest-lived monarchy of all was that of Libya: in 1951 the British got Sayyid Idris al-Sanusi, the ruler of their zone of control, Cyrenaica, proclaimed king, only to see him dispatched into exile eighteen years later.

The modernity of these monarchies is, however, evident in the broader international context. In the reorganization following World War I, choices were made as to the form of states being established in the region. The British favored monarchy in Iraq and Jordan, as they later did in Libya, whereas the French favored republics. This had little to do with the countries concerned and much to do with the constitutions of the metropolitan countries at the time: the French had not been loath to take over or create monarchies in the nineteenth century in Indochina and Mexico. The decision for the Egyptian ruler, Sultan Ahmad Fu'ad, to become a king, taken in 1922 when Egypt became formally independent, reflected a similar choice. In two other respects newly established militarized regimes chose monarchy: in Iran Reza Khan, who had initially favored a republic following Turkey, changed his mind, at least partly under pressure of the clerical establishment, whereas in Saudi Arabia the tribal emir of the al-Sauds decided, also for tactical reasons, mainly to deny the claims of the Hashemite king of the Hijaz to proclaim himself *malik* in 1926.[10] The impulsion for Arab rulers to do so at that time was all the greater because of the uncertainty caused by the abolition of the caliphate in 1924.

Turkey chose a republic, but we know from the evidence of the time that it was quite a close thing: Mustafa Kemal—Ataturk—consulted about what path to take and found opinion divided. He did not at first abolish the caliphate, only the sultanate. The decisive factor was that those old institutions were seen as unable to fulfill the national role of defending the interests of the people against foreign attack.[11] Such choices reflected not continuity but the combination of domestic calculation and international conformity to which these states were subjected. One can see how, in cases where monarchy fails, the factor of external defeat and challenge plays such a central role: the European and Far Eastern monarchies have fallen in this century largely due to defeat in war—in Russia, Austro-Hungary, Italy, China, and Japan. This was also the case in the Ottoman Empire, Egypt, and Libya. The one exception was Iran, where a set of powerful internal tensions, augmented by external financial inflows, undermined the Pahlavi regime. Yet even though tension between the Pahlavis and the society had endured for decades, only in 1978 did the Islamist opposition start to call for an "Islamic Republic" (*Jumhuriyi Islami*); the only political force calling for that hitherto had been the communist Tudeh Party, and it would seem that Khomeini took his lead from them.

COMPARISONS: REGIONAL AND INTERNATIONAL

The analysis of different origins, and of the broader Middle Eastern context, leads to the idea of comparing monarchies to each other and of monarchies to republican regimes. Examination of these eight cases, and of the conditions of their emergence and consolidation, raises the question of whether they are similar institutions. To some extent they are, but in many respects not. On the basis of the demonstration effect, the fact of their being different monarchies has to some degree a consolidating effect: the monarchs were disturbed by the fall of monarchs elsewhere and must retain the hope that those now surviving will continue. Yet by dint of their shared monarchical claims to legitimation there are also problems: the Saudis have their frictions with the other monarchs of the Gulf, especially when, as in the case of Kuwait, monarchs allow some elections, however controlled. Even more so, they surfaced during the reign of King Hussein of Jordan, descendant of a family with alternative claims in the western Peninsula. This very contemporary jostling was also evident in the claims each made to protection of holy places. King Hussein's attempt, in regard to his claims on the West Bank, to assert responsibility through the Jordanian-Palestinian agreement of 1985 for Jerusalem led the Saudi monarch in 1986 to proclaim himself *khadim al-haramayn* (custodian of Mecca and Medina).

In terms of origin and internal constitution, however, there are great differences between the Arab monarchies: Morocco and Oman are comparable as traditional sultanates turned into modern states by colonial support, whereas Jordan is a praetorian monarchy created ex nihilo or at least ex deserto by Britain after World War I. Saudi Arabia is a product of tribal conquest, whereas the smaller Gulf states are towns that became states thanks to colonial initiative and oil. The eight Arab monarchies therefore constitute not *one* but *four* different types of regime: transformed sultanate, praetorian monarchy, tribal military oligarchy, and monarchical city-state. This is as true in terms of how they were established, and the forms of legitimation they claim, as it is in terms of how they maintain themselves in power. Only two claims descend from the Prophet, but, as Gudrun Krämer points out, such a claim of sharifian descent is widespread and not a specific claim of monarchs. We are not looking at one single model of Muslim or Arab monarchy.

Yet there is the question of how the monarchies of the Arab world compare to non-Arab monarchs. Here again the answer is mixed. A glance at the broader pattern of colonial relationship to monarchy in Asia and Africa during the nineteenth and twentieth centuries shows that the European powers—British, French, Dutch—maintained or created monarchies when it suited them. Such was the case in Southeast Asia, India, and parts of Africa, such as Uganda, Lesotho, and Kano. The Middle East came under imperial control later, but when it did it was also favored, when deemed appropriate, with monarchical collaborators.

The evolution of the Moroccan state bears comparison to other Third World monarchies that arose in noncolonial countries, Nepal and Thailand in particular. Although distinct in not having been subject to colonial rule, in those two Asian states religion (Hinduism and Buddhism, respectively) provided the legitimation for autocracies that survived thanks to coalitions built with the armed forces and foreign support. The Thai monarch ruled as absolute autocrat until 1932, that of Nepal until 1990. The oil-dependent smaller emirs of the Gulf have an almost exact counterpart in the Southeast Asian sultanate of Brunei, an oil-producing state long protected by Britain where an early experiment in parliamentary government was stopped in 1962 by Sultan Umar Ali Sayf al-Din III. When it became independent in 1984, Brunei, with a population of 230,000, had an absolute monarchy, under Sultan Hasan al-Bulkiyya, legitimated by Islam and principles of Malayan monarchy. As with the Gulf, oil and foreign support against larger predatory neighbors go a long way to explaining the survival of the monarchical regime in Brunei. Jordan's monarchy was, in effect, a praetorian state established by European colonial powers. It is unique in its survival but not in the model: the French tried it in Mexico in the 1860s; the British installed and later reinstalled such a monarchy in Greece. It is King Hussein's survival—the result of astute politics and international support rather than his origins and the character of the regime—that requires explanation.

The Arab monarchies, of course, are distinct in two other respects. One, which is more than casual and raises interesting questions about the solidity of monarchy in the Middle East, is the remarkably high incidence of deposition, that is, replacement of one member of a ruling family by another. No one has, I think, ever quantified this, but the assumption of monarchies outside the Middle East has been that succession is clear and that once installed the monarch remains until death (or there is a regency in the event of illness). This has not been the pattern in the Middle East during the modern period: time and again we see the removal of reigning monarchs by relatives, often with foreign encouragement and for reasons other than ill health. Thus, in Saudi Arabia Abd al-Aziz, Ibn Saud's first successor, Saud, was effectively removed in 1962 after the Yemen Revolution. In Jordan, Abdallah's son Talal was prevented from taking office and dispatched to a sanatorium in Istanbul in 1952, after a brief period in power, in favor of his son. It was not clear at the time how much this was a result of medical factors or of Talal's anti-British sentiments. In Oman, Said bin Taymur, who himself had come to power in 1932 by deposing his father, was ousted by his son, Qabus, in 1970. In Abu Dhabi, Shakhbut was ousted in 1966; in Qatar Hamad al-Thani was removed in 1972; and his successor Khalifa al-Thani was deposed in 1995. In Bahrain, Isa al-Khalifa was deposed in 1923. The most spectacular case of deposition was in Iran in 1941, accompanied as it was by an invasion from north and south. In most cases there was, of course, a foreign role, if not foreign hand: one need not lapse into conspiracy theory to note that imperial interest played a role. This suggests that Middle Eastern monarchies are less absolute, less above manipulation, than those of other countries. Put another way, and drawing a distinction between monarchy and dynasty, the political systems being discussed here were more those of ruling families, with possible changes of ruler, than of monarchies, in the sense of consolidated, single rulers.

The other distinctive feature of Arab monarchies is more obvious: the lack of real constitutional evolution in the sense of effective limitation on the monarch's power. The monarchies of Europe and, more recently, those of Nepal and Thailand have under internal and international pressures come to accept the growth of parliamentary systems. This is where the most liberalized monarchies exist: Britain, Spain, Holland, Sweden, Denmark, and Norway. This is the model of modernized constitutional monarchy. Parliamentary developments under Arab monarchies have occurred everywhere except in the United Arab Emirates. In some cases (Oman, Saudi Arabia, Qatar), however, consultative councils amount to very little as yet. In Bahrain the parliament was suppressed in 1975 and not reconvened. In Kuwait, Jordan, and Morocco parliamentary politics does operate but within limits very clearly set by the monarchy. In contrast to the constitutional monarchies of Europe, the Middle Eastern monarch, backed by the armed forces, remains very much in charge and defines what political parties can and cannot do. This is linked to the patterns of rule in the nonmonarchical states. For it must be the case that one of the reasons for the survival of monarchy is the contrary demonstration effect, that is, the fates of the countries where republics have been established. Egypt's defeat in 1967, instability and extreme authoritarianism in

Iraq, and turmoil in Iran all serve as negative examples. The specificity of Arab monarchies is therefore part of the broader resistance to democracy in the Middle East as a whole.

Yet there are limits to how far monarchies can be analyzed as similar to republican states. The argument for presidential monarchy (Abd al-Nasir, Saddam, Qaddafi, Ali Abdullah Salih, and so forth) is frequently made.[12] It has some analytic force. These rulers are autocrats, like the monarchs; they appoint relatives and friends to positions of power, even as successors; and they promote cults of personality to mobilize support. The force of the comparison is, above all, a critical one, designed to trim the republican presidents of some of their illusions. As such it is valid. In a novel written by Saudi intellectual and diplomat Ghazi Alqosaibi (al-Qusaybi), *An Apartment Called Freedom*, we see a sympathetic account of the Arab nationalist intelligentsia of the 1950s but also scorn for the pretensions of the new rulers of Egypt.[13] We see the same critical and comparative point in other societies. In Russia, the Soviet leaders were denounced as czars; in China Mao was seen as an emperor; even in countries that never had a monarchy such delegitimation can occur, as in references in the United States to the "imperial" presidency and to "George III."

Yet there are also important differences. In the first place—and this is not trivial—the autocrats have not been able to appoint family members, let alone eldest sons, to succeed them or to serve as prime minister. The democracies of South Asia (India, Pakistan, Sri Lanka, Bangladesh) have gone much farther in the creation of such dynasties than have the republics of the Arab world. It is indeed worth noting what *did* happen to the children of Middle Eastern heads of state: Abd al-Nasir's children went into obscurity or opposition; Khomeini's son Ahmad led a quiet clerical opposition until his death in 1995; Inonu's son in Turkey became head of a small left-of-center party; Habib Bourguiba II lives in retirement in a Tunis suburb. Some Middle Eastern rulers—Saddam, Hafiz al-Asad, Qaddafi—have been grooming sons for some kind of influential role, but this would appear to be more as trusted supporters of their own rule. There is no sign of an effective hereditary principle here.[14] In the Iranian case it is particularly inapposite to compare Rafsanjani to the shah: whatever his informal influence before and after his two periods of presidency (1989–1997), Rafsanjani had a limited term in office and, within the pluralism of the Islamic republic, limited powers.

There are, moreover, differences in the ways in which monarchs and presidents can seek to mobilize support and implement policies. Presidents can create ruling parties; monarchs have more difficulty. Few remember the Rastkhiz Party of the shah.[15] The contrasted interventions of monarchs and presidents on the sensitive issue of birth control are illustrative in this regard. This argument may be strengthened by a counterfactual: if monarchy conveyed such benefits, and was so attractive to presidents, more might have tried to restore or recreate it. Saddam's flirtations with the Hashemite legacy aside, we have to go back to Reza Khan in 1925 to find a case of a republican ruler crowning himself.[16]

We can use many indices for contrasting means of legitimacy and use and abuse of power: economic policy is one, population policy another. Among the most important, however, is the use of repression. The monarchs ruled autocratically, and where they deemed it necessary they killed their opponents, as Ben Barka in Morocco, Nasir Said in Saudi Arabia, and successive generations of protesters in Bahrain have found out. But not all the monarchies have killed their opponents in extrajudicial ways: Kuwait, Qatar, and the United Arab Emirates have clean hands in this regard; Jordan used repression when challenged with overthrow in 1970. By contrast the republics have resorted to violence repeatedly and on a scale far greater than that of their monarchical predecessors: Abd al-Nasir and Qaddafi have been relatively low scorers in this regard, in judicial and extrajudicial forms. When it comes to the Ba'thi regime in Iraq and, to a significantly lesser extent, the Khomeini regime in Iran, then the contrast is to the disadvantage of the republics. Having mobilized the people into politics, and having thrown away an established system of legitimacy, the republicans have had to resort to violence to protect and legitimate their regime. Saddam Hussein has certainly scored higher than anyone else and seems to feel he has to continue to do so. But the contrast, in the case of the others, is not so clear. One exception to date, given too little credit, is Ali Abdallah Salih of Yemen, no friend of democracy but not a Saddam Hussein or Hafiz al-Asad, either. When the comparison is made not with the costs of regime maintenance but with that of establishing the regimes, then the costs look very different: the coups that brought Abd al-Nasir, Hafiz al-Asad, Qaddafi, even Saddam (in 1968 if not 1963) to power were relatively bloodless; the establishment of the kingdoms of Saudi Arabia, Iraq, and Iran were marked by widespread violence. The Moroccan regime has repeatedly resorted to violence against the demonstrations and insurrections it has faced.

PROSPECTS: AN ENDURING CONTINGENCY

The endurance of these monarchs is not just a matter for the past but also for the future. Here we should be cautious. The most pragmatic answer, once we have rid ourselves of any deterministic view of how Middle Eastern society will progress—be it toward republics, chaos, or "Islam"—is that the survival of the monarchies is contingent. Insofar as they can continue to meet the three criteria of survival—mobilization of economic resources, maintenance of a domestic support coalition, and management of international alliances—they can continue. By contrast, economic collapse, antagonism of the armed forces or other powerful domestic social interests, and confrontation with powerful regional or global forces could spell their end. In all of this, chance plays a role, be it in the vagaries of the international economic system or in the personalities of rulers. The latter is not all-important, nor is it trivial, any more than it is in the context of the republican leaderships. Highlighting the conditions for the monarchies to endure indicates what could cause difficulties in the future. One is delegitimation on the nationalist front: King Hussein balanced opposition forces most shrewdly over the years, and so did Hasan II, but their successors have to continue doing so. The Saudis are confronting Saddam Hussein, but they run the risk of appearing to be clients of Washington. In economic matters, the fact is that the oil-producing states and the non–oil-producing states face difficulties.

It is easy, and true, to say that Jordan and Morocco are better off by dint of not having oil. But they need money, and they need to find employment for their younger people. Per capita income is low, if not by Arab then by Mediterranean standards, and population pressure is rising. In the oil-producing states the era of money and security is over, even if there is oil in the ground for many decades to come. The issues of taxation, reduction of free services, and an end to gross corruption are present, unavoidable, and very difficult to confront. As for domestic coalitions, not least with the armed forces, this too is contingent. Rapacious Saudi princes, already in receipt of *khususiyyats* estimated to average $500,000 per year, do not win the hearts of Hijazi merchants and Najdi tribal recruits, let alone Shi'ites, to the armed forces; merchants in Kuwait and Bahrain resent the mismanagement of their oil revenues by the al-Sabahs and the al-Khalifas; all is far from being well in Oman because of endemic corruption and the lack of any successor generation. These societies, like many of the republics, can be considered kleptocracies, states run by a self-appointed elite that treats the state's finances as their own. Everyone knows it.

The question of the future also relates to the possibility of the restoration of monarchy. Here comparison may be the best place to start. Monarchies can be restored in some less-than-average circumstances: when they return from exile after war and occupation (as in Holland, Denmark, and Norway after World War II); or when they are associated with the restoration of democracy (Spain after 1975). But the overall record of monarchies returning is not a strong one, even where there is a clear royalist party within the country. In Greece as well as in Eastern European countries where monarchs were ousted by communism (Russia, Serbia, Romania, Bulgaria, and Albania), the monarchs have some support, but they are not serious contenders for power. The same would apply to other countries where monarchy has disappeared in this century: there is little clamor in China for the return of the Manchus, in Vietnam for the return of the Hue dynasty, or in Ethiopia for the return of the Solomonic family. Respect, interest, and nostalgia are present but restoration is not, and when monarchy is restored, as in Spain, it is not with the same power. If some of the Eastern European monarchies do get re-established—Serbia being the most likely candidate—then this will almost certainly also be the case.

If we look at Middle Eastern societies today there are cases where nostalgia—in some cases from independent sources, in some cases from on top—is detectable. Thus, in Iraq, Saddam sought to recruit the Hashemite past to his purposes, as he did Hamurrabi and the Quran; in Egypt the view of Faruk mellowed; in Iran people began to repeat the old saying *nur az maqbare miayad*—"light comes from his grave"; in Turkey there are articles in the press by writers evoking the benefits of the Ottoman period and the peace it brought—*Yeni Osmanlik* (New Ottomans). In Yemen the figure of the imam is, as it was during his time, both feared and respected, but that is not to say he might return to rule. In Afghanistan there has been much speculation, ever since the process of "national reconciliation" under the communist regime began in the mid-1980s, of a return of King Zahir from his exile in Rome. But that has not happened, and were he to go back he would find a country so transformed, so lacking in the levers of power and attendant balances with which he and his predecessors had ruled, that he would be unable to bring about internal peace. Echoes of monarchy emerge elsewhere: in the Afghan, *taliban* use of *emir al-mu'minin*, in the Islamists' interest, promoted by the "liberation party," *Hizb al-Tahrir;* in the caliphate; even in Israeli right-wing salutations to Ariel Sharon as king.[17] There is certainly a study to be done of how the deposed monarchies are viewed in literature, symbolism, and state presentation, and we can note than in almost all cases a mellowing is taking place. This mellowing reflects both the passage of time and political calculation, as well as the disappointments of the republican period. It does not seem to suggest that monarchy, in the sense of a dynastic autocracy, can return in any of these states, or that there is some cultural essence, inherent in the society and reproduced, that will lead them back to the institution. This is especially so in the country with the deepest and most continuous of monarchical traditions: Iran. It does not apply to Israel, the one country in the Middle East that has based its legitimacy, and claim to land, on the state established by a divinely sanctioned king: David.

For social scientists and historians of the Middle East the challenge of monarchy is essentially twofold. First, they must provide, as carefully as possible, an account of how the contemporary monarchical system emerged. Monarchy, like nationalism and religion, provides its own ideology of how it emerged and came to be as it is. But such narratives, usually involving an overstatement of historical continuity, mask the changes of symbol, power, and function that monarchies perform. The second challenge is that of analyzing how the societies in question function, including the ways in which monarchs have been able to manipulate domestic and international factors to maintain their positions. There are no certainties here, and each society has elements that distinguish it from others. The twentieth century has both created *and* destroyed monarchies, for reasons that historical and political analyses seek to explain. It is questionable how far the twenty-first century will create any new ones or restore those that have gone. Even if it does not, the challenge of analysis of how these rulers, and their relatives, maintain their positions will remain.

NOTES

1. Mehdi Ben Barka, *Option Revolutionnaire au Maroc* (Paris, 1964).

2. Lisa Anderson, "Absolutism and the Resilience of Monarchy in the Middle East," *Political Science Quarterly*, 106 (1991).

3. "During the Qajar reign monarchs had maintained a close connection with the people. Qajar shahs ruled acording to old tribal habits and sat with the people at lunch or in the mosque—since they were after all worshipping the same God. . . . The Pahlavis changed all that. Mohammad Reza Shah, like his father, was handed the crown and therefore lacked the tribal support that would have brought him close to the people. Unlike his father he grew up entirely sheltered and kept a great distance between himself and everyone else. The Shah's introversion, which eventually deteriorated into paranoia and egomania, was the fatal flaw in a man otherwise so conscious of his royal duties." Manucher Farmanfarmaian, *Blood and Oil* (New York: Random House, 1997), pp. 341–342.

4. On the emergence of the doctrine in France, see Albert Soboul, *The French Revolution, 1787–1799* (London: NLB, 1974), pp. 77ff.

5. *Al amr bil-ma'ruf wal-nahi an al-munkar,* Qur'an: 4.59.

6. Bernard Lewis, *The Political Language of Islam* (London: University of Chicago Press, 1988), pp. 53–56; Ami Ayalon, *Language and Change in the Arab Middle East* (Oxford: Oxford University Press, 1987), pp. 32–42. The relation between kingship and property in the root *mlk* is not, however, specific to Arabic or to Islamic tradition. In the Western European context it is evident in the two meanings of the word *domain*, i.e., are ruled *and* owned. In Chinese the word for *country* means "emperor's property." Significantly, perhaps, there in no distinction in Arabic between the words for *monarchy* and *kingship*—*malakiyya* serving for both. Yet as this discussion of the contemporary Arab world shows, only two of the eight monarchs are from their origins kings: Saudi Arabia and Jordan.

7. Leigh Douglas, *The Free Yemeni Movement* (Beirut: American University of Beirut Press, 1987).

8. Khomeini saw his role as "smasher" of these idols. In Persian one of his official titles was *bot-shekan*, the "idol-smasher." Thus, beyond being applied to all associated with the shah's regime, *taghut* was applied in particular to four people: the shah himself, U.S. President Jimmy Carter, Abu al-Hasan Bani Sadr, the first president of the Islamic Republic who broke with Khomeini in 1981; and Saddam Hussein. Khomeini considered that he had smashed the first three, but the fourth was harder to deal with.

9. Aziz al-Azmeh, *Muslim Kingship, Power, and the Sacred in Muslim, Christian, and Pagan Polities* (New York: I. B. Tauris, 1998).

10. Joseph Kostiner, *The Making of Saudi Arabia, 1916–1936: From Chieftaincy to Monarchical State* (Oxford: Oxford University Press, 1993).

11. Bernard Lewis, *The Emergence of Modern Turkey* (Oxford: Oxford University Press, 1961), pp. 251–253.

12. P. J. Vatikiotis, "Royals and Revolutionaries in the Middle East," *Middle East Lectures*, No. 2, Moshe Dayan Center for Middle Eastern and African Studies, Tel Aviv University, 1997.

13. Ghazi Algosaibi, *An Apartment Called Freedom* (London, 1996).

14. One partial qualification is that of the Arif brothers in Iraq: after the death of President Abd al-Salam Arif in 1966 he was replaced by his brother, Abd al-Rahman, himself ousted by the Ba'th in 1968.

15. Although it did resurface, in what we may also assume was a mistaken testimony to the demonstration effect of the shah's experiment, as a party in post-1991 Tajikistan.

16. The fate of others who have tried this—Jean-Claude Duvalier in Haiti, Bokassa in the Central African Republic, before that Napoleon—might also serve to discourage.

17. In Judaism monarchy has a religious association: God is the "King of Kings" (*melekh malkhei ha-mlakhim*). In contemporary Hebrew the term *melekh* is used both to denote king as ruler and as a generic, popular term of praise, be it of political leaders or football heroes. I am grateful to Joseph Kostiner for this information.

Bibliography

Abdallah, Anwar. *al-'Ulama' wal-'arsh, thana'iyyat al-Sulta fil-Sa'udiyya.* London: al-Rafid, 1955.

Abir, Mordechai. "The Consolidation of the Ruling Class and the New Elites in Saudi Arabia," *Middle East Studies*, 23 (1987).

———. *Saudi Arabia: Government, Society, and the Gulf Crises.* London: Routledge, 1993.

Abrahamian, Ervand. *Iran Between Two Revolutions.* Princeton: Princeton University Press, 1982.

———. *Khomeinism: Essays on the Islamic Republic.* Berkeley: University of California Press, 1993.

———. "The Crowd in Iranian Politics, 1905–1953," in H. Afshar (ed.). *Iran: A Revolution in Turmoil.* London: Macmillan, 1985.

Adams Schmidt, Dana. *Yemen: The Unknown War.* New York: Holt, Rinehart, and Winston, 1968.

Addleton, J. "Asian Expatriates—Coming Back," *The Middle East* (October 1991).

———. "The Impact of the Gulf War on Migration and Remittances in Asia and the Middle East," *International Migration*, 29 (1991).

Al-Adili, Mahmud Salih. *Al-Sa'udiyya al-namudhaj al-afdal . . . lil-hukm al-Islami (huquq wa-wajibat al-hukkam wal-mahkumin).* Tanta: Maktabat al-Azhar al-Haditha bi-Tanta, 1995.

Ahmad, A. "Class, Nation, and State: Intermediate Classes in Peripheral Societies," in D. L. Johnson (ed.). *Middle Classes in Dependent Countries.* London: Sage, 1985.

Ahmad, Ahmad Yusif. *Al-Dawr al-Masri fi al-Yaman.* Cairo: al-Hay'a al-Masriyya al-'Amma lil-Kitab, 1981.

Ahmad, Rif'at Sayyid. *Rasa'il Juhayman al-'Utaybi qa'id al-muqtahimin lil-masjid al-haram bi-Makka.* Cairo: Maktabat Madbuli, 1988.

Al-Ahnaf, M. "Maroc. Le code du statut personnel," *Maghreb-Machrek*, no. 145 (1994).

Ajami, Fouad. "Iran: The Impossible Revolution," *Foreign Affairs*, 67 (1988/89).

———. *The Arab Predicament: Arab Political Thought and Practice Since 1967.* Cambridge: Cambridge University Press, 1992.

———. "The End of Pan-Arabism," *Foreign Affairs*, 57 (1978/79).

Akhavi, Shahrough. *Religion and Politics in Contemporary Iran: Clergy-State Relations in the Pahlavi Period.* Albany: SUNY Press, 1980.

Algar, Hamid. "Imam Khomeini, 1902–1962: The Pre-Revolutionary Years," in Edmund Burke and Ira Lapidus (eds.). *Islam, Politics, and Social Movements.* Berkeley: University of California Press, 1988.

——. *Religion and State in Iran, 1785–1906: The Role of Ulama in the Qajar Period*. Berkeley: University of California Press, 1969.

Algosaibi, Ghazi. *An Apartment Called Freedom*. London, 1996.

Allen, Calvin. *Oman: The Modernization of the Sultanate*. Boulder: Westview Press, 1987.

Allman, James. "The Demography Transition in the Middle East and North Africa," in James Allman (ed.). *Woman's Status and Fertility in the Muslim World*. New York and London: Praeger Publishers, 1978.

Alshayeji, Abdullah. "Kuwait at Crossroads: The Quest for Democratization," *Middle East Insight*, 8 (1992).

Altorki, Soraya, and Donald Cole. *Arabian Oasis City: The Transformation of Unayzah*. Austin: University of Texas Press, 1989.

Amawi, Abla. "Democracy Dilemmas in Jordan," *Middle East Report*, 22 (1992).

——. "The 1993 Elections in Jordan," *Arab Studies Quarterly*, 16 (1994).

Amnesty International. *Jordan: Human Rights Protection After the State of Emergency*. London: Amnesty International, 1990.

Abu-Amr, Ziyad. *Islamic Fundamentalism in the West Bank and Gaza: Muslim Brotherhood and Islamic Jihad*. Bloomington: Indiana University Press, 1994.

Anderson, Benedict. *Imagined Communities: Reflections on the Origins and Spread of Nationalism*. New York: Verso, 1991.

Anderson, Lisa. "Absolutism and the Resilience of Monarchy in the Middle East," *Political Science Quarterly*, 106 (1991).

——. "Democracy in the Arab World: A Critique of the Political and Culture Approach," in Bahgat Korany, Rex Brynen, and Paul Noble (eds.). *Political Liberalization and Democratization in the Arab World. Vol. 1: Theoretical Perspective*. Boulder: Lynne Rienner Publishers, 1995.

——. "North Africa: Changes and Challenges," Special Issue on "Embattled Minorities Around the Globe," *Dissent* (Summer 1996).

Anderson, Perry. *Lineages of the Absolutist State*. London: Verso, 1974.

Antoun, Richard T. *Muslim Preacher in the Modern World: A Jordanian Case Study in Comparative Perspective*. Princeton: Princeton University Press, 1989.

el-Aoufi, Noureddine (ed.). *La Societe Civile au Maroc, Approches*. Rabat: SMER, 1992.

Apostolou, Andrew. "Stirrings of Political Debate," *The Middle East* (November 1992).

Arjomand, Said Amir. *The Shadow of God and the Hidden Imam*. Chicago: University of Chicago Press, 1984.

——. "The Shi'ite Hierarchy and the State in Pre-Modern Iran: 1785–1890," *European Journal of Sociology*, 22 (1981).

——. "The State and Khomeini's Islamic Order," *Iranian Studies*, 13 (1980).

——. *The Turban for the Crown: The Islamic Revolution in Iran*. New York: Oxford University Press, 1988.

Aruri, Naseer. *Jordan: A Study in Political Development 1921–1965*. The Hague: Nijhoff, 1972.

Asad, Nasir al-Din (ed.). *Ta'rikh Najd*. 2nd ed. Cairo: Dar al-Shuruq, 1985.

Asad, Talal. *Genealogies of Religion, Discipline, and Reasons of Power in Christianity and Islam*. Baltimore: Johns Hopkins University Press, 1993.

Ashraf, Ahmad. "Theocracy and Charisma: New Men of Power in Iran," *International Journal of Politics, Culture, and Society*, 4 (1990).

Asim, Ahmad. *Tarikh*. Istanbul: n.d.

Assiri, Abdul-Reda. *Kuwait's Foreign Policy: City-State in World Politics*. Boulder: Westview Press, 1990.

Attia, Attia Adel Moneim. "Oman," in Albert P. Blaustein and Gisbert H. Flanz (eds.). *Constitutions of the Countries of the World*. New York: Oceana, 1974.

Al-'Awda, Salman. *Hiwar hadi ma'a Muhammad al-Ghazali*. 3rd ed. Riyad: Dar al-Hijra lil-Nashr wal-Tawzi', 1990.

Axelrod, Laurence. "Tribesmen in Uniform: The Demise of the Fida'iyyun in Jordan, 1970–1971," *Muslim World*, 48 (1968).

Ayalon, Ami. *Language and Change in the Arab Middle East*. Oxford: Oxford University Press, 1987.

———. "Malik," *Encyclopedia of Islam*. Vol. 6. Leiden: Brill, 1987.

———. "Malik in Modern Middle Eastern Titulature," *Die Welt des Islam*, 23–24 (1984).

Ayubi, Nazih. *Overstating the Arab State: Politics and Society in the Middle East*. London: I. B. Tauris, 1995.

———. *Political Islam. Religion and Politics in the Arab World*. London: Routledge, 1991.

al-Azmeh, Aziz. *Muslim Kingship, Power, and the Sacred in Muslim, Christian, and Pagan Polities*. New York: I. B. Tauris, 1998.

———. "Wahhabite Polity," in I. R. Netton (ed.). *Arabia and the Gulf: From Traditional Society to Modern State*. Totowa, N.J.: Barnes and Noble Books, 1986.

Bagehot, Walter. *The English Constitution and Other Political Essays*. New York: Appleton, 1924.

Al-Baharna, Husain M. *The Arabian Gulf States: Their Legal and Political Status and Their International Problems*. Beirut: Librairie du Liban, 1975.

Bahrain, State of. Central Statistical Organization, Directorate of Statistics, *Statistical Abstract—1992*.

Baker, Raymond William. *Egypt's Uncertain Revolution Under Nasser and Sadat*. Cambridge: Harvard University Press, 1978.

Bakhash, Shaul. *The Reign of the Ayatollahs: Iran and the Islamic Revolution*. New York: Basic Books, 1986.

Balfour-Paul, Glen. *The End of Empire in the Middle East: Britain's Relinquishment of Power in Her Last Three Arab Dependencies*. New York: Cambridge University Press, 1991.

Banuazizi, Ali. "Iran's Revolutionary Impasse: Political Factionalism and Societal Resistance," *Middle East Report*, 24 (1994).

Baram, Amatzia. "The Radical Shi'ite Movement in Iraq," in Emanual Sivan and Menachem Friedman (eds.). *Religious Radicalism and Politics in the Middle East*. New York: SUNY Press, 1990.

Barghouti, Iyad. "The Islamists in Jordan and the Palestinian Occupied Territories," in Laura Guazzone (ed.). *The Islamic Dilemma: The Political Role of Islamist Movements in the Contemporary Arab World*. Reading, UK: Ithaca Press, 1995.

Barkey, Karen. *Bandits and Bureaucrats: The Ottoman Route to State Centralization*. Ithaca: Cornell University Press, 1994.

al-Basha, Hasan. *Al-Alqab al-Islamiyya fil-ta'rikh wal-watha'iq wa'l-athar*. Cairo: Maktaba al-Nahtha al-Missriah, 1957.

———. *Al-Funun al-Islamiyya wal-waza'if 'ala al-'Arabiyya*. Cairo: Maktabat al-Nahd al-Misriyya, 1966.

Batatu, Hanna. *The Old Social Classes and the Revolutionary Movements in Iraq*. Princeton: Princeton University Press, 1978.

————. "The Old Social Classes Revisited," in Robert A. Fernea and Wm. Roger Louis (eds.). *The Iraqi Revolution of 1958.* London: I. B. Tauris, 1991.

Bayat, Mangol. "Mahmud Taleqani and the Iranian Revolution," in Martin Kramer (ed.). *Shi'ism, Resistance, and Revolution.* Boulder: Westview Press, 1987.

al-Baydani, Abd al-Rahman. *'Azmat al-umma al-'arabiyya wa thawrat al-yaman.* N.p., 1983.

Bayne, E. A. *Persian Kingship in Transition.* New York: American Universities Field Staff, 1968.

Bean, Lee L., and A. G. Zofiry. "Marriage and Fertility in the Gulf Region: The Impact of Pro-Family, Pro-Natal Policies," Cairo Demographic Center, Working Papers, No. 36, Cairo, 1994.

Beblawi, Hazem. "The Rentier State in the Arab World," in Giacomo Luciani (ed.). *The Arab State.* London: Routledge, 1990.

Benani, Ahmed. "Legitimite du pouvoir au Maroc, consensus et contestation," in *Sou'al*, no. 6 (1987).

Ben Barka, Mehdi. *Option Revolutionnaire au Maroc.* Paris, 1966.

Bendix, Reinhard. *Kings or People: Power and the Mandate to Rule.* Berkeley: University of California Press, 1978.

————. *Nation-Building and Citizenship.* New York: Wiley, 1964.

Ben-Dor, Gabriel. "Jordan and Inter-Arab Relations," in Joseph Nevo and Ilan Pappe (eds.). *Jordan in the Middle East: The Making of a Pivotal State.* Ilford, UK: Frank Cass, 1994.

————. "Political Culture Approach to Middle East Politics," *International Journal of Middle East Studies*, 8 (1977).

————. "Prospects of Democratization in the Arab World: Global Diffusion, Regional Demonstration, and Domestic Imperatives," in Bahgat Korany, Rex Brynen, and Paul Noble (eds.). *Political Liberalization and Democratization in the Arab World. Vol. 1: Theoretical Perspective.* Boulder: Lynne Rienner Publishers, 1995.

————. *State and Conflict in the Middle East.* New York: Praeger, 1983.

————. "Stateness and Ideology in Contemporary Middle East Politics," *The Jerusalem Journal of International Relations*, 9 (1987).

————. "The Continuity of the Egyptian State and the Ambiguity of the Revolution," in Shimon Shamir (ed.). *Egypt from Monarchy to Republic: A Reassessment of Revolution and Change.* Boulder: Westview Press, 1995.

Be'eri, Eliezer. *Army Officers in Arab Politics and Society.* Jerusalem: Israel Universities Press, 1969.

Bengio, Ofra. "Faysal's Vision of Iraq: A Retrospect," in Asher Susser and Aryeh Shmuelevitz (eds.). *The Hashemites in the Modern Arab World.* London: Frank Cass, 1995.

————. "Iraq," in Ami Ayalon (ed.). *Middle East Contemporary Survey (MECS).* Vol. 13, 1989. Boulder and Tel Aviv: Westview Press and the Moshe Dayan Center for Middle Eastern and African Studies, Tel Aviv University, 1991.

Bennani-Chraibi, Monnia. *Soumis et rebelles: Les jeunes au Maroc.* Paris: CNRS, 1994.

Benomar, Jamal. "The Monarchy, the Islamist Movement, and Religious Discourse in Morocco," *Third World Quarterly*, 10 (1988).

Berger, Morroe. *Bureaucracy and Society in Modern Egypt.* Princeton: Princeton University Press, 1957.

Bill, James A. "Resurgent Islam in the Persian Gulf," *Foreign Affairs*, 63 (1984).

Bill, James A., and Carl Leiden. *Politics in the Middle East*. Boston: Little, Brown, 1984.

Bill, James A., and Robert Sprinborg. *Politics in the Middle East*. New York: Harper, 1994.

Binder, Leonard, et al. *Crises and Sequence in Political Development*. Princeton: Princeton University Press, 1971.

Birdwood, Lord. *Nuri al-Said: A Study in Arab Leadership*. London: Cassell, 1959.

Birks, J. S., and J. A. Rimmer. *Developing Education Systems in the Oil States of Arabia: Conflicts of Purpose and Focus*. Durham: Centre for Middle Eastern and Islamic Studies, 1984.

Birks, J. S., and C. A. Sinclair. *International Migration and Development in the Arab Region*. Geneva: ILO, 1980.

Birks, J. S., I. J. Seccombe, and C. A. Sinclair. "Labour Migration in the Arab States: Patterns, Trends, and Prospects," *International Migration*, 26 (1988).

Bligh, Alexander. "The Saudi Religious Elite (Ulama) as Participant in the Political System of the Kingdom," *International Journal of the Middle East*, 17 (1985).

Bocco, Riccardo, and Tariq Tell. "*Pax Britannica* in the Steppe: British Policy and the Transjordan Bedouin," in Eugene L. Rogan and Tariq Tell (eds.). *Village, Steppe, and State: The Social Origins of Modern Jordan*. London: British Academic Press, 1994.

Bosworth, C. E. "The Titulature of the Early Ghaznavids," *Oriens*, 15 (1962).

Brand, Laurie. "'In the Beginning Was the State. . .': The Quest for Civil Society in Jordan," in Augustus R. Norton (ed.). *Civil Society in the Middle East*. Leiden: E. J. Brill, 1995.

———. "Liberalization and Changing Policial Coalitions: The Bases of Jordan's 1990–1991 Gulf Crisis Policy," *Jerusalem Journal of International Relations*, 13 (1991).

Bromley, Simon. *Rethinking Middle East Politics*. Austin: University of Texas Press, 1994.

Bulloch, John. *The Shura Council in Saudi Arabia*. London: Gulf Center for Strategic Studies, 1993.

Burgat, Francois. *L'islamisme au Maghreb, La voix du Sud*. Paris: Carthala, 1989.

———. "Qadhdhafi's Ideological Framework," in Dirk Vandervalle (ed.). *Libya, 1969–1994*. New York: St. Martin's Press, 1995.

Burrowes, Robert D. *The Yemen Arab Republic: The Politics of Development, 1962–1986*. Boulder: Westview Press, 1987.

Butovsky, Avriel. "Language of the Egyptian Monarchy," *Harvard Middle Eastern and Islamic Review,* 1 (1994).

Camau, Michel (ed.). *Changements politiques au Maghreb*. Paris: Editions du Centre National de la Recherche Scientifique, 1991.

Chardin, Jean. *Voyage du Chevalier Chardin*. Tr. Roger Savory. Amsterdam, 1711.

Chaudhry, Kiren Aziz. "The Price of Wealth: Business and State in Labor Remittance and Oil Economics," *International Organization*, 43 (1989).

———. *The Price of Wealth: Economies and Institutions in the Middle East*. Ithaca: Cornell University Press, 1997.

Claisse, Alain. "Makhzen Traditions and Administrative Channels," in William Zartman (ed.). *The Political Economy of Morocco*. New York: Praeger, 1987.

Clements, Frank A. *Oman: The Reborn Land*. London: Longman, 1980.

Cohen, Amnon. *Political Parties in the West Bank Under the Jordanian Regime, 1949–1967*. Ithaca: Cornell University Press, 1982.

Cole, Donald P. *Nomads of the Nomads: The Al Murrah Bedouin of the Empty Quarter.* Arlington Heights, Ill.: AHM Publishing, 1975.

Combs-Schilling, M. E. *Sacred Performances: Islam, Sexuality, and Performance.* New York: Columbia University Press, 1989.

The Constitution of the Kingdom of Morocco, 1972.

Copeland, Miles. *The Game of Nations.* London: Weidenfeld and Nicholson, 1969.

Crystal, Jill. "Authoritarianism and Its Adversaries in the Arab World," *World Politics,* 46 (1994).

———. "Coalitions in Oil Monarchies: Kuwait and Qatar," *Comparative Politics,* 21–22 (1989).

———. *Oil and Politics in the Gulf: Rulers and Merchants in Kuwait and Qatar.* New York: Cambridge University Press, 1990.

Dabashi, Hamid. *Authority in Islam.* New Brunswick, N.J.: Transaction Publishers, 1993.

Dakhlia, Jocelyne. *Le Divan des rois. Le Politique et le Religieax dans l'Islam.* Paris: Aubier, 1998.

———. *Dalil al-mar'a al-urdunniyya fil-hayat al-'amma wal-siyasiyya.* Amman: Konrad-Adenauer-Stiftung, 1996.

Damis, John. "Sources of Political Stability in Modernizing Monarchical Regimes: Jordan and Morocco," in Constantine P. Danopoulos (ed.). *Civilian Rule in the Developing World: Democracy on the March?* Boulder: Westview Press, 1992.

Dann, Uriel. "Regime and Opposition in Jordan Since 1949," in Menahem Milson (ed.). *Society and Political Structure in the Arab World.* New York: Humanities Press, 1973.

———. *King Hussein and the Challenge of Arab Radicalism: Jordan, 1955–1967.* Oxford: Oxford University Press, 1989.

Darif, Muhammad. *Al-Islam al-siyasi fi l-maghrib, "muqaraba watha'iqiyya."* 3rd ed. Casablanca: maktabat al-umma, 1991.

———. *Jama'at al-'adl wal-ihsan.* Casablanca: manshurat al-majalla al-maghribiyya li-'ilm al-ijtima' al-siyasi, 1995.

Darwish, Sa'id. *al-Marhala al-Dimuaratiyya al-Jadida fil-Urdun.* Amman: al-Muassahah, 1990.

Davis, Eric. "Theorizing Statecraft and Social Change in Arab Oil Producing Countries," in Eric Davis and Nicolas Gavrielidis (eds.). *Statecraft in the Middle East: Oil, Historical Memory, and Popular Culture.* Miami: Florida International University Press, 1991.

Dawn, Ernest. *From Ottomanism to Arabism.* Urbana: University of Illinois Press, 1973.

De Gaulle, Charles. *Memoires de Guerre: L'Appel, 1940–1942.* Paris: Plon, 1954.

Dekmejian, R. Hrair. *Islam in Revolution: Fundamentalism in the Arab World.* Albany: Syracuse University Press, 1985.

———. "The Rise of Political Islamism in Saudi Arabia," *Middle East Journal,* 48 (1994).

Dieterich, Renate. *Transformation Oder Stagnation? Die Jordanische Demokratisierungspolitik seit 1989.* Hamburg: Deutsches Orient-Institut, 1999.

Dodge, Toby. *An Arabian Prince, English Gentlemen, and the Tribes East of the River Jordan: Abdullah and the Creation and Consolidation of the Trans-Jordanian State.* Occasional Paper 13, Centre of Near and Middle Eastern Studies, School of Oriental and African Studies, University of London, 1994.

Douglas, Leigh. *The Free Yemeni Movement, 1935–1962.* Beirut: American University of Beirut Press, 1987.

Doumato, Eleanor Abdella. "Women and the Stability of Saudi Arabia," *Middle East Report*, 21 (1991).

Dresch, Paul. *Tribes, Government, and History in Yemen.* New York: Oxford University Press, 1993.

Eickelman, Dale F. "Kings and People: Oman's State Consultative Council," *The Middle East Journal*, 38 (1984).

——. *The Middle East: An Anthropological Approach.* 2nd ed. Englewood Cliffs, N.J.: Prentice Hall, 1989.

Elger, Ralf. *Zentralismus und Autonomie: Gelehrte und Staat in Marokko, 1890–1931.* Berlin: K. Schwarz, 1994.

Elias, N. *The Civilizing Process.* Oxford: Basil Blackwell, 1982.

——. *The Court Society.* Oxford: Basil Blackwell, 1983.

Eliot, Matthew. *'Independent Iraq': The Monarchy and British Influence, 1941–1958.* London: I. B. Tauris, 1996.

Enayat, Hamid. *Modern Islamic Political Thought.* Austin: University of Texas Press, 1988.

Endo, M. "Saudization: Development in the Early 1990s and Prospects for the Rest of the Decade," *JIME Review* (1996).

Entelis, John P. *Culture and Counterculture in Moroccan Politics.* Boulder: Westview Press, 1989.

Esposito, John L., and John O. Voll. *Islam and Democracy.* New York: Oxford University Press, 1976.

Faath, Sigrid. "'Le Hassanisme.' Das marokkanische Konzept von Demokratie," *Wuquf*, 4–5 (1989–1990).

Faghfoori, Mohammad. "The Ulama-State Relations in Iran: 1921–1941," *International Journal of the Middle East*, 19 (1987).

Fandy, Mamoun Hamza. *State Islam and State Violence: The Case of Saudi Arabia.* Unpublished Ph.D. dissertation, Southern Illinois University at Carbondale, 1993 (Ann Arbor: University Microfilms).

Faour, Muhammad. "Fertility Policy and Family Planning in the Arab Countries," *Studies in Family Planning*, 20 (1989).

Farah, Tawfic (ed.). *Pan-Arabism and Arab Nationalism: The Continuing Debate.* Boulder: Westview Press, 1987.

Farmanfarmaian, Manucher. *Blood and Oil.* New York: Random House, 1997.

Farouk, Marion, and Peter Sluglett. "The Social Classes and the Origins of the Revolution," in Robert A. Fernea and Wm. Roger Louis (eds.). *The Iraqi Revolution of 1958: The Old Social Classes Revisited.* London: I. B. Tauris, 1991.

Fathi, Schirin H. *Jordan: An Invented Nation?* Hamburg: Deutsches Orient-Institut, 1994.

Filippani-Ronconi, Pio. "The Tradition of Sacred Kingship in Iran," in George Lenczowski (ed.). *Iran Under the Pahlavis.* Stanford: Hoover Institution Press, 1978.

Fischbach, Michael. "British Land Policy in Transjordan," in Eugene Rogan and Tariq Tell (eds.). *Village, Steppe, and State: The Social Origins of Modern Jordan.* London: British Academic Press, 1994.

Fischer, Michael. "Imam Khomeini: Four Levels of Understanding," in John Esposito (ed.). *Voices of Resurgent Islam.* Oxford: Oxford University Press, 1983.

Fleischer, Cornell. "Royal Authority, Dynastic Cyclism, and 'Ibn Khaldunism' in Sixteenth Century Ottoman Letters," *Journal of Asian and African Studies*, 18 (1983).

Floor, Willem. "The Revolutionary Character of Ulama: Wishful Thinking or Reality?" in Nikki Keddie (ed.). *Religion and Politics in Iran: Shi'ism, from Quietism to Revolution.* New Haven: Yale University Press, 1983.

Foulquier, Jean-Michel. *Arabe Seoudite: La dictature protegee.* Paris: Albin Michel, 1995.

Franklin, Rob. "Migrant Labor and the Politics of Development in Bahrain," *Merip Reports,* 15 (1985).

Freij, Hanna, Y. Leonard, and C. Robinson. "Liberalization, the Islamists, and the Stability of the Arab State: Jordan as a Case Study," *Muslim World,* 86 (1966).

Gabrieli, Francesco. *Tribu e Stato nell'antica poesia araba,* in his *L'Islam nella storia.* Bari: Edizioni del Centro Librario, 1966.

Gallman, Waldemar. *Iraq Under General Nuri, 1954–1958.* Baltimore: Johns Hopkins University Press, 1964.

Gaury, Gerald de. *Faisal: King of Arabia.* London: Barker, 1966.

———. *Rulers of Mecca.* New York: Dorset Press, 1991.

Gause, F. Gregory III. "The Gulf Conundrum: Economic Change, Population Growth, and Political Stability in the GCC States," *Washington Quarterly,* 20 (1997).

———. *The Oil Monarchies.* New York: Council on Foreign Relations, 1993.

———. "Gulf Regional Politics: Revolution, War, and Rivalry," in W. Howard Wriggins (ed.). *The Dynamics of Regional Politics: Four Systems on the Indian Ocean Rim.* New York: Columbia University Press, 1992.

———. *Oil Monarchies: Domestic and Security Challenges in the Arab Gulf States.* New York: Council on Foreign Relations, 1994.

———. *Saudi-Yemeni Relations: Domestic Structures and Foreign Influence.* New York: Columbia University Press, 1990.

———. "Sovereignty, Statecraft, and Stability in the Middle East," *Journal of International Affairs,* 4 (1992).

Gellner, Ernest. *Nations and Nationalism.* Ithaca: Cornell University Press, 1983.

———. "Tribalism and State in the Middle East," in Philip S. Khoury and Jospeh Kostiner (eds.). *Tribes and State Formation in the Middle East.* Berkeley: University of California Press, 1990.

Gellner, Ernest, and John Waterbury (eds.). *Patrons and Clients in Mediterranean Societies.* London: Duckworth, 1977.

Gerges, Fawwaz. "The Kennedy Administration and the Egyptian-Saudi Conflict in Yemen: Co-opting Arab Nationalism," *Middle East Journal,* 49 (1995).

———. *The Superpowers and the Middle East: Regional and International Politics, 1955–1967.* Boulder: Westview Press, 1994.

Ghabra, Shafeeq. "Voluntary Associations in Kuwait: The Foundation of a New System?" *Middle East Journal,* 45 (1991).

Gilbar, Gad G. *The Middle East Oil Decade and Beyond.* London: Frank Cass, 1997.

Glubb, John Bagot. *The Story of the Arab Legion.* London: Hodder and Stoughton, 1946.

Goldberg, Jacob. "Saudi Arabia," in Ami Ayalon (ed.). *Middle East Contemporary Survey (MECS).* Vol. 14 (1990). Boulder and Tel Aviv: Westview Press and The Moshe Dayan Center of Middle Eastern and African Studies, Tel Aviv University, 1992.

———. "The Shi'i Minority in Saudi Arabia," in Juan I. R. Cole and Nikki R. Keddie (eds.). *Shi'ism and Social Protest.* New Haven: Yale University Press, 1986.

Gordon, Joel. *Nasser's Blessed Movement.* New York: Oxford University Press, 1992.

Great Britain. Central Office of Information, Reference Division. *Aden and South Arabia.* June 1966.

Greenstein, Fred. "Personality and Politics: Problems of Evidence, Inference, and Conceptualization," in Seymour Martin Lipset (ed.). *Politics and the Social Sciences*. New York: Oxford University Press, 1969.

Grinaschi, M. "Quelques specimens de la litterature sassanide conserves dans les bibliotheques d'Istanbul," *Journal Asiatique*, vol. 254.

"Growing Concern over Dependence on Foreign Workers," *Arab Oil*, September 1983.

Gubser, Peter. "Balancing Pluralism and Authoritarianism," in Peter J. Chelkowski and Robert J. Pranger (eds.). *Ideology and Power in the Middle East*. Durham: Duke University Press, 1988.

Habermas, J. *Legitimation Crisis*. London: Heinemann, 1976.

Hairi, Abdul Hadi. *Shi'ism and Constitutionalism in Iran: A Study of the Role Played by the Persian Residents of Iraq in Iranian Politics*. Leiden: Brill, 1977.

Halliday, Fred. *Arabia Without Sultans*. London: Penguin Books, 1974.

Halpern, Manfred. "Middle Eastern Studies: A Review of the State of the Field with a Few Examples," *World Politics,* 15 (1962).

———. *The Politics of Social Change in the Middle East and North Africa*. Princeton: Princeton University Press, 1963.

———. "Toward Further Modernization of File Study of New Nations," *World Politics*, 17 (1964).

al-Hamad, Turki. "Tawhid al-jazira al-'arabiyya: dawr al-idiulujiyya wal-tanzim fi tahtim al-bunya al-'ijtima'iyya al-iqtisadiyya al-mu'iqa lil-wahda," *al-mustaqbal al-'arabi*, 93 (1986).

Hammoudi, Abdellah. *Master and Disciple: The Cultural Foundations of Moroccan Authoritarianism*. Chicago: Chicago University Press, 1997.

Hansen, Bent, and Samir Radwan. *Employment Opportunities and Equity in a Changing Economy: Egypt in the 1980s, a Labour Market Approach*. Geneva: ILO, 1982.

Harik, Ilya. "The Origins of the Arab State System," in Giacomo Luciani (ed.). *The Arab State*. London: Routledge, 1990.

al-Hasan, Hamza. *al-Shi'a fil-mamlaka al-'arabiyya al-sa'udiyya, al-'ahd al-sa'udi, 1913–1991. S.1: mu'assasat al-baqi' li-ihya' al-turath*, 1993.

Hashim, Ahmed. *The Crisis of the Iranian State*. London: Adelphi Papers No. 296, International Institute for Strategic Studies, 1995.

al-Hawali, Safar. *Kashf al-ghama 'an 'ulama' al-umma*. London: 1991.

Hawatmeh, George (ed.). *The Role of the Media in a Democracy: The Case of Jordan*. Amman: Center for Strategic Studies/Konrad Adenauer Foundation, 1994.

Heard-Bey, Frauke. *From Trucial States to United Arab Emirates*. London: Longman, 1982.

Hedayat, Mehdi Qoli. *Khaterat va Khatarat*. Tehran: Rangin, 1950/51.

Hegasy, Sonja. *Staat Öffentlichkeit und Zivilgesellschaft in Marokko*. Hamburg: Deutsches Orient Institute, 1997.

Heller, Mark, and Nadav Safran. *The New Middle Class and Regime Stability in Saudi Arabia*. Center for Middle East Studies, Harvard University, Harvard Middle East Papers, No. 1, 1985.

Helms, Christine Moss. *The Cohesion of Saudi Arabia: Evolution of Political Identity*. London: Croom Helm, 1981.

Henderson, Simon. *After King Fahd: Succession in Saudi Arabia*. Washington Institute for Near East Policy, Policy Paper No. 37, 1994.

Hijazi, I. *Nahwa 'Ilm Ijtima' 'Arabi*. Beirut: Center for Arab Unity Studies, 1986.

Hill, Allan G. "Population Growth in the Middle East and North Africa: Selected Policy Issues," in A. L. Udovich (ed.). *The Middle East: Oil, Conflict, and Hope.* Lexington: Lexington Books, 1976.

al-Hinai, Ali Masoud. *The Dynamics of Omani Foreign Policy: Omani-Gulf Relations, 1971–1985.* Unpublished dissertation, University of Kent at Canterbury (UK), 1991.

Holden, David, and Richard Johns. *The House of Saud: The Rise and Rule of the Most Powerful Dynasty in the Arab World.* New York: Holt, Rinehart, and Winston, 1981.

Hourani, Albert. *Arabic Thought in the Liberal Age, 1798–1939.* Cambridge: Cambridge University Press, rep. 1997.

———. *The Emergence of the Modern Middle East.* Berkeley: University of California Press, 1981.

Hourani, Mani (ed.). *Islamic Movements in Jordan.* Amman: al-Urdunn al-Jadid and Friedrich-Erbert-Stiftung, 1997.

Hudson, Michael C. "The Political Culture Approach to Arab Democratization: The Case for Bringing It Back In, Carefully," in Bahgat Korany, Rex Brynen, and Paul Noble (eds.). *Political Liberalization and Democratization in the Arab World. Vol. 1: Theoretical Perspective.* Boulder: Lynne Rienner Publishers, 1995.

———. *Arab Politics: The Search for Legitimacy.* New Haven: Yale University Press, 1977.

Human Rights Watch. *Empty Reforms: Saudi Arabia's New Basic Laws.* New York, Washington, D.C., 1992.

———. "Human Rights in Morocco," *Human Rights Watch/Middle East,* 7, October 1995.

Huntington, Samuel P. *Political Order in Changing Societies.* New Haven: Yale University Press, 1968.

Hurewitz, J. C. *Middle East Politics: The Military Dimension.* New York: Octagon Press, 1974.

Husayn, Abdullah bin. *Mudhakkirat.* Jerusalem: Matbaat Beit al-Mukades, 1945.

Hussein, King. *Uneasy Lies the Head: The Autobiography of His Majesty King Hussein I of the Hashemite Kingdom of Jordan.* New York: Bernard Geis Associates, 1962.

Huyette, Summer. *Political Adaptation in Saudi Arabia: A Study of the Council of Ministers.* Boulder: Westview Press, 1985.

Ibrahim, Saad Edin. "Crises, Elites, and Democratization in the Arab World," *Middle East Journal,* 47 (1993).

Inalcik, Halil. "Comment on 'Sultanism': Max Weber's Typification of the Ottoman Polity." Princeton Papers in Near Eastern Studies No. 1 (1992).

Isma'il, Jacqueline S. *Kuwait: Social Change in Historical Perspective.* New York: Syracuse University Press, 1982.

abu Jaber, Kamel S., and Schirin H. Fathi. "The 1989 Jordanian Parliamentary Elections," *Orient,* 31 (1990).

Joyce, Ann. "Interview with Sultan Qabus bin Sa'id Al Sa'id," *Middle East Policy,* 3 (1995).

al-Juzaylan, Abdullah. *al-Ta'rikh al-Sirri lil-Thawra al-Yamaniyya.* Cairo: Madbuli Bookstore, 1979.

Kadivar, Mohsen. *Nazariye-haye Doulat dar Fiqh-e Shi'e.* Tehran: Nashr-e Ney 1997/98.

al-Kaylani, Musa Zayd (ed.). *al-Harakat al-Islamiyya fil-Urdunn.* Amman: Dar al-Bashir, 1990.

Kaylani, Nabil M. "Politics and Religion in Uman: A Historical Overview," *International Journal of Middle Eastern Studies*, 10 (1979).

Kazemi, Farhad. "Civil Society and Iranian Politics," in Augustus R. Norton (ed.). *Civil Society in the Middle East*. Leiden: Brill, 1996.

Kechichian, Joseph A. "Islamic Revivalism and Change in Saudi Arabia: Juhayman al-'Utaybi's 'Letters' to the Saudi People," *Muslim World*, 80 (1990).

———. "The Role of the Ulama in the Politics of an Islamic State: The Case of Saudi Arabia," *International Journal of Middle Eastern Studies*, 18 (1986).

Keddie, Nikki. *Roots of Revolution: An Interpretive History of Modern Iran*. New Haven: Yale University Press, 1981.

———. "Religion, Society, and Revolution in Modern Iran," in Michael Bonine and Nikki Keddie (eds.). *Continuity and Change in Mordern Iran*. Albany: SUNY Press, 1981.

Kedourie, Elie. *Democracy and Arab Political Culture*. Washington, D.C.: Washington Institute for Near East Policy, 1992.

———. "Egypt and the Caliphate Question, 1915–1952," in Elie Kedourie (ed.). *The Chatham House Version and Other Middle Eastern Studies*. 2nd ed. Hanover, N.H.: University Press of New England, 1984.

———. *In the Anglo-Arab Labyrinth*. Cambridge: Cambridge University Press, 1976.

———. "The Genesis of the Egyptian Constitution of 1923," in Elie Kedourie (ed.). *The Chatham House Version and Other Middle Eastern Studies*. 2nd ed. Hanover, N.H.: University Press of New England, 1984.

———. *Politics in the Middle East*. London: Oxford University Press, 1992.

———. "The Kingdom of Iraq: A Retrospect," in Elie Kedourie (ed.). *The Chatham House Version and Other Middle Eastern Studies*. 2nd ed. Hanover, N.H.: University Press of New England, 1984.

Kerr, Malcolm. *The Arab Cold War*. 3rd ed. New York: Oxford University Press, 1971.

Khadduri, Majid. *Arab Contemporaries*. Baltimore: Johns Hopkins University Press, 1973.

———. *Arab Personalities in Politics*. Washington, D.C.: The Middle East Institute, 1981.

———. *Independent Iraq, 1932–1958*. Oxford: Oxford University Press, 1960.

Khalidi, Rashid, et al., eds. *The Origins of Arab Nationalism*. New York: Columbia University Press, 1991.

Khalidi, T. *Classical Arab Islam*. Princeton, N.J.: Darwin, 1985.

al-Khalil, Samir (pseud.). *Republic of Fear: The Inside Story of Saddam's Iraq*. New York: Pantheon Books, 1989.

Khomeini, Ayatollah Ruhollah. *Islam and Revolution: Writings and Declarations*. Trans. and anno. Hamid Algar. London: KPI, 1985.

———. *Kashf al-Asrar*. Tehran: Zaffar, 1979.

Khoury, Philip S. *Urban Notables and Arab Nationalism*. Cambridge: Cambridge University Press, 1983.

———. *Syria and the French Mandate*. Princeton: Princeton University Press, 1987.

Khuri, Fu'ad I., ed. *Leadership and Development in Arab Society*. Beirut: American University of Beirut, 1981.

———. *Tribe and State in Bahrain*. Chicago: University of Chicago Press, 1980.

Kingston, Paul. "Breaking the Patterns of Mandate: Economic Nationalism and State Formation in Jordan, 1951–1957," in Eugene Rogan and Tariq Tell (eds.). *Village, Steppe, and State: The Social Origin of Modern Jordan*. London: British Academic Press, 1994.

Kirkbride, Alec. *From the Wings: Amman Memoirs, 1947–1951*. London: Frank Cass, 1976.

Kishk, Muhammad Jallal. *al-Sa'udiyyun wa-l-hall al-Islami, masdar al-Shar'iyya lil-nizam al-Sa'udi*. 4th ed. Cairo: al-Matba'a al-Fanniyya, 1981.

Klieman, Aaron S. *Foundations of British Policy in the Arab World*. Baltimore: Johns Hopkins University Press, 1970.

Kohli, A. L., and Musa'ad al-Omaim. "Changing Patterns of Migration in Kuwait," *Population Bulletin of ESCWA* (Economic and Social Commission for Western Asia), 32, June 1988.

Kostiner, Joseph. *From Chieftaincy to Monarchical State: The Making of Saudi Arabia, 1916–1936*. New York: Oxford University Press, 1993.

———. "Kuwait," in Ami Ayalon (ed.). *Middle East Contemporary Survey (MECS)*. Vol. 15. Boulder and Tel Aviv: Westview Press and the Moshe Dayan Center for Middle Eastern Studies, Tel Aviv University, 1993.

———. "Shi'i Unrest in the Gulf," in Martin Kramer (ed.). *Shi'ism, Resistance, and Revolution*. Boulder and London: Westview Press and Mansell Publishing, 1987.

———. "State-Building and Radical Islam in Saudi Arabia: The Decline of 'Faysal's Order,' unpublished paper.

———. *The Struggle for South Yemen*. New York: St. Martin's Press, 1984.

———. "Transforming Dualities: Tribe and State Formation in Saudi Arabia," in Philip S. Khoury and Joseph Kostiner (eds.). *Tribes and State Formation in the Middle East*. Berkeley: University of California Press, 1990.

Krämer, Gudrun. "Cross-Links and Double Talk? Islamist Movements in the Political Process," in Laura Guazzone (ed.). *The Islamist Dilemma*. Reading, UK: Ithaca Press, 1995.

———. "The Integration of the Integrist: A Comparative Study of Egypt, Jordan, and Tunisia," in Ghassan Salame (ed.). *Democracy Without Democrats? The Renewal of Politics in the Muslim World*. New York: I. B. Tauris, 1994.

———. "Islamist Notions of Democracy," in Joel Beinin and Joe Stork (eds.). *Political Islam: Essays from Middle East Report*. Berkeley: University of California Press, 1997.

———. "Die Korrektur der Irrtuemer: Innerislamische Debatten um Theorie und Praxis der zeitgenossischen islamischen Bewegungen," *Zeitschrift der Deutschen Morgenlandischen Gesellschaft*, Suppl. 10 (1994).

———. "Techniques and Values: Contemporary Muslim Debates on Islam and Democracy," in Gema Martin Munoz (ed.). *Islam, Modernism, and the West: Cultural and Political Relations at the End of the Millennium*. New York: I. B. Tauris, 1999.

Kuhn, Thomas. *The Structure of Scientific Revolutions*. Chicago: University of Chicago Press, 1968.

Kuwait, State of. Ministry of Planning, Central Statistical Office, *Annual Statistical Abstract, 1981–1989*, various issues (Kuwait).

Lacey, Robert. *The Kingdom: Arabia and the House of Saud*. New York: Avon Books, 1981.

Lackner, Helen. *A House Built on Sand: A Political Economy of Saudi Arabia*. London: Ithaca Press, 1978.

Laitin, David. *Language Repertoires and State Construction in Africa*. Cambridge: Cambridge University Press, 1992.

Lajna min Tanzim al-Dubat al-Ahrar. *Asrar wa Watha'iq al-Thawra al-Yamaniyya*. Beirut: dar al-'awda, 1978.

Lambton, Ann. "A Reconsideration of the Position of the Marja' al-Taqlid and the Religious Institution," *Studia Islamica*, 1964.

———. *Qajar Persia*. Austin: University of Texas Press, 1987.

Lamchichi, Abderrahim. *Islam et Contestation au Maghreb*. Paris: L'Harmattan, 1991.

Lamote, Laurent (pseud.). "Domestic Politics and Strategic Intentions," in Patrick Clawson (ed.). *Iran's Strategic Intentions and Capabilities*. Washington, D.C.: National Defense University, 1994.

Landen, Robert G. *Oman Since 1856: Disruptive Modernization in a Traditional Arab Society*. Princeton: Princeton University Press, 1967.

LaPalombara, Joseph. *Politics Within Nations*. Englewood Cliffs, N.J.: Prentice Hall, 1974.

Lapidus, Ira. *A History of Islamic Societies*. New York: Cambridge University Press, 1988.

Lawson, Fred H. *Bahrain: The Modernization of Autocracy*. Boulder: Westview Press, 1989.

Layish, Aharon. "Saudi Arabian Legal Reform as a Mechanism to Moderate Wahhabi Doctrine," *Journal of the American Oriental Society*, 107 (1987).

Layne, Linda L. *Home and Homeland: The Dialogics of Tribal and National Identities in Jordan*. Princeton: Princeton University Press, 1994.

———. "Tribesmen as Citizens: 'Primordial Ties' and Democracy in Rural Jordan," in Linda Layne (ed.). *Elections in the Middle East: Implications of Recent Trends*. Boulder: Westview Press, 1987.

Legrain, Jean-François. "La Conference de Teheran," held 19–22 October 1991 to oppose the Madrid conference, *Maghreb-Machrek*, 15 (1991).

Lerner, Daniel. *The Passing of Traditional Society*. Glencoe, Ill.: Free Press, 1958.

Leveau, Remy. *Le fellah marocain defenseur du trone*. Paris: Presses de la FNSP, 1985.

———. "Le pouvoir marocain entre la repression et le dialogue," *Le Monde Diplomatique* (October 1993).

———. "Reussir la transition democratique au Maroc," *Le Monde Diplomatique* (October 1993).

———. "Stabilite du pouvoir monarchique et financement de la dette," *Maghreb-Machrek*, 11 (1987).

Lewis, Bernard. *The Emergence of Modern Turkey*. Oxford: Oxford University Press, 1961.

———. "Malik," *Cahiers de Tunisie, Tunis*, 35 (1987).

———. *The Political Language of Islam*. Chicago: Chicago University Press, 1989.

———. "Usurpers and Tyrants: Notes on Some Islamic Political Terms," in Roger M. Savory and Dionisius A. Agius (eds.). *Logos Islamikos: Studia Islamica in honerem Georgii Michaelis Wickens*. Papers in Medieval Studies 006, Toronto, Pontifical Institute of Medieval Studies, 1984.

Lienhardt, P. "The Authority of Shaykhs in the Gulf: An Essay in Nineteenth Century History," *Arabian Studies*, 2 (1975).

Looney, Robert E. *The Economic Development of Saudi Arabia: Consequences of the Oil Prices Decline*. Greenwich and London: JAI Press, 1990.

Louis, Roger. "The British and the Origins of the Revolution," in Robert A. Fernea and Wm. Roger Louis (eds.). *The Iraqi Revolution of 1958: The Old Social Classes Revisited*. London: I. B. Tauris, 1991.

———. *The British Empire in the Middle East*. Oxford: Clarendon Press, 1984.

Lunt, James. *Hussein of Jordan: A Political Biography*. London: Macmillan, 1989.

Lyall, Sir Charles, ed. and tr. *The Diwans of Abid b. al-Abras and Amir b. al-Tufayl.* London: Printed for the trustees of the E.J.W. Gibb Memorial by Luzac, 1913.

Maddy-Weitzman, Bruce. *The Crystallization of the Arab State System, 1945–1954.* Syracuse: Syracuse University Press, 1993.

Madelung, Wilferd. "The Assumption of the Title Shahanshah by the Buyids and the Reign of the Daylam Dawlat al-Daylam," *Journal of Near Eastern Studies,* 28 (1969).

al-Majid, Muhammad Abd. *al-Tamyiz al-ta'ifi fi al-sa'udiyya.* London: Rabitat 'Umum al-Shi'a fil-Sa'udiyya. n.d.

al-Majlis al-Ishtishari lil-Dawlat. *Abr 'Aq Min al-Zaman, 1981–1991.* Muscat: Dar Jaridat 'Uman, n.d.

Makki, Husayn. *Ta'rikh-e bist Saleh-e Iran.* Tehran, 1945.

Malcolm, John. *History of Persia.* London, 1815.

el-Mansour, M. "Les Qulemas et le Makhzen dans le Maroc Precolonial," in Robert Santucci (ed.). *Le Maroc actuel.* Paris, 1992.

Marlow, John. *Arab Nationalism and British Imperialism.* London: Cresset Press, 1961.

Marlow, Louise. "Kings, Prophets, and the 'Ulama' in Medieval Islamic Advice Literature," *Studia Islamica,* 81–82 (1995).

Marr, Phebe. *The Modern History of Iraq.* Boulder: Westview Press, 1985.

McLachlan, Keith. "Oil in the Persian Gulf Area," in Alvin J. Cottrell (ed.). *The Persian Gulf States: A General Survey.* Baltimore: Johns Hopkins University Press, 1980.

Meguid, Walid Abdel. "The Islamic Movement in Jordan and Palestine: The Case of the Muslim Brothers (al-Ikhwan al-Muslimin)," in Ola A. Abou Zeid (ed.). *Islamic Movements in a Changing World.* Cairo: Center for Political Research and Studies/Friedrich-Erbert-Stiftung, 1995.

Menashri, David. *Iran: A Decade of War and Revolution.* New York: Holmes and Meier, 1990.

———. *Iran in Revolution* (in Hebrew). Tel Aviv: Hakibutz Hameuhad, 1988.

———. *Revolution at a Crossroads: Iran's Domestic Politics and Regional Ambitions.* Washington, D.C.: Washington Institute for Near East Policy, 1997.

———. "Shi'ite Leadership: In the Shadow of Conflicting Ideologies," *Iranian Studies,* 13 (1980).

———. "Whither Iranian Politics? The Khatami Factor," in Patrick Clawson, et al. *Iran Under Khatami: A Political Economic and Military Assessment.* Washington, D.C.: Washington Institute for Near East Policy, 1998.

Migdal, Joel. *Strong Societies and Weak States.* Princeton: Princeton University Press, 1988.

al-Mithaq al-Watani wal-Tahawwul al-Dimuqrati fil-Urdun. Amman: al-Urdunn al-Jadid and Konrad-Adenauer-Stiftung, 1997.

Mohsen-Finan, Khadija. *Sahara occidental. Les enjeux d'un conflit regional.* Paris: CNRS, 1997.

Moore, Barrington. *Social Origins of Dictatorship and Democracy.* Harmondsworth: Penguin, 1969.

Morris, James. *Sultan in Oman: Venture into the Middle East.* New York: Pantheon, 1957.

Morris, Jan. *The Hashemite Kings.* London: Faber and Faber, 1956.

Mostowfi, Abdollah. *Sharh-e Zendegani-ye Man, ya Tarikh-e Ejtema'i va Edari Dowre-ye Qajariye.* Tehran: Zaddar, 1964.

Mottahedeh, Roy P. "The Islamic Movement: The Case of Democratic Inclusion," *Contention*, 4 (1995).

Mudhakkirat al-Nashia, Nashiat al-'Ulama' Lihukkam al-Sa'udiyya al-Umala. n.p., n.d.

Munson, Jr., Henry. *Religion and Power in Morocco*. New Haven: Yale University Press, 1993.

——. "The Social Base of Islamic Militancy in Morocco," *Middle East Journal*, 40 (1986).

Musa, Sulayman. *al-haraka al-'Arabiyya*. Beirut: Dar al-Tahar Lilnashir, 1970.

al-Muta'anni, *'Abd al-'Azim. Jarimat al-'asr. . .?!! qissat ihtilal al-masjid al-haram*. Cairo: Dar al-Ansar bil-Qahira, 1980.

Mutawi, Samir. *Jordan in the 1967 War*. Cambridge: Cambridge University Press, 1987.

Nafi, Zuhair Ahmed. *Economic and Social Development in Qatar*. London and Dover: Frances Pinter Publishers, 1983.

Nahost Jahrbuch 1994. Hamburg: Deutsches Orient Institut, 1995.

al-Nahwi, Adnan Ali. *Malamih al-Shura fil-Da'wa al-Islamiyya*. 2nd ed. Cairo: al-Farazdaq Press, 1984.

al-Najdi, Abu al-Bara. *al-Kawashif al-Jahiliyya fi Kufr al-Dawla al-Sa'udiyya*. Denmark: Al-Nur Islamic Beghandel, 1992.

al-Najjar, Baquer Salman. "Population Policies in the Countries of the Gulf Cooperation Council: Politics and Society," *Immigrants and Minorities*, 12 (1993).

al-Najjar, Muhammad Rajab. "Contemporary Trends in the Study of Folklore in the Arab Gulf States," in Eric Davis and Nicolas Gavrielides (eds.). *Statecraft in the Middle East: Oil, Historical Memory, and Popular Culture*. Miami: Florida International University Press, 1991.

abu-Namay, Rashed. "Constitutional Reform: A Systemization of Saudi Politics," *Journal of South Asian and Middle Eastern Studies*, 16 (1993).

——. "The Dynamics of Individual Rights and Their Prospective Development Under the New Constitution of Saudi Arabia," *Journal of South Asian and Middle Eastern Studies*, 18 (1995).

——. "The Recent Constitutional Reforms in Saudi Arabia," *International and Comparative Law Quarterly*, 42 (1993).

al-Naqib, Khaldun. *al-Mujtama' wal-Dawla fil-Khalij wal-Jazira al-'Arabiyya min Manzur Mukhtalaf*. Beirut: Markaz Dirasat al-Wahda al-'Arabiyya, 1987.

Nasr, Seyyed Hossein, Hamid Dabbashi, and Seyyed Vali Reza Nasr (eds.). *Expectation of the Millennium: Shi'ism in History*. Albany: SUNY Press, 1989.

Nasser, Gamal Abdul [Abd al-Nasir]. *Egypt's Liberation: The Philosophy of the Revolution*. Washington, D.C.: Public Affairs Press, 1955.

Nevo, Joseph, and Ilan Pape (eds.). *Jordan in the Middle East, 1948–1988: The Making of a Pivotal State*. London: Frank Cass, 1994.

Niblock, Tim. "Social Structure and the Development of the Saudi Arabian Political System," in T. Niblock (ed.). *State, Society, and Economy in Saudi Arabia*. London: Croom Helm, 1982.

Niun Abd al-Mun'im Mus'ad. "Jadaliyyat al-Istib'ad wal-Musharaka Muqarana bayna Jabhat al-Inqadh al-Islamiyya fil-Jaza'ir wa Jamma'at al-Ikhwan al-Muslimin fil-urdunn," *al-Mustaqbal al-'Arabi*, 13 (1991).

Nyrop, Richard F., et al. *Area Handbook for Saudi Arabia*. 3rd ed. Washington, D.C.: U.S. Government Printing Office, 1977.

Ochsenwald, William L. "Saudi Arabia and the Islamic Revival," *International Journal of Middle Eastern Studies*, 13 (1981).

Oman, Sultanate of. *Oman: A Modern State*. Muscat: Ministry of Information, 1988.

Owen, Roger. "Class and Class Politics in Iraq Before 1958: The 'Colonial and Post-Colonial State,'" in Robert A. Fernea and Wm. Roger Louis (eds.). *The Iraqi Revolution of 1958*. London: I. B. Tauris, 1991.

————. *Migrant Workers in the Gulf*. London: Minority Rights Group Ltd., 1985.

Pahlavi, Mohammad Reza [Shah]. *Enqelab-e Sefid*. Tehran, 1966.

Pahlavi, Farah. *My Thousand and One Days: An Autobiography*. London: W. H. Allen, 1978.

————. *Mission for My Country*. London: Hutchinson, 1961.

Parker, Richard. *North Africa: Regional Tensions and Strategic Concerns*. New York: Praeger, 1984.

Penrose, Edith Tilton. *Iraq: International Relations and National Development*. London and Boulder: Ernest Benn and Westview Press, 1978.

Peterson, J. E. *Oman in the Twentieth Century: Political Foundation of an Emerging State*. London and New York: Croom Helm and Barnes and Noble Books, 1978.

————. *The Arab Gulf States: Steps Toward Political Participation*. New York: Praeger, for the Center for Strategic and International Studies, Washington, D.C., 1988.

————. *Yemen: The Search for the Modern State*. Baltimore: Johns Hopkins University Press, 1982.

Philby, H. St. John. "The New Reign in Saudi Arabia," *Foreign Affairs*, 32 (1954).

Picard, E. "Arab Military in Politics: From Revolutionary Plot to Authoritarian State," in A. Dawisha and W. Zartman (eds.). *Beyond Coercion: The Durability of the Arab State*. London: Croom Helm, 1988.

Piscatori, James (ed.). *Islamic Fundamentalism and the Gulf Crisis*. Chicago: University of Chicago Press, 1992.

————. "Ideological Politics in Saudi Arabia," in James Piscatori (ed.). *Islam in the Political Process*. Cambridge: Cambridge University Press, 1983.

The Population Division of the UN Department of International Economic and Social Affairs and the UN Fund for Population Activities (UNFPA). *Population Policy Compendium: Bahrain*. New York, 1980.

Porath, Yehoshua. *In Search of Arab Unity, 1930–1945*. London: Frank Cass, 1986.

al-Qahtani, Fahd. *al-Islam wal-wataniyya al-Sa'udiyya*. London: Munazzamat al-Thawra al-Islamiyya, 1985.

al-Quisi, Issa. "Discrimination and Earning Differentials in the Kuwait Labor Market," Industrial Bank of Kuwait (IBK) Papers No. 29 (September 1998).

al-Rafi'i, Abd al-Rahman. *Thawrat 23 Yulyu—1952*. Cairo: Dar al-Ma'arif, 1959.

al-Rasheed, Madawi, and Loulouwa al-Rasheed. "The Politics of Encapsulation: Saudi Policy Towards Tribal and Religious Opposition," *Middle Eastern Studies*, 32 (1996).

Reissner, Johannes. "Die Besetzung der Grossen Moschee in Mekka," *Orient*, 21 (1980).

Rekhess, Elie. "The Iranian Impact on the Islamic Jihad Movement in the Gaza Strip," in David Menashri (ed.). *The Iranian Revolution and the Muslim World*. Boulder: Westview Press, 1990.

Repertoire Chronologique d'Epigraphie Arabe (RCEA). Cairo, 1931.

Richards, Alan, and John Waterbury (eds.). *A Political Economy of the Middle East: State, Class, and Economic Development*. Boulder: Westview Press, 1990.

al-Rifa'i, Mahmud. al-*Mashru' al-Islahi fil-Sa'udiyya: Qissat al-Hawali wal-'Awda.* n.p., 1995.

Robins, Philip J. "Politics and the 1986 Electoral Law in Jordan," in Rodney Wilson (ed.). *Politics and the Economy in Jordan.* London: Routledge, 1991.

Rosenfeld, Henry. "The Military Forces Used to Achieve and Maintain Power and the Meaning of Its Social Composition: Slaves, Mercenaries, and Townsmen," *Journal of the Royal Anthropological Institute*, 95 (1965).

———. "The Social Composition of the Military in the Process of State Formation in the Arabian Desert," *Journal of the Royal Anthropological Institute*, 95 (1965).

Roy, Olivier. *The Failure of Political Islam.* Cambridge: Harvard University Press, 1994.

Rubin, Barry. *The Arab States and the Palestine Question.* Syracuse: Syracuse University Press, 1981.

al-Rumaihi, Muhammad. "Harakat 1938 al-Islahiyya fil-Kuwayt wal-Bahrayn wa Dubbay," *Journal of the Gulf and Arabian Peninsula Studies*, 1 (1975).

Rush, Alan. *Al-Sabah: History and Genealogy of Kuwait's Ruling Family, 1752–1987.* London: Ithaca Press, 1987.

Ruzayq, Hamid bin Muhammad. *al-Fath al-Mubin fi Sirat al-Sada Al Bu Sa'idiyyin.* Cairo: 1977.

Sa'ati, Amin. *al-Shura fil-Mamlaka al-'Arabiyya al-Sa'udiyya min al-Malik 'Abd al-'Aziz ila al-Malik Fahd bin 'Abd al-'Aziz.* Cairo: al-Markaz al-Sa'udi lil-Dirasat al-Istratijiyya, 1991.

Sabah, Salim al Jabir. *Les Emirats du Golfe: Histoire d'un People.* Paris, 1980.

Sachedina, Abdulaziz. "Who Will Lead the Shi'a? Is the Crisis of Religious Leadership in Shi'ism Imagined or Real?" *Middle East Insight*, 11 (1995).

al-Sadat, Anwar. *In Search of Identity.* New York: Harper and Row, 1977.

Safran, Nadav. *Egypt in Search of Political Community.* Cambridge: Harvard University Press, 1961.

———. Saudi Arabia: *The Ceaseless Quest for Security.* Cambridge: Harvard University Press, 1985.

Salame, Ghassan. "Islam and Politics in Saudi Arabia," *Arab Studies Quarterly*, 9 (1987).

———. "Political Power and the Saudi State," in Albert Hourani, Philip Khouri, and Mary Wilson (eds.). *The Modern Middle East.* London: I. B. Tauris, 1993.

Salibi, Kamal. *The Modern History of Jordan.* London: I. B. Tauris, 1993.

al-Salimi, Nur al-Din 'Abdallah bin Humayd. *Tuhfat al-'Ayam Bi Sirat Ahl Uman.* Cairo: Matbaat al-Immam, 1966.

Satloff, Robert. *From Abdullah to Hussein; Jordan in Transition.* Oxford: Oxford University Press, 1994.

———. *Troubles on the East Bank: Challenges to the Domestic Stability of Jordan.* New York: Praeger, 1986.

Savory, Roger. "The Export of Ithna Ashari Shi'ism: Historical and Ideological Background," in David Menashri (ed.). *The Iranian Revolution and the Muslim World.* Boulder: Westview Press, 1990.

Sayegh, Fayez. *Arab Unity: Hope or Fulfillment?* New York: Devin-Adair, 1958.

Sayigh, Yezid. "Jordan in the 1980s: Legitimacy, Entity, and Identity," in Rodney Wilson (ed.). *Politics and the Economy in Jordan.* London: Routledge, 1991.

Sha'iri, Jammal. "tajribat al-Dimuqratiyya fil-Urdun," in Markaz Dirasat al-Wahda al-Arabiyya (ed.). *Azmat al-Dimokratiyya fil-Watan al-'Arabi.* Beirut, 1984.

Shams, Jallal. "Al-Fikr al-Idari fi Majlis al-Istishari li-dawlat 'Uman," *Al-Idari*, 4 (1982).

Sharabi, Hisham. *Nationalism and Revolution in the Arab World*. Princeton: Van Norstrand, 1966.

————. *Neopatriarchy: A Theory of Distorted Change in Arab Society*. New York: Oxford University Press, 1988.

al-Shaykh, Abd al-Rahman. *Intifadat al-Mintaqa al-Sharqiyya*. London: Munazamat al-Thawra al-Islamiyya, 1981.

Shirley, Edward G. (pseud.). "Fundamentalism in Power: Is Iran's Present Algeria's Future?" *Foreign Affairs*, 74 (1995).

————. "The Iran Policy Trap," *Foreign Affairs*, 74 (1995).

Sick, Gary. "A Sensitive Policy Toward Iran," *Middle East Insight*, 6 (1995).

Skeet, Ian. *Muscat and Oman: The End of an Era*. London: Faber and Faber, 1974.

Skocpol, T. "Rentier State and Shi'a Islam in the Iranian Revolution," *Theory and Society*, 2 (1982).

————. *States and Social Revolutions*. Cambridge: Cambridge University Press, 1979.

Soboul, Albert. *The French Revolution, 1787–1799*. London: NLB 1974.

Sorush, Abdul-Karim. "He Who Was Bazargan by Name and Not by Attribute," *Kiyan*, 4 (1995).

————. *Farbetar az Ideolojy*. Tehran: Sarat, 1993.

The Speeches of H. M. Sultan Qabus bin Said, Sultan of Oman, 1970–1990. 1991.

Stanton Russell, Sharon. "Politics and Ideology in Migration Policy Formulation: The Case of Kuwait," *International Migration Review*, 23 (1989).

Stookey, Robert W. *Yemen: The Politics of the Yemen Arab Republic*. Boulder: Westview Press, 1978.

Storrs, Ronald. *Orientations*. London: Nicholson and Watson 1937.

Susser, Asher. "Jordan," in Ami Ayalon (ed.). *Middle East Contemporary Survey (MECS)*. Vols. 15–17. Boulder and Tel Aviv: Westview Press and the Moshe Dayan Center for Middle Eastern Studies, Tel Aviv University, 1991 and 1993.

————. "Jordan," in Amy Ayalon and Bruce Maddy-Weitzman (eds.). *Middle East Contemporary Survey (MECS)*. Vol. 18. Boulder and Tel Aviv: Westview Press and the Moshe Dayan Center for Middle Eastern Studies, Tel Aviv University, 1996.

————. "Introduction," in Asher Susser and Aryeh Shmuelevitz (eds.). *The Hashemites in the Modern Arab World: Essays in Honour of the Late Professor Dann*. London: Frank Cass, 1995.

————. *On Both Banks of the Jordan: A Political Biography of Wasfi al-Tall*. London: Frank Cass, 1994.

Sutton, L. P. Elwell. "Reza Shah the Great: Founder of the Pahlavi Dynasty," in George Lenczowski (ed.). *Iran Under the Pahlavis*. Stanford: Hoover Institution Press, 1978.

Tabari, Muhammad. *Ta'rikh al-Rusul wal-Muluk*. Misr: Dar al-Ma'arif, 1960.

Tal, Lawrence. "Dealing with Radical Islam: The Case of Jordan," *Survival*, 37 (1995).

Talib, Hasan Abu. *Man yahkum al-Sa'udiyya?* Cairo: Sina' lil-nashr, 1990.

al-Tall, Tariq. "Al-ustura wasu' al-Fahm fi al-'Alaqat al-Urdunniyya-al-Filastiniyya," *Al-Siyasa al-Filastiniyya*, 3 (1996).

Tamimi, Azzam (ed.). *Power-Sharing Islam?* London: Liberty for Muslim World Publications, 1993.

Tangeaoui, Said. *Les entrepreneurs marocains. Pouvoirs, societe et modernite*. Paris: Karthala, 1994.

Taraki, Lisa. "Jordanian Islamists and the Agenda for Women: Between Discourse and Practice," *Middle Eastern Studies*, 32 (1996).

Tauber, Eliezer. "Rashid Rida's Political Attitudes During World War I," *Muslim World*, 65 (1995).

Teitelbaum, Joshua. *The Rise and Fall of the Hashemite Kingdom of Hijaz 1916–1925: A Failure of State Formation in the Arabian Peninsula.* Unpublished Ph.D. dissertation, Tel Aviv University, 1996.

———. "Saudi Arabia," in Ami Ayalon (ed.). *Middle East Contemporary Survey (MECS)*, Vol. 16–17. Boulder and Tel Aviv: Westview Press and the Moshe Dayan Center for Middle Eastern Studies, Tel Aviv University, 1995.

———. "The Saudis and the Hajj, 1916–1933: A Religious Institution in Turbulent Times." Unpublished M.A. thesis, Tel Aviv University, 1988.

Tessler, Mark. "Explaining the 'Surprises' of King Hassan II: The Linkage Between Domestic and Foreign Policy in Morocco: Part III: The Hassan-Peres Summit and Other Contacts with Israel," University Field Staff International Reports, Africa/Middle East, No. 40, 1986.

———. "Image and Reality in Moroccan Political Economy," in William I. Zartman (ed.). *The Political Economy of Morocco.* New York: Praeger, 1987.

Tétreault, Mary Ann. "Autonomy, Necessity, and the Small State: Ruling Kuwait in the Twentieth Century," *International Organization*, 45 (1991).

———. "Civil Society in Kuwait: Protected Spaces and Women's Rights," *Middle East Journal*, 47 (1993).

———. Kuwait's Economic Prospects," *Middle East Executive Reports* (January 1993).

Tilly, Charles (ed.). *The Formation of National States in Western Europe.* Princeton: Princeton University Press, 1975.

Timmerman, Kenneth R. "Kuwait's Real Elections," *Middle East Quarterly*, 2 (1996).

Tosy, Mohammed. "L'islam entre le controle de l'Etat et les debordements de la societe civile. Des nouveaux clercs aux nouveaux lieux de l'expression religieuse," in Robert Santucci (ed.). *Le Maroc actuel.* Paris: 1992.

———. "Monopolisation de la production symbolique et hierarchisation du champ politico-religieux au Maroc," in *Annuaire de l'Afrique du Nord 1979.* Paris: Centre National de la Recherche Scientifique, 1981.

Tosy, Mohammed, and Bruno Etienne. "La Da'wa au Maroc. Prolegomenes theorico-historiques," in Olivier Carre and Paul Dumont (eds.). *Radicalismes islamiques.* Vol. 2. Paris: L'Harmattan, 1986.

Townsend, John. *Oman: The Making of the Modern State.* London: Croom Helm, 1977.

Turner, Bryan S. *Max Weber from History to Modernity.* London: Routledge, 1993.

Tyan, Emile. *Institutions du droit public musulman.* Leiden: E. J. Brill, 1960.

Ubaydat, Muhammad Salim. *Athar al-jama'at al-Islamiyya al-mayolani khilal al-qarn al-'ishrin.* Amman: Maktabat al-Risala al-Haditha, 1989.

UNESCO. *Statistical Yearbook*, various issues, 1980–1994.

United Nations (UN), Department of International Economic and Social Affairs. *Case Studies in Population Policy: Kuwait.* Population Policy Paper, No. 15. New York: UN, 1988.

UN Economic and Social Commission for Western Asia (ESCWA). *Demographic and Related Socioeconomic Data Sheets for the Countries of the ESCWA*, No. 2. Beirut: ESCWA, 1978.

———. *Demographic Data Sheets*, various issues, 1982–1997.

————. *Expert Group Meeting on the Absorption of Returnees in the ESCWA Region with Special Emphasis on Opportunities in the Industrial Sector, Amman, 16–17 December 1991.* Amman: October 1992.

————. *Population Situation in the ESCWA Region, 1990.* Amman: ESCWA, 1992.

————. *Statistical Abstract of the ESCWA Region.* No. 16. New York: ESCWA, 1996.

————. *Survey of Economic and Social Developments in the ESCWA Region, 1995.* New York: UN Publications, 1996.

————. *Survey of Economic and Social Developments in the ESCWA Region, 1992.* Amman: ESCWA, October 1993.

al-Urdun al-Jadid Research Center. *Intikhabat 1989, Haqa'iq wa-Arqam.* Amman: al-Urdun al-Jadid Research Center, 1991.

————. *Intikhabat 1993, Dirasa Tahliliyya Raqamiyya.* Amman: al-Urdun al-Jadid Research Center, 1994.

Van Hear, Nicholas. *New Diasporas: The Mass Exodus, Dispersal, and Regrouping of Migrant Communities.* London: UCL Press, 1998.

Vatikiotis, P. J. *A History of Egypt.* 2nd ed. London: Weidenfeld and Nicholson, 1981.

————. *Nasser and His Generation.* London: Croom Helm, 1978.

————. "Royals and Revolutionaries in the Middle East," Middle East Lectures No. 2, Moshe Dayan Center for Middle Eastern and African Studies, Tel Aviv University, Tel Aviv, 1997.

Villier, Gerard de. *The Imperial Shah: An Informal Biography.* Boston: Little, Brown, 1976.

Vogel, Frank Edward. "Islamic Law and Legal System: Studies of Saudi Arabia." Unpublished Ph.D. thesis, Harvard University, 1993 (Ann Arbor: U.M.I.).

Waterbury, John. *The Commander of the Faithful: The Moroccan Political Elite—A Study in Segmented Politics.* New York: Columbia University Press, 1970.

al-Watha'iq al-Khasah Bi-Majlis Al-Shura, Al-Fatrah Al-Ula. Muscat: Majlis Al-Shura, 1991.

Wenner, Manfred W. *Modern Yemen, 1918–1966.* Baltimore: Johns Hopkins University Press, 1967.

Wilkinson, John. *The Imamate Tradition of Oman.* New York: Cambridge University Press, 1987.

Wilson, Mary C. *King Abdallah, Britain, and the Making of Jordan.* Cambridge: Cambridge University Press, 1987.

Winckler, Onn. "Demographic Developments and Population Policies in Bahrain," in Bruce Maddy-Weitzman (ed.). *Middle East Contemporary Survey (MECS),* Vol. 20. Boulder and Tel Aviv: Westview Press and the Moshe Dayan Center for Middle Eastern Studies, Tel Aviv University, 1998.

Winter, Michael. "Islam in the State: Pragmatism and Growing Commitment," in Shimon Shamir (ed.). *Egypt: From Monarchy to Republic.* Boulder: Westview Press, 1995.

World Bank. *World Tables.* 3rd ed. *Volume 2: Social Data from the Data Files of the World Bank.* Baltimore: Johns Hopkins University Press, 1984.

al-Yassini, Ayman. *Religion and State in the Kingdom of Saudi Arabia.* Boulder: Westview Press, 1985.

Yizraeli, Sarah. *The Remaking of Saudi Arabia.* Occasional Papers No. 2, Moshe Dayan Center for Middle Eastern and African Studies, Tel Aviv University, Tel Aviv, 1997.

Zahlan, Rosemarie Said. *The Making of the Modern Gulf States.* London: Unwin Hyman, 1989.

Zarnuqa, Salah Salim. *Anmat al-Istila' 'ala l-Sulta fil-duwwal al-'Arabiyya, 1950–1985.* 2nd ed.. Cairo: Maktabat Madbuli, 1993.

Zartman, William I. *Destiny of a Dynasty: The Search for Institutions in Morocco's Developing Society.* Columbia: University of South Carolina Press, 1964.

———. "King Hassan's New Morocco," in William I. Zartman (ed.). *The Political Economy of Morocco.* New York: Praeger, 1987.

———, (ed.). *Political Elites in Arab North Africa.* New York: Longman, 1982.

al-Zawi, Tahir Ahmad. *Jihad al-Abtal fi tarablus al-gharb.* Cairo: 1950.

Zonis, Marvin. *Majestic Failure: The Fall of the Shah.* Chicago: University of Chicago Press, 1991.

Zubaida, Sami. "Community, Class, and Minorities in Iraqi Politics," in Robert A. Fernea and Wm. Roger Louis (eds.). *The Iraqi Revolution of 1958.* London: I. B. Tauris, 1991.

JOURNALS AND NEWSPAPERS CITED

Al-Anba (Kuwait)
Arab Times
Bamdad
Al-Bayan (Dubai)
Cambio (Madrid)
Christian Science Monitor
Cumhuriyet
The Daily Telegraph
The Economist
Ettela'at
Financial Times
Foreign Report
Ha'aretz
Gulf States Newsletter
Al-Hayat
Al-Huquq
International Herald Tribune
Iran Times
Jahan-e Islam
al-Jazira al-'Arabiyya
The Jerusalem Report
Jomhuri-ye Islami
Jordan Times
Kayhan
Kiyan
Los Angeles Times
Al-Majalla
Al-Manar
The Middle East
Middle East Dialogue
Middle East Economic Digest
Middle East Newsletters, Gulf States
Le Monde

Al-Muharrir
Al-Muqtataf
Al-Musawwar
New Republic
New York Times
Al-Qabas
Al-Qibla
Salam
al-Sha'b
Al-Sharq al-Awsat
Al-Siyasa
Der Spiegel
al-Wasat
Washington Post
Al-Watan (Kuwait)
Al-Watan (Muscat)
Al-Watan al-'Arabi
Al-Wa'y

NEWS AGENCIES

Agence France Presse (AFP)
British Broadcasting Corporation, Summary of World Broadcasts (SWB)
Foreign Broadcasting Information Service (FBIS)
Kuwait News Agency (KUNA)
Reuters
Saudi Arabian Press Agency (SAMA)

The Contributors

Lisa Anderson is dean of the School of International and Public Affairs at Columbia University. She is author of *The State and Social Transformation in Tunisia and Libya, 1830–1980* (1986) and is the editor of *Transitions to Democracy* (forthcoming).

Ami Ayalon is associate professor, Department of Middle Eastern and African History, and senior research fellow at the Moshe Dayan Center, Tel Aviv University. He is author of *Language and Change in the Arab Middle East* (1987) and *The Press in the Arab Middle East, A History* (1995) and editor of *Middle East Contemporary Survey* (1988–1994).

Gabriel Ben-Dor is professor of political science and director of the Graduate Program in National Security Studies at the University of Haifa. He is a former rector of the university. The books he has authored or edited include *The Druzes in Israel: A Political Study* (1974), *State and Conflict in the Middle East* (1983), *Confidence Building in the Middle East* (1994), and the recent special issue of the annals of the American Academy of Political and Social Sciences entitled *Israel in Transition*.

F. Gregory Gause III is associate professor of political science at the University of Vermont and director of that university's Middle East Studies Program. He is the author of *Saudi-Yemeni Relations: Domestic Structures and Foreign Influence* (1990) and *Oil Monarchies: Domestic and Security Challenges in the Arab Gulf States* (1994).

Fred Halliday is professor of international relations at the London School of Economics and Political Science. His recent books include *Rethinking International Relations* (1994), *Islam and the Myth of Confrontation* (1996), and *Nation and Religion in the Middle East* (2000).

Joseph A. Kechichian is the CEO of Kechichian and Associates, LLC, a consulting partnership that provides analysis on the Arabian/Persian Gulf region.

His recent publications include *Oman and the World: The Emergence of an Independent Foreign Policy* (1995) and *The National Security of Saudi Arabia* (1996).

Joseph Kostiner is associate professor at the Department of Middle Eastern and African History and senior research fellow at the Moshe Dayan Center, Tel Aviv University. Among his recent publications are *From Chieftaincy to Monarchical State: The Making of Sauci Arabia, 1916–1936* (1993), *Tribes and State Formation in the Middle East* (coedited with Philip S. Khoury, 1991), and *Yemen: The Tortuous Quest for Unity* (1996).

Gudrun Krämer is professor of Islamic studies at the Free University in Berlin. She is the author of *Ägypten unter Mubarak* (1986) and *The Jews in Modern Egypt, 1914–1952* (1989). She is presently preparing a study of Islam, human rights, and democracy.

Remy Leveau is professor of political science at the Universite a l'IEP in Paris and at the Bologna campus of Johns Hopkins University. Among his books are *Le Fellah marocain defenseur du Trone* (1975), *Le sabre et le turban* (1993), *L'Algerie dans la guerre* (editor, 1995), *Islam(s) en Europe* (1995).

Bernard Lewis is Cleveland E. Dodge Professor of Near Eastern Studies Emeritus at Princeton University. Among his recent books are *The Muslim Discovery of Europe* (1982), *The Shaping of the Middle East* (1994), *The Middle East: A Brief History of the Last 2,000 Years* (1995), and *Multiple Identities of the Middle East* (1999).

Bruce Maddy-Weitzman is senior research fellow at the Moshe Dayan Center. He is author of *The Crystallization of the Arab State System: Inter-Arab Politics, 1945–1954* (1993), coeditor of *Religious Radicalism in the Greater Middle East* (1997), and editor of the Dayan Center's annual *Middle East Contemporary Survey*.

David Menashri is chairman and professor of the Department of Middle Eastern and African History, senior research fellow at the Moshe Dayan Center, and coordinator of the Parviz and Pouran Nazarian chair for modern Iranian studies, all at Tel Aviv University. He is author of *Revolution at a Crossroads: Iran's Domestic Politics and Regional Ambitions* (1997) and *Education and the Making of Modern Iran* (1992) and editor of *Central Asia Meets the Middle East* (1998).

Uzi Rabi is lecturer in the Department of Middle Eastern and African History at Tel Aviv University. His doctoral dissertation is entitled "The Emergence of the Omani State in the Twentieth Century: Tribal Entities in the Process of State Formation."

Asher Susser, senior research fellow at the Moshe Dayan Center and a former head of the center, is associate professor at the Department of Middle Eastern and African History, Tel Aviv University. His recent publications include *On Both Banks of the Jordan: A Political Biography of Wasfi al-Tall* (1994), *The Hashemites in the Modern Arab World* (coeditor, 1995), and editor of *Six Days, Thirty Years: New Perspectives on the Six Day War* (1999, in Hebrew).

Joshua Teitelbaum is research fellow at the Moshe Dayan Center and instructor in the overseas students program, Tel Aviv University. His recent works are "The Rise and Fall of the Hashimite Kingdom of the Hijaz, 1916–1925" (dissertation) and *Holier Than Thou: Saudi Arabia's Islamic Radicals* (forthcoming).

Onn Winckler is lecturer in the Department of Middle Eastern History at the University of Haifa. He is author of *Population Growth and Migration in Jordan* (1997) and *Demographic Developments and Population Policies in Ba'thist Syria* (1999). He is coeditor of *The Jordanian-Palestinian-Israeli Triangle: Smoothing the Path to Peace* (1998).

Index

quelling tribalism, 174–175; establishment of the Consultative Council, 203–206; external support, 291; increase in number of students, 245(table); modern governance style, 171–172; monarchic survival, 290; mortality and life expectancy rates, 243(table); nationalization of labor force, 246; newness of monarchy, 171; relations with Israel, 54; separation of power under Qabus and Tariq, 193–202; succession by deposition, 297; united religious and political authority, 176–177; workforce, 241(table), 251

Opposition, to monarchic regimes, 5–6, 34; failure of revolutionary regimes, 10; inevitability of revolution, 45–49; in Iran, 213–214, 218–219; Islamism as revolt, 279; Jordanian civil war, 100–101; "monarchies' resilience," 7–8; Muslim Brothers' peaceful opposition policy, 275; potential Moroccan, 277; to Saudi rule, 262–268; targeting ancient regimes, 71–74; uniting social and political groups, 47–48; Yemeni Revolution, 177–179, 289

Organization of Petroleum Exporting Countries (OPEC), 237

Ottoman Empire, 21; monarchical aspects of, 2–3; patrimonialism, 3–4; post-Ottoman regime options, 23–34; roots of Jordan's history, 88; royal titulature, 18

Oufkir, Muhammad, 121

Pahlavi, Mohammad Reza, 54, 55; absolutism of regime, 72; causality of overthrow, 45; religious minorities, 63

Pahlavi, Mohammad Reza, 302(n8); artificiality of, 38; Iran's anti-monarchic stance, 223–229; lack of coalitions, 291; lack of tribal support, 302(n3); policy failure of, 10; regime choice, 294; republicanism and, 215–218

Palestinian Liberation Organization (PLO), 99–100, 269, 271

Palestinians: as foreign labor, 250; Jordanian-Palestinian relations,

65–66, 91–92, 99–100, 103, 110–112; Jordan's civil war, 100–101; Muslim Brotherhood's support of, 273; recruitment by Abdullah I, 90–91

Pan-Arabism, 45, 91–92, 103

Parliament. See Constitutional monarchy

Patrimonialism, 3–5, 59–64, 93, 171–174

People's Islamic Bloc (Kuwait), 156

Persian Gulf states, 238–239; absolutism of regimes, 73; health services, 241–243; improving education, 244–245; inevitability of monarchic decline, 77–78; mortality and life expectancy rates, 243(table); nationalization of labor force, 245–250; Omani influence on, 188–191; as rentier states, 237. See also individual countries

Philby, H. St. John, 181

PLO. See Palestinian Liberation Organization

Pluralism, 259; religious police in Morocco, 276

Policy: foreign, 41, 209(n12); Muslim Brothers' peaceful opposition, 275; reflecting monarchies, 54–55

Political-religious power, 133

Population growth, 252

Primogeniture, 19

Pronatalist policies, 242

Prophet Muhammad. See Muhammad the Prophet

Qabus bin Sa'id: background and education, 209(n13), 210(n36); breaking with Tariq, 199; comparison with DeGaulle, 208(n2); controlling local tribes, 174–175; establishment of the Consultative Council, 203–206, 210(n34); Omani unification, 202–203; political modernization, 195–196; separation of Omani power under, 193–202; social modernization, 206–207; succession of monarchy, 187–188, 207–208

Qaddafi, Muammar, 42, 49

Qajar dynasty, 214–216, 302(n3)

Qarrash, Yusuf, 273

al-Qatami, Jasim, 156

About the Book

Though monarchies have been deemed obsolete by many observers, recent history testifies to their profound resilience. This volume offers an in-depth discussion of the fundamentals and performance of monarchies in the Middle East.

The authors focus on four themes: the roots and characteristics of Middle East monarchies, the causes of the collapse of some and the longevity of others, the performance of present-day monarchies, and the multiplicity of problems that they face. Case studies and comparative essays illustrate the varying capacities of the region's monarchies to cope with the successive challenges of modernity during the course of the twentieth century.

Joseph Kostiner is associate professor in the Department of Middle Eastern and African Studies and senior research associate at the Moshe Dayan Center for Middle Eastern and African Studies, Tel Aviv University. His many publications include *The Making of Saudi Arabia: From Chieftaincy to Monarchical State*, *Tribes and State Formation in the Middle East* (coedited with P. S. Khoury), and *Yemen: The Tortuous Quest for Unity, 1990–1994*.